READINGS IN
CHRISTIAN THEOLOGY

Readings in Christian Theology

Edited by
PETER C. HODGSON
and
ROBERT H. KING

FORTRESS PRESS Minneapolis

Acknowledgments are on pp. 407–13, which constitute an extension of
the copyright page.

Cover design: Pollock Design Group

Library of Congress Cataloging in Publication Data
Main entry under title:

Readings in Christian theology:

    Includes indexes.
    1. Theology, Doctrinal—Addresses, essays, lectures.
I. Hodgson, Peter Crafts, 1934–   II. King, Robert
Harlen, 1935–
BT10.R4 1985   230   84-48721
ISBN 0-8006-1849-1

AF 1-1849

18

CONTENTS

Preface   ix

I. Theology   1
   1. Farley: *Theologia*—The History of a Concept   1
   2. Ogden: What Is Theology?   15

II. Scripture and Tradition   31
   1. Origen: The Threefold Sense of Scripture   31
   2. Calvin: With the Aid of Spectacles   34
   3. Möhler: Tradition as the Living Word   37
   4. Hodge: The Protestant Rule of Faith   41
   5. Rahner: Scripture as the Church's Book   44
   6. Kelsey: The Function of Scripture   50

III. God   60
   1. Gregory of Nyssa: On the Trinity   60
   2. Anselm: The Attributes of God   64
   3. Thomas Aquinas: Language About God   69
   4. Hartshorne: The Divine Relativity   72
   5. Barth: The Humanity of God   78
   6. Tillich: Theism Transcended   81

IV. Revelation   88
   1. Augustine: Revelation as Illumination   88
   2. Luther: Revelation by Word and Spirit   91
   3. Tindal: Reason and Revelation   94
   4. Barth: Revelation as God's Self-Disclosure   97
   5. Bultmann: Revelation and Human Existence   101
   6. Rahner: The Supernatural Existential   104
   7. Pannenberg: Revelation and History   109
   8. Niebuhr: The Revelatory Image   112

V. Creation and Providence 118

    1. Augustine: In the Beginning God Created 118
    2. Calvin: God's Providence Governs All 123
    3. Spinoza: *Deus Sive Natura, Causa Omnium* 128
    4. Hegel: Without the World God Is Not God 132
    5. Ford: Divine Persuasion 136
    6. Tillich: God's Originating, Sustaining,
       and Directing Creativity 141

VI. Human Being 147

    1. Augustine: Body, Soul, Will, and the
       Image of God 147
    2. Schleiermacher: The Human Subject 153
    3. Barth: Christ and Adam 157
    4. Niebuhr: Human Beings as Creatures and Sinners 161
    5. Rahner: Persons as Free and Responsible Subjects 167

VII. Sin and Evil 176

    1. Augustine: Free Will and Sin 176
    2. Luther: Sin and Grace 180
    3. Tennant: Difficulties in the Classic Doctrine 185
    4. Kierkegaard: Sin as Despair 189
    5. Niebuhr: The Pride of Power 192
    6. Ricoeur: Paradox of the Servile Will 196
    7. Farrer: Beyond Augustinian Theodicy 199

VIII. Christ and Salvation 205

    1. The Nicene Creed: *Homousios* with the Father 205
    2. Athanasius: Truly Human, Truly God 205
    3. The Chalcedonian Definition: One Person,
       Two Natures 209
    4. Anselm: The Logic of Atonement 210
    5. Schleiermacher: The Work of Christ 217
    6. Bultmann: Faith in the Cross 221
    7. Barth: Lord as Servant, Servant as Lord 226
    8. Moltmann: The Crucified God 232

IX. The Church 237

    1. Cyprian: The Unity of the Church 237
    2. Thomas Aquinas: The Soul of the Church 239
    3. The Second Helvetic Confession: Christ the Sole Head
       of the Church 242

4. Schleiermacher: The Fellowship of Believers   247
5. Gustafson: The Church as a Human Community   250
6. Paris: The Black Christian Tradition   253
7. Gutiérrez: Sacrament of Liberation   259

X. The Sacraments   265

    1. Cyril of Jerusalem: Christian Initiation   265
    2. Ambrose: The Eucharistic Miracle   269
    3. Luther: Baptism and Faith   273
    4. Kant: Sacraments and the Moral Community   279
    5. Schmemann: Christ Our Eucharist   283
    6. Rahner: The Self-Communication of God   290

XI. The Spirit and the Christian Life   295

    1. Isaac of Syria: Directions on Spiritual Training   295
    2. Thomas Aquinas: Action and Contemplation   300
    3. John of the Cross and Teresa of Avila:
       The Mystical Way   304
    4. Law: Call to a Devout and Holy Life   312
    5. Rauschenbusch: Theology and the Social Gospel   317
    6. Williams: Christian Spirituality   320

XII. The Kingdom of God and Life Everlasting   323

    1. Irenaeus: New Heavens and a New Earth   323
    2. Origen: The Consummation of All Things   325
    3. Augustine: The Eternal Happiness of the Saints   329
    4. Schleiermacher: The Consummation of
       the Church and Personal Survival   333
    5. Bultmann: Jesus Christ as the Eschatological Event   338
    6. Tillich: *Kairos*   341
    7. Pannenberg: Eschatology and the Experience
       of Meaning   346
    8. Moltmann: The Resurrection as Hope   349

XIII. The Religions   351

    1. Justin Martyr: In Defense of Christianity   351
    2. Troeltsch: The Absoluteness and Relativity of
       Christianity   357
    3. Barth: Critique of Christianity as a Religion   362
    4. Pannenberg: Christianity in the History
       of Religions   368
    5. Cobb: Beyond Dialogue   375

CONTENTS

XIV. The Christian Paradigm: Alternative Visions   381

    1. Niebuhr: Radical Monotheism   381
    2. Cone: The Social Context of Theology   384
    3. Gutiérrez: Orthopraxis, Not Orthodoxy   388
    4. Ruether: The Prophetic, Iconoclastic Christ   393
    5. Hick: One God, Many Images   397
    6. Kaufman: Divine Power, Human Responsibility,
       and the Nuclear Threat   402

Acknowledgments   407

Index of Authors and Selections   415

PREFACE

This volume of readings is intended to supplement *Christian Theology: An Introduction to Its Traditions and Tasks*, which is appearing
concurrently in a newly updated edition. It brings together a rich
selection of works ranging from classical to contemporary and representing a diversity of theological views. The selections are organized
both topically and historically, and they are chosen for the most part
to illustrate specific themes in *Christian Theology*. So while they may
be read independently of that book, their primary purpose is to com-
plement the analysis and interpretation provided by it.

Most of the seminal thinkers of the Christian tradition are included in this collection of readings, some more prominently than
others. Augustine, for instance, is represented in five out of fourteen
chapters. This might seem excessive, yet he undoubtedly had more
to do with setting the terms of theological debate in the premodern
period than any other thinker; so he was in several instances the obvious choice to represent the classic view. Origen, Anselm, Aquinas,
Luther, and Calvin appear in more than one chapter as befits their
formative influence on Christian theology, but they could as well
have been included in many more. In making the selections, we have
tried to identify those thinkers whose contributions to the formulation of a particular doctrine were particularly decisive, recognizing
that many important contributors to the development of Christian
theology would of necessity have to be omitted.

With regard to the contemporary period, we have given a prominent
place to a few highly influential thinkers, notably Schleiermacher,
Barth, Rahner, and Tillich, while recognizing that others, such as Hegel, Kierkegaard, Bultmann, the Niebuhrs, and the representatives of
liberation theology are of almost equal importance. It has not been our
purpose, however, to provide representative selections from the works
of major theologians—present or past. Rather we have striven for a diversity and plurality of points of view, and at the same time have tried

to document the theological developments that have brought Christian reflection to its present state. Altogether, over fifty different authors are represented in some ninety selections.

With the exception of the first and last chapters, which present only contemporary views, each chapter may be said to represent a cross section of the tradition, beginning with one or more of the classical statements of a particular doctrine and tracing its development through the challenges and contributions of the modern period down to the present day. The reader in following this movement should not expect a steady progression toward a final resolution of all outstanding issues, but rather a broad exposure to significant points of controversy in respect to the doctrine. Thus, while some selections are included because they constitute the classic statement of a particular view, others are there simply to provoke thought. They may be read for their historical value or for their contribution to systematic reflection. The chapters themselves may be read in whole or in part, in the order in which they appear or some other order, as best serves the needs of the student.

The first chapter is different from the rest of the book in that it is comprised of only two rather extended programmatic essays, whereas the other chapters are made up of a larger selection of shorter readings. These two essays are oriented toward the discipline of theology as opposed to the subject matter typically encompassed by systematic theology; hence the issues considered are largely methodological. Since methodological issues arise out of engagement with a subject matter, those readers just beginning the study of theology may find it helpful to start with one or more of the chapters concerned with the content of theology and return to the first chapter at a later time. The concluding chapter also has a different function from the rest in that it offers a critical perspective on the conduct of theology in the present day, and a corrective to certain tendencies in Christian theology, particularly since the Enlightenment. It should stimulate reflection upon all of the preceding chapters.

The introductions to each selection have been intentionally kept brief in order to provide more space for the readings themselves. In the introductions no attempt has been made to give a biographical sketch of the author or to summarize the work from which the selection was taken. This sort of information, we believe, is best provided by the instructor or obtained from a standard reference work. We have tried to focus attention upon the argument, believing that each selection has something to say of intrinsic value, and that by attending to what is being said persons will be helped to advance their own constructive thinking. Because the selections even in translation cover such a broad historical period, there were in the originals considerable differences of style (including punctuation, spelling, capitalization, and footnoting). We have modified some of the texts in order to achieve a modicum of stylistic consistency but without seeking complete uniformity and without affecting the content. In particular, we have not attempted to render the selections gender-free, as we did the primary text, since to do so would have required substantial rewriting with the possibility of altering the original meaning. Biblical citations have been allowed to stand in the form given by the selected texts, without striving for consistency of style or translation. Where necessary, however, we have corrected chapter and verse references to correspond to modern English editions. Capitalization has been held to a minimum throughout, and footnotes in most cases either eliminated or incorporated into the body of the text (uniformly so in the case of biblical references). Editorial comments, where they appear, are set off by square brackets, while omitted passages are marked by ellipses.

We wish to express our appreciation to the original publishers for permission to use selections from their works. We hope that this sample of the best of the Christian tradition will inspire persons to read further in that tradition and to take up for themselves the task of constructive theology.

THE EDITORS

I. THEOLOGY

1. FARLEY: *THEOLOGIA*—THE HISTORY
OF A CONCEPT

In this selection, Edward Farley offers a brief history of the concept of theology (*theologia*) from the beginnings of Christian faith to the present. He uncovers two senses of the term: theology is both an actual knowledge of God (theology as "wisdom"), and a discipline or "science," which uses appropriate methods and issues in a body of teachings. While initially closely related, in the modern world these two senses fell apart as the unitary discipline of theology evolved into an aggregate of special sciences (only one of which retained the name "theology"), and as that aspect of theology offering wisdom was displaced by practical know-how and ministerial skills, so that *theologia* itself was lost. In the latter part of his work Farley offers a number of proposals for its recovery. Source: Edward Farley, *Theologia: The Fragmentation and Unity of Theological Education* (Philadelphia: Fortress Press, 1983), pp. 31–44, 162, 165–169.

The literature which pursues, interprets, and is entitled "theology" seems endless. Such a massive and complex articulation clearly indicates that the term *theology* is fundamentally ambiguous. This ambiguity does not simply mean that systematic theologians dispute the nature and method of theology, but rather that the term refers to things of entirely different *genres*. There are two fundamentally different premodern senses of the term. We must first review these senses and monitor the career of each sense before we are ready to consider the peculiarly modern usages. The two senses are these. First, theology is a term for an actual, individual cognition of God and things related to God, a cognition which in most treatments attends faith and has eternal happiness as its final goal. Second, theology is a term for a discipline, a self-conscious scholarly enterprise of understanding. In the former sense theology is a habit (*habitus*) of the human soul. In the latter it is a discipline, usually occurring in some sort of pedagogical setting. The ambiguity, the double reference and genre of the

1

term *theology* does not originate with theology itself, the church and its teachers. It is the outcome of a similar ambiguity and double reference occurring in the language of human "science" in premodern Western philosophy.

In the West the vision of human being as a cognitive animal, the vision of the possibility of science distinguished from opinion and rhetorical manipulation, is primarily the work of Plato and Aristotle. In Aristotle the term for knowledge, *episteme*, obtains the double meaning of true knowledge (contrasted with *doxa*, opinion) and an organized body of knowledge or deliberate inquiry producing such. *Episteme* can be quite properly translated both as knowledge and as science or discipline. The two senses were of course related. *Episteme* as knowledge meant a grasp of something's causes, hence the possibility of an inquiry (discipline) into causes. This same double meaning persisted in the Latin term which translated *episteme*, namely, *scientia*. *Scientia* thus means knowledge, a habit of the soul, by which the true is distinguished from the false. Citing pseudo-Grosseteste, Richard McKeon says that "knowledge (*scientia*) is a passion or a perfection resulting from the union of something intelligible and an intellectual power." But *scientia* can refer to the enterprise of investigation or reflection which produces the knowledge. And as these enterprises can be directed to different sorts of things, types of *sciences* arise.

It was this tradition and this language which was applied to the term *theologia* in medieval Christianity, and with the application came the double reference. Without clarifying the double usage, the question of whether or not theology is a science is not at all a clear question. And because of the double meaning, the ambiguity, there can be no straightforward history of "theology." Rather, there can be, on the one hand, a history of the church's claim that faith facilitates an individual cognitive act and, on the other, a history of interpretation (inquiry, argument, scholarship) in the church. And though related the two histories are not identical.

In the following brief exposition the two premodern senses of theology will be distinguished and the career of each one will be traced in three major periods—periods in which very different treatments of the particular sense in question emerge and with them new meanings. The one sense will here be called "theology/knowledge" and the other

2

sense "theology/discipline." Furthermore, it will be argued that the three periods are marked by changes in the institutional setting of theology (e.g., the rise of universities), and that there are correlations between the two senses in each period. The three periods do not coincide exactly with the conventional epochs of church history, but are distinguished by the prevailing institutional environments of theology. The first period covers early patristic and early medieval Christendom prior to the rise of the medieval universities. The second period ranges from the origin of the universities in the twelfth century (Bologna, Paris, Oxford) up to the so-called modern university, of which Halle is a prototype. In the third period the seminary arises, after Trent in Catholicism, and in the nineteenth century in Protestantism. Modeling itself on the Enlightenment-type university of Europe, the seminary developed faculties, disciplines, realms of scholarship parallel to the universities. Although the seminary is different from the university as an institution for the education of clergy, it too embodies and exemplifies what happened to theology in the third period.

The Early Christian Centuries

Theology/Knowledge

It may seem misleading to speak of theology in the period of the first eleven centuries of Christianity. The term itself rarely occurs, and when it does it refers to pagan authors, like Orpheus, who dealt with religion. The exceptions to this are occasional Greek fathers (Eusebius, pseudo-Dionysius) who mean by it the true, mystical knowledge of the one God. But however rare the term, the phenomenon itself, the knowledge of God, was very much a part of the Christian movement and Christian (patristic) literature. In other words a salvifically oriented knowledge of divine being was part of the Christian community and tradition long before it was named theology.

Theology/Discipline

The second sense of the term *theology* picks up that meaning of *episteme* and *scientia* which refers to a cognitive enterprise using appropriate methods and issuing in a body of teachings. Although this sort of thing had some existence in the church prior to the Middle Ages, it did not go by the name "theology." Some appropriation of classical learning had occurred in the church since the second century. And learning of a sort was promulgated in the monasteries. The door through which classical learning and classical literature entered monastic education was reading, memorizing, expounding, and meditating on scripture. Furthermore, the great teachers of the church from patristic times on had engaged in what now could be called inquiry, a discipline of thought and interpretation occurring in their commentaries on scripture and in their polemical and pedagogical writings. In Boethius's time this was more apt to be thought of as (Christian) philosophy. Whatever the term, there was in this early period, in addition to knowledge of God (the cognitive act, the illumined mind), the effort of discerning and setting forth the truth given to the world by God through Jesus. This effort had primarily the character of exposition, the interpretation of the received text from scripture or council. The truth of the revealed texts could be assumed, hence the task was to discern and properly formulate its meaning.

From the Middle Ages to the Enlightenment

From one point of view the period from the twelfth century to the Enlightenment and the modern university is an identifiable epoch in the history of Christianity. Even though another branch of Christianity, Protestantism, arose in that period, it still falls very much in this epoch and shares its characteristics. What gives the period its unity is the coming together of the classical patristic doctrinal scheme and the school. The result is the appropriation of learning, especially from philosophy, into a framework to explore and express the classical scheme. The result, in other words, is *theologia* as *scientia* in the distinctive scholastic sense of a method of demonstrating conclusions. The distinction between theology as knowledge and theology as discipline becomes sharpened. And as theology as discipline grows in the school, it is also opposed by those who see theology as a salvific knowledge. Prior to the universities were schools of another kind: palace schools, cathedral schools, monastic schools, traditional centers of learning, like Paris, which would become universities in the Middle Ages. And later in the university period are movements, especially the Renaissance, in which momentum is gathering toward the Enlightenment. Once the university came on the scene and with it the circle of Aristotelian sciences reformulated by Roger Bacon and others, a new literature arose —anticipated, however, by encyclopedic works of Cassiodorus and Isadore of Seville. Some writings described the circle of sciences and the place of *theologia* therein. In addition came works reflecting the new methods of inquiry in the schools, works of sentences, summas, introductions. And as the Thomist line developed theology more and more as a *scientia* in the sense of a discipline, a theoretical science, so came reaction against this from the Augustinian-monastic line (Bonaventure) which insisted that *theologia* had to do with the mind's road to God.

Theology/Knowledge

From its beginnings, the Christian community has laid claim to a knowledge of God, to a divine illumination of the human intellect operative in the salvation of the human being. Pseudo-Dionysius called this knowledge the "mystical theology." But in the second period, and with the coming of the universities and the renaissance of Aristotle, an appropriated philosophical scheme establishes the precedent of calling this knowledge of God *theologia*. The philosophical apparatus includes not only the concept of *episteme* but the Aristotelian anthropology of three powers of the soul. In that anthropology *episteme*, knowledge, is a *hexis*, one of the three states or enduring characteristics of the soul. Thus, for example, virtue in contrast to a particular act of virtue is an enduring, defining, structural feature of the human soul. The school theologians appropriated this anthropology, and translated *hexis* by the Latin term, *habitus*. Hence, they portrayed knowledge (*scientia*) as a habit, an enduring orientation and dexterity of the soul. It was natural then to see theology as a *habitus*, a cognitive disposition and orientation of the soul, a knowledge of God and what God reveals.

This meaning of *theologia* was not just a reflection of differences between one strand of medieval thinkers and another. Those like Thomas who thought of *theologia* as a discipline, a theoretical science, did not abandon the notion that it was also a cognitive state. The following definition attempts to capture the standard meaning of theology throughout this second period, from the twelfth through the seven-

5

teenth centuries: *theologia* is a state and disposition of the soul which has the character of knowledge. There were, of course, many debates about this throughout the period: between Thomists and Augustinians, Thomists and nominalists, Catholics and Protestants, Lutherans and Reformed, but the issue turned on what *kind* of knowledge (habit) theology was. And if there is a dominant position, it is that theology is a *practical*, not theoretical, habit having the primary character of wisdom. It is not our task here to sort out these controversies. The most important point is that in the second period theology characteristically refers to a practical, salvation-oriented (existential-personal) knowledge of God. It is not an easy point to grasp, since this usage of the term has been long absent from the Christian community, its churches and schools. . . .

Theology/Discipline

Regardless of how "theology" was conceived and carried out, there were in the church prior to the twelfth century enterprises of learning and teaching. There were "theologians" who engaged in controversy (Gottshalk, Erigena), refuted heresy, and even offered more or less systematic expositions of Christian doctrine (Origen). But prior to the twelfth century these enterprises were not thought of as a part of a "science" in the Aristotelian sense of a demonstrative undertaking. With the second period and the coming of the universities, this earlier learning, teaching, and exposition continued, but a great change took place in how they were conceived. Along with law, medicine, arts (including philosophy), "theology" names a faculty in a university and some ordered procedures which yield knowledge. It was not simply the direct cognitive vision of something given to it, a cognitive *habitus* of the soul, but a deliberate and methodical undertaking whose end was knowledge. Promoted especially by Thomas Aquinas and the schoolmen, theology in this sense became a discipline.

The transition of Christian learning and teaching based on scripture (*sacra pagina*) into an Aristotelian science (*sacra doctrina*), while primarily the work of Thomas and the thirteenth-century schoolmen, was made possible by a number of preceding historical accomplishments. The rise of *centers* of learning after the reform of Alcuin in connection with both cathedrals and monasteries was an important anticipation of the universities, most of which originate in the thirteenth through fifteenth centuries all over Europe. These abbey and cathedral schools were not only the settings for Peter Lombard, Abelard, Hugh of St. Victor, and Gilbert of la Porrée, whose work laid the foundations for theology as a discipline, but they were the recipients of the renaissance of Aristotle. The coming of Aristotle to Christian learning may have been the decisive catalyst for the precipitation of the new theological science, but it was not the only stimulus. The use of classical learning had long been accepted, even in the monastic schools. Such learning may have entered the schools as a servant, but it held the seeds of the independence later asserted in the Renaissance and Enlightenment.

One part of this classical learning was dialectic, serving initially as an instrument of exposition but then thematized by Abelard as an independent method. And with this comes the epoch-making distinction between commentary-exposition (*lectio*) and rational inquiry which uncovered what had been previously hidden (*quaestio*), between expounding the text and displaying the intelligibility of the content. In the beginning the questions had only an arbitrary order, but soon works appeared providing some rational sequence to the questions, a sequence which displayed the very structure of the articles of faith in relation to each other. . . .

From the Enlightenment to the Present

The third period covers roughly the seventeenth century to the present. In this period the two genres of theology continue but undergo such radical transformation that the original sense of theology as knowledge (wisdom) and as discipline virtually disappear from theological schools. Theology as a personal quality continues (though not usually under the term *theology*), not as a salvation-disposed wisdom, but as the practical know-how necessary to ministerial work. Theology as discipline continues, not as the unitary enterprise of theological study, but as one technical and specialized scholarly undertaking among others; in other words, as systematic theology. These developments are the outcome of theology's long career. They are peculiarly modern and, to some degree, even distinctively North American. But they are the result of events and movements occurring throughout the eighteenth and nineteenth centuries, and are not unrelated to the theology-as-Aristotelian-science development of the second period. . . .

Theology/Discipline: From Unitary Discipline to Aggregate of Specialties

In the narrower and more precise sense of the word, "Enlightenment" names a widespread eighteenth-century cultural movement in Western society which challenged traditional authority-oriented modes of thought and in their stead proffered critical, rational, and historical ways of understanding. In this narrow sense, there were Enlightenment theologians and philosophers who occupied a specific period of time and were the object of criticism by later thinkers. But in a broader sense Enlightenment is not simply a discrete period but a continuing part of modernity. Enlightenment introduced modes of thought into culture, education, and religion which are still very much with us in the form of ideals of scholarship, evidence, and criticism. With these ideals came the idea of the university in the modern sense, a community of free scholarship based on universal canons of evidence and inquiry.

It had been customary since the founding of the universities in the Middle Ages to differentiate the faculties: canon law, medicine, theology. Furthermore, within theology itself, the seventeenth century, drawing in part on the Middle Ages, applied all sorts of qualifying adjectives to the term *theology*. However it sounds, this nomenclature does not partition theology into scholarly disciplines or sciences in the modern sense. It rather designates different ways in which the cognitive *habitus* of the knowledge of divine things can be oriented to its object or on different aspects of that object which can be the subject of knowledge. In other words, theology itself was not divided into disciplines. In the eighteenth century two things occur which result in a totally new conception of theology/discipline. It is somewhat ironical that continental pietism played its own role in the rise of theology in the modern sense of specialized disciplines. Pietism attempted to correct a scholastic-scientific approach to the study of theology in which rational demonstrations were more central than faith and personal formation. Central to pietism was the individual's progress in spiritual matters, hence the emphasis on prayer and discipline as the setting of theological study. However, the pietists also wanted to correct any notion of the minister as primarily a knower, a resident scholastic theologian, hence they very much stressed preparation and training for specific tasks of ministry. This introduces, in addition to personal formation, a second telos of the study of theology: training for ministerial activities. This in turn sets the stage for conceiving the study of theology as a plurality of studies preparatory for such activities. It is not surprising, therefore, that theologians in the first half of the eighteenth century influenced by Spener and Francke are the very first to speak of theological *sciences*.

The primary movement, however, which effected the pluralization and specialization of theology was the Enlightenment. The Enlightenment was in part a revolt, an emancipation of thought and inquiry from institutional and even cognitive authorities. In pre-Enlightenment theologies, the *norms* for theology/discipline were the *articuli fidei* themselves. These doctrines of church tradition were not products, accomplishments of theology, but the *principia*, the givens. They were, accordingly, the norms for interpreting scripture and determining Christian responsibility and Christian truth. With the Enlightenment and the modern university came the ideal of autonomous science, of scholarship, proceeding under no other canons than proper evidence. With this came historical sense and historical-critical methods of interpretation. And these things in turn revolutionized the human and historical sciences into disciplines (sciences) in a new sense. A science was a cognitive enterprise working on some discrete region of objects under universal and critical principles. One result of this revolution was that new sciences, new bodies of data, and new methods were available to theology: philology, history, hermeneutics. In the mid-eighteenth century, Ernesti and Semler appropriated these for biblical interpretation. And once this happened it became apparent that the Bible itself could be the object of a "science," a collection to which critical, autonomous methods of interpretation could be applied. It was only a short step to realize the same thing was true about church history, about preaching, about dogmatic theology. . . .

Theology/Knowledge: From Sapiential Habitus to Practical Know-how

In the second period and especially in the Augustinian and monastic view, the end of the study of theology is salvific union with God. The rise of theology as an Aristotelian science in the medieval universities is a step toward the third period's pluralization of theology. What happens to theology as knowledge during the Enlightenment and after when theology names an aggregate of more or less independent sciences? The specialization of theology in the continental university creates a problem similar to high scholasticism. Monastics and pietists, Catholic and Protestant, suspect scholasticism of losing religion itself in a labyrinth of dialectic and ratiocination. Likewise, the university is suspected of training scholars at the expense of faith and the ministry. The pluralization and specialization of theology comes to resemble a new scholasticism. And it was a scholasticism with a much more severe problem than those inherent in medieval and seventeenth-century scholasticisms. In those times there was at least one unitary science to pursue, and it was correlative with an individual *habitus*, wisdom. But with its pluralization into sciences, theology as a disposition of the soul toward God simply drops out of "the study of theology." Furthermore, there is no unitary science but an aggregate of disciplines whose unity is their pertinence to the tasks of ministry. But concern for the individual's experience and faith and discontent with a merely academic approach to the study of theology has been present in schools of theology throughout the third period.

This concern has found three major expressions. The first is the attempt to make *each of the theological sciences* in some way personally relevant, pertaining to the faith, development, and life situations of the individual. A second is the attempt to create a special part of the educational experience called formation, a theme long present in Roman Catholic schools and recently flirted with in Protestant schools. The third and most pervasive expression is present in the unifying model of most theological schools where the tasks of the ministry are the *ratio studiorum*, the rationale for the disciplines. In that model there is a place for theology as a personal, cognitive disposition, the theology/knowledge genre. According to that model, it is necessary for the min-

ister or prospective minister to know certain things. This knowledge
is simply knowledge ordered toward and required by the tasks of ministry. . . .

Terminologically, the Enlightenment's pluralization of theological
study is determinative, so that theology has come to mean "systematic
theology." Its older usage as a disposition of the soul toward God has
been transformed, without retaining the word, into the know-hows
required for tasks of ministry. If the transformation of theology as a
discipline into a plurality of disciplines was primarily the work of the
post-Enlightenment, continental university, the transformation of
theology/knowledge into strategic know-how is primarily the work of
the twentieth-century seminary. Each of these transformations, however, pervades the programs of study of both seminaries and universities. . . .

The Recovery of Theologia

Theological understanding is not a theory or invention, something
wafted into existence by the theologian's magic wand. It names a dimension of the life of faith itself, the understanding required of faith as
it exists in various life contexts. . . .

We begin with what might turn out to be an axiom: the axiom of the
primacy of the situation in which theological understanding occurs.
Whatever is to be said about the independence and primacy of revelation in the order of knowledge and salvation, theological understanding is inevitably the understanding of an individual existing in an
already disposed biographical, social, and historical situation. One aspect of that situation may be the enduring structures of nature, the
fundamental ontology and existentiality of human being (Tillich), but
these do not exhaust the situation. The situation is always also a concrete situation and moment in the individual's biographical life set in a
social space and historical time. There is no other matrix of theological
understanding than this concrete situation. All theological work, be it
classically conciliar or parochial and individual, occurs from and in
the concrete situation.

It is the situation in which occur events and states of affairs which
constitute the individual's life and which evoke responses and interpretations. There is simply no way of conducting theology above the grid

11

of life itself. The dialectic of theological understanding is set in motion here, by the matters which evoke response and interpretation. To speak of the primacy of the situation in this sense is to say nothing of its *status* in theological understanding, whether or not its primacy qualifies it as a criterion, whether its primacy is a prison which faith cannot transcend. Nor does this describe a merely "secular" moment at the beginning which is empty of reference to revelation and redemption. The reason is that the understanding in question is preceded by and grounded in faith and its predispositions.

The references and imagery of faith are present prereflectively in the initial move of theological understanding, but not as explicit, self-conscious themes. But as we struggle to interpret and assess the situation, these prereflective references demand a hearing. Generally speaking, this is because the human being is in the world in the posture and reality of faith; its reading of the situation prompts it to self-consciously draw on the references of faith as guides to the interpretation and assessment of the situation. "References of faith" means simply the realities of faith carried in the imagery and even doctrinalizations of the ecclesial community. The matrix and unity of these realities is ecclesiality itself, a universalized form of a redemptive community. The first movement, then, of the dialectic of theological understanding is a thematization of the faith-world, of ecclesiality, of faith's language, references, realities. This movement attends to the total mythos of Christian faith, i.e., the essence of Christianity, the primary symbols, the themes of proclamation, the dogmas of tradition. Most traditional forms of education in the church have in fact focused on this moment, for instance, the Sunday school and a medieval cathedral school. This is the moment which draws on, and takes into account, the historical and distinctive content of tradition.

It was said earlier that the primacy of the situation was the primacy of a *matrix*, a context, not the primacy of a norm, a criterion, an ideal. But it is just this normativeness which unfaith would grant to the situation—the absolute status of what must be appeased, adapted to, satisfied. The self-oriented agendas, the principle of satisfaction, prompt the human being to grant not merely ontological but criteriological primacy to the situation. And at this point, in a second moment of the dialectic, faith intervenes, in what recently has been called a hermeneutics of suspicion. It repudiates the situation's claim to absoluteness (or the claims of elements in the situation) as it discerns its corruption and its relativity. In this second moment of theological understanding, the situation is refused normativeness and becomes a candidate for theological criticism. This is to say, it is viewed in relation to the transcendent, and therefore in both its creaturely and corrupted status. This moment of critique is exercised in a multiplicity of ways: as personal and autobiographical criticism, as ideological critique and the uncovering of injustice in the fabric of society. To use recent jargon, this second moment "raises the consciousness" to self-conscious awareness of the relativity and corruption of the situation.

If this dialectic stopped here, theological understanding would be simply the repudiation of one absolute criterion (the situation or its contents) on behalf of another, the historical tradition which disposes faith. The relative and corrupt cultural situation is contrasted to the absoluteness of tradition (Christianity, scripture, dogma, primary symbols, etc.). The peril of simply adapting to a particular situation, thus granting it autonomy, is replaced by the peril of adapting a situation to a heteronomous authority. But the dispositions of faith itself resist such an exchange. These dispositions are formed by a redemption which occurs in reference to the transcendent, the eternal, and they carry with them what Tillich calls the "Protestant principle" and what H. Richard Niebuhr calls radical monotheism.

Faith, accordingly, is prompted to refuse all absolutizations, all claims that human, historical, interpretive matters elude relativity and corruption. Hence, theological understanding would be incomplete, even self-destructive, if it failed to apply a hermeneutics of suspicion to its own tradition. For what in fact is that tradition? Even if it is granted the status of revelation, divine disclosure, it is something which occurred in the historical past. In other words, the tradition and its imagery, primary symbols, and dogmas originated in former concrete *situations*. In whatever sense it is divine work, it is clearly also a human work. To grant it the status of the eternal itself is simply one more idolatry. The third move, then, of theological dialectic is distancing and criticism in relation to tradition itself—the attempt to overcome the propensity to worship the norms. Again, to use modern jargon, one moment of the dialectic is a raising of the consciousness toward tradition itself. Only then are the elements in the tradition which serve oppression, ideology and the legitimization of privilege unmasked. Hence, the distancing we are talking about is informed not only by the critical temper of the Enlightenment but by the social criticism of the nineteenth and twentieth centuries.

According to this account of the dialectical spiral of the theological understanding, one set of moments elevates the content of the normative mythos (tradition) at work in faith itself. However, all that has been said so far is that theological understanding embraces both a self-conscious knowledge of that mythos and a self-conscious refusal to regard it as absolute. At this point theological understanding is in the ambivalent position of interpreting the mythos from two apparently competing perspectives, the one insisting on the normativeness, the other on its relativity of tradition. In this position the believer is not ready simply to return to the situation through the mythos. Hence, a fourth moment in the dialectic is called for which surmounts this impasse and grasps the mythos in its enduring reality and its power.

Any of these moments covers a vast terrain of possible tasks, issues, undertakings, and even sciences. This fourth moment, the determination of the normativeness of tradition, is no exception. What is discerned here is that about the persisting imagery, symbols, and doctrines of that mythos which expresses enduring truth. This truth pertains to more than simply the objective facticities of history or nature. As finally a truth about God and the presence of God, it has to do with what the world is and what human being is. Hence, one of the many specific tasks which would serve this moment in the dialectic is fundamental theology. This is not necessarily to claim that each moment in theological understanding is itself a discipline, a massive body of facts, data, and evidences. The point, rather, is that the dialectical reflection in which faith rises into understanding involves some grasp of the way in which the Christian mythos is a mirror of truth and reality. This truth and reality are inevitably present as the believer exists in the world in a self-conscious process of appraisal.

Theological understanding does not end with simply a relativizing critique of tradition. At that point nothing has yet happened to bring the assessed tradition into connection with the situation. Such an expression may be unfortunate. It sounds like a return to a theological pragmatism where the end of theological understanding is determined by a tradition whose autonomy was not really challenged in the third dialectical move. Medieval (neoplatonic and mystical) accounts of the believer's *itinerarium* decisively affirm the end and goal of that journey to be God and the vision of God. And yet few of them would formulate the matter in such as way as to obliterate creation. If the end is God, it is also God gracefully present among creatures working to fulfill ends which are theirs. Accordingly, what theological understanding discerns is "the kingdom of God," *the situation* as God undergirds it, pervades it, disposes it, lures it to its best possibilities. In this view, God is not a mere means to serve the autonomous situation nor is the situation ignored for the sake of a vision of God. This is why one hesitates to speak about the "object" of theological understanding. That language invites us to draw into the foreground something discrete: faith, revelation, God, Christianity, and so forth. Yet any of these things can be *theologia*'s object insofar as it functions as a generic term for the presence and activity of the sacred in the situation, the kingdom of God.

This final move of theological dialectic attempts to discern beyond the possibilities of corruption the place, legitimacy, beauty, redemptive possibilities, in short the theonomy, of the situation. And this is the case whether that situation be the individual's own concrete biographical life or a political situation of an oppressed people. Guiding this discernment is an assessed, de-absolutized tradition which has a disclosive character.

2. OGDEN: WHAT IS THEOLOGY?

This seminal essay sets forth a comprehensive definition of the meaning and method of Christian theology. Theology has a correlative structure because its task is to work out a "fully reflective understanding" of the Christian witness of faith in terms that are intelligible and relevant to human existence. While theology is a single movement of reflection, it has three distinctive moments, which allow for its differentiation into the disciplines of historical, systematic, and practical theology. The essay shows how these are related and advances a proposal for their unification. We give the full text except for the final two theses. Source: Schubert M. Ogden, "What Is Theology?" *The Journal of Religion* 52 (January 1972): 22–36.

1. *Theology, in the sense explicitly conveyed by the words "Christian theology," is the fully reflective understanding of the Christian witness of faith as decisive for human existence.*

One of the defining characteristics of theology, which it shares with philosophy in contrast to the special sciences, is that it necessarily includes reflection on its own conditions of possibility as a form of understanding. Thus the question of what theology is is itself a theological question, whose answer is subject to the same criteria of adequacy as any other theological statement. For reasons that will presently become clear, the theological understanding of theology peculiarly coincides with the philosophical, with the result that it is applicable in principle not only to Christian theology but also to the theological reflection cognate with any other witness of faith or religion. Moslem theology, for example, may be understood, *mutatis mutandis*, as the fully reflective understanding of Islam as similarly decisive for human existence.

But this primary sense of "theology" is not its only sense. It may also mean an integral part of philosophy's central task as metaphysics, in which case its meaning is explicated by the phrase "philosophical theology" (or, less happily, "natural theology"). This secondary sense is important because reflection discloses that philosophical theology is necessarily presupposed or implied by Christian theology—as well as, naturally, by the theology appropriate to every other religious tradition.

As for the phrase, "fully reflective understanding," it is intended to describe formally the mode or level of understanding that is properly theological. Since all understanding appears to involve some degree of reflection, "reflective understanding" by itself may understandably be considered a pleonasm. Yet, since reflectiveness clearly seems to be a matter of degree, addition of the adverb "fully" results in a significant expression, which makes explicit what is also intended by the unqualified phrase—namely, that reflection is, or should be, present to the highest degree in theological understanding. Implied thereby, of course, is that theology ought to exhibit at least some of the formal marks of any "science," including the methodical pursuit of its questions and the formulation of its answers in a precise conceptuality.

The ambiguity of the genitive phrase "the fully reflective understanding of the Christian witness of faith" is systematic and significant. Since Wilhelm Dilthey, it has been recognized that in the sciences of man (*Geisteswissenschaften*), to which theology clearly is most closely related, the relation of the inquirer to the object of his inquiry cannot be merely that of subject to object. Because the object of any such science is itself a meaningful human activity, and thus is or involves some mode of understanding, the only criteria of identity finally appropriate for specifying its regularities are those that it itself provides. Consequently, there can be no adequate understanding of such an activity as an object which is not also indirectly its fuller understanding of itself as a subject. It may be argued that the same is true *a fortiori* in the case of theology, since, rather like philosophy, its object is not this human activity or that, but the all-inclusive activity of witness, and thus human existence as such. In other words, the Christian witness of faith can become the object of theological understanding only insofar as it indirectly becomes the subject of such understanding as well. To this extent, there is a sound basis for the traditional formula in which theology is succinctly defined as *fides quaerens intellectum*.

It should also be noted that, since "the Christian witness of faith" can mean nothing other than the believing re-presentation of the witness of faith of Jesus of Nazareth, theology as here defined is, in effect, the fully reflective understanding of Jesus as the Christ. There can be no question that the affirmation, "Jesus is the Christ," is the constitutive affirmation of the Christian witness and, therefore, the integral object of theological reflection as well. Yet the task of theology as such is not simply to make this affirmation but also to understand it; and this consideration is important for a properly theological definition of theology itself.

2. *As such, theology presupposes as a condition of its possibility the correlation of the Christian witness of faith and human existence, both poles of which alike have a variable as well as a constant aspect.*

Like all reflective understanding, theology necessarily presupposes its own object, which in its case is the specifically Christian witness of faith. But, as has been indicated, this witness exists only in correlation with human existence, for which it claims to be decisive. In this, to be sure, the Christian witness of faith is no different from any other, since it is the essence of a religion to advance this claim and, as a consequence, to involve this correlation. As Whitehead puts it, "religion claims that its concepts, though derived primarily from special experiences, are yet of universal validity, to be applied by faith to the ordering of all experience. . . . It arises from that which is special, but it extends to what is general." So, too, with the Christian religion or witness of faith that theology presupposes: it is one expression of existence among others, which nevertheless claims to be decisive for the whole of such existence.

To speak in this way, however, evidently involves a high level of abstraction. Neither the Christian witness of faith nor the human existence with which it is correlated is ever given concretely in the way that the terms themselves suggest. The witness is present only in the form of all the various witnesses and kinds of witness, and the same is true of existence—insofar as it can be fully understood only through the whole of human history and all the forms of culture. In this sense, witness and existence alike have variable as well as constant aspects. Consequently, even if the object of theological reflection is one—namely, the one reality of human existence as decisively qualified by the Christian witness—its data are many, and that irreducibly.

3. *Because theological understanding itself must therefore be correlative in structure, it is subject to assessment by dual criteria of adequacy, which are likewise variable as well as constant in their specific requirements; accordingly, to be assessed as adequate, a theological statement must meet the two criteria of appropriateness and understandability as these may require in the given situation.*

If it is to reflect the correlation involved in the claim of the Christian witness to be decisive for human existence, theology itself must be correspondingly correlative in its very constitution. Both as a whole and in each of its parts, it must so interpret its many data as to vindicate this essential claim. This it can do only by exhibiting the witness of faith as expressive of *the* answer to the one fundamental question expressed or implied by all of man's life and history. But this implies in turn that the criteria of theological understanding or, more correctly, of the adequacy of theological statements, are necessarily double.

One such criterion requires that no theological statement be deemed adequate unless it is *appropriate*, in the sense that it represents the same understanding of faith as is expressed in the "datum discourse" of the Christian witness. A somewhat more technical way of formulating this requirement can be derived from a point made previously. In all understanding of understanding, such as is the task of theology along with philosophy and the sciences of man, the only appropriate criteria of identity and regularity are those provided in the first instance by the primary understanding. Although this does not mean that reflective understanding may employ no concepts or assertions other than those of its datum discourse, it does imply that the development of its conceptuality should never lose touch with the symbolism it is supposed to interpret. For this reason, a theological statement may be said to be appropriate only insofar as the understanding expressed by its concepts is that also expressed by the primary symbols of the witness of faith.

As for the other criterion, it requires that no theological statement be assessed as adequate which is not also *understandable*, in that it meets the relevant conditions of meaning and truth universally established with human existence. Since this is the criterion whose necessity in theology is likely to be denied or obscured, it is important to remove any doubt as to its derivation.

As we have seen, it is of the essence of the Christian witness that it claims to be decisive for human existence. Implied by this claim, however, is the further claim to truth—specifically, to the truth of the understanding of faith of which the symbols of the Christian witness are the primary expression. Furthermore, this understanding is held to be true because it meets the conditions of truth that are everywhere given with existence itself—as is evident from the fact that the witness of faith appeals simply to "every man's conscience in the sight of God" (2 Cor. 4:2). But this means that the requirement that theological statements be understandable, and thus universally meaningful and true, is far from merely the demand of an alien "rationalism." It is, in fact, the direct reflection at the level of full understanding of what the witness of faith itself essentially demands.

So to state the criteria of adequacy, however, abstracts altogether from the difficulty of applying them. We already touched on this difficulty when we recognized that the data of theological understanding with respect to both poles alike are irreducibly many. Since the one witness of faith is present only in all the many witnesses, which statements appropriately interpret it cannot be easy to determine. And so, also, in the matter of what statements are understandable; given the vast variety of history and culture, this is even harder to decide. The nub of the difficulty, of course, is that even the criteria themselves are open to variation in their specific requirements. Prior to the development of modern historical consciousness, it could be assumed that agreement with the received understanding of an allegedly infallible Scripture or dogma was a sufficient test of the appropriateness of a theological statement. But we now realize only too well that Scripture and dogma themselves, as well as any supposed understanding of them, are so thoroughly historical as to render any such test insufficient. Likewise, and for the same reason, we now recognize that what one epoch or culture accepts as criteria of meaning and truth by no means needs to be accepted by another. As a matter of fact, aware as we are that "uniqueness demonstrations" are hard to come by even in logic and mathematics, we know that even the most fundamental conditions of understandability may be subject to change.

All of which is to say that the two criteria of theological adequacy are situation-dependent as well as situation-invariant in what they require. Although in one aspect their requirements are always the same, in another they are constantly different, contingent on the possibilities and limitations of different historical situations. In general, their requirements in a situation are most likely to be discerned through intensive discussion with its best secular knowledge—in the case of appropriateness, the knowledge of history; in the case of understandability, that of philosophy and the special sciences. And yet, in neither case, is a theologian dependent on some other inquirer to specify these requirements. Although, given the situation, his only criteria must be universally applicable, he has his own role to play in determining such criteria; and it leaves ample room for offensive as well as defensive moves in the discussion with his secular colleagues.

4. *Insofar as a theological statement is adequate, and thus both appropriate and understandable, it is at once dogmatic and apologetic, as well as critical and constructive.*

In other words, such familiar phrases as "dogmatic theology," "apologetic theology," "critical theology," and "constructive theology" are all pleonasms, which are significant only to the extent that "theology" is always open to misunderstanding in one respect or another. Properly speaking, a theology that was not dogmatic would be no theology at all in the relevant sense of the word; for, as we have seen, the first requirement of the theology of any religion is that its statements give appropriate expression to the same understanding of faith as is expressed in the witness or "dogma" it presupposes as its object. Similarly, in the case of a theology that was not apologetic or not critical and constructive; since it would then fail to be understandable or would be deficiently reflective, it would be lacking in one or the other of theology's essential qualifications and insofar not really be theology. None of which is to deny, naturally, that in different situations theology may be quite correctly viewed more under one aspect than another —as when, as at present, for instance, there is a new appreciation for its inescapable apologetic task, or the detailed criticism of particular questions is held to be more important than the development of comprehensive systems.

5. *Although theology is a single movement of reflection, it has three distinct moments, which allow for its differentiation into the interrelated disciplines of historical, systematic, and practical theology.*

Up to this point, theology has been considered simply as such and without differentiation to make clear that, behind the complexity of the field as it has developed historically, there is, after all, but one movement of reflection having one integral task. Among other reasons that could be given for emphasizing this is that its recognition is essential to effective control of the growth of specialization, which has not always contributed to the advancement of theological understanding.

Still, the unity of such understanding is itself complex, so that the self-differentiation of theology is to a considerable extent natural and of good effect. With all its limitations, the advantages of a division of labor are clear, and theology has as much reason to claim them as any other form of reflective understanding. In fact, it has even more reason, since, from the standpoint of its logic, it is a field-encompassing field. Its unity is a unity-in-diversity involving three distinct moments, each centering in a logically different kind of question. Accordingly, its differentiation into the three main disciplines of historical, systematic, and practical theology is fully allowed for by its own essential constitution.

Yet, for all their differences, the three disciplines are thoroughly interrelated in that their respective questions and answers all fall within the horizon of a single inquiry. Thus, as we shall see, each discipline is in its own way correlative in structure, and its statements are subject to assessment by generally the same two criteria of adequacy.

6. *Historical theology, which includes exegetical theology as a special case, answers the general question, "What has the Christian witness of faith already been as decisive for human existence?"; as such, it is cognate with all other historical inquiries and subject to common criteria of understandability.*

It is important here to recall the point made earlier that the witness of faith is present concretely only in the form of the many actual witnesses and kinds of witness. By "witnesses" is meant simply the meanings expressed by all the individuals and groups that have in fact borne testimony to the Christian understanding of faith. But by *"kinds* of witness," account is also taken of the fact that there always have been, because there always must be, any number of ways in which such testimony has been borne. Indeed, it belongs to the very nature of faith that there is no human activity, and hence no form of culture, that does not in some way bear witness to it. In general, however, one may distinguish between the *explicit* witness of faith, which is borne by religion as one form of culture among others, and the *implicit* witness of faith, which is borne somehow by all the remaining cultural forms. To say, then, that the question of historical theology is what the Christian witness of faith has already been is to say that it is concerned with the reflective understanding of the history of the Christian religion, its beliefs, rites, social organization, and theology, together with the rest of human activity and culture so far as historically shaped thereby.

Saying this, however, should already make clear why historical theology is cognate with historical inquiry in general and assessable by the same criteria of meaning and truth. The Christian religion is obviously continuous with the history of religion generally, which is, in turn, of a piece with all the rest of the human story. Consequently, to understand Christian history, as historical theology is called to do, is to be engaged in discussion at every point with the general secular study of man's religious and cultural past.

Among the other things this implies is that the inquiry of historical theology, also, finally takes place within a larger horizon. Just as study of the past in general is ultimately for the sake of authentic existence in the present and the future, so study of the past as specifically Christian serves the same ulterior end. This is not to deny, naturally, that all historical inquiry, including that of historical theology, has its own autonomous structure firmly grounded in the logically different kind of question it attempts to answer. As a matter of fact, the rule applies here with particular force, that the larger cause is best served by those who are free to serve it in their own unique way. Still, like all historical inquiries, historical theology is but part of a whole, which should to some extent determine its character. Not only should it always be sensitive in its choice of topics for research to the needs of the entire field, but it should never be content with merely exhibiting the past for its own sake. From this it follows that its most essential task is the provision of accurate and readable translations of significant texts, together with critical interpretations that risk expressing the meaning of such texts in contemporary terms.

In the special case of exegetical theology, all that has been said about historical theology in general fully applies. Even the study of Holy Scripture is nothing other than historical study, continuous at every point from data to methods both with the study of Christianity and thence with the comprehensive understanding of the entire human past. And yet, in the nature of the case, the texts of the Old and the New Testaments have a peculiar place in theological reflection. Like other historical traditions, the Christian tradition is heterogeneous in composition to the extent that, through special acts of self-definition, certain of its elements have acquired a normative significance in relation to some or all of the rest. Unique among such elements is the canon of Scripture, which from an early time has in one way or another exercised the authority within the tradition of a universal norm—as appears from its historic designation as *norma non normata*. Consequently, by far the largest part of the Christian past may be plausibly regarded as the history of scriptural interpretation—provided, of course, interpretation is taken broadly enough to cover not only *theoria* but *praxis*, as well as the rest of man's self-expression. Furthermore, the critical interpretation of Scripture, toward which the whole of historical theology converges, is just the point of first importance for the other theological disciplines; for, with all the difficulties of applying it, agreement with the witness of Scripture is still the primary test of the appropriateness of theological statements, practical as well as systematic. There can be no question, then, that historical study of the Scriptures is in a way special, and that it is sufficiently special to have some claim to constitute a fourth discipline of theological inquiry. If such a claim has not been honored here, it is simply because the unity of exegesis with historical theology generally seems an even more important consideration.

Finally, we may note it is by no means accidental that historical theology is the first of the three disciplines to be considered. For, as Harnack rightly insisted, if history never has the last word in theology, it always has the first.

7. *Systematic theology, including what is sometimes distinguished as moral theology, answers all questions of the type, "What is the Christian witness of faith as decisive for human existence?"; since it therefore consists in a reflective understanding of reality itself, it is more or less closely related to all the other systematic inquiries of philosophy and the special sciences and is understandable by the same criteria.*

Although historical theology itself properly engages in critical interpretation (*Sachkritik*), including the expression of historical meanings in contemporary terms, it still is something different from systematic theology. Nor is the difference simply that historical theology interprets the *many* witnesses and kinds of witness, while it is reserved to systematic theology to essay interpretations of the *one* witness of faith itself. Historical theology has every reason to concern itself with the one as well as the many, and to do so without in the least encroaching on systematic theology. For the real difference between the two disciplines is logical: the difference between expressing what has already been said or meant by others and expressing what is properly said or meant by all, whether or not anyone up to now has ever actually said it. In other words, the distinctive task of systematic theology is to express at the level of full reflectiveness the understanding of faith, and hence the understanding of reality itself, decisively attested by the Christian witness.

That the understanding of faith (*genitivus subiectivus*) is also and as such an understanding of reality (*genitivus obiectivus*) hardly requires

24

explanation. "To have faith" is, at the least, "to believe," and thus to be committed to some understanding of the way things really are. Moreover, because the Christian witness of faith claims to be decisive for human existence, it also claims, in effect, to represent the understanding of reality that is true; that means, as we have seen, the same understanding universally given with existence as such, and thus also properly expressed by the systematic forms of reflection generally. Accordingly, if the claim of the Christian witness is warranted, its systematic interpretation, insofar as it is appropriate to its scriptural norm, should also be understandable—in that it both confirms and is confirmed by the cognate understanding of reality represented by philosophy and the special sciences. In this sense, the achievement of a systematic theology which is understandable as well as appropriate is a vindication of the claim of the Christian witness to represent the truth of human existence.

For reasons already given, the possibility of such an achievement is in the nature of the case situation-dependent, in that it is always a matter of the opportunities and limitations of a particular historical context. Yet, clearly, there are also definite limits imposed by the essential meaning of the Christian witness itself. Just where these limits lie is no doubt far more difficult to determine than has commonly been assumed. All sorts of beliefs once held to be essential to the Christian witness have since proved inessential, and critically interpreting them has only freed theology for more appropriate interpretations of what faith understands. Still, the Christian witness historically has represented a definite understanding of the nature of reality—of God, the world and man—with which certain other understandings are quite evidently incompatible. This is particularly obvious to us today, when the conflict of Christian beliefs with the secularistic claims made by many in our secular culture is undeniable. But, even in our situation, the task of systematic theology remains in principle the same: to achieve an understanding of the Christian witness that, however different it may be from all previous witnesses and their theological interpretations, appropriately grasps their essential meaning; and that, with whatever differences from current philosophical and scientific opinions, is understandable by the same criteria of meaning and truth to which they, too, are subject.

To understand the character of our present situation, however, is to recognize the centrality of systematic theology among the three disciplines. I referred earlier to the peculiarity of theological reflection, which it shares with the philosophical—that it is required to reflect on its own conditions of possibility as a form of understanding. Since it is this very possibility that the claims of modern secularism have now made problematic, it is not surprising that theologians have recently had to give considerable attention to the various aspects of this basic problem. Yet, significantly, such reflection has not only commonly been done by systematicians, but is also generally allowed to be the responsibility of their discipline. And this with good reason; for the task of self-reflection, which is essential to theology and which the present situation has made crucial, is quite properly a systematic task. Unlike the special sciences, theology is such that its content and its method are finally not two questions but one. Therefore, it is only fitting that the discipline to which it belongs to express faith's understanding of reality in concepts that are at once appropriate and understandable should also be responsible for the methodology of the entire field. Nor is this the only reason systematic theology occupies a central place. Not only does it reflectively establish the methods of the other disciplines, but it even contributes to their respective contents—in the case of historical theology, by providing the conceptuality required by its critical interpretations; and in the case of practical theology, by providing the first principles necessary to its particular conclusions.

Once again, then, we may note a direct correspondence between the relations of the three disciplines among themselves and their place in our consideration here. In fact, we may even appropriate the suggestion of Heinrich Ott and picture systematic theology as the keystone in the one "hermeneutical arch" of theological understanding.

8. *Practical theology, which should be understood much more comprehensively than is commonly the case, answers the general question, "What should the Christian witness of faith now become as decisive for human existence?"; accordingly, it is continuous with all other inquiries of the same logical type, especially the sciences of man and the various arts, sharing identical criteria of meaning and truth.*

Many, if not all, of the handicaps under which practical theology usually labors are due to its being conceived far too narrowly. Ordinarily, the only task assigned to it is to reflect on the shape to be given to the explicit witness of faith through the forms of religion, and that solely in relation to the official functions of the ordained ministry. Thus not only is it generally thought to be of value principally to clergy—present and prospective—but experience in the ministerial office is often supposed to be the main qualification for engaging in it. Not surprisingly, then, practical theologians frequently strike their colleagues as suffering from real inferiority as well as feelings thereof —their discipline apparently consisting in little more than an assortment of clerical techniques. But none of this is as unavoidable as its prevalence may tempt one to think. For, as we have seen, there is vastly more to the witness of faith than the explicit witness of religion, and it is easy to show that the only primary form of Christian ministry is that of the whole people of God. Consequently, there are the best reasons for striking at the root of practical theology's difficulties by conceiving it much more inclusively—namely, as reflective understanding of the responsibilities of Christian witness as such in the present situation.

Needless to say, such a conception allows for practical theology still having the task ordinarily assigned to it. Insofar as the expression of faith through proper religious forms is an abiding responsibility of Christian witness, practical theology has every right to concern itself with the present possibilities of such expression. Nor is there any reason why it should not give special attention to the functions of the ministerial office, so long as that office remains central to the explicit witness of the Christian community. But, on a comprehensive conception of its responsibility, all of this remains but a part—in fact, the smaller part—of practical theology. Its far larger task is also to reflect on the present possibilities of the *implicit* witness of faith in all its different modes. Thus, for example, among the most important issues that practical theology today is called to consider are those raised by the role of the community of witness, both gathered and dispersed, in a period of rapid social change and rising expectations among "the wretched of the earth." How ought Christians today, as individuals and through institutions, to think, speak, and act so as to respect the limitations of their situation, while yet fully exploiting its unique possibilities of human authenticity? Something like this must be the paradigmatic question of practical theology in our time, else its concern with the specifically religious and clerical be a mere abstraction torn from its total context.

In short, the scope of theology's practical discipline is as broad as the whole of man's cultural self-expression, and it properly considers every form of human activity as potentially bearing the contemporary witness of faith. This is the reason its natural *Gesprächspartner* are all the sciences of man and the various arts (including law, medicine, business, government, education, etc.) that in any way have to do with the realization of human good.

With so broad a scope, practical theology may at first appear to lack the integrity of a single discipline. But, as in the case of historical theology, there is one point toward which all its tasks converge. We have learned that theology as such is correlative in structure because it is reflective understanding of the given correlation of witness and existence. Furthermore, it should be clear that, while all three of its disciplines reflect this same correlation, each stands in a different relation to its two poles. Systematic theology is distinctive in that it reflects neither pole in itself but precisely their correlation, whereas historical theology peculiarly reflects the pole of witness, practical theology, that of existence. Yet, just as historical theology converges on critical interpretation of the normative witness of Scripture, so practical theology is one in the way each of its different tasks is related to the other pole of existence—namely, by contributing to one comprehensive understanding of the present human situation in its limitations and possibilities. And this, of course, is just the point where practical theology is of prime importance for its sister disciplines; for it is for the sake of this situation and its authentic possibilities that all theological reflection finally exists, even as it is in its terms that all theological statements—whether historical or systematic—must somehow become understandable.

It is altogether fitting, therefore, that practical theology should stand last in our consideration of the three disciplines. For, with even better reason than Schleiermacher, we, too, may say that "practical theology is the crown of theological study."

9. *Given the differentiation of theology into its three disciplines and their still further specialization into an indefinite number of special*

inquiries, there arises the urgent task, essential to all disciplines and specialties alike, of fundamental theology.

At the advanced stage of development which theology in general has now attained, the disadvantages of the division of labor whereby such development has alone become possible are not to be denied. As in other fields of understanding, the growth of specialization has tended toward a situation where individual inquirers know more and more about less and less, with a resulting fragmentation of the field and the breakdown of communication within it. Bad as such a situation may be in any case, it is disastrous in the case of theology. For, encompassing though it certainly is, theology still is a single field constituted by an integral movement of reflective understanding. Consequently, given this situation, it becomes a pressing responsibility of everyone working within the field to assist in recovering its essential unity.

Yet, since differentiation as such and even specialization neither can nor should be simply repealed, the only way in which this may be done is by taking up the task that is here called "fundamental theology": reflection undertaken within each of the specialties and disciplines directed toward formulating their respective first principles and thereby reestablishing communication among them. In the nature of the case, this kind of fundamental reflection, especially as it pertains to method, will seem particularly incumbent on systematic theology, which doubtless explains why "fundamental theology" is commonly used to designate a task or specialty peculiar to the systematic discipline. But to leave the task here so designated solely in the hands of systematicians is seriously to underestimate the problem that gives rise to it. Aside from the fact that systematic theology is fully as much a part of the problem as any of the other disciplines or specialties, little is gained by a few of its specialists' projecting schemes of unity that their colleagues feel justified in ignoring for the sake of their own special inquiries. Since the problem itself is a problem of the whole field, its solution as well belongs to the field as a whole. And, while this almost certainly means that a number of individuals must make it the object of their special attention, these individuals must be found within each of the three disciplines.

10. *Theological understanding as such, and thus all its disciplines and specialties as well, is in a broad sense "practical," in that, in un-*

derstanding the witness of faith as decisive for human existence, it, too, is ordered quite directly to the realization of man's authenticity.

Here the commentary may be brief, since this is simply the necessary conclusion of what has already been said. Although all forms of reflective understanding, even the most "theoretical," are in the broadest sense "practical," in that they are ultimately for the sake of authentic existence, they obviously differ insofar as they serve this ulterior end more or less directly. Thus, as compared with the special sciences—including the sciences of man—such arts as law, medicine, business, or education have to do rather more directly with the realization of human good. In somewhat the same way, theology, too, is as a whole "practical"; for, while it is ordered not merely to some particular aspect of man's good, but to the comprehensive end of authenticity itself, it nevertheless serves that end quite directly. The reason for this, of course, is the eminently practical character of the witness of faith, which alone makes theological understanding either possible or necessary. Because this witness advances the claim to be decisive for human existence, theology can adequately reflect it only by sharing the same existential finality. Accordingly, even when it is most theoretical, theology can be itself only by being just what it has traditionally been described as being: *sapientia eminens practica.*

II. SCRIPTURE AND TRADITION

1. ORIGEN: THE THREEFOLD SENSE
OF SCRIPTURE

One of the great interpreters of scripture, Origen established the allegorical method of exegesis that lasted at least until the Reformation. Convinced that the Bible was divinely inspired and infallible, and having proved to his own satisfaction that much of it could not be intended in its literal sense, he argued that, just as a human being is made up of three parts—body, soul and spirit—so also scripture must have a threefold sense—literal, moral, and spiritual. Source: Origen, *On First Principles*, Book 4, Chaps. 1–3, trans. G. W. Butterworth (London: SPCK, 1936; r.p. Gloucester, Mass.: Peter Smith, 1973), pp. 256, 264, 267, 269, 271–72, 275–76, 277–78, 293–94, 295, 296–97. Date of original composition: 219–225.

Now in our investigation of these important matters we do not rest satisfied with common opinions and the evidence of things that are seen, but we use in addition, for the manifest proof of our statements, testimonies drawn from the scriptures which we believe to be divine, both from what is called the Old Testament and also from the New, endeavoring to confirm our faith by reason. We have not yet, however, discussed the divine character of the scriptures. Well then, let us deal in a brief manner with a few points concerning them, bringing forward in this connection the reasons that influence us to regard them as divine writings. And first of all, before we make use of statements from the writings themselves and from the events disclosed in them, let us speak of Moses, the Hebrew lawgiver, and of Jesus Christ, the introducer of the saving doctrines of Christianity. . . .

Now when we thus briefly demonstrate the divine nature of Jesus and use the words spoken in prophecy about him, we demonstrate at the same time that the writings which prophesy about him are divinely inspired and that the words which announce his sojourning here and his teaching were spoken with all power and authority and that this is the reason why they have prevailed over the elect people taken from among the nations. And we must add that it was after the advent of Jesus that the inspiration of the prophetic words and the spiritual nature of Moses' law came to light. For before the advent of Christ it was not at all possible to bring forward clear proofs of the divine inspiration of the old scriptures. But the advent of Jesus led those who might have suspected that the law and the prophets were not divine to the clear conviction that they were composed by the aid of heavenly grace. . . .

Just as providence is not abolished because of our ignorance, at least for those who have once rightly believed in it, so neither is the divine character of scripture, which extends through all of it, abolished because our weakness cannot discern in every sentence the hidden splendor of its teachings, concealed under a poor and humble style. For "we have a treasure in earthen vessels, that the exceeding greatness of the power of God may shine forth" (2 Cor. 4:7) and may not be reckoned as coming from us who are but men. For if it had been the hackneyed methods of demonstration used among men and preserved in books that had convinced mankind, our faith might reasonably have been supposed to rest in the wisdom of men and not in the power of God (see 1 Cor. 2:5). But now it is clear that "the word and the preaching" have prevailed among the multitude "not in persuasive words of wisdom, but in demonstration of the Spirit and of power" (1 Cor. 2:4). . . .

Now that we have spoken cursorily about the inspiration of the divine scriptures it is necessary to discuss the manner in which they are to be read and understood, since many mistakes have been made in consequence of the method by which the holy documents ought to be interpreted not having been discovered by the multitude. . . . [The text continues with examples of those who have misinterpreted the scriptures, especially Jews and heretics.]

Now the reason why all those we have mentioned hold false opinions and make impious or ignorant assertions about God appears to be nothing else but this, that scripture is not understood in its spiritual sense, but is interpreted according to the bare letter. On this account we must explain to those who believe that the sacred books are not the works of men, but that they were composed and have come down to us as a result of the inspiration of the Holy Spirit by the will of the

Father of the universe through Jesus Christ, what are the methods of interpretation that appear right to us, who keep to the rule of the heavenly Church of Jesus Christ through the succession from the Apostles. . . .

The right way, . . . as it appears to us, of approaching the scriptures and gathering their meaning, is the following, which is extracted from the writings themselves. We find some such rule as this laid down by Solomon in the Proverbs concerning the divine doctrines written therein: "Do thou portray them threefold in counsel and knowledge, that thou mayest answer words of truth to those who question thee" (Prov. 22:20, 21).

One must therefore portray the meaning of the sacred writings in a threefold way upon one's own soul, so that the simple man may be edified by what we call the *flesh* of the scripture, this name being given to the obvious interpretation; while the man who has made some progress may be edified by its *soul*, as it were; and the man who is perfect and like those mentioned by the apostle ("We speak wisdom among the perfect; yet a wisdom not of this world, nor of the rulers of this world, which are coming to nought; but we speak God's wisdom in a mystery, even the wisdom that hath been hidden, which God foreordained before the worlds unto our glory" [1 Cor. 2:6–7])—this man may be edified by the *spiritual law* (see Rom. 7:14), which has "a shadow of the good things to come" (Heb. 10:1). For just as man consists of body, soul and spirit, so in the same way does the scripture, which has been prepared by God to be given for man's salvation. . . .

Since there are certain passages of scripture which, as we shall show in what follows, have no bodily sense at all, there are occasions when we must seek only for the soul and the spirit, as it were, of the passage. . . . [There follow numerous examples.]

We have mentioned all these instances with the object of showing that the aim of the divine power which bestowed on us the holy scriptures is not that we should accept only what is found in the letter; for occasionally the records taken in a literal sense are not true, but actually absurd and impossible, and even with the history that actually happened and the legislation that is in its literal sense useful there are other matters interwoven.

But someone may suppose that the former statement refers to all the scriptures, and may suspect us of saying that because some of the history did not happen, therefore none of it happened; and because a certain law is irrational or impossible when taken literally, therefore no laws ought to be kept to the letter; or that the records of the Saviour's life are not true in a physical sense; or that no law or commandment of his ought to be obeyed. We must assert, therefore, that in regard to some things we are clearly aware that the historical fact is true. . . . [Indeed,] the passages which are historically true are far more numerous than those which are composed with purely spiritual meanings. . . .

When, therefore, as will be clear to those who read, the passage as a connected whole is literally impossible, whereas the outstanding part of it is not impossible but even true, the reader must endeavor to grasp the entire meaning, connecting by an intellectual process the account of what is literally impossible with the parts that are not impossible but are historically true, these being interpreted *allegorically* in common with the parts which, so far as the letter goes, did not happen at all. For our contention with regard to the whole of divine scripture is, that it all has a spiritual meaning, but not all a bodily meaning; for the bodily meaning is often proved to be an impossibility. Consequently the man who reads the divine books reverently, believing them to be divine writings, must exercise great care. . . .

2. CALVIN: WITH THE AID OF SPECTACLES

While adhering to the classical scripture principle, and indeed offering lengthy proofs of the "credibility" of scripture, Calvin regards the "secret testimony of the Spirit" as the highest proof. Moreover, rather than simply containing a body of divinely revealed information, scripture is like a pair of "spectacles" with which we are able to "read" the knowledge of God that is already confusedly present in nature and our minds. Source: John Calvin, *Institutes of the Christian Religion*, Book 1, Chaps. 6–7, ed. J. T. McNeill, trans. F. L. Battles (Philadelphia: Westminster Press, 1960), Vol. 1, pp. 69–70, 75–76, 78–79. Date of original publication: 1536–59.

That brightness which is borne in upon the eyes of all men both in heaven and on earth is more than enough to withdraw all support from men's ingratitude—just as God, to involve the human race in the same guilt, sets forth to all without exception his presence portrayed in his creatures. Despite this, it is needful that another and better help be added to direct us aright to the very Creator of the universe. It was not in vain, then, that he added the light of his Word by which to become known unto salvation; and he regarded as worthy of this privilege those whom he pleased to gather more closely and intimately to himself. For because he saw the minds of all men tossed and agitated, after he chose the Jews as his very own flock, he fenced them about that they might not sink into oblivion as others had. With good reason he holds us by the same means in the pure knowledge of himself, since otherwise even those who seem to stand firm before all others would soon melt away. Just as old or bleary-eyed men and those with weak vision, if you thrust before them a most beautiful volume, even if they recognize it to be some sort of writing, yet can scarcely construe two words, but with the aid of spectacles will begin to read distinctly; so Scripture, gathering up the otherwise confused knowledge of God in our minds, having dispersed our dullness, clearly shows us the true God. This, therefore, is a special gift, where God, to instruct the church, not merely uses mute teachers but also opens his own most hallowed lips. Not only does he teach the elect to look upon a god, but also shows himself as the God upon whom they are to look. He has from the beginning maintained this plan for his church, so that besides these common proofs he also put forth his Word, which is a more direct and more certain mark whereby he is to be recognized. . . .

A most pernicious error widely prevails that Scripture has only so much weight as is conceded to it by the consent of the church. As if the eternal and inviolable truth of God depended upon the decision of men! For they mock the Holy Spirit when they ask: Who can convince us that these writings came from God? Who can assure us that Scripture has come down whole and intact even to our very day? Who can persuade us to receive one book in reverence but to exclude another, unless the church prescribe a sure rule for all these matters? What reverence is due Scripture and what books ought to be reckoned within its canon depend, they say, upon the determination of the church. . . .

But such wranglers are neatly refuted by just one word of the apostle. He testifies that the church is "built upon the foundation of the prophets and apostles" (Eph. 2:20). If the teaching of the prophets and apostles is the foundation, this must have had authority before the church began to exist. Groundless, too, is their subtle objection that, although the church took its beginning here, the writings to be attributed to the prophets and apostles nevertheless remain in doubt until decided by the church. For if the Christian church was from the beginning founded upon the writings of the prophets and the preachings of the apostles, wherever this doctrine is found, the acceptance of it —without which the church itself would never have existed—must certainly have preceded the church. It is utterly vain, then, to pretend that the power of judging Scripture so lies with the church that its certainty depends upon churchly assent. Thus, while the church receives and gives its seal of approval to the Scriptures, it does not thereby render authentic what is otherwise doubtful or controversial. But because the church recognizes Scripture to be the truth of its own God, as a pious duty it unhesitatingly venerates Scripture. As to their question—How can we be assured that this has sprung from God unless we have recourse to the decree of the church?—it is as if someone asked: Whence will we learn to distinguish light from darkness, white from black, sweet from bitter? Indeed, Scripture exhibits fully as clear evidence of its own truth as white and black things do of their color, or sweet and bitter things do of their taste. . . .

Credibility of doctrine is not established until we are persuaded beyond doubt that God is its author. Thus, the highest proof of Scripture derives in general from the fact that God in person speaks in it. The prophets and apostles do not boast either of their keenness or of anything that obtains credit for them as they speak; nor do they dwell upon rational proofs. Rather, they bring forward God's holy name, that by it the whole world may be brought into obedience to him. Now we ought to see how apparent it is not only by plausible opinion but by clear truth that they do not call upon God's name heedlessly or falsely. If we desire to provide in the best way for our consciences—that they may not be perpetually beset by the instability of doubt or vacillation, and that they may not also boggle at the smallest quibbles—we ought to seek our conviction in a higher place than human reasons, judgments, or conjectures, that is, in the secret testimony of the Spirit. True, if we wished to proceed by arguments, we might advance many

36

things that would easily prove—if there is any god in heaven—that the law, the prophets, and the gospel come from him. Indeed, ever so learned men, endowed with the highest judgment, rise up in opposition and bring to bear and display all their mental powers in this debate. Yet, unless they become hardened to the point of hopeless impudence, this confession will be wrested from them: that they see manifest signs of God speaking in Scripture. From this it is clear that the teaching of Scripture is from heaven. And a little later we shall see that all the books of sacred Scripture far surpass all other writings. Yes, if we turn pure eyes and upright senses toward it, the majesty of God will immediately come to view, subdue our bold rejection, and compel us to obey. . . .

3. MÖHLER: TRADITION AS THE LIVING WORD

The founder of the nineteenth-century Catholic Tübingen School wrote a great work in comparative "symbolics," in which he examined the doctrinal differences between Catholics and Protestants. Möhler is also in many respects a forerunner of the twentieth-century Catholic renewal. In this selection he argues that, whereas Protestants appeal to Holy Scripture as the source of saving knowledge, Catholics appeal to the church, which *interprets* scripture and is the bearer of the "living word," *tradition.* At certain points we have modernized the translation, which was made only a few years after the work was originally published in German in 1832, but have made no changes in the text. Source: Johann Adam Möhler, *Symbolism, or Exposition of the Doctrinal Differences between Catholics and Protestants, as Evidenced by Their Symbolic Writings,* Book 1, Chap. 5, trans. James B. Robertson (New York: Edward Dunigan, 1844), pp. 349–52, 358–60.

The main question, which we have now to answer, is this: how does man attain to possession of the true doctrine of Christ; or, to express ourselves in a more general, and at once more accurate, manner, how does man obtain a clear knowledge of the institute of salvation, proffered in Christ Jesus? The Protestant says, by searching Holy Writ, which is infallible; the Catholic, on the other hand, replies, by the Church, in which alone man arrives at the true understanding of Holy Writ. In a more minute exposition of his views, the Catholic continues: doubtless the Sacred Scriptures contain *divine* communications, and, consequently, the pure truth: whether they contain *all* the truths, which in a religious and ecclesiastical point of view are necessary, or at least very useful to be known, is a question which does not yet come under consideration. Thus, the Scripture is God's unerring word: but however the predicate of inerrability may belong *to it, we ourselves* are not exempt from error; nay, we only become so when we have unerringly received the word, which is in *itself* inerrable. In this reception of the word, human activity, which is fallible, has necessarily a part.

But, in order that, in this transit of the divine contents of the Sacred Scriptures into possession of the human intellect, no gross illusion or general misrepresentation may occur, it is taught, that the Divine Spirit, to which are entrusted the guidance and vivification of the Church, becomes, in its union with the human spirit in the Church, a peculiarly Christian tact, a deep sure-guiding feeling, which, as it abides in truth, leads also into all truth. By a confiding attachment to the perpetuated apostleship, by education in the Church, by hearing, learning, and living within her pale, by the reception of the higher principle, which renders her eternally fruitful, a deep interior sense is formed that alone is fitted for the perception and acceptance of the written word, because it entirely coincides with the sense in which the Sacred Scriptures themselves were composed. If, with such a sense acquired in the Church, the sacred volume be perused, then its general essential import is conveyed unaltered to the reader's mind. Nay, when instruction through the apostleship, and the ecclesiastical education in the way described, takes place in the individual, the Sacred Scriptures are not even necessary for our acquisition of their general contents.

This is the ordinary and regular course. But errors and misunderstandings, more or less culpable, will never fail to occur; and, as in the times of the apostles, the word of God was combated out of the word of God, so this combat has been renewed at all times. What, under such circumstances, is the course to be pursued? How is the Divine Word to be secured against the erroneous conceptions that have arisen? The general sense decides against particular opinion—the judgment of the Church against that of the individual: *the Church interprets the Sacred Scriptures.* The Church is the body of the Lord: it is, in its universality, his visible form—his permanent, ever-renovated, humanity—his eternal revelation. He dwells in the community; all his promises, all his gifts are bequeathed to the community—but to no individuals, as such, since the time of the apostles. This general sense, this ecclesiastical consciousness is tradition, in the subjective sense of the word. What then is tradition? The peculiar Christian sense existing in the Church, and transmitted by ecclesiastical education; yet this sense is not to be conceived as detached from its subject-matter—nay, it is formed in and by this matter, so it may be called a full sense. Tradition is the living word, perpetuated in the hearts of believers. To this sense, as the general sense, the interpretation of Holy Writ is entrusted. The declaration, which it pronounces on any controverted subject, is the judgment of the Church; and, therefore, the Church is judge in matters of faith. Tradition, in the objective sense, is the general faith of the Church through all ages, manifested by outward historical testimonies; in this sense, tradition is usually termed the *norma*, the standard of Scriptural interpretation—the rule of faith. . . .

Ages passed by, and with them the ancient sects; new times arose, bringing along with them new schisms in the Church. The formal principles of all these productions of egotism were the same; all asserted that Holy Writ, abstracted from tradition and from the Church, is at once the sole source of religious truth, and the sole standard of its knowledge for the individual. This formal principle, common to all parties separated from the Church—to the Gnostic of the second century, and the Albigensian and Vaudois of the twelfth, to the Sabellian of the third, the Arian of the fourth, and the Nestorian of the fifth century—this principle, we say, led to the most contradictory belief. What indeed can be more opposite to each other than Gnosticism and Pelagianism, than Sabellianism and Arianism? The very circumstance, indeed, that one and the same formal principle can be applied to every possible mode of belief; or rather that this belief, however contradictory it may be in itself, can still make use of that formal principle, should alone convince every one that grievous errors must here lie concealed, and that between the individual and the Bible a mediating principle is wanting.

What is indeed more striking than the fact that every later religious sect does not deny that the Catholic Church, in respect to the parties that had previously seceded from her, has in substance right on her side, and even recognizes in these cases her dogmatic decisions; while on the other hand, it disputes her formal principles? Would this ecclesiastical doctrine, so formed and so approved of, have been possible without the peculiar view the Church entertained of herself? Does not the one determine the other? With joy the Arian recognizes what has been decided by the Church against the Gnostics; but he does not keep in view the manner in which she proceeded against them; and he will not consider that those dogmas on which he agrees with the Church, she would not have saved and handed down to his time, had she acted according to those formal principles which he requires of her, and on which he stands. The Pelagian and the Nestorian embrace also, with the most undoubting faith, the decisions of the Church against the Arians. But as soon as the turn comes to either, he becomes as it were stupified, and is inconsiderate enough to desire the matter of Christian doctrine without the appropriate ecclesiastical form—without that form, consequently, by the very neglect whereof those parties, to which he is most heartily opposed, have fallen on the adoption of their articles of belief. It was the same with Luther and Calvin. The pure Christian dogmas, in opposition to the errors of the Gnostics, Paulicians, Arians, Pelagians, Nestorians, Monophysites and others, they received with the most praiseworthy firmness and fervency of faith. But, when they took a fancy to deliver their theses on the relations between faith and works, between free-will and grace, or however else they may be called, they trod (as to form) quite in the footsteps of those whom they execrated, and when they were able to obtain possession of their persons, even burned them.

This accordingly is the doctrine of Catholics. You will obtain the knowledge full and entire of the Christian religion only in connection with its essential form, which is the Church. Look at the Scripture in an ecclesiastical spirit, and it will present you an image perfectly resembling the Church. Contemplate Christ in and with his creation—the Church; the only adequate authority; the only authority representing him, and you will then stamp his image on your soul. Should it, however, be stated, in ridicule of this principle, that it were the same as to say, "Look at the Bible through the spectacles of the Church," be not disturbed, for it is better for you to contemplate the star by the aid of a glass than to let it escape your dull organ of vision, and be lost in mist and darkness. Spectacles, besides, you must always use, but only beware lest you get them constructed by the first casual glass-grinder, and fixed upon your nose. . . .

4. HODGE: THE PROTESTANT RULE OF FAITH

The founder of the "Princeton Theology" sets forth a Protestant scholastic version of the scripture principle, or of what he calls "the Protestant rule of faith," arguing for the inspiration and infallibility of scripture with great force and clarity. His arguments have been refined and modified by modern fundamentalism and evangelicalism, but not essentially altered or improved. Source: Charles Hodge, *Systematic Theology* (New York: Charles Scribner's Sons, 1872; reprint 1960 by Eerdmans), Vol. 1, pp. 151, 152, 153–54, 155, 156–57, 163, 165, 166.

All Protestants agree in teaching that "the word of God, as contained in the Scriptures of the Old and New Testaments, is the only infallible rule of faith and practice." . . . [There follow quotations from the symbols and creeds of the Protestant churches.]

From these statements it appears that Protestants hold, (1) That the Scriptures of the Old and New Testaments are the word of God, written under the inspiration of the Holy Spirit, and are therefore infallible, and of divine authority in all things pertaining to faith and practice, and consequently free from all error whether of doctrine, fact, or precept. (2) That they contain all the extant supernatural revelations of God designed to be a rule of faith and practice to his Church. (3) That they are sufficiently perspicuous to be understood by the people, in the use of ordinary means and by the aid of the Holy Spirit, in all things necessary to faith or practice, without the need of any infallible interpreter. . . .

The infallibility and divine authority of the Scriptures are due to the fact that they are the word of God; and they are the word of God because they were given by the inspiration of the Holy Ghost.

The nature of inspiration is to be learned from the Scriptures; from their didactic statements, and from their phenomena. There are certain general facts or principles which underlie the Bible, which are assumed in all its teachings, and which therefore must be assumed in its interpretation. We must, for example, assume, (1) That God is not the unconscious ground of all things; nor an unintelligent force; nor a name for the moral order of the universe; nor mere causality; but a Spirit,—a self-conscious, intelligent, voluntary agent, possessing all the attributes of our spirits without limitation, and to an infinite degree. (2) That he is the creator of the world, and extra-mundane, existing before, and independently of it; not its soul, life, or animating principle; but its maker, preserver, and ruler. (3) That as a spirit he is everywhere present, and everywhere active, preserving and governing all his creatures and all their actions. (4) That while both in the external world and in the world of mind he generally acts according to fixed laws and through secondary causes, he is free to act, and often does act immediately, or without the intervention of such causes, as in creation, regeneration, and miracles. (5) That the Bible contains a divine, or supernatural revelation. The present question is not, whether the Bible is what it claims to be; but what does it teach as to the nature and effects of the influence under which it was written?

On this subject the common doctrine of the Church is, and ever has been, that inspiration was an influence of the Holy Spirit on the minds of certain select men, which rendered them the organs of God for the infallible communication of his mind and will. They were in such a sense the organs of God, that what they said God said.

This definition includes several distinct points. First. Inspiration is a supernatural influence. It is thus distinguished, on the one hand, from the providential agency of God, which is everywhere and always in operation; and on the other hand, from the gracious operations of the Spirit on the hearts of his people. According to the Scriptures, and the common views of men, a marked distinction is to be made between those effects which are due to the efficiency of God operating regularly through second causes, and those which are produced by his immediate efficiency without the intervention of such causes. The one class of effects is natural; the other, supernatural. Inspiration belongs to the latter class. It is not a natural effect due to the inward state of its subject, or to the influence of external circumstances.

No less obvious is the distinction which the Bible makes between the gracious operations of the Spirit and those by which extraordinary gifts are bestowed upon particular persons. Inspiration, therefore, is not to be confounded with spiritual illumination. They differ, first, as to their subjects. The subjects of inspiration are a few selected persons; the subjects of spiritual illumination are all true believers. And, secondly, they differ as to their design. The design of the former is to render certain men infallible as teachers; the design of the latter is to render men holy. . . .

Second. The above definition assumes a difference between revelation and inspiration. They differ, first, as to their object. The object of revelation is the communication of knowledge. The object or design of inspiration is to secure infallibility in teaching. Consequently they differ, secondly, in their effects. The effect of revelation was to render its recipient wiser. The effect of inspiration was to preserve him from error in teaching. These two gifts were often enjoyed by the same person at the same time. That is, the Spirit often imparted knowledge, and controlled [it] in its communication orally or in writing to others. . . .

A third point included in the Church doctrine of inspiration is, that the sacred writers were the organs of God, so that what they taught, God taught. It is to be remembered, however, that when God uses any of his creatures as his instruments, he uses them according to their nature. He uses angels as angels, men as men, the elements as elements. Men are intelligent voluntary agents; and as such were made the organs of God. The sacred writers were not made unconscious or irrational. The spirits of the prophets were subject to the prophets (1 Cor. 14:32). They were not like calculating machines which grind out logarithms with infallible correctness. The ancients, indeed, were accustomed to say, as some theologians have also said, that the sacred writers were as pens in the hand of the Spirit; or as harps, from which he drew what sounds he pleased. These representations were, however, intended simply to illustrate one point, namely, that the words uttered or recorded by inspired men were the words of God. The Church has never held what has been stigmatized as the mechanical theory of inspiration. The sacred writers were not machines. Their self-consciousness was not suspended; nor were their intellectual powers superseded. Holy men spake as they were moved by the Holy Ghost. It was men, not machines; not unconscious instruments, but living, thinking, willing minds, whom the Spirit used as his organs. . . .

The fourth element of the Church doctrine on this subject [is that inspiration extends equally to all parts of Scripture]. This means, first, that all the books of Scripture are equally inspired. All alike are infallible in what they teach. And secondly, that inspiration extends to all the contents of these several books. It is not confined to moral and religious truths, but extends to the statements of facts, whether scientific, historical, or geographical. It is not confined to those facts the importance of which is obvious, or which are involved in matters of doctrine. It extends to everything which any sacred writer asserts to be true. . . .

The view presented above is known as the doctrine of plenary inspiration. Plenary is opposed to partial. The Church doctrine denies that inspiration is confined to parts of the Bible; and affirms that it applies to all the books of the sacred canon. It denies that the sacred writers were merely partially inspired; it asserts that they were fully inspired as to all that they teach, whether of doctrine or fact. This of course does not imply that the sacred writers were infallible except for the special purpose for which they were employed. They were not imbued with plenary knowledge. As to all matters of science, philosophy, and history, they stood on the same level with their contemporaries. They were infallible only as teachers, and when acting as the spokesmen of God. . . . Nor does the Scriptural doctrine on this subject imply that the sacred writers were free from errors in conduct. Their infallibility did not arise from their holiness, nor did inspiration render them holy. Balaam was inspired, and Saul was among the prophets. David committed many crimes, although inspired to write psalms. Peter erred in conduct at Antioch; but this does not prove that he erred in teaching. The influence which preserved him from mistakes in teaching was not designed to preserve him from mistakes in conduct. . . .

5. RAHNER: SCRIPTURE AS THE CHURCH'S BOOK

The distinguished Catholic theologian Karl Rahner argues that scripture is an expression of the self-constitution of the church in the apostolic age, and that it derives its inspiration and authority from the fact that God is the author of the church. As such there can be no conflict between scripture and tradition, since scripture itself is the fundamental moment in the formation of the church's tradition. Source: Karl Rahner, *Foundations of Christian Faith: An Introduction to the Idea of Christianity*, trans. William V. Dych (New York: Crossroad, 1978), pp. 371, 373–78. Date of original publication: 1976.

We regard [scripture] as the church's book, the book in which the church of the beginning always remains tangible as a norm for us in the concrete. Indeed it is norm which is already distinguished from those things which are found in the original church but which cannot have a normative character for our faith and for the life of the later church. If the church in every age remains bound to its origins in its faith and in its life; if the church as the community of faith in the crucified and risen Jesus is itself to be in its faith and in its life the eschatological and irreversible sign of God's definitive turning to the world in Jesus Christ, a sign without which Jesus Christ himself would not signify God's irreversible coming into the world and would not be the absolute savior; and if this church of the beginning objectifies itself in scriptural documents at least in fact, and also does so necessarily given the historical and cultural presuppositions in which the church came to be, then in all of this together we have a point of departure for understanding the essence of scripture.

It is also a point of departure from whose perspective we can arrive at an adequate and at the same time a critical understanding of what is really meant by the inspiration of scripture and by a binding canon of scripture. Since scripture is something derivative, it must be understood from the essential nature of the church, which is the eschatological and irreversible permanence of Jesus Christ in history. It is to be understood from this perspective as something normative in the church. . . .

During the apostolic age the real theological essence of the church is constituted in a historical process in which the church comes to the fullness of this essence and to the possession of this essence in faith. This self-constitution of the essence of the church until it reaches its full historical existence (and it is not until then that it can fully be the norm for the future church) implies written objectifications. Therefore this process is *also*, but not exclusively, the process of the formation of the canon: the church objectifies its faith and its life in written documents, and it recognizes these objectifications as so pure and so successful that they are able to hand on the apostolic church as a norm for future ages. From this perspective there is no insuperable difficulty with the fact that the formation of these writings and the knowledge that they are representative as objectifications of the apostolic church do not simply coincide in time, and that the formation of the canon was not finished until the post-apostolic age. In this understanding the canonicity of scripture is established by God insofar as he constitutes the church through the cross and the resurrection as an irreversible event of salvation, and the pure objectifications of its beginning are constitutive for this church. . . .

From this perspective, or so it seems to us, we can also clarify what is called "inspiration" in the church's doctrine on scripture. In the documents of the church it is said again and again that God is the *auctor* (author) of the Old and New Testaments as scripture. The school theology, which is at work in the encyclicals of Leo XIII and up to those of Pius XII, tried time and time again to clarify by means of psychological theories how God himself is the *literary* author or the writer of Holy Scripture. And it tried to formulate and to clarify the doctrine of inspiration in such a way that it becomes clear that God is the literary author of scripture. This, however, did not deny (and the Second Vatican Council affirmed it explicitly) that this understanding of God's authorship and of inspiration may not reduce the human authors of these writings merely to God's secretaries, but rather it grants them the character of a genuine literary authorship of their own.

This interpretation of the inspired nature of scripture which we have done no more than sketch can of course be understood in such a way that even today one does not necessarily have to accuse it of being mythological. We would have to recall in this connection what we said in the fifth chapter about the unity between transcendental revelation and its historical objectification in word and in writing, and about the knowledge of the success of these objectifications. In any case it cannot be denied in the Catholic church that God is the author of the Old and New Testaments. But he does not therefore have to be understood as the literary author of these writings. He can be understood in a variety of other ways as the author of scripture, and indeed in such a way that in union with grace and the light of faith scripture can truly be called the word of God. This is true especially because, as we said elsewhere, even if a word *about* God is caused by God, it would not by this very fact be a word *of God* in which God offers himself. It would not be such a word *of God* if this word did not take place as an objectification of God's self-expression which is effected by God and is borne by grace, and which comes to us without being reduced to our level because the process of hearing it is borne by God's Spirit.

If the church was founded by God himself through his Spirit and in Jesus Christ, if the *original* church as the norm for the future church is the object of God's activity in a qualitatively unique way which is different from his preservation of the church in the course of history, and if scripture is a constitutive element of this original church as the norm for future ages, then this already means quite adequately and in both a positive and an exclusive sense that God is the author of scripture and that he inspired it. Nor at *this* point can some special psychological theory of inspiration be appealed to for help. Rather we can simply take cognizance of the actual origins of scripture which follow for the impartial observer from the very different characteristics of the individual books of scripture. The human authors of Holy Scripture work exactly like other human authors, nor do they have to know anything about their being inspired in reflexive knowledge. If God wills the original church as an indefectible sign of salvation for all ages, and wills it with an absolute, formally pre-defining and eschatological will within salvation history, and hence if he wills with this quite definite will everything which is constitutive for this church, and this includes in certain circumstances scripture in a preeminent way, then he is the inspirer and the author of scripture, although the inspiration of scripture is "only" a moment within God's primordial authorship of the church.

From the doctrine that Holy Scripture is inspired theology and the official doctrine of the church derive the thesis that scripture is inerrant. We can certainly say with the Second Vatican Council (*Dei Verbum*, art. 11): "Therefore, since everything asserted by the inspired authors or sacred writers must be considered to be asserted by the Holy Spirit, we must profess of the books of scripture that they teach with certainty, with fidelity and without error the truth which God wanted recorded in the sacred writings for the sake of our salvation." But if because of the very nature of scripture as the message of salvation we acknowledge the inerrancy of scripture first of all in this global sense, we are still far from having solved all of the problems and settled all of the difficulties about the meaning and the limits of this statement which can be raised because of the actual state of the scriptural texts. The inerrancy of scripture was certainly understood earlier in too narrow a sense, especially when inspiration was interpreted in the sense of verbal inspiration, and the sacred writers were only regarded as God's secretaries and not as independent and also historically conditioned literary authors. That difficulties still exist here in the understanding and in the exact interpretation of the church's doctrine on the inerrancy of scripture is shown even by the history of the conciliar text just cited. It follows from this history that the Council evidently wanted to leave open the question whether the phrase about the truth which God wanted to have recorded *for the sake of our salvation* is supposed to restrict or to explicate the meaning of the sentence.

We cannot of course treat and answer all of these questions and difficulties in detail here, especially since we cannot go into individual scriptural texts which raise special difficulties with regard to their "truth." We shall have to leave them to the introductory disciplines and to exegesis. Nor can we go into the question here whether in the papal encyclicals of the last century and up to Pius XII the doctrine on the inerrancy of scripture was not understood here and there in a too narrow and materialistic sense. It is also obvious that much of what was said elsewhere in this book, for example, about the inerrancy of Christ and the inerrancy of real dogmas in the teaching of the church, can have its corresponding validity in this question too.

We only want to say here very briefly: scripture in its unity and totality is the objectification of God's irreversible and victorious offer of salvation to the world in Jesus Christ, and therefore in its unity and totality it cannot lead one away from God's truth in some binding way. We must read every individual text within the context of this single whole in order to understand its true meaning correctly. Only *then* can it be understood in its real meaning, and only then can it really be grasped as "true." The very different literary genre of the individual books must be seen more clearly than before and be evaluated in establishing the real meaning of individual statements. (For example, in the

New Testament stories it is not impossible in certain circumstances that we find forms of midrash and that they were originally intended to be such, so that according to scripture's own meaning the "historical" truth of a story can be relativized without any qualms.) Scriptural statements were expressed within historically and culturally conditioned conceptual horizons, and this must be taken into account if the question of what is "really" being said in a particular text is to be answered correctly. In certain circumstances it can be completely legitimate to distinguish between the "correctness" and the "truth" of a statement. Nor may we overlook the question whether the really binding meaning of a scriptural statement does not change if a particular book has its origins outside the canon as the work of some individual, and then is taken into the totality of the canonical scriptures.

Just as by the very nature of the case there is an analogy of faith which is a hermeneutical principle for the correct interpretation of individual statements in the official teaching of the church, so that the individual statement can only be understood correctly within the unity of the church's total consciousness of the faith, so too and in an analogous sense, or as a particular instance of this principle, there is also an *analogia scripturae* or an analogy of scripture which is a hermeneutical principle for interpreting individual texts of scripture. If there is a "hierarchy of truths," that is, if a particular statement does not always have the same objective and existential weight which another statement has, then this has to be taken into account in interpreting individual scriptural statements. This does not mean that the statement which is "less important" in relation to another statement has to be qualified as incorrect or as false.

If we grant the validity of and apply these similar principles, which follow from the very nature of the case and from the nature of human speech and are not the principles of a cheap "arrangement" or a cowardly attempt to cover up difficulties, then we certainly do not inevitably have to get into the difficulty of having to hold that particular statements of scripture are "true" in the meaning which is really intended and is intended in a binding way, although a sober and honest exegesis might declare that they are incorrect and erroneous in the sense of a negation of the "truth." . . .

Insofar as the church's teaching office in later ages continues to be bound permanently to the original church's consciousness of the faith which is the constitutive beginning of the church as a whole, and insofar as this consciousness has been objectified in an authentic and pure way in Holy Scripture, the teaching office does not stand above scripture. Rather it only has the task of giving witness to the truth of scripture, of maintaining this truth in a vital way, and of always interpreting it anew in historically changing horizons of understanding as the one truth which always remains the same.

If everything which has been said so far is understood correctly (and would be developed more clearly), then there also follows the correct understanding of the relationship between scripture and tradition. Scripture itself is the concrete process and the objectification of the original church's consciousness of the faith, and by means of it this consciousness of the faith is "transmitted" to later ages of the church. The formation of the canon is a process whose legitimacy cannot be established by scripture alone, but rather it is itself a fundamental moment in the tradition. Conversely, the Second Vatican Council refused to make tradition a second source for us today which exists by itself alongside scripture, a source which testifies to individual, material contents of faith which have no foundation at all in scripture. However much the more precise relationship between scripture and tradition still needs a great deal of further theological clarification, it is perhaps obvious from what has already been said earlier that the "scripture alone" of the Reformation is no longer a doctrine which distinguishes and separates the churches. For Evangelical theology too recognizes that scripture is the objectification of the original church's living consciousness of the faith, and is so in the midst of a very clear pluralism in the original church's preaching and in the theologies which are found there. This pluralism can ultimately be held together in unity only by the church's single and living consciousness of the faith.

6. KELSEY: THE FUNCTION OF SCRIPTURE

In this article David Kelsey summarizes and further develops the constructive thesis of his book *The Uses of Scripture in Recent Theology* (1975). The thesis is that scripture has authority to the extent that it functions in the church to shape new human identities and transform individual and communal life. It can be understood theologically to function this way because it is God who is "active" in scripture—not God "saying" or "revealing" (the classic images), but God "shaping identity," "using" the uses of scripture toward a specific end. In the first two propositions, Kelsey sets forth certain theological presuppositions; our selection begins with the third. Source: David H. Kelsey, "The Bible and Christian Theology," *Journal of the American Academy of Religion* 48 (September 1980): 393–99, 400–401.

Biblical writings are scripture when and insofar as they
function in the common life of the Christian
community to shape individual and communal life
and thereby author new identities and, for that reason
and on that basis, also function to authorize
theological proposals. This is its de facto authority.

In a Christian community it is precisely the biblical writings which, as used in a great variety of activities that comprise the common life of the community, provide the images, concepts, principles, parables, etc., that serve to evoke, nurture, and correct the dispositions, beliefs, policies, emotions, etc., that are basic to the identities of members of the community and to the identity of the community itself. When used in these ways they may be said often to "author" new personal identities.

The distinction between "biblical writing" and "scripture" no doubt is artificial; but it is useful to make a central point about the relation between Bible and theology. To describe a writing as a "biblical writing" is to identify it as one of a set of more or less ancient writings customarily published together as the Bible and historically rooted partly in the religious life of ancient Israel and partly in the religious life of the early Christian church. It is a suitable subject for all sorts of literary and historical study.

To describe precisely the same texts as "scripture" in the sense I am stipulating here, is to say something else. Biblical writings are "scripture" only in tradition where "tradition" is understood as active tradition (*actus tradendi*), the act of handing on from person to person a promise and a call through use of these texts. In part (another part will be discussed in the next section), to say "This is our scripture" is to say "These are the texts that present to us the promise and call that define our communal identity." It is a "self-involving" expression. That is, to call these texts "scripture" is to commit oneself to a particular community and to shaping one's identity by the dispositions, beliefs, emotions, etc., that go with trusting the promises and responding to the call. So too, to say more objectively "These are the Christian scriptures" is to report that these texts are texts that define the identity of the Christian community and which the community is committed to using in its common life in ways that will nurture and reform its common life and the individual lives of its members.

This brings out two further points. First, it means that to call certain texts "scripture" is to acknowledge that they are authoritative de facto in the church and that that authority is *functional*. That is, its authority consists in its functioning to "author" or shape decisively communal and individual identities. And to call them "scripture" is to say that the community is in fact committed to use them in this way in the course of Christian *praxis*.

Second, this brings out that biblical texts function as "scripture" in quite *diverse* ways. Different activities employing scripture address different capacities in the users—sometimes it is the affections that are addressed, sometimes capacities for reflective thought, sometimes capacities for regulating behavior, sometimes not capacities at all but deep sufferings or exuberant spirits. In the process different aspects of the texts, often of the very same texts, may be especially attended to: sometimes historical truth claims or theological beliefs explicitly proposed or apparently implicit in the text; sometimes stories taken as historical reports and sometimes stories (even the same stories) taken as paradigms for guiding behavior or for construing our experience; sometimes laws and moral principles as injunctions and sometimes simply as part of a legalistic history by contrast to which the radical character of grace is highlighted. It seems to be the case that some texts, though certainly not all, have been used in the common life of the Christian community with attention to several of their aspects which are not centrally related to the evident intent of their authors or their literary genre. Thus, a passage from a writing of Paul may have been intended by Paul to address a particular moral problem in a specific congregation under very concrete conditions and written in the genre of "epistle" that has its own conventions governing how it would have been construed in its original setting by its original recipients. But it may be so used in various activities in the common life of later Christian communities that attention has focused chiefly on images and metaphors Paul happened to use, taken now to illuminate the significance of Jesus or the nature of God's relationship to the human family; or attention may focus in the context of another activity on individual sentences that are taken as asserting theological truths rich with further theological implications, even though Paul was not there developing a system of ideas or making a theological argument. *What is attended to in a passage of scripture tends to be determined more by what human capacities or needs are being addressed by the activity in which the text is being used as scripture than by the apparent or historically reconstructible "original" point of the text.*

Biblical writings are scripture insofar as they are used in the activities comprising the common life of the Christian community, most basically, as those activities that serve to "author" the identities of the community and of its members: it is *for that reason* that they *also* serve to "authorize" theological proposals. Doing theology is one of the activities that comprise the common life of the Christian community. Theological proposals are made to the end that the ways in which the community presents itself in speech and action may be examined as to their faithfulness to the community's calling. In order to do that, theological proposals must be made concerning how best to characterize that call and the promise in which it is grounded, and further proposals made of the criteria by which "faithfulness" to the call may be evaluated. Inasmuch as this is rational self-criticism, these proposals must be backed by arguments. Since that call and promise, and the array of dispositions, beliefs, emotions, etc., that goes with them, are brought to bear on persons' identities by Christian scripture, i.e., by the way biblical writings are used in the common life of the Christian community, it is necessary that arguments in support of theological proposals appeal to passages of scripture to help authorize them, i.e., appeal to them as authority. But that will usually be an *indirect* authorizing. A proposal may well be directly authorized by some experience or warranted belief that has no grounding in scripture. Its relevance to the proposal, however, may be shown—if challenged—by appeal to scripture. In such a case, the biblical writing authorizes the theological proposal, but only indirectly.

However, this illuminates only the de facto relationship of Christian scripture to Christian theology, viz., that given its functions in the community, it also helps authorize theological proposals. It is necessary to go beyond this to justify this by showing that scripture's authoritative relationship to theology is, so to speak, de jure. To do that is to make a specifically *theological* proposal *about* scripture, i.e., a proposal about its relationship to God.

Biblical writings ought to be used in the common life of the Christian community (and hence in doing theology too) because the power of God's kingly rule graciously shapes human identity and empowers new forms of life in persons through scripture, i.e., through the uses of biblical writings in the community's common life. This is the ground of its authority de jure.

This is a theological claim for scripture's de jure authority. It is not enough that as a matter of fact biblical writings are used in certain ways in the community's common life, including use in doing theology. Such de facto authority is either an arbitrary *ascription* of authority to those texts by the community or else it is an *acknowledgment* by the community that they *ought* so to be used, i.e., that they have authority de jure. The latter is the case.

I believe Schubert Ogden is correct in his recent application to scriptural authority of the analysis of the meaning of de jure authority commonly given in philosophy of authority, viz., that de jure authority is "rule-conferred authority." Authority is legitimate, i.e., has a *right* to be acknowledged, only when there are rules that govern legitimation of authority. Thus, a de jure authority and those who acknowledge its authority are in one respect on the same level: they both stand under the authority of the rules that determine that, in another respect, the acknowledger ought to be subordinate to the authority. Hence scripture is "normed norm." Its authority as norm is itself normed by rule(s) that confer on it its authority.

Whence comes the rule(s) in the case of scripture's authority in the common life of the Christian community and in Christian theology? The answer can only be given *theologically* in the strictest sense, i.e., in the form of a claim about the relation of *God* to scripture. One way (but not necessarily the only way) in which the eschatological rule of God impinges on persons' lives is through God's "use" of the uses of scripture in activities comprising the common life of the Christian community. Biblical texts are scripture, we said, only in active tradition, i.e., the act of handing on the promise and call; but that is true only as tradition is actually a concrete mode in which God is present to human life. *In tradition*, biblical writings have authority, but the authority derives not in the first instance from their "content," but rather from the *end* to which they are used, viz., by God's power to empower new human identities.

This is to house a "doctrine of scripture" in the context of a doctrine of God. More exactly, to invoke a classical distinction, it belongs with a discussion of the work of God appropriated to the Third Person rather than with a discussion of the work of God appropriated to the Second Person.

From the earliest period in Christian history revelation has been taken as the middle term between scripture and theology. And revelation has been discussed as part of an explication of the incarnation of the Second Person, the Logos, the principle of intelligibility and of communication between the Creator and creatures. The content of God's disclosure was then said to be recorded in biblical writings inspired by God in such a way that their statement of this content is without error, and in no way relative to the cultural setting of their writing nor to the personalities of their human authors. Theology's task is to republish that content in concise and systematic fashion. Thus scripture's de jure authority for theology was grounded in the work of the Logos, the Second Person of the Triune Godhead. To be sure, in the context of a trinitarian understanding of God, revelation is an act of the Triune Godhead, and so is not without the work of the Holy Spirit. Nevertheless, it has been customary to "appropriate" it to the Son. As Gerhard Ebeling pointed out in a now classic essay first presented thirty years ago, this view trades on the application of "both physical and metaphysical, historical and metahistorical categories to the event of revelation," with the result that the metaphysical and metahistorical categories locate revelatory events in a special *historia sacra* alongside secular history and assessable only by different standards than secular history. In turn, then, biblical writings, as the oracular communication of revelation, are themselves located outside the bibliography of secular writings and, insofar as they are revelatory, are assessable only by other standards than nonbiblical writings. There seem to be two decisive objections to this: methodologically, it involves historical study of the biblical writings in intellectually dishonest special pleading. Theologically, it involves a docetic picture of the involvement of God the revealer in the actual world with its thoroughgoing historical and cultural conditioning of all human phenomena.

By and large modern theology preserved the traditional pattern of making God the revealer the middle term between scripture and theology. But it sought to avoid these objections by insisting that the content of revelation is not specific information about God, but God *himself*, God as "Thou" self-disclosed to us in an I-Thou encounter in Jesus of Nazareth. Accordingly, the conditioned character of biblical writings can be fully acknowledged. They only witness to or symbolize that disclosure. They thereby convey the content of revelation, the word of God (Barth), or the kerygma (Bultmann), or the message (Tillich). Theology's task is not to republish that content, for that content is stated in ways that are tied to long dead cultures. Rather it is to translate it in ways intelligible to a modern hearer. But no actual biblical words or sentences may be identified with that content. Indeed, every effort to *state* it in some way traduces it. It turns out that "word," "kerygma," "message," are *ciphers*. They do not designate any determinate content at all. Rather, they signal the occurrence of an act or an event in which personal existence is transformed (Bultmann) or the ontic structure of reality and history is transformed (Barth) or both (Tillich). And when scripture is used as the basis for proclamation, the "word" or "kerygma" may be communicated, that is, human life now may in some way be caught up in that same act or event. But this way of putting the matter itself has serious drawbacks. Several scholars with quite different theological perspectives have pointed out that the concept of revelation on which this proposal rests cannot adequately include and synthesize the variety of ways in which biblical writings speak of God communicating with persons and is in any case incoherent with a major theme in those writings that God's being (in contradistinction to information about God) can be revealed, if at all, only at the end of history (cf. Barr; Downing; Pannenberg). Secondly, this way of putting things seems to make unintelligible how biblical writings can bear on theological proposals so as to authorize them. That about biblical writings which is said to be theologically important ("word"/"kerygma"/ "message") is systematically elusive. It cannot be formulated. Hence it cannot be used as a norm by which to assess the adequacy of a theological proposal. Thus neither the traditional nor the modern way of grounding the de jure authority of scripture in the revelatory work of the Second Person is available to us.

What matters is that the de jure authority of scripture be grounded in God's relation to it. The suggestion made here is that it be seen as grounded, not in the relation to scripture that God assumes as self-revealer, traditionally appropriated to the Second Person, but in the relation to scripture that God assumes as sanctifier and transformer of human identity, traditionally appropriated to the Third Person. This is not proposed on the grounds that biblical writings are "holy objects" evoking awe, nor on the grounds that sometimes their use is the occasion for the entering of the sacred into the midst of the profane. Nor is it proposed on the grounds that the biblical writings were in some sense "inspired" by God. These may all be true, but none of them is necessary for the biblical writings to be de jure authoritative scripture. That is, none of them needs be true in order that, by various uses of the writings, God may empower new human identities.

Seen this way, what is authoritative about scripture is not a systematizable set of doctrines about transcendent states of affairs and about arcane metahistorical histories, nor is it a systematically elusive "word." It is a heterogeneous collection of images, parables, metaphors, principles for action, beliefs, emotion-concepts, etc., each of which is determinately particular and concrete. It is their concreteness that creates the need to do theology, for it is never simply self-evident how to speak or act today in one's own setting in ways that follow the "grammar" they exhibit in their own setting. It is their heterogeneity that obliges every one who does theology to make a theological judgment about what is central to that heterogeneity, what can serve as a norming norm by which to select, order, and interrelate the scripture to which appeal is made.

The norming norm guiding the construal and use of scripture (as normed norm) in theology is the actuality of the inauguration in and for the world of the eschatological rule of God in the resurrection of the crucified Jesus. This makes it both necessary and possible that as scripture is used to authorize theological proposals its "polyphonic variety" be respected.

One way in which God's rule bears on persons, empowering new forms of life, is *in* the course of "active tradition" *by* means of "passive tradition." The "passive tradition" is immensely diverse. Its component documents originated in different historical periods and cultures. They often exhibit theological beliefs that seem mutually exclusive. Where they seem to make historical claims they are of varying reliability. In all their diversity, the biblical writings may nonetheless be "scripture," used to authorize theological proposals to the extent that they can be shown to have some relation to the actuality of God's eschatological rule in and for the world. This point can be illustrated only in the sketchiest way here.

The traditions about the ministry, life, death, and resurrection appearances of Jesus clearly have a sort of centrality. Where they are narratives, they may be construed as rendering concretely the peculiar and concrete *way* in which God's eschatological rule was inaugurated. The subtle dialectic between crucifixion and resurrection must rule what is said about God and God's rule, especially what is said about God's power. And it must govern what is said about dispositions, emotions, and beliefs appropriate to the presence of this rule, and especially how "hope" is understood. Since Christian identity is called into being as a response to precisely this actuality, the narratives about Jesus clearly *focus* all else that is to be said about suitable dispositions, emotions, beliefs, etc., and focuses uses of other traditions in the biblical writings. Furthermore, since these beliefs, attitudes, dispositions, etc., are relative to an individual human life, clearly the truth of some historical fact claims is a necessary condition of their appropriateness. Here one fact *is* of ultimate importance so far as the identity of the Christian community and its members is concerned. But it does not follow that all biblical writings must be construed and used "Christocentrically" or that they are authoritative only as they "bear Christ" (Luther). . . .

Rigorous academic historical and critical study of biblical texts, study of their history and study of their historical accuracy, bears in obvious and decisive ways on every use of any passage of biblical writing employed to help authorize a theological proposal. Clearly no proposal can be warranted by appeal to a historical claim either made about scripture or made on the basis of biblical claims if the claim has been discredited by historical research. Critical textual study can sharpen our grasp of nuance, especially of biblical emotion-, disposition-, attitude-, and other concepts, helping us to avoid archaizing assimilations, e.g., of blessedness to happiness, or faith to "basic trust." So, too, it can identify tensions between different texts that might too easily be assimilated to each other, and it can bring to light tensions within a text as it now stands. But neither historical study of the texts nor careful and, in its own way, rigorous reading of the text as it now is can validate or invalidate any plausible proposal such as the one made throughout this paper, viz., that it is the inauguration of God's kingly rule that lies at the heart of the various forms of Christian existence and Christian beliefs. That is a judgment about what the "Christian thing" is basically all about. Scripture may be construed and used in light of it. But any biblical text adduced in an argument to show that it is wrong or inadequate would itself be used and construed within the horizon of another and competing such general judgment, and hence not be decisive.

III. GOD

1. GREGORY OF NYSSA: ON THE TRINITY

Following in the tradition of Origen, Gregory belonged to a group of fourth-century theologians credited with securing the final triumph of Nicene orthodoxy over Arianism and Apollinarianism. In this selection, he defends the trinitarian conception of God against the charge that it amounts to belief in three separate gods by appealing to the unity of divine action. Source: Gregory of Nyssa, "An Answer to Ablabius: That We Should Not Think of Saying There Are Three Gods," *Christology of the Later Fathers,* ed. E. R. Hardy (Philadelphia: Westminster Press, 1954), pp. 259–64. Date of original composition: 375.

Most people think that the word "Godhead" refers to God's nature in a special way. Just as the heaven, the sun, or any other of the world's elements is denoted by a proper name which signifies its subject, so they say that, in reference to the transcendent and divine nature, the word "Godhead" is fitly applied, like some proper name, to what it represents. We, however, following the suggestions of Holy Scripture, have learned that his nature cannot be named and is ineffable. We say that every name, whether invented by human custom or handed down by the Scriptures, is indicative of our conceptions of the divine nature, but does not signify what that nature is in itself. It is not very difficult to prove that this is the case. For, even without going into their origins, you will find that all terms that refer to the created world are accidentally applied to their subjects. We are content, in whatever way, to signify things by their names so as to avoid confusion in our knowledge of the things we refer to. But whatever terms there are to lead us to the knowledge of God, each of them contains a particular idea of its own; and you will not find any word among the terms especially applied to God which is without some meaning. From this it is clear that the divine nature in itself is not signified by any of these terms. Rather is some attribute declared by what is said. For we say, perhaps, that the divine is incorruptible or powerful or whatever else we are in the habit of saying. But in each of these terms we find a particular idea which by thought and expression we rightly attribute to the divine nature, but which does not express what that nature essentially is. For the subject, whatever it may be, is incorruptible, but our idea of incorruptibility is this: that that which is is not resolved into decay. In saying, then, that he is incorruptible, we tell what his nature does not suffer. But what that is which does not suffer corruption we have not defined. Or again, even if we say he is the creator of life, while we indicate by the expression what it is he creates, we do not reveal by the word what creates it. By the same principle, we find in all other cases that the significance attaching to divine names lies either in their forbidding wrong conceptions of the divine nature or in their teaching right ones. But they do not contain an explanation of the nature in itself.

We perceive, then, the varied operations of the transcendent power, and fit our way of speaking of him to each of the operations known to us. Now one of these is the power of viewing and seeing, or, one might say, of beholding (*theatikē*). By it God surveys all things and oversees them all. He discerns our thoughts, and by his power of beholding penetrates even what is invisible. From this we suppose that "Godhead" (*theotēs*) is derived from "beholding" (*thea*), and that by general custom and the teaching of the Scriptures, he who is our beholder (*theatēs*) is called God (*theos*). Now if anyone admits that to behold and see are the same thing, and that the God who oversees all things both is and is called the overseer of the universe, let him consider whether this operation belongs to one of the persons we believe to constitute the holy Trinity, or whether the power extends to the three persons. For if our interpretation of "Godhead" is the right one, and the things which are seen are said to be beheld (*theata*), and that which beholds them is called God (*theos*), no one of the persons of the Trinity could properly be excluded from this form of address on the ground of the meaning of the word. For Scripture attributes sight equally to Father, Son, and Holy Spirit. David says, "See, O God our defender" (Ps. 84:9). From this we learn that the power of sight is proper to the idea of God so far as he is conceived. For David said, "See, O Lord." But Jesus, too, sees the thoughts of those who condemn him because he forgives men's sins on his own authority. For it says, "Jesus, seeing their thoughts" (Matt. 9:4). And in reference to the Holy Spirit, Peter says to Ananias, "Why has Satan filled your heart to lie to the Holy Spirit?" (Acts 5:3). Thus he shows that the Holy Spirit, by whom the secret was disclosed to Peter, was a faithful witness and privy to what Ananias dared to do in secret. For Ananias became a thief of his own property, imagining he was escaping everyone's notice and hiding his sin. But the same moment the Holy Spirit was in Peter and discerned his degraded and avaricious intention and himself gave Peter the power to penetrate the secret; which he clearly could not have done had he been unable to discern what is hidden. . . .

We have fairly well proved by our argument that the word "Godhead" does not refer to a nature, but to an operation. Perhaps, then, someone might with a good cause adduce the following reason why men who share the same profession with one another can be counted and referred to in the plural, while the deity is spoken of in the singular as one God and one Godhead, despite the fact that the three persons are not excluded from the significance attaching to "Godhead." He might argue that in the case of men, even if many share the same operation, each one separately and by himself undertakes the matter at hand. By his individual action each contributes nothing to the others engaged in the same task. For if there are many orators, their pursuit, being identical, bears the same name despite their plurality. Yet each one who follows this pursuit goes about it on his own. This one pleads in his special way, that one in his. In the case of men, therefore, since we can differentiate the action of each while they are engaged in the same task, they are rightly referred to in the plural. Each is distinguished from the others by his special environment and his particular way of handling the task.

With regard to the divine nature, on the other hand, it is otherwise. We do not learn that the Father does something on his own, in which the Son does not co-operate. Or again, that the Son acts on his own without the Spirit. Rather does every operation which extends from God to creation and is designated according to our differing conceptions of it have its origin in the Father, proceed through the Son, and reach its completion by the Holy Spirit. It is for this reason that the word for the operation is not divided among the persons involved. For the action of each in any matter is not separate and individualized. But whatever occurs, whether in reference to God's providence for us or to the government and constitution of the universe, occurs through the three persons, and is not three separate things.

We can grasp this by reference to a single instance. From him, I say, who is the source of gifts, all things that share in this grace have obtained life. When, then, we inquire whence this good gift came to us, we find through the guidance of the Scriptures that it was through the Father, the Son, and the Holy Spirit. But though we take it for granted that there are three persons and names, we do not imagine that three different lives are granted us—one from each of them. Rather is it the same life which is produced by the Father, prepared by the Son, and depends on the will of the Holy Spirit.

Thus the holy Trinity brings to effect every operation in a similar way. It is not by separate action according to the number of the persons; but there is one motion and disposition of the good will which proceeds from the Father, through the Son, to the Spirit. For we do not call those who produce a single life three life-givers; nor do we say they are three good beings who are seen to share the same goodness; nor do we speak of them in the plural reference to all their other attributes. In the same way we cannot enumerate as three gods those who jointly, inseparably, and mutually exercise their divine power and activity of overseeing us and the whole creation. . . .

As we have already said, the principle of the overseeing and beholding (*theatikēs*) power is a unity in Father, Son, and Holy Spirit. It issues from the Father, as from a spring. It is actualized by the Son; and its grace is perfected by the power of the Holy Spirit. No activity is distinguished among the persons, as if it were brought to completion individually by each of them or separately apart from their joint supervision. Rather is all providence, care and direction of everything, whether in the sensible creation or of heavenly nature, one and not three. The preservation of what exists, the rectifying of what is amiss, the instruction of what is set right, is directed by the holy Trinity. But it is not divided into three parts according to the number of the persons acknowledged by the faith, so that each operation, viewed by itself, should be the work of the Father alone, or of the Only-begotten by himself, or of the Holy Spirit separately. But while, as the apostle says (1 Cor. 12:11), the one and the same Spirit distributes his benefits to each one severally, this beneficent movement of the Spirit is not without beginning. Rather do we find that the power we conceive as preceding it, namely, the only-begotten God, effects everything. Apart from him nothing comes into being; and again, this source of goodness issues from the Father's will.

Every good thing and everything we name as good depends on the power and purpose which is without beginning. And it is brought to completion by the power of the Holy Spirit and through the only-begotten God, immediately and independent of time. No delay exists or is to be conceived in the movement of the divine will from the Father through the Son and to the Holy Spirit. Now the Godhead is one of these good names and concepts; and hence the word cannot be rightly used in the plural, since the unity of operation forbids the plural number.

The Savior of all men, especially of believers, is spoken of by the apostle (1 Tim. 4:10) as one. Yet no one argues from this expression that the Son does not save believers, or that those who share in salvation receive it apart from the Spirit. But God who is over all is the Savior of all, while the Son brings salvation to effect by the grace of the Spirit. Yet on this account Scripture does not call them three Saviors, although salvation is recognized to come from the holy Trinity. In the same way they are not three gods according to the meaning we have given to the term "Godhead," although this expression attaches to the holy Trinity. . . .

2. ANSELM: THE ATTRIBUTES OF GOD

Called the "Father of Scholasticism," Anselm prepared the way for the full flowering of medieval thought with his judicious application of philosophical reasoning to problems of Christian belief. In these selections from his *Monologium*, Chaps. 16–18, 25, he discusses the attributes of God in relation to the being of God, and in particular analyzes the attributes of simplicity, eternity, and immutability. Source: *St. Anselm*, trans. S. N. Deane (La Salle, Ill.: Open Court, 1951), pp. 64–70, 84–85. Date of original composition: 1076.

For this being it is the same to be just that it is to be
justice; and so with regard to attributes that can be
expressed in the same way: and none of these shows of
what character, or how great, but what this being is.

But perhaps, when this being is called just, or great, or anything like these, it is not shown what it is, but of what character, or how great it is. For every such term seems to be used with reference to quantity or magnitude; because everything that is just is so through justness, and so with other like cases, in the same way. Hence, the supreme nature itself is not just, except through justness.

It seems, then, that by *participation* in this quality, that is, justness, the supremely good substance is called just. But, if this is so, it is just through another, and not through itself. But this is contrary to the truth already established, that it is good, or great, or whatever it is at all, through itself and not through another. So, if it is not just, except through justness, and cannot be just, except through itself, what can be more clear than that this nature is itself justness? And, when it is said to be just through justness, it is the same as saying that it is just through itself. And, when it is said to be just through itself, nothing else is understood than that it is just through justness. Hence, if it is inquired what the supreme nature, which is in question, is in itself, what truer answer can be given, than *justness?*

We must observe, then, how we are to understand the statement, that the nature which is itself justness is just. For, since a man cannot be justness, but can possess justness, we do not conceive of a just man as *being* justness, but as possessing justness. Since, on the other hand, it cannot properly be said of the supreme nature that it possesses justness, but that it is justness, when it is called just it is properly conceived of as being justness, but not as possessing justness. Hence, if, when it is said to be justness, it is not said of what character it is, but *what* it is, it follows that, when it is called just, it is not said of what character it is, but what it is.

Therefore, seeing that it is the same to say of the supreme being, that it is just and that it is justness; and, when it is said that it is justness, it is nothing else than saying that it is just; it makes no difference whether it is said to be justness or to be just. Hence, when one is asked regarding the supreme nature, what it is, the answer, *just*, is not less fitting than the answer, *justness*. Moreover, what we see to have been proved in the case of justness, the intellect is compelled to acknowledge as true of all attributes which are similarly predicated of this supreme nature. Whatever such attribute is predicated of it, then, it is shown, not of what character, or how great, but *what* it is.

But it is obvious that whatever good thing the supreme nature is, it is in the highest degree. It is, therefore, supreme being, supreme justness, supreme wisdom, supreme truth, supreme goodness, supreme greatness, supreme beauty, supreme immortality, supreme incorruptibility, supreme immutability, supreme blessedness, supreme eternity, supreme power, supreme unity; which is nothing else than supremely being, supremely living, etc.

It is simple in such a way that all things that can be
said of its essence are one and the same in it: and
nothing can be said of its substance except in terms of
what it is.

Is it to be inferred, then, that if the supreme nature is so many goods, it will therefore be compounded of more goods than one? Or is it true, rather, that there are not more goods than one, but a single good described by many names? For, everything which is composite requires for its subsistence the things of which it is compounded, and, indeed, owes to them the fact of its existence, because, whatever it is, it is through these things; and they are not what they are through it, and therefore it is not at all supreme. If, then, that nature is compounded of more goods than one, all these facts that are true of every composite must be applicable to it. But this impious falsehood the whole cogency of the truth that was shown above refutes and overthrows, through a clear argument.

Since, then, that nature is by no means composite, and yet is by all means those so many goods, necessarily all these are not more than one, but are one. Any one of them is, therefore, the same as all, whether taken all at once or separately. Therefore, just as whatever is attributed to the essence of the supreme substance is one; so this substance is whatever it is essentially in one way, and by virtue of one consideration. For, when a man is said to be a material body, and rational, and human, these three things are not said in one way, or in virtue of one consideration. For, in accordance with one fact, he is a material body; and in accordance with another, rational; and no one of these, taken by itself, is the whole of what man is. That supreme being, however, is by no means anything in such a way that it is not this same thing, according to another way, or another consideration; because, whatever it is essentially in any way, this is all of what it is. Therefore, nothing that is truly said of the supreme being is accepted in terms of quality or quantity, but only in terms of *what* it is. For, whatever it is in terms of either quality or quantity would constitute still another element, in terms of what it is; hence, it would not be simple, but composite.

It is without beginning and without end.

From what time, then, has this so simple nature which creates and animates all things existed, or until what time is it to exist? Or rather, let us ask neither from what time, nor to what time, it exists; but is it without beginning and without end? For, if it has a beginning, it has this either from or through itself, or from or through another, or from or through nothing.

But it is certain, according to truths already made plain, that in no wise does it derive existence from another, or from nothing; or exist through another, or through nothing. In no wise, therefore, has it had inception through or from another, or through or from nothing.

Moreover, it cannot have inception from or through itself, although it exists from and through itself. For it so exists from and through itself, that by no means is there one essence which exists from and through itself, and another through which, and from which, it exists. But, whatever begins to exist from or through something, is by no means identical with that from or through which it begins to exist. Therefore, the supreme nature does not begin through or from itself.

Seeing, then, that it has a beginning neither through nor from itself, and neither through nor from nothing, it assuredly has no beginning at all. But neither will it have an end. For, if it is to have end, it is not supremely immortal and supremely incorruptible. But we have proved that it is supremely immortal and supremely incorruptible. Therefore, it will not have an end.

Furthermore, if it is to have an end, it will perish either willingly or against its will. But certainly that is not a simple, unmixed good, at whose will the supreme good perishes. But this being is itself the true and simple, unmixed good. Therefore, that very being, which is certainly the supreme good, will not die of its own will. If, however, it is to perish against its will, it is not supremely powerful, or all-powerful. But cogent reasoning has asserted it to be powerful and all-powerful. Therefore, it will not die against its will. Hence, if neither with nor against its will the supreme nature is to have an end, in no way will it have an end.

Again, if the supreme nature has an end or a beginning, it is not true eternity, which it has been irrefutably proved to be above.

Then, let him who can conceive of a time when this began to be true, or when it is not true, namely, that something was destined to be; or when this shall cease to be true, and shall not be true, namely, that something has existed. But, if neither of these suppositions is conceivable, and both these facts cannot exist without truth, it is impossible even to conceive that truth has either beginning or end. And then, if truth had a beginning, or shall have an end; before it began it was true that truth did not exist, and after it shall be ended it will be true that truth will not exist. Yet, anything that is *true* cannot exist without truth. Therefore, truth existed before truth existed, and truth will exist after truth shall be ended, which is a most contradictory conclusion. Whether, then, truth is said to have, or understood not to have, beginning or end, it cannot be limited by any beginning or end. Hence, the same follows as regards the supreme nature, since it is itself the supreme truth. . . .

It cannot suffer change by any accidents.

But does not this being, which has been shown to exist as in every way substantially identical with itself, sometimes exist as different from itself, at any rate, accidentally? But how is it supremely immutable, if it can, I will not say, *be*, but, be conceived of, as variable by virtue of accidents? And, on the other hand, does it not partake of accident, since even this very fact that it is greater than all other natures and that it is unlike them seems to be an accident in its case (*illi accidere*)? But what is the inconsistency between susceptibility to certain facts, called *accidents,* and natural immutability, if from the undergoing of these accidents the substance undergoes no change?

For, of all the facts, called accidents, some are understood not to be present or absent without some variation in the subject of the accident —all colors, for instance—while others are known not to effect any change in a thing either by occurring or not occurring—certain relations, for instance. For it is certain that I am neither older nor younger than a man who is not yet born, nor equal to him, nor like him. But I shall be able to sustain and to lose all these relations toward him, as soon as he shall have been born, according as he shall grow, or undergo change through divers qualities.

It is made clear, then, that of all those facts, called accidents, a part bring some degree of mutability in their train, while a part do not impair at all the immutability of that in whose case they occur. Hence, although the supreme nature in its simplicity has never undergone such accidents as cause mutation, yet it does not disdain occasional expression in terms of those accidents which are in no wise inconsistent with supreme immutability; and yet there is no accident respecting its essence, whence it would be conceived of, as itself variable.

Whence this conclusion, also, may be reached, that it is susceptible of no accident; since, just as those accidents, which effect some change by their occurrence or non-occurrence, are by virtue of this very effect of theirs regarded as being true *accidents,* so those facts, which lack a like effect, are found to be improperly called accidents. Therefore, this essence is always, in every way, substantially identical with itself; and it is never in any way different from itself, even accidentally. But, however it may be as to the proper signification of the term *accident,* this is undoubtedly true, that of the supremely immutable nature no statement can be made, whence it shall be conceived of as mutable. . . .

3. THOMAS AQUINAS: LANGUAGE ABOUT GOD

The publication of the *Summa Theologica* of Thomas Aquinas marked the culmination of several centuries of speculation regarding the nature of God. While better known for his five "proofs" for the existence

of God, Thomas's most important contribution to current thinking about
God is probably his discussion of theological language. For it is there
that he sets forth his famous doctrine of analogy, in which he affirms our
capacity to speak meaningfully of God while recognizing that words used
in this way cannot mean the same as in ordinary usage. Source: Thomas
Aquinas, *Summa Theologica* Ia. 13, 5–6 (Blackfriars ed., Vol. 3, trans.
Herbert McCabe [London: Eyre & Spottiswoode, 1964], pp. 61–71).
Date of original composition: 1266 ff.

Are Words Used Univocally or Equivocally of God and Creatures?

It is impossible to predicate anything univocally of God and creatures. Every effect that falls short of what is typical of the power of its
cause represents it inadequately, for it is not the same kind of thing as
the cause. Thus what exists simply and in a unified way in the cause
will be divided up and take various different forms in such effects—as
the simple power of the sun produces many different kinds of lesser
things. In the same way, as we said earlier, the perfections which in
creatures are many and various pre-exist in God as one.

The perfection of words that we use in speaking of creatures all differ
in meaning and each one signifies a perfection as something distinct
from all the others. Thus when we say that a man is wise, we signify
his wisdom as something distinct from the other things about
him—his essence, for example, his powers or his existence. But when
we use this word about God we do not intend to signify something distinct from his essence, power or existence. When "wise" is used of a
man, it so to speak contains and delimits the aspect of man that it signifies, but this is not so when it is used of God; what it signifies in God
is not confined by the meaning of our word but goes beyond it. Hence
it is clear that the word "wise" is not used in the same sense of God and
man, and the same is true of all other words, so they cannot be used
univocally of God and creatures.

Yet although we never use words in exactly the same sense of creatures and God we are not merely equivocating when we use the same
word, as some have said, for if this were so we could never argue from
statements about creatures to statements about God—any such argument would be invalidated by the fallacy of equivocation. That this
does not happen we know not merely from the teachings of the philos-

ophers who prove many things about God but also from the teaching of St. Paul, for he says, "The invisible things of God are made known by those things that are made" (Rom. 1:20).

We must say, therefore, that words are used of God and creatures in an *analogical* way, that is in accordance with a certain order between them. We can distinguish two kinds of analogical or "proportional" uses of language. Firstly there is the case of one word being used of two things because each of them has some order or relation to a third thing. Thus we use the word "healthy" of both a diet and a complexion because each of these has some relation to health in a man, the former as a cause, the latter as a symptom of it. Secondly there is the case of the same word used of two things because of some relation that one has to the other—as "healthy" is used of the diet and the man because the diet is the cause of the health in the man.

In this way some words are used neither univocally nor purely equivocally of God and creatures, but analogically, for we cannot speak of God at all except in the language we use of creatures, and so whatever is said both of God and creatures is said in virture of the order that creatures have to God as to their source and cause in which all the perfections of things pre-exist transcendently.

This way of using words lies somewhere between pure equivocation and simple univocity, for the word is neither used in the same sense, as with univocal usage, nor in totally different senses, as with equivoca-tion. The several senses of a word used analogically signify different re-lations to some one thing, as "health" in a complexion means a symptom of health in a man, and in a diet means a cause of that health. . . .

Are Words Predicated Primarily of God or of Creatures?

Whenever a word is used analogically of many things, it is used of them because of some order or relation they have to some central thing. In order to explain an extended or analogical use of a word it is necessary to mention this central thing. Thus you cannot explain what you mean by a "healthy" diet without mentioning the health of the man of which it is the cause; similarly you must understand "healthy" as applied to a man before you can understand what is meant by a "healthy complexion" which is the symptom of that health. The primary application of the word is to the central thing that has to be understood first; other applications will be more or less secondary in so far as they approximate to this use.

Thus all words used *metaphorically* of God apply primarily to creatures and secondarily to God. When used of God they signify merely a certain parallelism between God and the creature. When we speak metaphorically of a meadow as "smiling" we only mean that it shows at its best when it flowers, just as a man shows at his best when he smiles: there is a parallel between them. In the same way, if we speak of God as a "lion" we only mean that, like a lion, he is mighty in his deeds. It is obvious that the meaning of such a word as applied to God depends on and is secondary to the meaning it has when used of creatures.

This would be the case for non-metaphorical words too if they were simply used, as some have supposed, to express God's causality. If, for example, "God is good" meant the same as "God is the cause of goodness in creatures" the word "good" as applied to God would have contained within its meaning the goodness of the creature; and hence "good" would apply primarily to creatures and secondarily to God.

But we have already shown that words of this sort do not only say how God is a cause, they also say what he is. When we say he is good or wise we do not simply mean that he causes wisdom or goodness, but that he possesses these perfections transcendently. We conclude, therefore, that from the point of view of what the word means it is used primarily of God and derivatively of creatures, for what the word means—the perfection it signifies—flows from God to the creature. But from the point of view of our use of the word we apply it first to creatures because we know them first. That, as we have mentioned already, is why it has a way of signifying that is appropriate to creatures.

4. HARTSHORNE: THE DIVINE RELATIVITY

In the modern period, the classical doctrine of God has come under persistent attack on both metaphysical and religious grounds. Emphasizing the relatedness of God to the world, modern theologians have tended to be critical of traditional notions of the absoluteness, independence, and self-sufficiency of God. The philosopher Charles Hartshorne is representative of this development with his argument for the "process" model of God. Source: Charles Hartshorne, *The Divine Relativity* (New Haven: Yale University Press, 1948), pp. 18–24.

Of course one is free to mean by "absolute" whatever is supreme or most excellent. But then one is not free to use the same word, without warning, for the nonrelative, for what is independent, immutable, impassive, and the like. It is not self-evident that independence (or immutability) as such *is* excellence, and that excellence as such *is* independence. On the contrary, as I hope in this first chapter to show, excellence or value has a dimension of dependence as well as of independence, and there is no basis for the venerable doctrine that supreme independence will constitute supreme excellence of every kind. To resolve the paradoxes connected with the contrast between relative and absolute we must, I shall argue, admit that the "absolute" is not identical with the supreme being or God, but in a strict sense is infinitely less than the supreme, and in fact is a certain kind of constituent within it. If this admission seems as much a paradox as any which it is designed to remove, the reason is that sufficient attention has not been paid to the definition of "absolute" as simply "what is nonrelative." Why must the nonrelative be more than, or even as much as, the relative? Why must a mere term be more than or equal to a term which involves relations, and hence other terms as relata?

But, it will be said, by God we mean, or for religion we require, not simply a supreme or most excellent but a perfect being. And how can a perfect being change (as it must if relations to the changing world are internal to it)? This argument I counter with a dilemma.

The perfect being either does, or does not, include the totality of imperfect things. If it does, then it is inferior to a conceivable perfection whose constituents would be more perfect. (There is no meaning to the idea of a greatest possible totality of imperfect things.) If the perfect does *not* include the totality of imperfect things, then the total reality which is "the perfect *and* all existing imperfect things" is a greater reality than the perfect alone. If it be said that the perfect, though it does not include the imperfect things, does include their values, whatever is good in them, the reply is that the existence of the imperfect must then be strictly valueless, adding nothing to the sum of values, and might

73

exactly as well not be as be. He who says this implies that God did no good thing when he created the world, and that our human existence is metaphysically useless and meaningless. The only way to escape this is to admit that the perfect-*and*-the-imperfect is something superior to the perfect "alone"—or as independent of the imperfect.

Which horn of this dilemma shall we grasp? If perfection is defined as that which in no respect could conceivably be greater, and hence is incapable of increase, then we face paradox on either hand. But suppose we define the perfect, or supremely excellent or good, as that individual being (in what sense "individual" will appear later) than which no *other individual* being could *conceivably* be greater, but which *itself*, in another "state," could become greater (perhaps by the creation within itself of new constituents). Otherwise expressed, let us define perfection as an excellence such that rivalry or superiority on the part of other individuals is impossible, but self-superiority is not impossible. Or again, let us say that the perfect is the "self-surpassing surpasser of all." This formula resolves the dilemma. For suppose the self-surpassing surpasser of all has the power of unfailingly enjoying as its own constituents whatever imperfect things come to exist. Then it will be bound to possess in its own unity all the values which the imperfect things severally and separately achieve, and therefore it is bound to surpass each and every one of them. Thus it is certain of superiority to any "other individual." It must, in any conceivable state of existence, be the "most excellent being."

By speaking of the perfect as "enjoying" the values of things, I mean to exclude the idea of a mere collection of all things. The surpasser of all others must be a single individual enjoying as his own all the values of all other individuals, and incapable of failing to do so. For this, it is enough to suppose that the being is bound to have adequate knowledge of events when and as they occur, and thereafter. For adequately to know values is to possess them; and to surpass the values of other beings it is enough to possess the values of every one of them from the time these values exist. There is no need to possess them in advance of the others; or to possess them eternally, unless a being which surveys all time eternally is itself a conceivable being—which this essay seeks to disprove. To surpass other conceivable beings, there is no need to surpass inconceivable beings, as they would be if they were, which they are not, conceivable. Even the least of beings surpasses mere nonsense.

I shall hope to show in this chapter that religion does not need perfection in any other sense than that called for by our formula. (If my use of the term "perfection" be objected to, I ask that the phrase "transcendent excellence" be mentally substituted. I would have used "transcendence" were it not usually contrasted to immanence, a contrast here not directly relevant. And I know of no term except "perfect" which connotes superiority to all possible others.) Meanwhile, I wish to point out that, although the self-surpassing surpasser of all must obviously be in some aspect relative, it does not follow that it is in *no* aspect absolute. For to be capable of self-increase in *some* respect does not imply capacity to increase in every respect. Indeed, it is logically self-evident that in two respects such increase is excluded by our definition. To be absolutely guaranteed superiority to absolutely every other individual that comes to exist is an absolute maximum in certainty and universality of superiority. Moreover, this certainty and universality are intelligible only in terms of such attributes as omniscience (ideal knowledge), and we shall see that as "relational types" these are absolute in the strictest sense.

The absolute aspect of perfection, as above defined, may be symbolized as A-perfection. The relative aspect correspondingly becomes R-perfection. The common element of "perfection," neutral as between A and R, is "surpasses all others in all conceivable states of existence."

Since the relativity of the all-surpassing is a unique and supreme case, it needs a special title. I propose the terms, Surrelative and Surrelativism, for this kind of relativity and the doctrine asserting it. The letter R has the convenience of being able to suggest another feature of the theory, which is that the relativity of the surrelative is also the reflexivity of its all-surpassingness. It surpasses itself, as well as everything else; with the difference that it surpasses others simultaneously, but itself only in a subsequent state.

Is this conception acceptable to religion? To answer this question significantly we must consider not mere verbal habits common among

theologians, however reputable, but the *values* that can be detected
—other than the mere value of familiar or high-sounding words—beneath the use of religious terms like perfect or absolute.

Why is it religiously significant that God be supposed absolute? The
reason is at least suggested by the consideration that absoluteness is
requisite for complete reliability. What is relative to conditions may
fail us if the conditions happen to be unfavorable. Hence if there is to
be anything that *cannot* fail, it must be nonrelative, absolute, in those
respects to which "reliability" and "failure" have reference. But it is
often not noted that this need not be every respect or aspect from
which God's nature can be regarded. For there may be qualities in
God whose relativity or variability would be neutral to his reliability.
To say of a man that (as human affairs go) his reliability is established
refers not to every quality of the man, but only to certain principles ex-
hibited in his otherwise highly variable behavior. We do not mean that
if something comes close to his eye he will not blink, or that if he is
given bad-tasting food he will enjoy it as much as better fare. We mean
that his fixed intention to act according to the requirements of the general welfare will not waver, and that his wisdom and skill in carrying
out this aim will be constant. But in all this there is not only no implication that conditions will not have effect upon the man, but the very
plain implication that they will have plenty of effect. Skill in one set of
circumstances means one form of behavior, in another set another
form, and the same is true of the intention to serve the general good.
Of course, one may argue that complete fixity of good intention and
complete constancy of skill imply every other sort of fixity as well. But
this has never yet been definitely shown by careful, explicit reasoning,
and anything less is inappropriate in as difficult a subject as we are
dealing with. General hunches will not do.

A typically invalid argument in this connection is that unless God
surveys at once the whole of time and thus is independent of change,
he cannot be relied upon to arrange all events with due regard to their
relations to all that has gone before and all that is to come after. This
argument either rests on an equivocation or it destroys all religious
meaning for the divine reliability. For, if it is meant in any clear sense,
it implies that every event has been selected by deity as an element in
the best of all possible worlds, the ideal total pattern of all time and all

existence. But this ideal pattern includes all acts of sin and the most hideous suffering and catastrophe, all the tragedies of life. And what then becomes of the ideas of human responsibility and choice, and of the notion that some deeds ought not to have taken place? These are only the beginning of the absurdities into which the view thrusts us. To mitigate these absurdities theologians introduce various more or less subtle equivocations. Would they not do better to take a fresh start (as indeed many have done) and admit that we have no good religious reason for positing the notion of providence as an absolute contriving of all events according to a completely detailed plan embracing all time? The religious value of such a notion is more negative than positive. It is the mother of no end of chicanery (see the book of Job for some examples), of much deep feeling of injustice (the poor unfortunate being assured that God has deliberately contrived everything as exactly the best way events could transpire), and of philosophical quagmires of paradox and unmeaning verbiage. The properly constituted man does not want to "rely" upon God to arrange all things, including our decisions, in accordance with a plan of all events which fixes every least detail with reference to every other that ever has happened or ever "is to" happen. How many atheists must have been needlessly produced by insistence upon this arbitrary notion, which after all is invariably softened by qualifications surreptitiously introduced *ad hoc* when certain problems are stressed! We shall see later that the really usable meaning of divine reliability is quite different and is entirely compatible with a profound relativity of God to conditions and to change. For the present, I suggest that all we can assert to have obvious religious value is the faith that God is to be relied upon to do for the world all that ought to be done for it, and with as much survey of the future as there ought to be or as is ideally desirable, leaving for the members of the world community to do for themselves and each other all that they ought to be left to do. We cannot assume that what ought to be done for the world by deity is everything that ought to be done at all, leaving the creatures with nothing to do for themselves and for each other. Nor can we assume that the ideal survey of what for us at least constitutes the future is one which fully defines it in every detail, leaving no open alternatives of possibility. So far from being self-evidently of religious value, these assumptions, viewed in the light of history, seem clearly of extreme disvalue. Yet they are often either asserted, or not unequivocally denied or avoided, in the intemperate insistence upon the total absoluteness of deity.

5. BARTH: THE HUMANITY OF GOD

Shortly after the First World War, Karl Barth stunned his contemporaries with a commentary on Romans in which he called for a radically transcendent view of God as a corrective to the more immanent view espoused by liberal theology. Some years later he shifted direction again, reaffirming God's relationship to humanity, though from a strictly christological perspective. Source: Karl Barth, *The Humanity of God*, trans. J. N. Thomas and T. Wieser (Richmond: John Knox Press, 1960), pp. 47–52. Originally delivered as a lecture in 1956.

Who and what God is—this is what in particular we have to learn better and with more precision in the new change of direction in the thinking and speaking of evangelical theology, which has become necessary in the light of the earlier change. But the question must be, who and what is God *in Jesus Christ*, if we here today would push forward to a better answer.

Beyond doubt God's *deity* is the first and fundamental fact that strikes us when we look at the existence of Jesus Christ as attested in the Holy Scripture. And God's deity in Jesus Christ consists in the fact that God himself in him is the *subject* who speaks and acts with sovereignty. He is the free One in whom all freedom has its ground, its meaning, its prototype. He is the initiator, founder, preserver, and fulfiller of the covenant. He is the sovereign Lord of the amazing relationship in which he becomes and is not only different from man but also one with him. He is also the creator of him who is his partner. He it is through whose faithfulness the corresponding faithfulness of his partner is awakened and takes place. The old Reformed Christology worked that out especially clearly in its doctrine of the "hypostatic union": God is on the throne. In the existence of Jesus Christ, the fact that God speaks, gives, orders, comes absolutely first—that man hears, receives, obeys, can and must only follow this first act. In Jesus Christ man's freedom is wholly enclosed in the freedom of God. Without the condescension of God there would be no exaltation of man. As the Son of God and not otherwise, Jesus Christ is the Son of Man. This sequence is irreversible. God's independence, omnipotence, and eternity, God's holiness and justice and thus God's deity, in its original and proper form, is the power leading to this effective and visible sequence in the existence of Jesus Christ: superiority preceding subordination. Thus we have here no universal deity capable of being reached conceptually, but this concrete deity—real and recognizable in the *descent* grounded in that sequence and peculiar to the existence of Jesus Christ.

But here there is something even more concrete to be seen. God's high freedom in Jesus Christ is his freedom for *love*. The divine capacity which operates and exhibits itself in that superiority and subordination is manifestly also God's capacity to bend downwards, to attach himself to another and this other to himself, to be together with him. This takes place in that irreversible sequence, but in it is completely real. In that sequence there arises and continues in Jesus Christ the highest communion of God with man. God's deity is thus no prison in which he can exist only in and for himself. It is rather his freedom to be in and for himself but also with and for us, to assert but also to sacrifice himself, to be wholly exalted but also completely humble, not only almighty but also almighty mercy, not only Lord but also servant, not only judge but also himself the judged, not only man's eternal king but also his brother in time. And all that without in the slightest forfeiting his deity! All that, rather, in the highest proof and proclamation of his deity! He who *does* and manifestly *can* do all that, he and no other is the living God. So constituted is his deity, the deity of the God of Abraham, Isaac, and Jacob. In Jesus Christ it is in this way operative and recognizable. If he is the Word of truth, then the truth of God is exactly this and nothing else.

It is when we look at Jesus Christ that we know decisively that God's deity does not exclude, but includes his *humanity*. Would that Calvin had energetically pushed ahead on this point in his Christology, his doctrine of God, his teaching about predestination, and then logically also in his ethics! His Geneva would then not have contained so much bitterness. It would then not be so easy to play a Heinrich Pestalozzi and, among his contemporaries, a Sebastian Castellio off against him. How could God's deity exclude his humanity, since it is God's freedom for love and thus his capacity to be not only in the heights but also in the depths, not only great but also small, not only in and for himself but also with another distinct from him, and to offer himself to him? In his deity there is enough room for communion with man. Moreover God has and retains in his relation to this other one the unconditioned priority. It is his act. *His* is and remains the first and decisive Word, *his* the initiative, *his* the leadership. How could we see and say it otherwise when we look at Jesus Christ in whom we find man taken up into communion with God? No, God requires no exclusion of humanity, no non-humanity, not to speak of inhumanity, in order to be truly God. But we may and must, however, look further and recognize the fact that actually his deity *encloses humanity in itself.* This is not the fatal Lutheran doctrine of the two natures and their properties. On the contrary, the essential aim of this doctrine is not to be denied at this point but to be adopted. It would be the false deity of a false God if in his deity his humanity did not also immediately encounter us. Such false deities are by Jesus Christ once for all made a laughingstock. In him the fact is once for all established that God does not exist without man.

It is not as though God stands in need of another as his partner, and in particular of man, in order to be truly God. "What is man, that thou art mindful of him, and the son of man that thou dost care for him?" Why should God not also be able, as eternal love, to be sufficient unto himself? In his life as Father, Son, and Holy Spirit he would in truth be no lonesome, no egotistical God even without man, yes, even without the whole created universe. And he must more than ever be not *for* man; he *could*—one even thinks he *must*—rather be against him. But that is the mystery in which he meets us in the existence of Jesus Christ. He wants in his freedom actually not to be without man but *with* him and in the same freedom not against him but *for* him, and that apart from or even counter to what man deserves. He wants in fact to be man's partner, his almighty and compassionate Savior. He chooses to give man the benefit of his power, which encompasses not only the high and the distant but also the deep and the near, in order to maintain communion with him in the realm guaranteed by his deity. He determines to love him, to be his God, his Lord, his compassionate Preserver and Savior to eternal life, and to desire his praise and service.

In this divinely free volition and election, in this sovereign decision (the ancients said, in his decree), God is *human*. His free affirmation of man, his free concern for him, his free substitution for him—this is God's humanity. We recognize it exactly at the point where we also first recognize his deity. Is it not true that in Jesus Christ, as he is attested in the Holy Scripture, genuine deity includes in itself genuine humanity? There is the father who cares for his lost son, the king who does the same for his insolvent debtor, the Samaritan who takes pity on the one who fell among robbers and in his thoroughgoing act of compassion cares for him in a fashion as unexpected as it is liberal. And this is the act of compassion to which all these parables as parables of the kingdom of heaven refer. The very One who speaks in these parables takes to his heart the weakness and the perversity, the helplessness and the misery, of the human race surrounding him. He does not despise men, but in an inconceivable manner esteems them highly just as they are, takes them into his heart and sets himself in their place. He perceives that the superior will of God, to which he wholly subordinates himself, requires that he sacrifice himself for the human race, and seeks his honor in doing this. In the mirror of this humanity of Jesus Christ the humanity of God enclosed in his deity reveals itself. Thus God is as he is. Thus he affirms man. Thus he is concerned about him. Thus he stands up for him. The God of Schleiermacher cannot show mercy. The God of Abraham, Isaac, and Jacob can and does. If Jesus Christ is the Word of Truth, the "mirror of the fatherly heart of God" (Martin Luther), then Nietzsche's statement that man is something that must be overcome is an impudent lie. Then the truth of God is, as Titus 3:4 says, his loving-kindness and nothing else.

6. TILLICH: THEISM TRANSCENDED

Employing what he called the "method of correlation," Paul Tillich developed a systematic theology explicitly directed to the existential questions of his day. His most controversial ideas, however, had to do with God. Taking a position at variance with both liberal and conservative assumptions, he espoused a nonliteral, nontheistic view of God which some have found to be indistinguishable from atheism. Source: Paul Tillich, *The Courage To Be* (New Haven: Yale University Press, 1952), pp. 182–90.

Theism can mean the unspecified affirmation of God. Theism in this sense does not say what it means if it uses the name of God. Because of the traditional and psychological connotations of the word God such an empty theism can produce a reverent mood if it speaks of God. Politicians, dictators, and other people who wish to use rhetoric to make an impression on their audience like to use the word God in this sense. It produces the feeling in their listeners that the speaker is serious and morally trustworthy. This is especially successful if they can brand their foes as atheistic. On a higher level people without a definite religious commitment like to call themselves theistic, not for special purposes but because they cannot stand a world without God, whatever this God may be. They need some of the connotations of the word God and they are afraid of what they call atheism. On the highest level of this kind of theism the name of God is used as a poetic or practical symbol, expressing a profound emotional state or the highest ethical idea. It is a theism which stands on the boundary line between the second type of theism and what we call "theism transcended." But it is still too indefinite to cross this boundary line. The atheistic negation of this whole type of theism is as vague as the theism itself. It may produce an irreverent mood and angry reaction of those who take their theistic affirmation seriously. It may even be felt as justified against the rhetorical-political abuse of the name God, but it is ultimately as irrelevant as the theism which it negates. It cannot reach the state of despair any more than the theism against which it fights can reach the state of faith.

Theism can have another meaning, quite contrary to the first one: it can be the name of what we called the divine-human encounter. In this case it points to those elements in the Jewish-Christian tradition which emphasize the person-to-person relationship with God. Theism in this sense emphasizes the personalistic passages in the Bible and the Protestant creeds, the personalistic image of God, the word as the tool of creation and revelation, the ethical and social character of the kingdom of God, the personal nature of human faith and divine forgiveness, the historical vision of the universe, the idea of a divine purpose, the infinite distance between creator and creature, the absolute separation between God and the world, the conflict between holy God and sinful man, the person-to-person character of prayer and practical devotion. Theism in this sense is the nonmystical side of biblical religion and historical Christianity. Atheism from the point of view of this theism is the human attempt to escape the divine-human encounter. It is an existential—not a theoretical—problem.

Theism has a third meaning, a strictly theological one. Theological theism is, like every theology, dependent on the religious substance which it conceptualizes. It is dependent on theism in the first sense insofar as it tries to prove the necessity of affirming God in some way; it usually develops the so-called arguments for the "existence" of God. But it is more dependent on theism in the second sense insofar as it tries to establish a doctrine of God which transforms the person-to-person encounter with God into a doctrine about two persons who may or may not meet but who have a reality independent of each other.

Now theism in the first sense must be transcended because it is irrelevant, and theism in the second sense must be transcended because it is one-sided. But theism in the third sense must be transcended because it is wrong. It is bad theology. This can be shown by a more penetrating analysis. The God of theological theism is a being beside others and as such a part of the whole of reality. He certainly is considered its most important part, but as a part and therefore as subjected to the structure of the whole. He is supposed to be beyond the ontological elements and categories which constitute reality. But every statement subjects him to them. He is seen as a self which has a world, as an ego which is related to a thou, as a cause which is separated from its effect, as having a definite space and an endless time. He is a being, not being-itself. As such he is bound to the subject-object structure of reality, he is an object for us as subjects. At the same time we are objects for him as a subject. And this is decisive for the necessity of transcending theological theism. For God as a subject makes me into an object which is nothing more than an object. He deprives me of my subjectivity because he is all-powerful and all-knowing. I revolt and try to make *him* into an object, but the revolt fails and becomes desperate. God appears as the invincible tyrant, the being in contrast with whom all other beings are without freedom and subjectivity. He is equated with the recent tyrants who with the help of terror try to transform everything into a mere object, a thing among things, a cog in the machine they control. He becomes the model of everything against which existentialism revolted. This is the God Nietzsche said had to be killed because nobody can tolerate being made into a mere object of absolute knowledge and absolute control. This is the deepest root of atheism. It is an atheism which is justified as the reaction against theological theism and its disturbing implications. It is also the deepest root of the existentialist despair and the widespread anxiety of meaninglessness in our period.

Theism in all its forms is transcended in the experience we have called absolute faith. It is the accepting of the acceptance without somebody or something that accepts. It is the power of being-itself that accepts and gives the courage to be. This is the highest point to which our analysis has brought us. It cannot be described in the way the God of all forms of theism can be described. It cannot be described in mystical terms either. It transcends both mysticism and personal encounter, as it transcends both the courage to be as a part and the courage to be as oneself.

The ultimate source of the courage to be is the "God above God"; this is the result of our demand to transcend theism. Only if the God of theism is transcended can the anxiety of doubt and meaninglessness be taken into the courage to be. The God above God is the object of all mystical longing, but mysticism also must be transcended in order to reach him. Mysticism does not take seriously the concrete and the doubt concerning the concrete. It plunges directly into the ground of being and meaning, and leaves the concrete, the world of finite values and meanings, behind. Therefore it does not solve the problem of meaninglessness. In terms of the present religious situation this means that Eastern mysticism is not the solution of the problems of Western existentialism, although many people attempt this solution. The God above the God of theism is not the devaluation of the meanings which doubt has thrown into the abyss of meaninglessness; he is their potential restitution. Nevertheless absolute faith agrees with the faith implied in mysticism in that both transcend the theistic objectivation of a God who is a being. For mysticism such a God is not more real than any finite being, for the courage to be such a God has disappeared in the abyss of meaninglessness with every other value and meaning.

The God above the God of theism is present, although hidden, in every divine-human encounter. Biblical religion as well as Protestant theology are aware of the paradoxical character of this encounter. They are aware that if God encounters man God is neither object nor subject and is therefore above the scheme into which theism has forced him. They are aware that personalism with respect to God is balanced by a transpersonal presence of the divine. They are aware that forgiveness can be accepted only if the power of acceptance is effective in man—biblically speaking, if the power of grace is effective in man. They are aware of the paradoxical character of every prayer, of speaking to somebody to whom you cannot speak because he is not "somebody," of asking somebody of whom you cannot ask anything because he gives or gives not before you ask, of saying "thou" to somebody who is nearer to the I than the I is to itself. Each of these paradoxes drives the religious consciousness toward a God above the God of theism.

The courage to be which is rooted in the experience of the God above the God of theism unites and transcends the courage to be as a part and the courage to be as oneself. It avoids both the loss of oneself by participation and the loss of one's world by individualization. The acceptance of the God above the God of theism makes us a part of that which is not also a part but is the ground of the whole. Therefore our self is not lost in a larger whole, which submerges it in the life of a limited group. If the self participates in the power of being-itself it receives itself back. For the power of being acts through the power of the individual selves. It does not swallow them as every limited whole, every collectivism, and every conformism does. This is why the Church, which stands for the power of being-itself or for the God who transcends the God of the religions, claims to be the mediator of the courage to be. A church which is based on the authority of the God of theism cannot make such a claim. It inescapably develops into a collectivist or semicollectivist system itself.

But a church which raises itself in its message and its devotion to the God above the God of theism without sacrificing its concrete symbols can mediate a courage which takes doubt and meaninglessness into itself. It is the Church under the Cross which alone can do this, the Church which preaches the Crucified who cried to God who remained his God after the God of confidence had left him in the darkness of doubt and meaninglessness. To be as a part in such a church is to receive a courage to be in which one cannot lose one's self and in which one receives one's world.

Absolute faith, or the state of being grasped by the God beyond God, is not a state which appears beside other states of the mind. It never is something separated and definite, an event which could be isolated and described. It is always a movement in, with, and under other states of the mind. It is the situation on the boundary of man's possibilities. It is this boundary. Therefore it is both the courage of despair and the courage in and above every courage. It is not a place where one can live, it is without the safety of words and concepts, it is without a name, a church, a cult, a theology. But it is moving in the depth of all of them. It is the power of being, in which they participate and of which they are fragmentary expressions.

One can become aware of it in the anxiety of fate and death when the traditional symbols, which enable men to stand the vicissitudes of fate and the horror of death have lost their power. When "providence" has become a superstition and "immortality" something imaginary that which once was the power in these symbols can still be present and create the courage to be in spite of the experience of a chaotic world and a finite existence. The Stoic courage returns but not as the faith in universal reason. It returns as the absolute faith which says Yes to being without seeing anything concrete which could conquer the nonbeing in fate and death.

And one can become aware of the God above the God of theism in the anxiety of guilt and condemnation when the traditional symbols that enable men to withstand the anxiety of guilt and condemnation have lost their power. When "divine judgment" is interpreted as a psychological complex and forgiveness as a remnant of the "father-image," what once was the power in those symbols can still be present and create the courage to be in spite of the experience of an infinite gap between what we are and what we ought to be. The Lutheran courage returns but not supported by the faith in a judging and forgiving God. It returns in terms of the absolute faith which says Yes although there is no special power that conquers guilt. The courage to take the anxiety of meaninglessness upon oneself is the boundary line up to which courage to be can go. Beyond it is mere non-being. Within it all forms of courage are re-established in the power of the God above the God of theism. *The courage to be is rooted in the God who appears when God has disappeared in the anxiety of doubt.*

IV. REVELATION

1. AUGUSTINE: REVELATION AS
ILLUMINATION

Augustine exercised a major influence not only on the theology of his day but also on most subsequent theology. In his homilies on the Gospel of John, he developed the themes that would characterize the medieval and classical understanding of revelation. Jesus Christ is the light of God which illumines the darkness of the human intellect and enables it to know God. Source: Augustine, *Lectures on the Gospel According to St. John*, trans. John Gibb and James Innes, *Nicene and Post-Nicene Fathers*, First Series (New York: Christian Literature Co., 1886–90; reprinted by Eerdmans), Vol. 7, pp. 20–21. Date of original composition: 416.

"In the beginning was the Word." In what beginning? "And the Word was with God." And what word? "And the Word was God." Was then perhaps this Word made by God? No. For "the same was in the beginning with God." What then? Are the other things which God made not like unto the Word? No: because "all things were made by him, and without him was not anything made." In what manner were all things made by him? Because "that which was made in him was life"; and before it was made there was life. That which was made is not life; but in the art, that is, in the wisdom of God, before it was made, it was life. That which was made passes away; that which is in wisdom cannot pass away. There was life, therefore, in that which was made. And what sort of life, since the soul also is the life of the body? Our body has its own life; and when it has lost it, the death of the body ensues. Was then the life such as this? No; but "the life was the light of men." Was it the light of cattle? For this light is the light of men and of cattle. There is a certain light of men: let us see how far men differ from the cattle, and then we shall understand what is the light of men. Thou dost not differ from the cattle except in intellect; do not glory in anything besides. Dost thou presume upon thy strength? By the wild beasts thou art surpassed. Upon thy swiftness dost thou presume? How great beauty is there in the feathers of a peacock! Wherein then art thou better? In the image of God. Where is the image of God? In the mind, in the intellect. If then thou art in this respect better than the cattle, that thou hast a mind by which thou mayest understand what the cattle cannot understand; and therein a man, because better than the cattle; the light of men is the light of minds. The light of minds is above minds and surpasses all minds. This was that life by which all things were made.

Where was it? Was it here? Was it with the Father, and was it not here? Or, what is more true, was it both with the Father and here also? If then it was here, wherefore was it not seen? Because "the light shineth in darkness, and the darkness comprehended it not." Oh men, be not darkness, be not unbelieving, unjust, unrighteous, rapacious, avaricious lovers of this world: for these are the darkness. The light is not absent, but you are absent from the light. A blind man in the sunshine has the sun present to him, but is himself absent from the sun. Be ye not then darkness. For this is perhaps the grace regarding which we are about to speak, that now we be no more darkness, and that the apostle may say to us, "We were sometimes darkness, but now light in the Lord" (Eph. 5:8). Because then the light of men was not seen, that is, the light of minds, there was a necessity that a man should give testimony regarding the light, who was not in darkness, but who was already enlightened; and nevertheless, because enlightened, not the light itself, "but that he might bear witness of the light." For "he was not that light." And what was the light? "That was the true light which enlightened every man that cometh into this world." And where was that light? "In this world it was." And how was it "in this world"? As the light of the sun, of the moon, and of lamps, was that light thus in the world? No. Because "the world was made by him, and the world knew him not"; that is to say, "the light shineth in darkness, and the darkness comprehended it not." For the world is darkness; because the lovers of the world are the world. For did not the creature acknowledge its Creator? The heavens gave testimony by a star (Matt. 2:2); the sea gave testimony, and bore its Lord when he walked upon it (Matt. 14:26); the winds gave testimony, and were quiet at his bidding (Matt. 23:27); the earth gave testimony, and trembled when he was crucified (Matt.

27:51). If all these gave testimony, in what sense did the world not know him, unless that the world signifies the lovers of the world, those who with their hearts dwell in the world? And the world is evil, because the inhabitants of the world are evil; just as a house is evil, not because of its walls, but because of its inhabitants.

"He came unto his own"; that is to say, he came to that which belonged to himself; "and his own received him not." What, then, is the hope, unless that "as many as received him, to them gave he power to become the sons of God"? If they become sons, they are born; if born, how are they born? Not of flesh, "nor of blood, nor of the will of the flesh, nor of the will of man; but of God they are born." Let them rejoice, therefore, that they are born of God; let them believe that they are born of God; let them receive the proof that they are born of God: "And the Word became flesh, and dwelt among us." If the word was not ashamed to be born of man, are men ashamed to be born of God? And because he did this, he cured us; and because he cured us, we see. For this, "that the Word was made flesh, and dwelt among us," became a medicine unto us, so that as by earth we were made blind, by earth we might be healed; and having been healed, might behold what? "And we beheld," he says, "his glory, the glory as of the Only-begotten of the Father, full of grace and truth."

"John beareth witness of him, and crieth, saying, this was he of whom I spake, he that cometh after me is made before me." He came after me, and he preceded me. What is it, "He is made before me"? He preceded me. Not was made before I was made, but was preferred before me, this is "he was made before me." Wherefore was he made before thee, when he came after thee? "Because he was before me." Before thee, O John! What great thing to be before thee! It is well that thou dost bear witness to him; let us, however, hear himself saying, "Even before Abraham, I am" (John 8:58). But Abraham also was born in the midst of the human race: there were many before him, many after him. Listen to the voice of the Father to the Son: "Before Lucifer I have begotten thee" (Ps. 110:3). He who was begotten before Lucifer himself illuminates all. A certain one was named Lucifer, who fell; for he was an angel and became a devil; and concerning him the Scripture said, "Lucifer, who did arise in the morning, fell" (Isa. 14:27). And why was he *Lucifer*? Because, being enlightened, he gave forth light. But for what reasons did he become dark! Because he abode not in the truth (John 8:44). Therefore he was before Lucifer, before every one that is enlightened; since before every one that is enlightened, of necessity he must be by whom all are enlightened who can be enlightened.

2. LUTHER: REVELATION BY WORD AND SPIRIT

In his challenge to the ecclesiastical system of his day, Luther argued that Christian faith and theology should be based not on the authority of the church but on the Word of God. Appropriately enough some of his most important insights are found in his commentaries on scripture. In this selection from his commentary on Galatians, he argues that "particular" knowledge of God—the knowledge of redemption—cannot be found in nature but is given only by the Word and the Holy Spirit. Source: Martin Luther, *Lectures on Galatians—1535*, in *Luther's Works*, Vol. 26, ed. Jaroslav Pelikan (St. Louis: Concordia Publishing House, 1963), pp. 399–402. Written in 1531, this commentary was first published in 1535.

God does not want to be known except through Christ; nor, according to John 1:18, can he be known any other way. Christ is the offspring promised to Abraham; on him God founded all his promises. Therefore Christ alone is the means, the life, and the mirror through which we see God and know his will.

Through Christ God announces his favor and mercy to us. In Christ we see that God is not a wrathful taskmaster and judge but a gracious and kind father, who blesses us, that is, who delivers us from the law, sin, death, and every evil, and endows us with righteousness and eternal life through Christ. This is a sure knowledge of God and a true divine conviction, which does not deceive us but portrays God himself in a specific form, apart from which there is no God. . . .

Formerly, when you did not know God, you were in bondage (Gal. 4:8).

By nature all men have the general knowledge that there is a God, according to the statement in Rom. 1:19–20: "To the extent that God

91

can be known, he is known to them. For his invisible nature, etc." Besides, the forms of worship and the religions that have been and remained among all nations are abundant evidence that at some time all men have had a general knowledge of God. Whether this was on the basis of nature or from the tradition of their parents, I am not discussing it at the moment.

But . . . someone may raise the objection: "If all men know God, why does Paul say that before the proclamation of the Gospel the Galatians did not know God?" I reply: There is a twofold knowledge of God: the general and the particular. All men have the general knowledge, namely, that God is, that he has created heaven and earth, that he is just, that he punishes the wicked, etc. But what God thinks of us, what he wants to give and to do to deliver us from sin and death and to save us—which is the particular and the true knowledge of God—this men do not know. Thus it can happen that someone's face may be familiar to me but I do not really know him, because I do not know what he has in his mind. So it is that men know naturally that there is a God, but they do not know what he wants and what he does not want. For it is written (Rom. 3:11): "No one understands God"; and elsewhere (John 1:18): "No one has ever seen God," that is, no one knows what the will of God is. Now what good does it do you to know that God exists if you do not know what his will is toward you? Here different people imagine different things. The Jews imagine that it is the will of God that they should worship God according to the commandment of the Law of Moses; the Turks, that they should observe the Koran; the monk, that he should do what he has learned to do. But all of them are deceived and, as Paul says in Rom. 1:21, "become futile in their thinking"; not knowing what is pleasing to God and what is displeasing to him, they adore the imaginations of their own heart as though these were true God by nature, when by nature these are nothing at all.

Paul indicates this when he says: "When you did not know God, that is, when you did not know what the will of God is, you were in bondage to beings that by nature are no gods; that is, you were in bondage to the dreams and imaginations of your own hearts, by which you made up the idea that God is to be worshiped with this or that ritual." From the acceptance of this major premise, "There is a God," there came all the idolatry of men, which would have been unknown in the world without the knowledge of the Deity. But because men had this natural knowledge about God, they conceived vain and wicked thoughts about God apart from and contrary to the Word; they embraced these as the very truth, and on the basis of these they imagined God otherwise than he is by nature. Thus a monk imagines a God who forgives sins and grants grace and eternal life because of the observance of his rule. That God does not exist anywhere. Therefore the monk neither serves nor worships the true God; he serves and worships one who by nature is no God, namely, a figment and idol of his own heart, his own false and empty notion about God, which he supposes to be the surest truth. But even reason itself is obliged to admit that a human opinion is not God. Therefore whoever wants to worship God or serve him without the Word is serving, not the true God but, as Paul says, "one who by nature is no god." . . .

But now that you have come to know God, or rather to
be known by God (Gal. 4:9).

Paul corrects his first sentence ("now that you have come to know God") or rather inverts it this way: "or rather to be known by God." For he was afraid that they might lose God altogether. It is as though he were saying: "Alas, the situation has now come to the point that you do not even know God correctly, because you are returning from grace to the law. Nevertheless, God still knows you." As a matter of fact, our knowing is more passive than active; that is, it is more a matter of being known than of knowing. Our "activity" is to permit God to do his work in us; he gives the Word, and when we take hold of this by the faith that God gives, we are born as sons of God. Therefore the statement, "You have come to be known by God," means "You have been visited by the Word; you have been granted faith and the Holy Spirit, by whom you have been renewed." Therefore even with the words "You have come to be known by God" he is disparaging the righteousness of the law and denying that we obtain a knowledge of God because of the worthiness of our works. "For no one knows the Father except the Son and anyone to whom the Son chooses to reveal him" (Matt. 11:27). And again (Isa. 53:11): "By his knowledge shall he make many to be accounted righteous, for he shall bear their iniquities." Therefore our knowledge about God is purely passive.

3. TINDAL: REASON AND REVELATION

In the seventeenth century, the deists launched a major attack on the classical doctrine of revelation in the name of reason. One of the most influential members of this group, Matthew Tindal, argued that reason and revelation are not inconsistent and moreover that nothing can be true by revelation which reason knows to be false. In this selection, he offers a dialogue between a critic (A) and a defender (B) of traditional religion. Source: Matthew Tindal, "Christianity as Old as Creation," in *Deism: An Anthology*, ed. Peter Gay (Princeton: D. Van Nostrand Company, Inc., 1968), pp. 112–13, 117–20. We have modernized spelling, punctuation, and capitalization, but otherwise the text is unchanged from its original form, which was published in 1730.

B. In my opinion you lay too great a stress on fallible reason, and too little on infallible revelation; and therefore I must needs say, your arguing wholly from reason would make some of less candor than myself take you for an errant free-thinker.

A. Whatever is true by reason can never be false by revelation; and if God can't be deceived himself, or be willing to deceive men, the light he has given to distinguish between religious truth and falsehood cannot, if duly attended to, deceive them in things of so great moment.

They who do not allow reason to judge in matters of opinion or speculation are guilty of as great absurdity as the Papists, who will not allow the senses to be judges in the case of transubstantiation, though a matter directly under their cognizance; nay, the absurdity, I think, is greater in the first case, because reason is to judge whether our senses are deceived. And if no texts ought to be admitted as a proof in a matter contrary to sense, they ought certainly as little to be admitted in any point contrary to reason.

In a word, to suppose anything in revelation inconsistent with reason, and, at the same time, pretend it to be the will of God, is not only to destroy that proof on which we conclude it to be the will of God, but even the proof of the being of a God; since if our reasoning faculties duly attended to deceive us, we can't be sure of the truth of any one proposition; but everything would be alike uncertain, and we should forever fluctuate in a state of universal skepticism: which shows how absurdly they act who, on pretense of magnifying tradition, endeavor to weaken the force of reason (though to be sure they always except their own), and thereby foolishly sap the foundation to support the superstructure; but as long as reason is against men, they will be against reason. We must not, therefore, be surprised to see some endeavor to reason men out of their reason; though the very attempt to destroy reason by reason is a demonstration men have nothing but reason to trust to.

And to suppose anything can be true by revelation, which is false by reason, is not to support that thing, but to undermine revelation; because nothing unreasonable, nay, what is not highly reasonable, can come from a God of unlimited, universal, and eternal reason. As evident as this truth is, yet that shall not hinder me from examining in a proper place whatever you can urge from revelation. And give me leave to add that I shall not be surprised if, for so laudable an attempt as reconciling reason and revelation, which have been so long set at variance, I should be censured as a free-thinker; a title that, however invidious it may seem, I am far from being ashamed of; since one may as well suppose a man can reason without thinking at all, as reason well without thinking freely. . . .

B. I don't think we ought to have the same regard for reason as men had formerly, when that was the sole rule God had given them for the government of their actions; since now we Christians have two supreme, independent rules, *reason* and *revelation*; and both require an absolute obedience.

A. I can't see how that is possible; for if you are to be governed by the latter, that supposes you must take everything on trust, or merely because it's said by those for whose dictates you are to have an implicit faith. For to examine into the truth of what they say is renouncing their authority; as on the contrary, if men are to be governed by their reason, they are not to admit anything farther than as they see it reasonable. To suppose both consistent is to suppose it consistent to take, and not to take, things on trust.

To receive religion on the account of authority supposes that if the authority promulgated a different religion, we should be obliged to receive it; and indeed, it's an odd jumble to prove the truth of a book by the truth of the doctrines it contains, and at the same time conclude those doctrines to be true because contained in that book; and yet this is a jumble everyone makes who contends for man's being absolutely governed both by reason and authority.

What can be a fuller evidence of the sovereignty of reason than that all men, when there is anything in their traditional religion which in its literal sense can't be defended by reason, have recourse to any method of interpretation, though ever so forced, in order to make it appear reasonable. . . .

In a word, when men, in defending their own or attacking other traditionary religions, have recourse to the nature or reason of things, does not that show they believe the truth of all traditionary religions is to be tried by it, as being that which must tell them what is true or false in religion? And were there not some truths relating to religion of themselves so evident as that all must agree in them, nothing relating to religion could be proved, everything would want a farther proof; and if there are such evident truths, must not all others be tried by their agreement with them? And are not these the tests by which we are to distinguish the only true religion from the many false ones? And do not all parties alike own [that] there are such tests drawn from the nature of things, each crying [that] their religion contains everything worthy, and nothing unworthy of having God for its author, thereby confessing that reason enables them to tell what is worthy of having God for its author. And if reason tells them this, does it not tell them everything that God can be supposed to require?

In short, nothing can be more certain than that there are some things in their own nature good, some evil, and others neither good nor evil; and for the same reason [that] God commands the good and forbids the evil, he leaves men at liberty in things indifferent, it being inconsistent with his wisdom to reward the observance of such things, and with his goodness to punish for not observing them. And as he could have no end in creating mankind but their common good, so they answer the end of their creation who do all the good they can. And to enable men to do this, God has given them reason to distinguish good from evil, useful from useless things, or, in other words, has made them moral agents, capable of discerning the relations they stand in to God and one another, and the duties resulting from these relations, so necessary to their common good. And consequently, religion, thus founded on these immutable relations, must at all times, and in all places, be alike immutable; since external revelation, not being able to make any change in these relations, and the duties that necessarily result from them, can only recommend and inculcate these duties; except we suppose that God at last acted the tyrant and imposed such commands as the relations we stand in to him, and one another, no ways require.

To imagine any external revelation not to depend on the reason of things is to make things give place to words, and implies that, from the time this rule commenced, we are forbid to act as moral agents in judging what is good or evil, fit or unfit; and that we are to make no other use of our reason than to see what is the literal meaning of texts; and to admit that only to be the will of God, though ever so inconsistent with the light of nature and the eternal reason of things. Is not this to infer there's nothing good or evil in itself, but that all depends on the will of an arbitrary being, which, though it may change every moment, is to be unalterably found in such a book?

All divines, I think, now agree in owning that there's a law of reason antecedent to any external revelation, that God can't dispense, either with his creatures or himself, for not observing; and that no external revelation can be true that in the least circumstance, or minutest point, is inconsistent with it. If so, how can we affirm any one thing in revelation to be true until we perceive by that understanding which God has given us to discern the truth of things, whether it agrees with this immutable law or not?

If we can't believe otherwise than as things appear to our understandings, to suppose God requires us to give up our understandings (a matter we can't know but by using our understanding) to any authority whatever, is to suppose he requires impossibilities. And our self-evident notions being the foundation of all certainty, we can only judge of things, as they are found to be more or less agreeable to them; to deny this on any pretense whatever can serve only to introduce a universal skepticism.

4. BARTH: REVELATION AS GOD'S SELF-DISCLOSURE

In response to the collapse of nineteenth-century theological liberalism, Barth renewed the Reformation claim that theological knowledge should be grounded solely on the objective reality of God's self-disclosure in the Word. He began his *Church Dogmatics* by reinterpreting the doctrine of revelation in terms of three forms of the Word of God—Jesus Christ, scripture, and proclamation. In this selection he takes up the question whether there is a basis in human nature for receiving the Word of God. Source: Karl Barth, *Church Dogmatics*, Vol. 1/1, ed. G. W. Bromiley and T. F. Torrance (Edinburgh: T. & T. Clark, 1975), pp. 191, 193–94, 196. Date of original publication: 1932.

Primarily and originally the Word of God is undoubtedly the Word that God speaks by and to himself in eternal concealment. We shall have to return to this great and inalienable truth when we develop the concept of revelation in the context of the doctrine of the Trinity. But undoubtedly, too, it is the Word that is spoken to men in revelation, Scripture and preaching. Hence we cannot speak or think of it at all without remembering at once the man who hears and knows it. The Word of God, Jesus Christ, as the being of the Church, sets us ineluctably before the realization that it was and will be men who are intended and addressed and therefore characterized as recipients but as also themselves bearers of this Word. The Word of God thus sets us before the so-to-speak anthropological problem: How then can men be this? Before the "so-to-speak" anthropological problem, I said, and I indicated thereby that it can be called this only with some reserve. Or is this not so? Shall we say unreservedly that the question of the possibility of the knowledge of God's Word is a question of anthropology? Shall we ask what man generally and as such, in addition to all else he can do, can or cannot do in this regard? Is there a general truth about man which can be made generally perceptible and which includes within it man's ability to know the Word of God? We must put this question because an almost invincible development in the history of Protestant theology since the Reformation has led to an impressive affirmative answer to this question in the whole wing of the Church that we have called Modernist. . . .

The question is whether this event ranks with the other events that might enter man's reality in such a way that to be able to enter it actually requires on man's part a potentiality which is brought by man as such, which consists in a disposition native to him as man, in an organ, in a positive or even a negative property that can be reached and discovered by self-reflection, by anthropological analysis of his existence, in short, in what philosophy of the Kantian type calls a faculty.

It might also be that this event did not so much presuppose the corresponding possibility on man's part as bring it with it and confer it on man by being event, so that it is man's possibility without ceasing (as such) to be wholly and utterly the possibility proper to the Word of God and to it alone. We might also be dealing with a possibility of knowledge which can be made intelligible as a possibility of man, but, in contrast to all others, only in terms of the object of knowledge or the reality of knowledge and not at all in terms of the subject of knowledge, i.e., man as such. In the light of the nature of God's Word, and especially of what we said [above] about its purposiveness or pertinence, its being aimed at man, its character as an address to man, we must decide against the first view and in favor of the second. From this standpoint, the same that concerns us here, we had to understand the Word of God as the act of God's free love and not as if the addressed and hearing man were in any way essential to the concept of the Word of God. That man is the recipient of God's Word is, to the extent that it is true, a fact, and it cannot be deduced from anything we might previously know about God's nature. Even less, of course, can it be deduced from anything we previously knew about the nature of man. God's Word is no longer grace, and grace itself is no longer grace, if we ascribe to man a predisposition towards this Word, a possibility of knowledge regarding it that is intrinsically and independently native to him. But the same results from what was said in the same passage about the content of the Word of God addressed to man.

We then made the assertion that this content, whatever it might be *in concretissimo* for this man or that man, will always be an authentic and definitive encounter with the Lord of man, a revelation which man cannot achieve himself, the revelation of something new which can only be told him. It will also be the limitation of his existence by the absolute "out there" of his Creator, a limitation on the basis of which he can understand himself only as created out of nothing and upheld over nothing. It will also be a radical renewal and therewith an obviously radical criticism of the whole of his present existence, a renewal and a criticism on the basis of which he can understand himself only as created out of nothing and upheld over nothing. It will also be a radical renewal and therewith an obviously radical criticism of the whole of his present existence, a renewal and a criticism on the basis of which he can understand himself only as a sinner living by grace and therefore as a lost sinner closed up against God on his side. Finally it will be the presence of God as the One who comes, the Future One in the strict sense, the Eternal Lord and Redeemer of man, a presence on the basis of which he can understand himself only as hastening towards this future of the Lord and expecting him. To be sure, it is not these formulae which describe the real content of the Word of God, but the content of the Word which God himself speaks and which he does so always as these formulae indicate, the real content of the real Word of God, that tells man also that there can be no question of any ability to hear or understand or know on his part, of any capability that he the creature, the sinner, the one who waits, has to bring to this Word, but that the possibility of knowledge corresponding to the real Word of God has come to him, that it represents an inconceivable *novum* compared to all his ability and capability, and that it is to be understood as a pure fact, in exactly the same way as the real Word of God itself. . . .

The fact of God's Word does not receive its dignity and validity in any respect or even to the slightest degree from a presupposition that we bring to it. Its truth for us, like its truth in itself, is grounded absolutely in itself. The procedure in theology, then, is to establish self-certainty on the certainty of God, to measure it by the certainty of God, and thus to begin with the certainty of God without waiting for the validating of this beginning by self-certainty. When that beginning is made, but only when it is made, it is then, but only subsequently, incidentally and relatively validated by the necessary self-certainty. In other words, in the real knowledge of God's Word, in which alone that beginning is made, there also lies the event that it is possible, that that beginning can be made. Again, we do not base this rejection of the Cartesian way on a better philosophy. In relation to this object, the object of theology, we are content to say that one must affirm the possibility of its knowledge by men in this way and no other. Men can know the Word of God because and insofar as God wills that they know it, because and insofar as there is over against God's will only the impotence of disobedience, and because and insofar as there is a revelation of God's will in his Word in which the impotence of disobedience is set aside. . . . If one wants to call the problem of the knowability of the Word of God an anthropological problem, the reference must be to a

Church (or theological) anthropology. The question is not how man in general and as such can know God's Word. This question is pointless, for vis-à-vis the Word of God there is no man in general and as such; the Word of God is what it is as it is concretely spoken to this or that specific man. The question is how these men to whom it is concretely spoken can know it. And our answer must be that they can do so when the ability is given to them by the Word itself.

5. BULTMANN: REVELATION AND HUMAN EXISTENCE

Rudolf Bultmann made important contributions to both biblical scholarship and theology. He argued that the New Testament message was embedded in mythological language and that in order for it to speak to modern people it must be reinterpreted or "demythologized." He employed the categories of the existentialist philosopher Martin Heidegger to reinterpret the gospel, especially in its Pauline and Johannine forms. His emphasis throughout is on the self-knowledge that comes through revelation. Source: Rudolf Bultmann, "The Concept of Revelation in the New Testament," in *Existence and Faith: Shorter Writings of Rudolf Bultmann*, ed. Schubert M. Ogden (Cleveland: World Publishing Co., 1960), pp. 85–88. Date of original publication: 1929.

What, then, has been revealed? Nothing at all, so far as the question concerning revelation asks for doctrines—doctrines, say, that no man could have discovered for himself—or for mysteries that become known once and for all as soon as they are communicated. On the other hand, however, *everything has been revealed, insofar as man's eyes are opened concerning his own existence and he is once again able to understand himself.* It is as Luther says: "Thus, in going out of himself, God brings it about that we go into ourselves; and through knowledge of him he brings us to knowledge of ourselves." There is no other light shining in Jesus than has always already shined in the creation. Man learns to understand himself in the light of the revelation of redemption not a bit differently than he always already should understand himself in face of the revelation in creation and the law— namely, as God's creature who is limited by God and stands under God's claim, which opens up to him the way to death or to life. If the revelation in Jesus means salvation as an understanding of oneself in him, then the revelation in creation meant nothing other than this understanding of oneself in God in the knowledge of one's own creatureliness.

Therefore, the Johannine Jesus, at the conclusion of the farewell discourses, can say that the fulfillment of revelation is that no one needs any longer to ask questions (John 16:23 f.). Man always asks questions because he does not understand himself; if he does understand himself, however, all questioning ceases. He then is transparent to himself; he has become "light." For if Jesus is the "light" that enlightens every man, this does not mean that he gives them a capacity for knowledge (or strengthens such a capacity), by means of which the things of the world may be illumined, but rather that he gives them the light through which they may understand themselves. "Awake, O sleeper, and arise from the dead and Christ shall give you light" (Eph. 5:14). "For once you were darkness, but now you are light in the Lord" (Eph. 5:8; cf. 2 Cor. 3:18, 4:6). This is the condition of "fullness of joy" in which all questioning ceases and everything is understood (John 15:11, 16:24, 17:13).

Revelation does not provide this self-understanding, however, as a world-view that one grasps, possesses, and applies. Indeed, it is precisely in such views that man *fails* to understand himself, because he looks upon himself as something simply given and tries to understand himself as a part of the world that lies before him. Revelation does not mediate a world-view, but rather addresses the individual as an existing self. That he thereby learns to understand himself means that he learns to understand his now, the moment, as a now that is qualified by the proclamation. For existence in the moment is his authentic being. And just as little as the proclamation communicates something that happened in a certain place and at a certain time, but rather says what has occurred to the person being addressed, so little is faith the knowledge of some fact within the world or the willingness to hold some remarkable dogma to be true. Rather it is the obedience that obeys God not in general or *in abstracto*, but in the concrete now. The man of faith understands his now as one who comes out of a sinful past and therefore stands under God's judgment, but also as one who is freed from this past by the grace that encounters him in the word. Thus he for the first time sees the other person as his neighbor and in under-

standing the neighbor understands himself. Such faith is something
that man does, but it is never something that has been done, never a
work that he produces or accomplishes. Rather it is the momentary act
in which he lays hold of himself in his God-given freedom. And the
man of faith understands himself only in such an act.

Thus it becomes completely clear that revelation is an act of God,
an *occurrence*, and not a communication of supernatural knowledge.
Further, it is clear that revelation reveals *life*, for it frees man from
what is provisional and past and gives him the future. Even so, it is
clear that *Christ* is revelation and that revelation is the *word*; for these
two are one and the same. Christ is not the act of God's love as a fact
within the world that one can find some place and demonstrate to be
an "act of love." All possible demonstrations that the historical Jesus
loved this man or that, many men or all men, do not say what has to
be said, i.e., what is said by the proclamation of Christ—that God has
loved us in Christ and reconciled us to himself (2 Cor. 5:18; John
3:18). For the love directed to *me*—and this alone can make me a new
creature—cannot be demonstrated by historical observation. It can
only be promised to me directly; and this is what is done by the proclamation. To go behind the Christ who is preached is to misunderstand
the preaching; it is only in the word, as the one who is preached, that
he encounters us, that the love of God encounters us in him. But once
again, it must be emphasized that the word is what it is—namely,
revelation—not because of its timeless content, but rather as an address that is brought to us here and now by common ordinary men.
Therefore, *faith* also, like the word, is revelation because it is only real
in this occurrence and otherwise is nothing. It is no disposition of the
human soul, no being convinced, but rather the answer to an address.

It is also completely clear how *the righteousness of God* is *revealed*;
namely, neither as an idea nor as a condition that is brought about in
us, a quality that is produced in us. Rather it is awarded to us and will
be awarded to us in the address that encounters us. As we should obey
the word, so also should we "obey" the righteousness of God (Rom.
6:18, 10:3). Thus the interpretation of the Reformers is correct: righteousness is "imputed" to us as *justitia aliena*. And so it also becomes
clear that and how *love* is revealed. For it would be a misunderstanding
of *justitia aliena* to suppose that the rightwised sinner is only looked at

"as if" he were righteous. No! he *is* righteous, even if he really *is* so only when righteousness is awarded to him. But if he *is* righteous, then he understands himself and sees his neighbor and knows what he owes him (Rom. 13:8).

Then there is indeed a *knowledge* that is also given in revelation, however little the latter is a supernatural arrangement for communicating remarkable doctrines. I am given a knowledge, namely, of myself, of my immediate now, in which and for which the word of proclamation is spoken to me. Thus it is not an observer's knowledge, not a world-view in which man is interpreted as a phenomenon within the world on the basis of certain general principles of explanation, but rather a knowledge that is only opened up to me in laying hold of the possibility for understanding myself that is disclosed in the proclamation; it is a knowledge that is only real in the act of faith and love. And if such knowledge can also be explicated theologically, still theological knowledge always has a "dialectical" character, in the sense, namely, that as a knowledge that is preserved it is always spurious, however "correct" it may be, and that it is only genuine when the act of faith is realized in it, when the resolve to exist in faith is carried through to the end. For "whatever does not proceed from faith is sin" (Rom. 14:23).

6. RAHNER: THE SUPERNATURAL EXISTENTIAL

Rahner has attempted to reinterpret classical Roman Catholic theology in response to such modern figures as Immanuel Kant. Like Bultmann, he uses the work of Heidegger to construct his theology. He has sought especially to determine what it is in the structure of human being that makes revelation or "supernatural communication" a possibility. Source: Karl Rahner, *Foundations of Christian Faith: An Introduction to the Idea of Christianity,* trans. William V. Dych (New York: Crossroad, 1978), pp. 126–30.

The statement, "man is the event of God's absolute self-communication," does not refer to some reified objectivity "in man." Such a statement is not a categorical and ontic statement, but an ontological statement. It expresses in words the subject as such, and therefore the subject in the depths of his subjectivity, and hence in the depths of his transcendental experience. Christian teaching, which becomes conceptual in reflexive, human words in the church's profession of faith, does not simply inform man of the content of this profession from without and only in concepts. Rather it appeals to reality, which is not only said, but also given and really experienced in man's transcendental experience. Hence it expresses to man his own self-understanding, one which he already has, although unreflexively.

In order to understand this thesis we must first of all consider that the thesis proposed here about the innermost and ultimate characteristic of our basic statement that man is the event of God's absolute self-communication does not refer to a statement which is valid only for this or that group of people as distinguished from others, for example, only for the baptized or the justified as distinguished from pagans or sinners. Without prejudice to the fact that it speaks of a free and unmerited grace, of a miracle of God's free love for spiritual creatures, the statement that man as subject is the event of God's self-communication is a statement which refers to absolutely all men, and which expresses an existential of every person. Such an existential does not become merited and in this sense "natural" by the fact that it is present in *all* men as an existential of their concrete existence, and is present prior to their freedom, their self-understanding and their experience. The gratuity of a reality has nothing to do with the question whether it is present in many or only in a few people.

What we said about God's self-communication being supernatural and unmerited is not threatened or called into question by the fact that this self-communication is present in *every* person at least in the mode of an offer. The love of God does not become less a miracle by the fact that it is promised to all men at least as an offer. Indeed only what is given to everybody realizes the real essence of grace in a radical way. Something gratuitous which is given to one and denied to another is really by its very nature something which falls within the realm of possibility for everyone precisely because it is given to one and is denied to another to whom it could also have been given. Hence such an understanding satisfies only the notion of something unmerited by the individual, but not the notion of something supernatural which essentially transcends the natural.

The supernatural, then, does not cease to be supernatural if, at least in the mode of an offer to man's freedom, it is given to everyone who is a being of unlimited transcendentality as a fulfillment essentially transcending the natural. In this sense everyone, really and radically *every* person must be understood as the event of a supernatural self-communication of God, although not in the sense that every person necessarily accepts in freedom God's self-communication to man. Just as man's essential being, his spiritual personhood, in spite of the fact that it is and remains an inescapable given for every free subject, is given to his freedom in such a way that the free subject can possess himself in the mode of "yes" or in the mode of "no," in the mode of deliberate and obedient acceptance or in the mode of protest against this essential being of his which has been entrusted to freedom, so too the existential of man's absolute immediacy to God in and through this divine self-communication as permanently offered to freedom can exist merely in the mode of an antecedent offer, in the mode of acceptance and in the mode of rejection.

The mode in which God's self-communication is present with respect to human freedom does not nullify the real presence of this self-communication as something offered. For even an offer merely as antecedently given or as rejected by freedom must not be understood as a communication which could exist, but does not. It must rather be understood as a communication which has really taken place, and as one by which freedom as transcendental is and remains always confronted really and inescapably.

God's self-communication is given not only as gift, but also as the necessary condition which makes possible an acceptance of the gift which can allow the gift really to be God, and can prevent the gift in its acceptance from being changed from God into a finite and created gift which only represents God, but is not God himself. In order to be able to accept God without reducing him, as it were, in this acceptance to our finiteness, this acceptance must be borne by God himself. God's self-communication as offer is also the necessary condition which makes its acceptance possible.

If, then, man is to have something to do with God as God is in his own self, and if in his freedom he is to open or close himself to God's self-communication without this response reducing God himself to the level of man, then God's self-communication must always be present in man as the prior condition of possibility for its acceptance. This is true insofar as man must be understood as a subject who is capable of such an acceptance, and therefore is also obligated to it. And conversely: without prejudice to its gratuity, God's self-communication must be present in every person as the condition which makes its personal acceptance possible. This presupposes only that the possibility of such a personal acceptance of God is acknowledged in principle for man because God in his universal salvific will has offered and destined this fulfillment not only for some, but for all men, a fulfillment which consists in the fully realized acceptance of this divine self-communication.

It follows from this that God's offer of himself belongs to all men and is a characteristic of man's transcendence and his transcendentality. Therefore God's self-communication as an offer, and as something given prior to man's freedom as a task and as the condition of freedom's highest possibility, also has the characteristics which all of the elements in man's transcendental constitution have.

Such an element in man's transcendental constitution is not the object of an individual, a posteriori and categorical experience of man *alongside of* other objects of his experience. Basically and originally man does not encounter this supernatural constitution as an object. The supernatural constitution of man's transcendentality due to God's offer of self-communication is a modality of his original and unthematic subjectivity. Hence this modality can at most, if at all, be made thematic in a subsequent reflection and objectified in a subsequent concept. Such a supernatural transcendentality is just as inconspicuous and can be just as much overlooked, suppressed, denied and falsely interpreted as everything else which is transcendentally spiritual in man. This antecedent self-communication of God which is prior to man's freedom means nothing else but that the spirit's transcendental movement in knowledge and love towards the absolute mystery is borne by God himself in his self-communication in such a way that this movement has its term and its source not in the holy mystery as eternally distant and as a goal which can only be reached asymptotically, but rather in the God of absolute closeness and immediacy.

Therefore God's self-communication in grace, as a modification of transcendence in and through which the holy mystery, that mystery by which transcendence is intrinsically opened and borne, is present in its own self and in absolute closeness and self-communication, cannot by simple and individual acts of reflection and psychological introspection be differentiated from those basic structures of human transcendence which we tried to present in the second chapter of our reflections. The absolutely unlimited transcendence of the natural spirit in knowledge and freedom along with its term, the holy mystery, already implies by itself such an infinity in the subject that the possession of God in absolute self-communication does not really fall outside of this infinite possibility of transcendence, although it remains gratuitous. Therefore the transcendental experience of this abstract possibility on the one hand and the experience of its radical fulfillment by God's self-communication on the other cannot be clearly and unambiguously differentiated simply by the direct introspection of an individual as long as the history of freedom in its acceptance or rejection is still going on, and hence as long as this fulfillment through self-communication has not yet reached its culmination in the final and definitive state which we usually call the immediate vision of God.

Transcendental experience, including its modality as grace, and reflection upon transcendental experience are no more the same thing conceptually than self-consciousness and objectified, thematic knowledge of something which we are conscious of are the same thing. In our case there are two special reasons why God's self-communication in grace as a modification of our transcendentality is not reflexive and cannot be made reflexive. First, on the side of the addressee of this self-communication, because of the unlimited nature of the subjective spirit already in its natural state; and, secondly, on the side of God's self-communication, because of the unfulfilled state of this self-communication, that is, because it has not yet become the vision of God.

We can describe the transcendental experience of God's self-communication in grace, or, to put it differently, the dynamism and the finalization of the spirit as knowledge and love towards the immediacy of God, which dynamism is of such a kind that, because of God's self-communication, the goal itself is also the very power of the movement (we usually call this movement grace), we can describe this experience along with the essence of this spiritual dynamism adequately only by saying: in grace the spirit moves within its goal (because of God's self-communication) towards its goal (the beatific vision). Consequently, it cannot be concluded from the impossibility of identifying it directly and with certainty in individual reflection that this self-communication of God is absolutely beyond the subject and his consciousness, and is postulated *only* by a dogmatic theory imposed on man from without. What we are really dealing with is a transcendental experience which gives evidence of itself in human existence and is operative in that existence.

7. PANNENBERG: REVELATION AND HISTORY

A major theological voice in the last half of the twentieth century has been that of the German theologian Wolfhart Pannenberg. In the early 1960s, he and several other young theologians, biblical scholars, and church historians challenged the dominant interpretation of revelation espoused by neo-Reformation theology. According to Pannenberg, revelation is best understood not in terms of "sacred history," to which only a privileged few have access, but universal history open to all. Source: Wolfhart Pannenberg, "Dogmatic Theses on the Doctrine of Revelation," in *Revelation As History*, ed. Wolfhart Pannenberg, trans. David Granskou (New York: Macmillan, 1968), pp. 135–39. Date of original publication: 1961.

We are ordinarily urged to think of revelation as an occurrence that man cannot perceive with natural eyes and that is made known only through a secret mediation. The revelation, however, of the biblical God in his activity is no secret or mysterious happening. An understanding that puts revelation into contrast to, or even conflict with, natural knowledge is in danger of distorting the historical revelation into a gnostic knowledge of secrets.

In the Old Testament discussion about the self-vindication of Jahweh, it is his acts in history that were the events through which Jahweh proved his deity to all peoples, not just to Israel. What Jahweh accomplished in history cannot be written off as the imagination of the pious soul, for its inherent meaning of revealing the deity of Jahweh is impressed on everyone.

In this way Paul can say: "By the open statement of truth we would commend ourselves to every man's conscience in the sight of God" (2 Cor. 4:2). H. Schulte has noted with justice that Paul is not sharing a secret knowledge after the manner of the gnostics. "The Gospel is no dialectic play between the state of revelation and hiddenness, but is fully revealed." It is not without significance that Paul uses the philosophical term "conscience" in this passage.

In a similar vein, Paul can speak of those who do not wish to see the truth that is manifest. The fact that some do not believe does not mean that the gospel is accessible to only a few, but that "the god of this world has blinded the minds of the unbelievers" (2 Cor. 4:4) so that they cannot see the truth of the revelation of God in the fate of Jesus, a revelation that is available to all. Nothing must mute the fact that all truth lies right before the eyes, and that its appropriation is a natural consequence of the facts. There is no need for any additional perfection of man as though he could not focus on the "supernatural" truth with his normal equipment for knowing. The event, which Paul witnessed, took place totally within the realm of that which is humanly visible. In particular, the Holy Spirit is not an additional condition without which the event of Christ could not be known as revelation. Bultmann has rightly insisted that Paul never describes faith as a gift of the Spirit, but rather that the Spirit is described as the gift received by means of faith, in that which the gospel proclaims, which for its own part belongs to the sphere of the Spirit so long as it relates to the eschatological event. The paradox that there are persons who will not see this most evident truth does not absolve theology and proclamation from the task of stressing and showing the ordinary, and in no way supernatural, truth of God's revelation in the fate of Jesus. Theology has no reason or excuse to cheapen the character and value of a truth that is open to general reasonableness.

To say that the knowledge of revelation is not supernatural does not mean that man is only confirming what he already knows through the force of his own intellect. In this respect, no one comes to the knowledge of God by his own reason or strength. This is not only true about the knowledge of God, but about other experiences that we have. The divinely revealed events and the message that reports these events brings man to a knowledge he would not have by himself. And these events *do* have transforming power. When these are taken seriously for what they are, and in the historical context to which they belong, then they speak their own language, the language of facts. God has proved his deity in this language of facts. Naturally, these experiences are not to be treated as naked facts, but are to be seen in their traditio-historical context. If we are to take these facts seriously, nothing ought to be inserted so as to allow them to be seen in a way different from what would naturally emerge. That these and also other events are veiled from many men, indeed, from most men, does not mean that this truth is too high for them, so that their reason must be supplemented by other means of knowing. Rather, it means that they must use their reason in order to see correctly. If the problem is not thought of in this way, then the Christian truth is made into a truth for the in group, and the church becomes a gnostic community.

The history of Israel all the way to the resurrection is a series of very special events. Thus they communicate something that could not be gotten out of other events. The special aspect is the event itself, not the attitude with which one confronts the event. A person does not bring faith with him to the event as though faith were the basis for finding the revelation of God in the history of Israel and of Jesus Christ. Rather, it is through an open appropriation of these events that true faith is sparked.

This is not to say that faith is made superfluous by the knowledge of God's revelation in the events that demonstrate his deity. Faith has to do with the future. This is the essence of trust. Trust primarily directs itself toward the future, and the future justifies, or disappoints. Thus a person does not come to faith blindly, but by means of an event that can be appropriated as something that can be considered reliable. True faith is not a state of blissful gullibility. The prophets could call Israel to faith in Jahweh's promises and proclaim his prophecy because Israel had experienced the dependability of their God in the course of a long history. The Christian risks his trust, life, and future on the fact of God's having been revealed in the fate of Jesus. This presupposition must be as certain as possible to him. Otherwise who could expect to obtain a participation in the life that has been manifested in Jesus, if such a presupposition were not oriented to the future?

There is a consequence for the Christian proclamation from this point. The proclamation of Christ presents, for those who hear it, a fact (taken to be reasonably and reliably true) that in the fate of Jesus of Nazareth, God has been revealed to all men. The proclamation of the

111

gospel cannot assert that the facts are in doubt and that the leap of faith must be made in order to achieve certainty. If this sort of assertion were allowed to stand, then one would have to cease being a theologian and Christian. The proclamation must assert that the facts are reliable and that you can therefore place your faith, life, and future on them.

The knowledge of God's revelation in the history demonstrating his deity must also be the basis of faith. Faith does not need to worry that this knowledge has been altered because of shifts in historical research, just as long as this current image of the facts of history allows him to reassess and to participate in the events that are fundamental to it. This far-reaching independence of faith from the particular form of historical knowledge out of which it has come is founded on the fact that, in the act of trust, faith transcends its own picture of the event. The event has its own foundation in that it relies on the God who reveals himself in it. In the trusting surrender of his existence, the faithful man is thrust beyond his own theological formulations and opened to new and better understandings of history, which are the basis for his life. It is through such faith that the patriarchs of Israel had a part in the fulfillment, in Jesus Christ of the promises given to them, a fulfillment very different from anything that they might have been able to imagine. Through such faith, men have a part in the same history of God even though their ideological formulations of the history of God are irreconcilable. Such men are not only reciprocally bound to each other through faithful participation in the one history, but are also bound to those men who have no understanding of what the two are arguing about. Nevertheless, only the knowledge of God's revelation can be the foundation of faith, no matter how confused or mixed with doubt such knowledge might be. It should also be emphasized that it is not knowledge, but the resulting faith in God that secures participation in salvation.

8. NIEBUHR: THE REVELATORY IMAGE

H. Richard Niebuhr occupies a central place in the development of twentieth-century theology. Influenced by the work of Ernst Troeltsch, he accepted historical relativism, yet sought to base his theology on the revelation of God in history. The key to his resolution of this apparent contradiction resides in his highly original insight into the role of the religious imagination. Source: H. Richard Niebuhr, *The Meaning of Revelation* (New York: Macmillan, 1941), pp. 109–16.

By revelation in our history, then, we mean that special occasion which provides us with an image by means of which all the occasions of personal and common life become intelligible. What concerns us at this point is not the fact that the revelatory moment shines by its own light and is intelligible in itself but rather that it illuminates other events and enables us to understand them. Whatever else revelation means it does mean an event in our history which brings rationality and wholeness into the confused joys and sorrows of personal existence and allows us to discern order in the brawl of communal histories. Such revelation is no substitute for reason; the illumination it supplies does not excuse the mind from labor; but it does give to that mind the impulsion and the first principles it requires if it is to be able to do its proper work. In this sense we may say that the revelatory moment is revelatory because it is rational, because it makes the understanding of order and meaning in personal history possible. Through it a pattern of dramatic unity becomes apparent with the aid of which the heart can understand what has happened, is happening and will happen to selves in their community. Why we must call this a dramatic pattern and how it differs from the conceptual patterns of the observer's reason can be most clearly indicated through an examination of the way in which the heart uses it to understand life's meaning.

First of all, the revelatory moment is one which makes our past intelligible. Through it we understand what we remember, remember what we have forgotten and appropriate as our own past much that seemed alien to us. In the life of an individual a great occasion may make significant and intelligible the apparently haphazard course of his earlier existence; all that has happened to him may then assume continuity and pattern as it is related to the moment for which he knows himself to have been born. So prophets, being called to prophecy, may understand with Jeremiah how birth and nurture were for them an ordination to their office or an Augustine may see blessing even in the "sin which brought so great a salvation." When Israel focussed its varied and disordered recollections of a nomad past, of tribal bickerings and alien tyrannies in the revelatory event of its deliverance and choice to be a holy people, then it found there hitherto unguessed meaning and unity. What had been a "tale told by an idiot, full of sound and fury, signifying nothing," became a grand epic; every line, stanza and canto fell into its proper place. The tribal chants, the legends of the unheroic past were not forgotten; they were remembered in a new connection; meanings hitherto hidden became clear. To be sure, the labor of prophets and poets and priests who searched the memories of Israel and ordered them with the aid of the revelatory image was necessary before a unified understanding could be achieved. They had to carry the light of revelation into their past; revelation did not excuse the reasoning heart from toil but equipped it with the instrument whereby it could understand what it remembered. So the Scriptures were written not as the history of revelation only but as the history of Israel understood and unified by means of revelation. The labor of Israel in seeking to understand the past has never been completed, being continued by the rabbis of a later and the present day; but the revelatory occasion and idea have remained constant.

In the Christian church the function of the revelation in Jesus Christ has been similar. Through it the early apostles understood and interpreted the memories not only of Hebrew but also of Gentile Christians. The whole past of the human race assumed for them a unity and significance that had been lacking in the national and religious recollections of men. That Jesus had been born in the fullness of time meant that all things which had gone before seemed to conspire toward the realization of this event. Not only the religion of the Hebrews but the philosophy of the Greeks also was now intelligible as prophecy of the coming of a great salvation. The work of the apostles has been carried on through the following ages of the church. The rise and fall of pagan empires as well as the destiny of the chosen people, Socrates' martyrdom as well as Jeremiah's, the wanderings of Greeks as well as of Hebrews, have come to be understood not simply as illustrations of a general principle of creative love and judgment in history but as parts of one inclusive process. The work has not been completed, for the past is infinite, and thought, even with the aid of revelation, is painful, and doubt assails the human heart. But for the Christian church the whole past is potentially a single epic. In the presence of the revelatory occasion it can and must remember in tranquillity the long story of human ascent from the dust, of descent into the sloughs of brutality and sin, the nameless sufferings of untold numbers of generations, the groaning and travailing of creation until now—all that otherwise is remembered only with despair. There is no part of that past that can be ignored or regarded as beyond possibility of redemption from meaninglessness. And it is the ability of the revelation to save all the past from senselessness that is one of the marks of its revelatory character.

By reasoning on the basis of revelation the heart not only understands what it remembers but is enabled and driven to remember what it had forgotten. When we use insufficient and evil images of the personal or social self we drop out of our consciousness or suppress those memories which do not fit in with the picture of the self we cherish. We bury our follies and our transgressions of our own law, our departures from our own ideal, in the depths of our unconsciousness. We also forget much that seems to us trivial, since it does not make sense when interpreted by means of the idolatrous image. We do not destroy this past of ours; it is indestructible. We carry it with us; its record is written deep into our lives. We only refuse to acknowledge it as our true past and try to make it an alien thing—something that did not happen to our real selves. So our national histories do not recall to the consciousness of citizens the crimes and absurdities of past social conduct, as our written and unwritten autobiographies fail to mention our shame. But this unremembered past endures. An external view can see its embodiment in the boundaries of nations, in the economic status of groups, such as that of Negroes in America, in folkways and customs whose origins have been forgotten, in national policies and in personal habits. When we live and act in accordance with our inward social constitution in which there are class and race divisions, prejudices, assumptions about the things we can and cannot do, we are constrained by the unconscious past. Our buried past is mighty; the ghosts of our fathers and of the selves that we have been haunt our days and nights though we refuse to acknowledge their presence.

The revelatory event resurrects this buried past. It demands and permits that we bring into the light of attention our betrayals and denials, our follies and sins. There is nothing in our lives, in our autobiographies and our social histories, that does not fit in. In the personal inner life revelation requires the heart to recall the sins of the self and to confess fully what it shuddered to remember. Every great confession, such as Augustine's or St. Paul's, indicates how this rationalizing of the past takes place. And every social history, not least that of the church itself, when recollected in the light of revelation, becomes a confession of sin. It is true that in this realm the work of revelation has never been completed and that, indeed, in many spheres it has not even been started. Yet it is also true that for Christians critical history of self and community, wherein the forgotten past is recollected, is the possible and necessary consequence of revelation.

The third function of revelation with respect to the past we may call appropriation. When men enter into a new community they not only share the present life of their new companions but also adopt as their own the past history of their fellows. So immigrants do not become true members of the American community until they have learned to call the Pilgrims and the men of 1776 their fathers and to regard the torment of the Civil War as somehow their own. Where common memory is lacking, where men do not share in the same past there can be no real community, and where community is to be formed common memory must be created; hence the insistence on the teaching of history in modern national communities. But by the aid of such provincial memories only partial pasts can be appropriated and only limited human communities can be formed. To Christians the revelatory moment is not only something they can all remember as having happened in their common past, be they Hebrews or Greeks, slaves or free, Europeans or Africans or Americans or Asiatics, medieval men or modern. It becomes an occasion for appropriating as their own the past of all human groups. Through Jesus Christ Christians of all races recognize the Hebrews as their fathers; they build into their lives as Englishmen or as Americans, as Italians or Germans, the memories of Abraham's loyalty, of Moses' heroic leadership, of prophetic denunciations and comfortings. All that has happened to the strange and wandering people of God becomes a part of their own past. But Jesus Christ is not only the Jew who suffered for the sins of Jews and so for our own sins; he is also the member of the Roman world-community through whom the Roman past is made our own. The history of empire through which his life and death must be understood is the history of our empire. Beyond all that, he is the man through whom the whole of human history becomes our history. Now there is nothing that is alien to us. All the struggles, searchings after light, all the wanderings of all the peoples, all the sins of men in all places become parts of our past through him. We must remember them all as having happened in and to our community. Through Christ we become immigrants into the empire of God which extends over all the world and learn to remember the history of that empire, that is of men in all times and places, as our history.

V. CREATION AND PROVIDENCE

1. AUGUSTINE: IN THE BEGINNING
GOD CREATED

Books 11 through 14 of Augustine's *City of God* offer a classic treatment of the creation of the world as the beginning of salvation history. The following selections articulate the fundamental difference between Creator and creature, the view that the world and time had a specific beginning, the hierarchical ordering of creation culminating in the human creature, God's governance of all that exists, and the origin of evil. Source: Augustine, *The City of God*, Book 11, Chaps. 4, 6, 16–18, in *The Fathers of the Church: Writings of Saint Augustine*, Vol. 7, trans. G. G. Walsh and G. Monahan (Washington, D.C.: Catholic University of America Press, 1952), pp. 190–93, 195–96, 211–14. Date of original composition: 413–26.

Of all visible things, the universe is the greatest; of all invisible realities, the greatest is God. That the world exists we can see; we believe in the existence of God. But there is no one we can more safely trust than God himself in regard to the fact that it was he who made the world. Where has he told us so? Nowhere more distinctly than in the Holy Scriptures where his prophet said: "In the beginning God created the heavens and the earth" (Gen. 1:1). Well, but was the prophet present when God made heaven and earth? No; but the Wisdom of God by whom all things were made was there. And this Wisdom, entering into holy souls, makes of them the friends and prophets of God and reveals to them, silently and interiorly, what God has done.

They are taught, also, by the angels of God who "always behold the face of the Father" (Matt. 18:10) and are commissioned to announce his will to others. Among these prophets was the one who announced in writing: "In the beginning God created the heavens and the earth." And it was so fitting that faith in God should come through such a witness that he was inspired by the same Spirit of God, who had revealed these truths to him, to predict, far in advance, our own future faith.

But, why did it please the eternal God to create heaven and earth at that special time, seeing that he had not done so earlier? If the purpose of those who pose this question is to protest that the world is eternal, without beginning, and, therefore, not created by God, then they are far from the truth and are raving with the deadly disease of irreligion. For, quite apart from the voice of the prophets, the very order, changes, and movements in the universe, the very beauty of form in all that is visible, proclaim, however silently, both that the world was created and also that its Creator could be none other than God whose greatness and beauty are both ineffable and invisible.

There are those who say that the universe was, indeed, created by God, denying a "temporal" but admitting a "creational" beginning, as though, in some hardly comprehensible way, the world was made, but made from all eternity. Their purpose seems to be to save God from the charge of arbitrary rashness. They would not have us believe that a completely new idea of creating the world suddenly occurred to him or that a change of mind took place in him in whom there can be no change.

I do not see, however, how this position is consistent with their stand in other matters, especially in regard to the soul. For, if, as they must hold, the soul is co-eternal with God, they have no way to explain how a completely new misery can begin in an eternally existing soul.

For, if they say that its misery and happiness ceaselessly alternate, then they are obliged to conclude that this alternation will go on forever. Thus, an absurdity follows: though the soul is called blessed, it will not be so in fact, since it foresees its future misery and disgrace; and, even if it does not foresee its future disgrace or misery but thinks that it will be happy forever, its happiness will depend upon deception. And this is as foolish a statement as could possibly be made.

But, if they suppose that the soul has been alternately happy and unhappy through infinite ages but that, from now on, being set free, it will never return to its former misery, they are, in fact, convinced that the soul was never truly blessed but that at last it begins to enjoy a new and genuine happiness. Thus, they admit that something new, important, and remarkable happens within the soul which had never occurred to it before from all eternity. And, if they deny that God's eternal providence included the cause of this new experience of the soul, they likewise deny that he is the author of its beatitude—which is an abominable piece of impiety. If, on the other hand, they claim that by a new decree God determined that the soul should be eternally blessed, how can they show that he is free from that mutability which even they repudiate?

Finally, if they say that the soul was created in time but will not perish in any future time, like numbers which begin with "one" but never end, and, therefore, that having experienced misery, it will be freed from it, never again to return to it, they will surely have no hesitation in admitting that this is compatible with the immutability of God's decision. This being so, they should also believe that the world could be made in time without God who made it having to change the eternal decision of his will. . . .

The distinguishing mark between time and eternity is that the former does not exist without some movement and change, while in the latter there is no change at all. Obviously, then, there could have been no time had not a creature been made whose movement would effect some change. It is because the parts of this motion and change cannot be simultaneous, since one part must follow another, that, in these shorter or longer intervals of duration, time begins. Now, since God, in whose eternity there is absolutely no change, is the creator and ruler of time, I do not see how we can say that he created the world after a space of time had elapsed unless we admit, also, that previously some creature had existed whose movements would mark the course of time.

Again, sacred and infallible Scripture tells us that in the beginning God created heaven and earth in order. Now, unless this meant that nothing had been made before, it would have been stated that whatever else God had made before was created in the beginning. Undoubtedly, then, the world was made not in time but together with time. For, what is made in time is made after one period of time and before another, namely, after a past and before a future time. But, there could have been no past time, since there was nothing created by whose movements and change time could be measured.

The fact is that the world was made simultaneously with time, if, with creation, motion and change began. Now this seems evident from the order of the first six or seven days. For, the morning and evening of each of these days are counted until on the sixth day all that had been created during this time was complete. Then, on the seventh day, in a mysterious revelation, we are told that God ceased from work. As for these "days," it is difficult, perhaps impossible to think—let alone to explain in words—what they mean. . . .

Among all things which somehow exist and which can be distinguished from God who made them, those that live are ranked higher than those that do not, that is to say, those that have the power of reproduction or even of appetite are above those which lack this faculty. In that order of living things, the sentient are superior to the non-sentient, for example, animals to trees. Among sentient beings, the intelligent are higher than the non-intelligent, as with men and cattle. Among the intelligent, the immortal are superior to the mortal, as angels to men.

This is the hierarchy according to the order of nature. However, we have another and variable standard of values which is based on utility. By this standard, sometimes we so prefer certain non-sentient things to others which are sentient that, had we the power, we would annihilate these latter, reckless of the place they hold in the pattern of nature or wilfully sacrificing them to our own convenience. For, who would not rather have food in his house than mice, money than fleas? This is less astonishing when we recall that, in spite of the great dignity of human nature, the price for a horse is often more than that for a slave and the price for a jewel more than that for a maid.

Thus, a person who evaluates according to reason has far more freedom of choice than one who is driven by want or drawn by passion. For, reason can see the gradation of things in an objective hierarchy of values, while necessity must consider them as means to an end. Reason seeks for what seems true in the light of the intellect, while passion craves for what seems pleasant to the senses.

So, too, in evaluating rational natures, the weight, so to speak, of will and love is so great that, although in the order of nature angels are higher than men, in the scale of morality good men outweigh bad angels.

We are right to understand "beginning" in the following text as referring to the Devil's nature, not to his malice: "This is the beginning of the creation of God" (Job 40:19). For, undoubtedly, before we can have the canker of maliciousness, there must have been a nature that was not previously cankered. Moreover, any canker is so contrary to nature that it must be harmful. In fact, departure from God would not be a defect except in a being whose nature it was to be united with God. Thus, even a bad will is clear evidence of a good nature.

Now, God is not only the supremely beneficent creator of good natures, but also the just ruler of evil wills. So, while creatures can use a good nature for a bad purpose, he can use bad wills for a good one. Thus, God has brought it to pass that the Devil, who was good by creation but evil by choice, should be cast down from heaven and be mocked by the angels whenever the temptations of the Devil which are meant to injure the saints turn to their profit.

It was because God foresaw, in creating the Devil, both the future malice and the good which he would draw from it, that the Psalmist says: "This sea dragon which thou hast formed to play therein" (Ps. 104:26). The point here is that, while God, in his goodness, made the Devil good, he found a way, by his foresight, to use the Devil's future wickedness.

God would never have created a single angel—not even a single man—whose future wickedness he foresaw, unless, at the same time, he knew of the good which could come of this evil. It was as though he meant the harmony of history, like the beauty of a poem, to be enriched by antithetical elements. For, the figure of speech called "antithesis" is the most elegant among the ornaments of rhetoric. The Latin for *antitheta* would be *opposita* or, better, *contraposita*; and although these words are not in common use, Latin, like every other language in the world, adopts this ornament of style. Thus, even the Apostle Paul in his Second Epistle to the Corinthians uses antitheses with rhetorical effect: "With the armor of justice on the right hand and on the left; in honor and dishonor, in evil report and good report; as deceivers and yet truthful, as unknown and yet well known, as dying and behold, we live, as chastised but not killed, as sorrowful yet always rejoicing, as poor yet enriching many, as having nothing yet possessing all things" (2 Cor. 6:7–10).

Now, just as this kind of antithesis lends beauty to literary style, so, in the antitheses of history, there is a rhetoric not of words, but of facts, that makes for beauty. This is the idea which the Book of Ecclesiasticus expresses clearly as follows: "Good is set against evil, and life against death; so also is the sinner against a just man. And so look upon all the works of the Most High. Two and two, and one against another" (Ecclus. 33:14–15).

2. CALVIN: GOD'S PROVIDENCE GOVERNS ALL

Calvin is the last great proponent of the theological "consensus" with respect to the doctrines of creation and providence. His particular interest is in God's sovereign, providential governance of all that happens, especially in human affairs, directing everything toward a foreordained, salvific end. Belief in fortune, chance, or fate has no place in Christian theology. These passages make clear the "logic of sovereignty" that governs Calvin's thought and much of the tradition. Source: John Calvin, *Institutes of the Christian Religion*, Book 1, Chap. 16, ed. J. T. McNeill, trans. F. L. Battles (Philadelphia: Westminster Press, 1960), Vol. 1, pp. 197–203, 207–9. Date of original publication: 1536–59.

God by his power nourishes and maintains the world
created by him, and rules its several parts by his
providence.

Moreover, to make God a momentary Creator, who once for all finished his work, would be cold and barren, and we must differ from profane men especially in that we see the presence of divine power shining as much in the continuing state of the universe as in its inception. For even though the minds of the impious too are compelled by merely looking upon earth and heaven to rise up to the Creator, yet faith has its own peculiar way of assigning the whole credit for creation to God. To this pertains that saying of the apostle's to which we have referred before, that only "by faith we understand that the universe was created by the word of God" (Heb. 11:3). For unless we pass on to his providence—however we may seem both to comprehend with the mind and to confess with the tongue—we do not yet properly grasp what it means to say: "God is Creator." . . .

But faith ought to penetrate more deeply, namely, having found him Creator of all, forthwith to conclude he is also everlasting Governor and Preserver—not only in that he drives the celestial frame as well as its several parts by a universal motion, but also in that he sustains, nourishes, and cares for, everything he has made, even to the least sparrow (cf. Matt. 10:29). . . .

That this difference may better appear, we must know that God's providence, as it is taught in Scripture, is opposed to fortune and fortuitous happenings. Now it has been commonly accepted in all ages, and almost all mortals hold the same opinion today, that all things come about through chance. What we ought to believe concerning providence is by this depraved opinion most certainly not only beclouded, but almost buried. Suppose a man falls among thieves, or wild beasts; is shipwrecked at sea by a sudden gale; is killed by a falling house or tree. Suppose another man wandering through the desert finds help in his straits; having been tossed by the waves, reaches harbor; miraculously escapes death by a finger's breadth. Carnal reason ascribes all such happenings, whether prosperous or adverse, to fortune. But anyone who has been taught by Christ's lips that all the hairs of his head are numbered (Matt. 10:30) will look farther afield for a cause, and will consider that all events are governed by God's secret plan. And concerning inanimate objects we ought to hold that, although each one has by nature been endowed with its own property, yet it does not exercise its own power except insofar as it is directed by God's ever-present hand. These are, thus, nothing but instruments to which God continually imparts as much effectiveness as he wills, and according to his own purpose bends and turns them to either one action or another.

And truly God claims, and would have us grant him, omnipotence—not the empty, idle, and almost unconscious sort that the Sophists imagine, but a watchful, effective, active sort, engaged in ceaseless activity. Not, indeed, an omnipotence that is only a general principle of confused motion, as if he were to command a river to flow through its once-appointed channels, but one that is directed toward individual and particular motions. For he is deemed omnipotent, not because he can indeed act, yet sometimes ceases and sits in idleness, or continues by a general impulse that order of nature which he previously appointed; but because, governing heaven and earth by his providence, he so regulates all things that nothing takes place without his deliberation. For when, in the Psalms, it is said that "he does whatever he wills" (Ps. 115:3), a certain and deliberate will is meant. For it would be senseless to interpret the words of the prophet after the manner of the philosophers, that God is the first agent because he is the beginning and cause of all motion; for in times of adversity believers comfort themselves with the solace that they suffer nothing except by God's ordinance and command, for they are under his hand. . . .

At the outset, then, let my readers grasp that providence means not that by which God idly observes from heaven what takes place on earth, but that by which, as keeper of the keys, he governs all events. Thus it pertains no less to his hands than to his eyes. And indeed, when Abraham said to his son, "God will provide" (Gen. 22:8), he meant not only to assert God's foreknowledge of a future event, but to cast the care of a matter unknown to him upon the will of him who is wont to give a way out of things perplexed and confused. Whence it follows that providence is lodged in the act; for many babble too ignorantly of bare foreknowledge. Not so crass is the error of those who attribute a governance to God, but of a confused and mixed sort, as I have said, namely, one that by a general motion revolves and drives the system of the universe, with its several parts, but which does not specifically direct the action of individual creatures. Yet this error, also, is not tolerable; for by this providence which they call universal, they teach that nothing hinders all creatures from being contingently moved, or man from turning himself hither and thither by the free choice of his will. And they so apportion things between God and man that God by his power inspires in man a movement by which he can act in accordance with the nature implanted in him, but he regulates his own actions by the plan of his will. Briefly, they mean that the universe, men's affairs, and men themselves are governed by God's might but not by his determination. I say nothing of the Epicureans (a pestilence that has always filled the world) who imagine that God is idle and indolent; and others just as foolish, who of old fancied that God so ruled above the middle region of the air that he left the lower regions to fortune. As if the dumb creatures themselves do not sufficiently cry out against such patent madness!

For now I propose to refute the opinion (which almost universally obtains) that concedes to God some kind of blind and ambiguous motion, while taking from him the chief thing: that he directs everything by his incomprehensible wisdom and disposes it to his own end. And so in name only, not in fact, it makes God the Ruler of the universe because it deprives him of his control. What, I pray you, is it to have control but so to be in authority that you rule in a determined order those things over which you are placed? Yet I do not wholly repudiate what is said concerning universal providence, provided they in turn grant me that the universe is ruled by God, not only because he watches over the order of nature set by himself, but because he exercises especial care over each of his works. It is, indeed, true that the several kinds of things are moved by a secret impulse of nature, as if they obeyed God's eternal command, and what God has once determined flows on by itself.

At this point we may refer to Christ's statement that from the very beginning he and the Father were always at work (John 5:17); and to Paul's teaching that "in him we live, move, and have our being" (Acts 17:28); also, what the author of the Letter to the Hebrews says, meaning to prove the divinity of Christ, that all things are sustained by his mighty command (Heb. 1:3). But they wrongly conceal and obscure by this excuse that special providence which is so declared by sure and clear testimonies of Scripture that it is a wonder anyone can have doubts about it. And surely they who cast over it the veil of which I spoke are themselves compelled to add, by way of correction, that many things take place under God's especial care. But they wrongly restrict this to particular acts alone. Therefore we must prove God so attends to the regulation of individual events, and they all so proceed from his set plan, that nothing takes place by chance. . . .

Those who wish to cast odium upon this doctrine defame it as the Stoics' dogma of fate. This charge was once hurled at Augustine. Even though we are unwilling to quarrel over words, yet we do not admit the word "fate," both because it is one of those words whose profane novelties Paul teaches us to avoid (1 Tim. 6:20), and because men try by the odium it incurs to oppress God's truth. Indeed, we are falsely and maliciously charged with this very dogma. We do not, with the Stoics, contrive a necessity out of the perpetual connection and intimately related series of causes, which is contained in nature; but we make God the ruler and governor of all things, who in accordance with his wisdom has from the farthest limit of eternity decreed what he was going to do, and now by his might carries out what he has decreed. From this we declare that not only heaven and earth and the inanimate creatures, but also the plans and intentions of men, are so governed by his providence that they are borne by it straight to their appointed end.

What then? you will ask. Does nothing happen by chance, nothing by contingency? I reply: Basil the Great has truly said that "fortune" and "chance" are pagan terms, with whose significance the minds of the godly ought not to be occupied. For if every success is God's blessing, and calamity and adversity his curse, no place now remains in human affairs for fortune or chance. . . .

Yet since the sluggishness of our mind lies far beneath the height of God's providence, we must employ a distinction to lift it up. Therefore I shall put it this way: however all things may be ordained by God's plan, according to a sure dispensation, for us they are fortuitous. Not that we think that fortune rules the world and men, tumbling all things at random up and down, for it is fitting that this folly be absent from the Christian's breast! But since the order, reason, end, and necessity of those things which happen for the most part lie hidden in God's purpose, and are not apprehended by human opinion, those things, which it is certain take place by God's will, are in a sense fortuitous. For they bear on the face of them no other appearance, whether they are considered in their own nature or weighed according to our knowledge and judgment. Let us imagine, for example, a merchant who, entering a wood with a company of faithful men, unwisely wanders away from his companions, and in his wandering comes upon a robber's den, falls among thieves, and is slain. His death was not only foreseen by God's eye, but also determined by his decree. For it is not said that he foresaw how long the life of each man would extend, but that he determined and fixed the bounds that men cannot pass (Job 14:5). Yet as far as the capacity of our mind is concerned, all things therein seem fortuitous. What will a Christian think at this point? Just this: whatever happened in a death of this sort he will regard as fortuitous by nature, as it is; yet he will not doubt that God's providence exercised authority over fortune in directing its end. The same reckoning applies to the contingency of future events. As all future events are uncertain to us, so we hold them in suspense, as if they might incline to one side or the other. Yet in our hearts it nonetheless remains fixed that nothing will take place that the Lord has not previously foreseen.

3. SPINOZA: *DEUS SIVE NATURA, CAUSA OMNIUM*

The seventeenth-century philosopher Benedict de Spinoza posed a radical challenge to consensus theism by developing a system of pantheistic naturalism. In this view there is no substantial difference between God and the cosmos. There is only one substance, infinite and eternal, lacking no ontological perfection, an inexhaustibly creative being from which an infinite number of things necessarily flow. There are religious reasons for calling this being God, but philosophically it may properly be called nature: hence "God or nature," *Deus sive natura*. We begin these selections with Spinoza's famous distinction between *natura naturans* ("nature naturing"), the one substance that is God or nature, and *natura naturata* ("nature natured"), the modes of creation and the infinitely many particular things of the created order. In this frame of reference, Spinoza is able to reaffirm the traditional doctrines of God's causality, necessary activity, providence, and predestination. Source: Benedict de Spinoza, *Short Treatise on God, Man, and His Well-Being* (c. 1660), Chaps. 8, 3–6, in *Spinoza: Selections*, ed. John Wild (New York: Charles Scribner's Sons, 1930), pp. 66–70, 72–73, 75–76, 80–81.

Here, before we proceed to something else, we shall briefly divide the whole of nature—namely, into *natura naturans* and *natura naturata*. By *natura naturans* we understand a being that we conceive clearly and distinctly through itself, and without needing anything beside itself (like all the attributes which we have so far described), that is, God. The Thomists likewise understand God by it, but their *natura naturans* was a being (so they called it) beyond all substances.

The *natura naturata* we shall divide into two, a general, and a particular. The general consists of all the modes which depend immediately on God, of which we shall treat in the following chapter; the particular consists of all the particular things which are produced by the general mode. So that the *natura naturata* requires some substance in order to be well understood. . . .

We shall now begin to consider those attributes [of God] which we

128

called *propria*. And, first of all, how God is a cause of all things.

Now, we have already said above that one substance cannot produce another; and that God is a being of whom all attributes are predicated; whence it clearly follows that all other things can by no means be, or be understood, apart from or outside him. Wherefore we may say with all reason *that God is a cause of all things.*

As it is usual to divide the efficient cause in eight divisions, let me, then, inquire how and in what sense God is a cause.

First then, we say that he is an emanative or productive cause of his works; and, insofar as there is activity, an active or operating cause, which we regard as one and the same, because they involve each other.

Secondly, he is an immanent, and not a transeunt cause, since all that he produces is within himself, and not outside him, because there is nothing outside him.

Thirdly, God is a free cause, and not a natural cause, as we shall make clear and manifest when we come to consider whether God can omit to do what he does, and then it will also be explained wherein true freedom consists.

Fourthly, God is a cause through himself and not by accident; this will become more evident from the discussion on predestination.

Fifthly, God is a principal cause of his works which he has created immediately, such as movement in matter, etc.; in which there is no place for a subsidiary [instrumental] cause, since this is confined to particular things; as when he dries the sea by means of a strong wind, and so forth in the case of all particular things in nature.

The subsidiary provoking cause is not [found] in God, because there is nothing outside him to incite him. The predisposing cause, on the other hand, is his perfection itself; through it he is a cause of himself, and, consequently, of all other things.

Sixthly, God alone is the first or initial cause, as is evident from our foregoing proof.

Seventhly, God is also a universal cause, but only insofar as he produces various things; otherwise this can never be predicated of him, as he needs no one in order to produce any results.

Eighthly, God is the proximate cause of the things that are infinite, and immutable, and which we assert to have been created immediately

129

by him, but, in one sense, he is the remote cause of all particular things.

We deny that God can omit to do what he does, and we shall also prove it when we treat of predestination; when we will show that all things necessarily depend on their causes. But, in the second place, this conclusion also follows from the perfection of God; for it is true, beyond a doubt, *that God can make everything just as perfect as it is conceived in his idea*; and just as things that are conceived by him cannot be conceived by him more perfectly than he conceives them, so all things can be made by him so perfect that they cannot come from him in a more perfect condition. Again, when we conclude that God could not have omitted to do what he has done, we deduce this from his perfection; because, in God, it would be an imperfection to be able to omit to do what he does; we do not, however, suppose that there is a subsidiary provoking cause in God that might have moved him to action, for then he were not God. . . . True freedom is only, or no other than [the status of being] the first cause, which is in no way constrained or coerced by anything else, and which through its perfection alone is the cause of all perfection; consequently, if God could omit to do this, he would not be perfect: for the ability to omit doing some good, or accomplishing some perfection in what he does, can have no place in him, except through defect. . . .

The second attribute, which we call a *proprium* [of God] is his providence, which to us is nothing else than the striving which we find in the whole of nature and in individual things to maintain and preserve their own existence. For it is manifest that no thing could, through its own nature, seek its own annihilation, but, on the contrary, that every thing has in itself a striving to preserve its condition, and to improve itself. Following these definitions of ours we, therefore, posit a *general* and a *special providence*. The general [providence] is that through which all things are produced and sustained insofar as they are parts of the whole of nature. The special providence is the striving of each thing separately to preserve its existence [each thing, that is to say], considered not as a part of nature, but as a whole [by itself]. This is explained by the following example: All the limbs of man are provided for, and cared for, insofar as they are parts of man, this is general providence; while special [providence] is the striving of each separate limb (as a whole in itself, and not as a part of man) to preserve and maintain its own well-being. . . .

[Against the attributes of divine providence and predestination, some people object:] how is it possible that God, who is said to be supremely perfect, and the sole cause, disposer, and provider of all, nevertheless permits such confusion to be seen everywhere in nature? Also, why has he not made man so as not to be able to sin?

Now, in the first place, it cannot be rightly said that there is confusion in nature, since nobody knows all the causes of things so as to be able to judge accordingly. This objection, however, originates in this kind of ignorance, namely, that they have set up general ideas, with which, they think, particular things must agree if they are to be perfect. These ideas, they state, are in the understanding of God, as many of Plato's followers have said, namely, that these general ideas (such as rational, animal, and the like) have been created by God; and although those who follow Aristotle say, indeed, that these things are not real things, only things of reason, they nevertheless regard them frequently as [real] things, since they have clearly said that his providence does not extend to particular things, but only to kinds; for example, God has never exercised his providence over Bucephalus, etc., but only over the whole genus horse. They say also that God has no knowledge of particular and transient things, but only of the general, which, in their opinion, are imperishable. We have, however, rightly considered this to be due to their ignorance. For it is precisely the particular things, and they alone, that have a cause, and not the general, because they are nothing.

God then is the cause of, and providence over, particular things only. If particular things had to conform to some other nature, then they could not conform to their own, and consequently could not be what they truly are. For example, if God had made all human beings like Adam before the fall, then indeed he would only have created Adam, and no Paul nor Peter; but no, it is just perfection in God, that he gives to all things, from the greatest to the least, their essence, or, to express it better, that he has all things perfectly in himself.

As regards the other [objection], why God has not made mankind so that they should not sin, to this it may serve [as an answer], that whatever is said about sin is only said with reference to us, that is, as when we compare two things with each other, or [consider one thing] from different points of view. For instance, if someone has made a clock precisely in order to strike and to show the hours, and the mechanism quite fulfils the aims of its maker, then we say that it is good, but if it does not do so, then we say that it is bad, notwithstanding that even then it might still be good if only it had been his intention to make it irregular and to strike at wrong times.

We say then, in conclusion, that Peter must, as is necessary, conform to the idea of Peter, and not to the idea of *man*; good and evil, or sin, these are only modes of thought, and by no means things, or any thing that has reality, as we shall very likely show yet more fully in what follows. For all things and works which are in nature are perfect.

4. HEGEL: WITHOUT THE WORLD GOD IS NOT GOD

Although powerfully influenced by Spinoza, Hegel drew back from any pantheistic identification of God and the world. Rather he attempted to understand God's relation to the world as the outward actualization of the moment of difference or otherness that is already present within the divine life, represented in the tradition by the trinitarian symbol of the Son. The non-serious divine "play of love with itself" becomes deadly serious when it takes on the determinacy of other-*being*, of actual separation and rupture. In order for God to become a living, actual God, as distinguished from being merely a logically complete God, the moment of creation, of divine finitization, is necessary. In this sense, "without the world God is not God." Our selections are from two parts of Hegel's philosophy of religion lectures—the first being a passage from the 1824 lectures in Part I ("The Concept of Religion"), the second a passage from the 1827 lectures in Part III ("The Consummate Religion"). Source: G. W. F. Hegel, *Lectures on the Philosophy of Religion*, ed. P. C. Hodgson (Berkeley: University of California Press, 1984ff.), Vol. 1, pp. 307–9; Vol. 3, pp. 271–74, 291–94.

I

The finite is . . . an essential moment of the infinite in the nature of God; and it may consequently be said that God is the very being who finitizes himself, who posits determinations within himself. God creates a world, that is, he wills a world, he thinks a world, and determines himself—outside him[self] there is nothing to determine; that is, he determines himself, he posits for himself an other over against himself, so that there is God and there is the world—they are two. In this relationship God himself is held fast as the finite over against another finite, but the truth is that this world is only an appearance in which he possesses himself. Without the moment of finitude there is no life, no subjectivity, no living God. God creates, he is active: therein lies the distinguishing, and with distinction the moment of finitude is posited. This subsistence of the finite, however, must be sublated once more. On this view there are two kinds of infinity, the true infinite, and the merely bad infinite of the understanding. Thus the finite is a moment of the divine life. . . .

This might initially strike us as ungodly, but it is also to be found in the commonest representations of God, for we are accustomed to regarding him as creator of the world. God creates the world out of nothing; i.e., outside the world there is nothing sensible, nothing external, for the world is externality itself. Only God is, but God [is] only by virtue of his being mediated with himself. God wills the finite, posits it as his other and so himself becomes an other of himself, a finite, for he is confronted by an other. But this other is the contradiction of what he is. It is of God, for it is *his* other, and is therefore determined as the other of God. It is the other and the not-other, it dissolves itself, it is not itself but an other, it is its own ruination. But other-being vis-à-vis God has in consequence disappeared, and God recognizes himself therein, by reason of which he maintains himself as what he has made of himself by his own effort. God is this inward movement, and only by virtue of so being is he a living God. However, the subsistence of finitude must accordingly not be adhered to, but also sublated. God *is* movement toward the finite, and, by sublating the finite, movement toward himself.[1]

Propositional forms are no longer valid here. "God is infinite," or "Spirit is infinite," and "I am finite"—these are false, defective expressions. For God is likewise the finite and I am likewise the infinite; God returns to himself in the I as what sublates itself as finite, and he *is* God only as this return. Without the world God is not God.[2] . . . The finite

---

1. [*Ed.*] This paragraph is from a freely edited notebook of the 1824 lectures by H. G. Hotho.
2. [*Ed.*] This sentence and the preceding one are from the Hotho notebook.

is not actual being, it is not something subsistent; similarly the infinite is not fixed. These definitions do not express the nature of spirit; they must rather be grasped only as moments of the process. . . .

II

The absolute, eternal idea is:

(1) First, in and for itself, God in his eternity before the creation of the world and outside the world.

(2) Secondly, God creates the world and posits the separation. He creates both nature and finite spirit. What is thus created is at first an other, posited outside of God. But God is essentially the reconciling to himself of what is alien, what is particular, what is posited in separation from him. He must restore to freedom and to his truth what is alien, what has fallen away in the idea's self-diremption, in its falling away from itself. This is the path and the process of reconciliation.

(3) In the third place, through this process of reconciliation, spirit has reconciled with itself what it distinguishes from itself in its act of diremption, or primal division, and thus it is the Holy Spirit, the Spirit [present] in its community.

These are not external distinctions, which *we* have made merely in accord with what we are; rather they are the activity, the developed vitality, of absolute spirit itself. It is itself its eternal life, which is a development and return of this development into itself; this vitality in development, this actualization of the concept, is what we have now to consider. . . . [Hegel's consideration of the first moment is omitted; the selection continues with the second moment.]

Eternal being-in-and-for-itself is what discloses itself, determines itself, divides itself, posits itself as what is differentiated from itself, but the difference is at the same time constantly sublated. Thereby actual being in and for itself constantly returns into itself—only in this way is it spirit. What is distinguished is defined in such a way that the distinction immediately disappears, and we have a relationship of God, of the idea, merely to himself. The act of differentiation is only a movement, a play of love with itself, which does not arrive at the seriousness of other-being, of separation and rupture. The other is to this extent defined as "Son"; in terms of sensibility, what-has-being-in-and-for-itself is defined as love, while in a higher mode of determinacy, it is defined as spirit that is present to itself and free. In the idea as thus specified, the determination of the distinction is not yet complete, since it is only abstract distinction in general. We have not yet arrived at distinction in its own proper form; [here] it is just one determinate characteristic. The distinguished elements are posited as the same; they have not yet come to be defined so that they are distinctly determined.

From this side the primal division of the idea is to be conceived in such a way that the other, which we have also called "Son," obtains the determination of the other as such—that this other exists as a free being for itself, and that it appears as something actual, as something that exists outside of and apart from God. Its ideality, its eternal return into actual being in and for itself, is posited in the first form of identity, the idea, in an immediate and identical way. Otherness is requisite in order that there may be difference; it is necessary that what is distinguished should be the otherness as an entity. Only the absolute idea determines itself and is certain of itself as absolutely free within itself because of this self-determination. For this reason its self-determination involves letting this determinate [entity] exist as something tree, something independent, or as an independent object. It is only for the being that is free that freedom *is*; it is only for the free human being that an other has freedom too. It belongs to the absolute freedom of the idea that, in its act of determining and dividing, it releases the other to exist as a free and independent being. This other, released as something free and independent, is *the world* as such.

The truth of the world is only its *ideality*—for it is not true that it possesses genuine actuality. Its nature is to *be*, but only in an *ideal* sense; it is not something eternal in itself but rather something created, whose being is only posited. For the world to be means to have being only for an instant, so to speak, but also to sublate this its separation or estrangement from God. It means to return to its origin, to enter into the relationship of spirit, of love—to *be* this relationship of spirit, or love, which is the third element. The second element is, therefore, the process of the world in love by which it passes over from fall and separation into reconciliation.

This is the second element—the creation of the world. The first element, within the idea, is only the relationship of the Father to the Son in eternal reconciliation, or, alternatively, non-reconciledness, because no fall is present yet. But the *other* also obtains the determinacy of other-*being*, of an actual entity. It is in the Son, in the determina-

135

tion of distinction, that the advance to further distinction occurs, that distinction comes into its own as [true] diversity. . . .

Looked at from this standpoint, [this] other is not the Son but rather the external world, the finite world, which is outside the truth—the world of finitude, where the other has the form of being, and yet by its nature is only the *heteron* [other], the determinate, what is distinct, limited, negative. The finite world is the side of distinction as opposed to the side that remains in unity; hence it divides into the *natural world* and the world of *finite spirit*. On its own account, nature enters into relationship only with humanity, not with God, for nature is not knowledge. God is spirit; nature knows nothing of spirit. It is created by God, but of itself it does not enter into relationship with him—in the sense that it is not possessed of knowledge. It stands in relation only to humanity, and in this relationship it provides what is called the dependent side of humanity. But to the extent that thinking recognizes that nature is created by God, that understanding and reason are within it, nature is known by thinking human beings. To that extent it is posited in relation to the divine, because its truth is recognized.

5. FORD: DIVINE PERSUASION

The process view of God already anticipated by Hegel was fully articulated by Alfred North Whitehead and his theological followers. Process theism, responding in part to the experience of radical evil in the twentieth century, represents a dramatic break with classical doctrines of God. God is viewed as neither unchanging nor independent of the world; and the world is not controlled by God, although it is guided or "lured" toward the realization of divine aims through divine "persuasion." In this selection, Lewis Ford attempts to demonstrate the nature of God's influence upon the world and the implications this has for the role and responsibilities of human beings in bringing about the good. Source: Lewis S. Ford, "Divine Persuasion and the Triumph of the Good," in *Process Philosophy and Christian Thought*, ed. Delwin Brown, Ralph James, and Gene Reeves (New York: Bobbs-Merrill Co., 1971), pp. 288–91, 297–98.

We contend that divine power is neither coercive nor limited, though we agree that God does not wholly control finite actualities. This means we must recognize their contention that process theism does preclude any *necessary* guarantee that good will triumph on the stage of worldly endeavor. Yet should there be such a guarantee? Far from being required by theism, we shall argue that such a philosophical guarantee would undermine genuine religious commitment, and that the ultimate redemption from evil moves on a very different plane. With respect to any such guarantee we find, as Kant did on another occasion, that it becomes "necessary to deny knowledge, in order to make room for faith." . . .

But power may be defined more broadly as the capacity to influence the outcome of any process of actualization, thereby permitting both persuasive and coercive power. Coercive power directly influences the outcome, since the process must conform to its control. Persuasive power operates more indirectly, for it is effective in determining the outcome only to the extent that the process appropriates and reaffirms for itself the aims envisioned in the persuasion. Thus the measure of control introduced differs; coercive power and control are commensurate, while persuasive power introduces the additional variable of acceptance by the process in actualization. That God's control is in fact limited by the existence of evil would signify a limited coercive power, but it is compatible with unlimited persuasive power.

Whitehead's thesis is that God possesses no coercive power at all. Whether limited or unlimited, such power is incompatible with divine perfection. In the official formulation of Christian doctrine, Whitehead complains, "the deeper idolatry, of the fashioning of God in the image of the Egyptian, Persian, and Roman imperial rulers, was retained. The Church gave unto God the attributes which belonged exclusively to Caesar." The concept of divine coercive power, both in its pure and modified forms, has led to grave difficulties.

Consider the extreme instance in which God is conceived as exerting unlimited coercive power, thereby controlling and determining all things. God is the master potter, moulding the clay of the world by the force of his creative activity, except that God has no need of any clay with which to work; he makes his own. On this exception the analogy breaks down, for the potter's vase asserts its own reality apart from the human potter precisely because it had already existed separately as clay. Could a world moulded completely by God's coercive power assert any independent existence of its own? To do so the world must possess some power. Pure coercive power transforms *creatio ex nihilo* into *creatio ex deo*, with the world possessing no more independent actuality than an idea in the divine mind would have. Even if it were to exist apart from the divine mind, it could not enrich God's experience, for he fully experiences in imagination any world he could completely determine.

Most views of divine power are less extreme, but they all share the same basic defects insofar as they ascribe coercive power to God. To the extent that God exercises such power, creaturely freedom is restricted, the reality of the world is diminished, and the divine experience is impoverished. Creaturely freedom is all important, for without it God is deprived of the one thing the world can provide which God alone cannot have: a genuine social existence. Abandoning the angelic marionettes who merely echo his thought as further extensions of his own being, God has elected to enter into dialogue with sinful, yet free, men.

Divine persuasive power maximizes creaturely freedom, respecting the integrity of each creature in the very act of guiding that creature's development toward greater freedom. The image of God as the craftsman, the cosmic watchmaker, must be abandoned. God is the husbandman in the vineyard of the world, fostering and nurturing its continuous evolutionary growth throughout all ages; he is the companion and friend who inspires us to achieve the very best that is within us. God creates by persuading the world to create itself. Nor is this persuasion limited by any defect, for as Plato pointed out long ago, the real good is genuinely persuasive, in contrast to the counterfeit of the apparent good we confront on all sides.

This vision appears to many as too bold, for it seems to ascribe mind and consciousness to all beings. In ordinary discourse only those who are consciously sensitive to the directives and promptings of others can be persuaded, although we are beginning to recognize the subliminal influence of the "hidden persuaders." Whitehead is urging us to broaden our understanding of persuasion, for otherwise we lack the means for penetrating the nature of creation. Without the alternative of divine persuasion, we confront two unwelcome extremes: divine determinism or pure chance. In neither instance can God create. If determined by God, the world lacks all ontological independence. It makes no difference even if God only acts through the secondary causes of the natural order. To exist apart from God, either the world as a whole or its individual parts must possess a self-activity of its own. This self-activity is denied to the world as a whole if God is its primary (coercive) cause, and it is denied to the individual parts if they are determined by the secondary causes of the natural order acting in God's stead. Chance, on the other hand, ignores God's role in the evolutionary advance entirely and renders this advance itself unintelligible. We need not anthropocentrically imagine the evolutionary process to culminate in man, for it is quite conceivable that in time it might bypass man and the entire class of mammals to favor some very different species capable of a greater complexity than man can achieve; if not here on earth, then in some other planetary system. Nevertheless it seems impossible to deny that there has been an evolutionary advance in the sense of increasing complexity of order over the past several billion years. This increasing complexity cannot be satisfactorily accounted for simply in terms of the chance juxtaposition of component elements, and calls for a transcendent directing power constantly introducing richer possibilities of order for the world to actualize. God proposes, and the world disposes. This response is the necessary self-activity of the creature by which it maintains its own existence. The creature may or may not embody the divine urge toward greater complexity, but insofar as that ideal is actualized, an evolutionary advance has been achieved. Any divine power which so influences the world without violating its integrity is properly called persuasive, while the necessary self-activity of the creature insures the spontaneity of response. This spontaneity may be minimal for protons and electrons, but in the course of the evolutionary advance, sustained until now, it has manifested itself in ever richer forms as the vitality of living cells, the conscious activity of the higher animals, and the self-conscious freedom of man. Spontaneity has matured as freedom. On this level it becomes possible for the increasing complexity of order to be directed toward the achievement of civilization, and for the means of divine persuasion to become ethical aspiration. The devout will affirm that in the ideals we envision we are being persuaded by God, but this self-conscious awareness is not necessary for its effectiveness. Not only we ourselves, but the entire created order, whether consciously or unconsciously, is open to this divine persuasion, each in its own way. . . .

Is there then any ultimate triumph of good? The Christian and the

Jew alike wait with confident expectation for that day when the wolf shall lie down with the lamb. Classical theism, construing omnipotence in terms of coercive power, provides a philosophical guarantee that that day will in fact come to pass, or argues that it is already taking place (Leibniz' best of all possible worlds). This guarantee, however, transforms a confident expectation into a determinate fact, whether that fact be regarded as present or future. From the standpoint of faith, this appears to be nothing more than an emphatic underscoring of an intense trust in God. From the standpoint of logic, however, the fact of the triumph of good vitiates all need to strive for it. As in the case of the Marxist vision of a classless society, if its coming is inevitable, why must we work for it?

In process theism the future is an open risk. God is continuously directing the creation toward the good, but his persuasive power is effective only insofar as the creatures themselves affirm that good. Creaturely evil is an ever-present contingency, unless Origen is correct that we cannot resist the grace of God forever. On the other hand, the absence of any final guarantee now makes it genuinely possible for the expectation of the good to become a matter of faith. By faith I do not mean its rationalistic counterfeit: a belief based upon insufficient evidence. Rather I mean what Kierkegaard meant by truth for the existing individual: "an objective uncertainty held fast in an appropriation-process of the most passionate inwardness." Faith is belief in spite of doubt, sustained by trust, loyalty, and devotion. The future is now doubtful, risky, uncertain. Yet the theist is sustained by his confident expectation that if we as creatures all have faith in God, that is, if all rely upon his guidance (given in the initial aim of each occasion), trusting him sufficiently to actualize the good which he proposes as novel possibility, then the good *will* triumph. The continued persistence of evil, both in man and in the natural order, testifies to the very fragmentary realization of creaturely faith in God. Nonetheless we may hope that the grace of God may be received and permeate all beings, and in that hope do our part in the great task. Such hope prohibits other worldly withdrawal, but calls upon us to redouble our efforts to achieve the good in this world with all its ambiguities for good and evil.

Faith in this sense is reciprocal. Just as the world must trust God to provide the aim for its efforts, so God must trust the world for the achievement of that aim. As Madden and Hare point out, "he is apparently so weak that he cannot guarantee his own welfare." This is true to the Biblical image of God's vulnerability toward man's waywardness. We read that "God repented that he had made man, and it grieved him to his heart" (Gen. 6:6). Israel remembers God's suffering and anguish over his chosen people, a suffering most poignantly revealed to the Church in the crucifixion of Jesus of Nazareth. The world is a risky affair for God as well as for us. God has taken that risk upon himself in creating us with freedom through persuasion. He has faith in us, and it is up to us to respond in faith to him.

6. TILLICH: GOD'S ORIGINATING, SUSTAINING, AND DIRECTING CREATIVITY

In working out a contemporary theological interpretation of the doctrine of creation, Tillich seeks to avoid the pitfalls of both classical theism, which in modernity tends to devolve into deism, and Spinozistic pantheism, which in modernity devolves into naturalism. God's relation to the world is one of an originating, sustaining, and directing creativity—a creativity by which God transcends the world precisely through his immanence within it as the power of being. Source: Paul Tillich, *Systematic Theology*, Vol. 1 (Chicago: University of Chicago Press, 1951), pp. 252–54, 261–63, 264, 266–67.

The divine life is creative, actualizing itself in inexhaustible abundance. The divine life and the divine creativity are not different. God is creative because he is God. Therefore, it is meaningless to ask whether creation is a necessary or a contingent act of God. Nothing is necessary for God in the sense that he is dependent on a necessity above him. His aseity implies that everything which he is he is through himself. He eternally "creates himself," a paradoxical phrase which states God's freedom. Nor is creation contingent. It does not "happen" to God, for it is identical with his life. Creation is not only God's freedom but also his destiny. But it is not a fate; it is neither a necessity nor an accident which determines him.

The doctrine of creation is not the story of an event which took place "once upon a time." It is the basic description of the relation between

God and the world. It is the correlate to the analysis of man's finitude. It answers the question implied in man's finitude and in finitude generally. In giving this answer, it discovers that the meaning of finitude is creatureliness. The doctrine of creation is the answer to the question implied in the creature as creature. This question is asked continually and is always answered in man's essential nature. The question and the answer are beyond potentiality and actuality, as all things are in the process of the divine life. But actually the question is asked and is *not* answered in man's existential situation. The character of existence is that man asks the question of his finitude without receiving an answer. It follows that even if there were such a thing as natural theology, it could not reach the truth of God's creativity and man's creatureliness. The doctrine of creation does not describe an event. It points to the situation of creatureliness and to its correlate, the divine creativity.

Since the divine life is essentially creative, all three modes of time must be used in symbolizing it. God *has* created the world, he *is* creative in the present moment, and he *will* creatively fulfil his *telos*. Therefore, we must speak of originating creation, sustaining creation, and directing creation. This means that not only the preservation of the world but also providence is subsumed under the doctrine of the divine creativity.

(a) God's originating creativity. . . . The classical Christian doctrine of creation uses the phrase *creatio ex nihilo*. The first task of theology is an interpretation of these words. Their obvious meaning is a critical negation. God finds nothing "given" to him which influences him in his creativity or which resists his creative *telos*. The doctrine of *creatio ex nihilo* is Christianity's protection against any type of ultimate dualism. That which concerns man ultimately can only be that on which he ultimately depends. Two ultimates destroy the ultimacy of concern. This negative meaning of *creatio ex nihilo* is clear and decisive for every Christian experience and assertion. It is the mark of distinction between paganism, even in its most refined form, and Christianity, even in its most primitive form.

The question arises, however, whether the term *ex nihilo* points to more than the rejection of dualism. The word *ex* seems to refer to the origin of the creature. "Nothing" is what (or where) it comes from. Now "nothing" can mean two things. It can mean the absolute negation of being (ouk on), or it can mean the relative negation of being (me on). If ex nihilo meant the latter, it would be a restatement of the Greek doctrine of matter and form against which it is directed. If ex nihilo meant the absolute negation of being, it could not be the origin of the creature. Nevertheless, the term ex nihilo says something fundamentally important about the creature, namely, that it must take over what might be called "the heritage of nonbeing." Creatureliness implies nonbeing, but creatureliness is more than nonbeing. It carries in itself the power of being, and this power of being is its participation in being-itself, in the creative ground of being. Being a creature includes both the heritage of nonbeing (anxiety) and the heritage of being (courage). It does not include a strange heritage originating in a half-divine power which is in conflict with the power of being-itself.

The doctrine of creation out of nothing expresses two fundamental truths. The first is that the tragic character of existence is not rooted in the creative ground of being; consequently, it does not belong to the essential nature of things. In itself finitude is not tragic, that is, it is not doomed to self-destruction by its very greatness. Therefore, the tragic is not conquered by avoiding the finite as much as possible, that is, by ontological asceticism. The tragic is conquered by the presence of being-itself within the finite. The second truth expressed in this doctrine is that there is an element of nonbeing in creatureliness; this gives insight into the natural necessity of death and into the potentiality but not necessity of the tragic.

Two central theological doctrines are based on the doctrine of creation, namely, incarnation and eschatology. God can appear within finitude only if the finite as such is not in conflict with him. And history can be fulfilled in the eschaton only if salvation does not presuppose elevation above finitude. The formula creatio ex nihilo is not the title of a story. It is the classical formula which expresses the relation between God and the world. . . .

(b) God's sustaining creativity. Man actualizes his finite freedom in unity with the whole of reality. This actualization includes structural independence, the power of standing upon one's self, and the possibility of resisting the return to the ground of being. At the same time, actualized freedom remains continuously dependent on its creative ground. Only in the power of being-itself is the creature able to resist nonbeing. Creaturely existence includes a double resistance, that is, resistance against nonbeing as well as resistance against the ground of being in which it is rooted and upon which it is dependent. Traditionally the relation of God to the creature in its actualized freedom is called the preservation of the world. The symbol of preservation implies the independent existence of that which is preserved as well as the necessity of protection against threats of destruction. The doctrine of the preservation of the world is the door through which deistic concepts easily creep into the theological system. The world is conceived as an independent structure which moves according to its own laws. God certainly created the world "in the beginning" and gave it the laws of nature. But after its beginning he either does not interfere at all (consistent deism) or only occasionally through miracles and revelation (theistic deism), or he acts in a continual interrelationship (consistent theism). In these three cases, it would not be proper to speak of sustaining creation.

Since the time of Augustine, another interpretation of the preservation of the world is given. Preservation is continuous creativity, in that God out of eternity creates things and time together. Here is the only adequate understanding of preservation. It was accepted by the Reformers; it was powerfully expressed by Luther and radically worked out by Calvin, who added a warning against the deistic danger which he anticipated. This line of thought must be followed and made into a line of defense against the contemporary half-deistic, half-theistic way of conceiving God as a being alongside the world. God is essentially creative, and therefore he is creative in every moment of temporal existence, giving the power of being to everything that has being out of the creative ground of the divine life. There is, however, a decisive difference between originating and sustaining creativity. The latter refers to the given structures of reality, to that which continues within the change, to the regular and calculable in things. Without the static element, finite being would not be able to identify itself with itself or anything with anything. Without it, neither expectation, nor action for the future, nor a place to stand upon would be possible; and therefore being would not be possible. The faith in God's sustaining creativity is the faith in the continuity of the structure of reality as the basis for being and acting.

The main current of the modern world view completely excluded the awareness of God's sustaining creativity. Nature was considered a system of measurable and calculable laws resting in themselves without beginning or end. The "well-founded earth" was a safe place within a safe universe. Although no one would deny that every special thing was threatened by nonbeing, the structure of the whole seemed beyond such a threat. Consequently, one could speak of *deus sive natura*, a phrase which indicates that the name "God" does not add anything to what is already involved in the name "nature." One may call such ideas "pantheistic"; but, if one does, one must realize that they are not much different from a deism which consigns God to the fringe of reality and relegates to the world the same independence which it has in naturalistic pantheism. The symbol of God's sustaining creativity has disappeared in both cases. Today the main trend of the modern world view has been reversed. The foundations of the self-sufficient universe have been shaken. The questions of its beginning and end have become theoretically significant, pointing to the element of nonbeing in the universe as a whole. At the same time, the feeling of living in an ultimately secure world has been destroyed through the catastrophes of the twentieth century and the corresponding existentialist philosophy and literature. The symbol of God's sustaining creativity received a new significance and power. . . .

(c) *God's directing creativity*. . . . The concept "the purpose of creation" should be replaced by "the *telos* of creativity"—the inner aim of fulfilling in actuality what is beyond potentiality and actuality in the divine life. One function of the divine creativity is to drive every creature toward such a fulfilment. Thus directing creativity must be added to originating and sustaining creation. It is the side of the divine creativity which is related to the future. The traditional term for directing creativity is "providence." . . .

Providence means a fore-seeing (*pro-videre*) which is a fore-ordering ("seeing to it"). This ambiguity of meaning expresses an ambiguous feeling toward providence, and it corresponds to different interpretations of the concept. If the element of foreseeing is emphasized, God becomes the omniscient spectator who knows what will happen but who does not interfere with the freedom of his creatures. If the element of foreordering is emphasized, God becomes a planner who has ordered everything that will happen "before the foundations of the world"; all natural and historical processes are nothing more than the execution of this supratemporal divine plan. In the first interpretation the creatures make their world, and God remains a spectator; in the second interpretation the creatures are cogs in a universal mechanism, and God is the only active agent. Both interpretations of providence must be rejected. Providence is a permanent activity of God. He never is a spectator; he always directs everything toward its fulfilment. Yet God's directing creativity always creates through the freedom of man and through the spontaneity and structural wholeness of all creatures. Providence works through the polar elements of being. It works through the conditions of individual, social, and universal existence, through finitude, nonbeing, and anxiety, through the interdependence of all finite things, through their resistance against the divine activity and through the destructive consequences of this resistance. All existential conditions are included in God's directing creativity. They are not increased or decreased in their power, nor are they canceled. Providence is not interference; it is creation. It uses all factors, both those given by freedom and those given by destiny, in creatively directing everything toward its fulfilment. Providence is a *quality* of every constellation of conditions, a quality which "drives" or "lures" toward fulfilment. Providence is "the divine condition" which is present in every group of finite conditions and in the totality of finite conditions. It is not an additional factor, a miraculous physical or mental interference in terms of supranaturalism. It is the quality of inner directedness present in every situation. The man who believes in providence does not believe that a special divine activity will alter the conditions of finitude and estrangement. He believes, and asserts with the courage of faith, that no situation whatsoever can frustrate the fulfilment of his ultimate destiny, that nothing can separate him from the love of God which is in Christ Jesus (Romans, chap. 8).

VI. HUMAN BEING

1. AUGUSTINE: BODY, SOUL, WILL, AND THE IMAGE OF GOD

According to the theology of history developed by Augustine in *The City of God*, the dynamics of history are generated by a struggle between two "cities." The distinction between the two cities is based on his view of human nature, and especially the role of will in human nature. He develops this view by way of commentary on the Genesis account of the creation and fall of Adam. Source: Augustine, *The City of God*, Book 13, Chaps. 2, 3, 24; Book 14, Chaps. 1, 5, 6, 11, 13, 27, in *Fathers of the Church: Writings of Saint Augustine*, Vol. 7, ed. G. G. Walsh and G. Monahan (Washington, D.C.: Catholic University of America Press, 1952), pp. 299–300, 302, 340–41, 343–46, 347, 356, 358, 375–76, 380–81, 409. Date of original composition: 413–26.

Adam's Sin and Its Consequences

It seems to me that I ought to examine more carefully the nature of death. For, although the human soul is, in a true sense, immortal, nonetheless it, too, can suffer its own sort of death. It is said to be immortal because it can never, in the least degree, cease to live and perceive. The body, on the other hand, is mortal because it can be deprived entirely of life and because, of itself, it has no power to live. Death comes to the soul when God abandons it, just as death comes to the body when the soul departs.

There is also a total death for man, a death of body and soul, namely, when a soul, abandoned by God, abandons the body. In this case, the soul has no life from God and the body has no life from the soul. The consequence of such total death is the second death, so called on the authority of divine revelation (Rev. 2:11; 20:14; 21:8). . . .

While the first parents were so created that, had they not sinned, they would have experienced no kind of death, nevertheless, these first sinners were so punished that all of their descendants were to be subject to the same penalty of death. . . . Such was the greatness of the guilt that the punishment so impaired human nature that what was originally a penal condition for the first parents who sinned became a natural consequence in all of their descendants.

Man is not produced from man in the same way that he was created from the dust. Dust was but the material out of which man was made, while a man is the parent of his child. Earth and flesh are not identical, even though the latter was made from the former, but parent and offspring are identical in having the same human nature. Hence, when the first couple was punished by the judgment of God, the whole human race, which was to become Adam's posterity through the first woman, was present in the first man. . . .

This first man, then, who was formed from the dust of the earth or from slime (since the dust was moistened dust), this "dust of the earth," to use the exact expression of Scripture, became a living body when he received a soul, according to the Apostle's words: "And this man became a living soul."

But, it is objected, Adam had a soul already for, otherwise, he would not have been called a man, since a man is not a body only nor a soul only but a being consisting of the two. Now, it is true that the soul is not the entire man, but only his better part; nor is the body the entire man, but merely his inferior part. Only when body and soul are in union can we speak of a man. However, either part, even when it is mentioned separately, can be used for a man, for in everyday speech no one can be blamed for saying "That man is dead and is now in peace or in pain"—although this can be said strictly only of his soul. We also say: "That man is buried in such or such a place"—although this applies only to his body. . . .

What we need to understand is how a man can be called, on the one hand, the image of God and, on the other, is dust and will return to dust. The former relates to the rational soul which God by his breathing or, better, by his inspiration communicated to man, meaning to the body of man; but the latter refers to the body such as God formed it from dust into the man to whom a soul was given that it might become a living body, that is, that man might become a living soul. But, what our Lord wanted us to understand when he breathed on his disciples, saying: "Receive the Holy Spirit," was that the Holy Spirit is the Spirit not only of the Father but also the Spirit of the only-begotten Son himself. For, in fact, one and the same Spirit is the Spirit of both the Father and the Son—not a creature but the Creator, and forming with them the Trinity: Father, Son and Holy Spirit. . . .

We find that Holy Scripture is accustomed to use both phrases— "living soul" and "the breath of life"—in regard even to beasts. . . . Hence, the only real question here is: What need was there to add "living," since the soul cannot exist without being alive? Or what need was there to add "of life" after the word "breath"? The answer to these questions is that Scripture regularly uses the terms "living soul" and "breath of life" to signify animals or animated bodies that are clearly capable of sensation on account of a soul, but, on the contrary, when there was a question of the creation of man, the ordinary usage of Holy Scripture is forgotten. There is now an altogether special mode of expression which is meant to imply that when man was created he received in addition a rational soul not produced from water and earth like the souls of other animals, but created by the breath of God, and that, nevertheless, man was so made as to live, just like the other animals, in an animal body, but in one which is animated by a human soul. It was of the other animals that Scripture says: "Let the earth bring forth the living soul," and likewise says of this animal soul that it has the "breath of life." . . .

In a previous chapter . . . we saw that the natural body, to use the Apostle's expression, in which the first man, Adam, was created was not so created that under no conditions could it die, but in such a way that it would not die unless man sinned. But the body which, by the life-giving spirit, will become spiritual and immortal will under no conditions be able to die. It will be immortal, just as a created soul is immortal, for, even though a soul can be said to be dead when sin deprives it of that special kind of life which is the Spirit of God that could have enabled the soul to live wisely and blessedly, nevertheless, even in sin the soul does not cease to live, however miserably, a life of its own, because it is immortal by creation. . . .

On the other hand, men who are sharers in the grace of God and fellow citizens with the holy angels abiding in beatitude will be so clothed with spiritual bodies as to be saved forever from sin and death. Yet, while invested with an immortality like the angels' which can never be lost by sin, the nature of their flesh will remain the same, without a trace, however, of any remnant of corruption or clumsiness. . . .

Two Loves Originate Two Different Cities

I have already said, in previous Books, that God had two purposes in deriving all men from one man. His first purpose was to give unity to the human race by the likeness of nature. His second purpose was to bind mankind by the bond of peace, through blood relationship, into one harmonious whole. I have said further that no member of this race would ever have died had not the first two—one created from nothing and the second from the first—merited this death by disobedience. The sin which they committed was so great that it impaired all human nature—in this sense, that the nature has been transmitted to posterity with a propensity to sin and a necessity to die. Moreover, the kingdom of death so dominated men that all would have been hurled, by a just punishment, into a second and endless death had not some been saved from this by the gratuitous grace of God. This is the reason why, for all the difference of the many and very great nations throughout the world in religion and morals, language, weapons, and dress, there exist no more than the two kinds of society, which, according to our Scriptures, we have rightly called the two cities. One city is that of men who live according to the flesh. The other is of men who live according to the spirit. Each of them chooses its own kind of peace and, when they attain what they desire, each lives in the peace of its own choosing. . . .

We ought not, therefore, to blame our sins and defects on the nature of the flesh, for this is to disparage the Creator. The flesh, in its own kind and order, is good. But what is not good is to abandon the goodness of the Creator in pursuit of some created good, whether by living deliberately according to the flesh, or according to the soul, or according to the entire man, which is made up of soul and flesh and which is the reason why either "soul" alone or "flesh" alone can mean a man. . . .

Man's will, then, is all-important. If it is badly directed, the emotions will be perverse; if it is rightly directed, the emotions will be not merely blameless but even praiseworthy. The will is in all of these affections; indeed, they are nothing else but inclinations of the will. For, what are desire and joy but the will in harmony with things we desire?

And what are fear and sadness but the will in disagreement with the things we abhor?

The consent of the will in the search for what we want is called desire; joy is the name of the will's consent to the enjoyment of what we desire. So, too, fear is aversion from what we do not wish to happen, as sadness is a disagreement of the will with something that happened against our will. Thus, according as the will of a man is attracted or repelled by the variety of things which he either seeks or shuns, so is it changed or converted into one or other of these different emotions. . . .

The good will, then, is a work of God, since man was created by God with a good will. On the contrary, the first bad will, which was present in man before any of his bad deeds, was rather a falling away from the work of God into man's own works rather than a positive work itself; in fact, a fall into bad works, since they were "according to man" and not "according to God." Thus, this bad will or, what is the same, man in so far as his will is bad is like a bad tree which brings forth these bad works like bad fruit.

A bad will, however, contrary as it is to nature and not according to nature, since it is a defect in nature, still belongs to the nature of which it is a defect, since it has no existence apart from this nature. This nature, of course, is one that God has created out of nothing, and not out of himself, as was the case when he begot the Word through whom all things have been made (John 1:3). Though God has fashioned man from the dust of the earth, that same dust, like all earthly matter, has been made out of nothing. And it was a soul made out of nothing which God united to the body when man was created. . . .

Our first parents only fell openly into the sin of disobedience because, secretly, they had begun to be guilty. Actually, their bad deed could not have been done had not bad will preceded it; what is more, the root of their bad will was nothing else than pride. For, "pride is the beginning of all sin" (Eccl. 10:13). And what is pride but an appetite for inordinate exaltation? Now, exaltation is inordinate when the soul cuts itself off from the very source to which it should keep close and somehow makes itself and becomes an end to itself. This takes place when the soul becomes inordinately pleased with itself, and such self-pleasing occurs when the soul falls away from the unchangeable good which ought to please the soul far more than the soul can please itself.

Now, this falling away is the soul's own doing, for, if the will had merely remained firm in the love of that higher immutable good which lighted its mind into knowledge and warmed its will into love, it would not have turned away in search of satisfaction in itself and, by so doing, have lost that light and warmth. . . .

Our first parents, then, must already have fallen before they could do the evil deed, before they could commit the sin of eating the forbidden fruit. For such "bad fruit" could come only from a "bad tree" (cf. Matt. 7:18). That the tree became bad was contrary to its nature, because such a condition could come about only by a defection of the will, which is contrary to nature. Notice, however, that such worsening by reason of a defect is possible only in a nature that has been created out of nothing. In a word, a nature is a nature because it is something made by God, but a nature falls away from that which is because the nature was made out of nothing.

Yet, man did not so fall away from being as to be absolutely nothing, but, in so far as he turned himself toward himself, he became less than he was when he was adhering to him who is supreme being. Thus, no longer to be in God but to be in oneself in the sense of to please oneself is not to be wholly nothing but to be approaching nothingness. . . .

The point here is that the first man had been so constituted that if, as a good man, he had relied on the help of God, he could have overcome the bad angel, whereas he was bound to be overcome if he proudly relied on his own will in preference to this wisdom of his maker and helper, God; and he was destined to a merited reward if his will remained firm with the help of God, and to an equally deserved doom if his will wavered because of his desertion from God. Notice here that, whereas the reliance on the help of God was a positive act that was only possible by the help of God, the reliance on his own will was a negative falling away from favors of divine grace, and this was a possibility of his own choice.

There is an analogy to this in living. The act of living in a body is a positive act which is not a matter of choice but is only possible by the help of nourishment; whereas the choice not to live in the body is a negative act which is in our human power, as we see in the case of suicide. Thus, to remain living as one ought to live was not a matter of

152

choice, even in Eden, but depended on the help of God, whereas to live ill, as one ought not to live, was in man's power; therefore, man was justly responsible for the cutting short of his happiness and the incurring of the penalty that followed.

2. SCHLEIERMACHER: THE HUMAN SUBJECT

It is characteristic of theology in the modern period to give a distinctly "subjective" turn to the interpretation of traditional doctrines. Nowhere is this characteristic more evident than in the writings of Schleiermacher, who prefaces his major work, *The Christian Faith*, with an analysis of human consciousness. This conception of the human subject then provides the interpretive principle for his work as a whole. Source: Friedrich Schleiermacher, *The Christian Faith*, § 4, ed. H. R. Mackintosh and J. S. Stewart (Edinburgh: T. & T. Clark, 1928), pp. 12–17. Date of original publication of the 2d edition: 1830.

The common element in all howsoever diverse
expressions of piety, by which these are conjointly
distinguished from all other feelings, or, in other words,
the self-identical essence of piety, is this: the
consciousness of being absolutely dependent, or, which
is the same thing, of being in relation with God.

In any actual state of consciousness, no matter whether it merely accompanies a thought or action or occupies a moment for itself, we are never simply conscious of our selves in their unchanging identity, but are always at the same time conscious of a changing determination of them. The ego in itself can be represented objectively; but every consciousness of self is at the same time the consciousness of a variable state of being. But in this distinction of the latter from the former, it is implied that the variable does not proceed purely from the self-identical, for in that case it could not be distinguished from it. Thus in every self-consciousness there are two elements, which we might call respectively a self-caused element and a non-self-caused element; or a being and a having-by-some-means-come-to-be. The latter of these presupposes for every self-consciousness another factor besides the ego, a factor which is the source of the particular determination, and without which the self-consciousness would not be precisely what it is. But this other is not objectively presented in the immediate self-consciousness

153

with which alone we are here concerned. For though, of course, the double constitution of self-consciousness causes us always to look objectively for an other to which we can trace the origin of our particular state, yet this search is a separate act with which we are not at present concerned. In self-consciousness there are only two elements: the one expresses the existence of the subject for itself, the other its co-existence with an other.

Now to these two elements, as they exist together in the temporal self-consciousness, correspond in the subject its *receptivity* and its (spontaneous) *activity*. If we could think away the co-existence with an other, but otherwise think ourselves as we are, then a self-consciousness which predominantly expressed an affective condition of receptivity would be impossible, and any self-consciousness could then express only activity—an activity, however, which, not being directed to any object, would be merely an urge outwards, an indefinite "agility" without form or color. But as we never do exist except along with an other, so even in every outward-tending self-consciousness the element of receptivity, in some way or other affected, is the primary one; and even the self-consciousness which accompanies an action (acts of knowing included), while it predominantly expresses spontaneous movement and activity, is always related (though the relation is often a quite indefinite one) to a prior moment of affective receptivity, through which the original "agility" received its direction. To these propositions assent can be unconditionally demanded; and no one will deny them who is capable of a little introspection and can find interest in the real subject of our present inquiries.

The common element in all those determinations of self-consciousness which predominantly express a receptivity affected from some outside quarter is the *feeling of dependence*. On the other hand, the common element in all those determinations which predominantly express spontaneous movement and activity is the *feeling of freedom*. The former is the case not only because it is by an influence from some other quarter that we have come to such a state, but particularly because we *could* not so become except by means of an other. The latter is the case because in these instances an other is determined by us, and without our spontaneous activity could not be so determined. . . .

Let us now think of the feeling of dependence and the feeling of freedom as *one*, in the sense that not only the subject but the corresponding other is the same for both. Then the total self-consciousness made up of both together is one of *reciprocity* between the subject and the corresponding other. Now let us suppose the totality of all moments of feeling, of both kinds, as one whole: then the corresponding other is also to be supposed as a totality or as one, and then that term "reciprocity" is the right one for our self-consciousness in general, inasmuch as it expresses our connection with everything which either appeals to our receptivity or is subjected to our activity. And this is true not only when we particularize this other and ascribe to each of its elements a different degree of relation to the twofold consciousness within us, but also when we think of the total "outside" as one, and moreover (since it contains other receptivities and activities to which we have a relation) as one together with ourselves, that is, as a *world*. Accordingly our self-consciousness, as a consciousness of our existence in the world or of our co-existence with the world, is a series in which the feeling of freedom and the feeling of dependence are divided. But neither an absolute feeling of dependence, i.e., without any feeling of freedom in relation to the co-determinant, nor an absolute feeling of freedom, i.e., without any feeling of dependence in relation to the co-determinant, is to be found in this whole realm. If we consider our relations to nature, or those which exist in human society, there we shall find a large number of objects in regard to which freedom and dependence maintain very much of an equipoise: these constitute the field of equal reciprocity. There are other objects which exercise a far greater influence upon our receptivity than our activity exercises upon them, and also vice versa, so that one of the two may diminish until it is imperceptible. But neither of the two members will ever completely disappear. The feeling of dependence predominates in the relation of children to their parents, or of citizens to their fatherland; and yet individuals can, without losing their relationship, exercise upon their fatherland not only a directive influence, but even a counter-influence. And the dependence of children on their parents, which very soon comes to be felt as a gradually diminishing and fading quantity, is never from the start free from the admixture of an element of spontaneous activity towards the parents: just as even in the most absolute autocracy the ruler is not without some slight feeling of dependence. It is the same in the case of nature: towards all the forces of nature—even, we may say, towards the heavenly bodies—we ourselves do, in the same sense in which they influence us, exercise a counter-influence, however minute. So that our whole self-consciousness in relation to the world or its individual parts remains enclosed within these limits.

There can, accordingly, be for us no such thing as a feeling of absolute freedom. He who asserts that he has such a feeling is either deceiving himself or separating things which essentially belong together. For if the feeling of freedom expresses a forthgoing activity, this activity must have an object which has been somehow given to us, and this could not have taken place without an influence of the object upon our receptivity. Therefore in every such case there is involved a feeling of dependence which goes along with the feeling of freedom, and thus limits it. The contrary could only be possible if the object altogether came into existence through our activity, which is never the case absolutely, but only relatively. But if, on the other hand, the feeling of freedom expresses only an inward movement of activity, not only is every such individual movement bound up with the state of our stimulated receptivity at the moment, but, further, the totality of our free inward movements, considered as a unity, cannot be represented as a feeling of absolute freedom, because our whole existence does not present itself to our consciousness as having proceeded from our own spontaneous activity. Therefore in any temporal existence a feeling of absolute freedom can have no place. As regards the feeling of absolute dependence which, on the other hand, our proposition does postulate: for just the same reason, this feeling cannot in any wise arise from the influence of an object which has in some way to be *given* to us; for upon such an object there would always be a counter-influence, and even a voluntary renunciation of this would always involve a feeling of freedom. Hence a feeling of absolute dependence, strictly speaking, cannot exist in a single moment as such, because such a moment is always determined, as regards its total content, by what is *given*, and thus by objects towards which we have a feeling of freedom. But the self-consciousness which accompanies all our activity, and therefore, since that is never zero, accompanies our whole existence, and negatives absolute freedom, is itself precisely a consciousness of absolute dependence; for it is the consciousness that the whole of our spontaneous activity comes from a source outside of us in just the same sense in which anything towards which we should have a feeling of absolute freedom must have proceeded entirely from ourselves. But without any feeling of freedom a feeling of absolute dependence would not be possible.

As regards the identification of absolute dependence with "relation to God" in our proposition: this is to be understood in the sense that the *whence* of our receptive and active existence, as implied in this self-consciousness, is to be designated by the word "God," and that this is for us the really original signification of that word. . . . In the first instance God signifies for us simply that which is the co-determinant in this feeling and to which we trace our being in such a state; and any further content of the idea must be evolved out of this fundamental import assigned to it. Now this is just what is principally meant by the formula which says that to feel oneself absolutely dependent and to be conscious of being in relation with God are one and the same thing; and the reason is that absolute dependence is the fundamental relation which must include all others in itself. This last expression includes the God-consciousness in the self-consciousness in such a way that, quite in accordance with the above analysis, the two cannot be separated from each other.

3. BARTH: CHRIST AND ADAM

As a reaction to what he perceived to be the excesses of subjectivism, Barth undertook to ground the whole of theology, including anthropology, in the self-revelation of God in Jesus Christ. This selection, from his commentary on Romans 5, explicitly addresses the theme of human nature. Source: Karl Barth, *Christ and Adam*, trans. T. A. Smail (New York: Harper & Brothers, 1956), pp. 86–94. Date of original publication: 1952.

Jesus Christ is the secret truth about the essential
nature of man, and even sinful man is still essentially
related to him. That is what we have learned from
Rom. 5:12–21.

Now we shall try to summarize our conclusions: We have seen how, according to vv. 1–11, Jesus Christ is a sharply-defined individual, and how, as such, he is clearly the representative of an undetermined multitude of other men. In his life and destiny he represents and anticipates their life and their destiny so that they, without ceasing to be distinct individuals, must make their life an image and reflection of his life and must work out the destiny that overtook them in him. They have to identify themselves with him, because he has already identified himself with them. There is no question of any merging or any confusion between him and them, but neither can there be any question of any abstraction or separation. He in his individuality is theirs, and so they in their individuality can only be his. The ineffaceable distinction between him and them is the guarantee of their indissoluble unity with him. They as receivers are subordinated and yet indissolubly related to him as giver; they as members are subordinated and yet indissolubly united to him as head.

But vv. 1–11 only speak of Jesus Christ and those who *believe* in him. If we read that first part of the chapter by itself, we might quite easily come to the conclusion that for Paul Christ's manhood is significant only for those who are united to him in faith. We would then have no right to draw any conclusion about the relationship between Christ and *man as such*, from what Paul says about the "religious" relationship between Christ and Christians. We could not then expect to find in the manhood of Christ the key to the essential nature of man.

But in vv. 12–21 Paul does not limit his context to Christ's relationship to believers but gives fundamentally the same account of his relationship to all men. The context is widened from Church history to world history, from Christ's relationship to Christians to his relationship to all men. It should be noted that in these verses there is no further mention of faith or even of the gift of the Holy Spirit, and that the first person plural which is continually used in vv. 1–11 is here (with the exception of the last phrase of v. 21) replaced by a quite general third person plural. What is said here applies generally and universally, and not merely to one limited group of men. Here "religious" presuppositions are not once hinted at. The fact of Christ is here presented as something that dominates and includes all men. The nature of Christ objectively conditions human nature and the work of Christ makes an objective difference to the life and destiny of all men. Through Christ grace overflows upon them, bringing them pardon and justification and opening before them a prospect of life with God.

In short, "grace rules," as it is put in v. 21. And all that is in exact correspondence to what happens to human nature in its objective relationship to Adam. There sin rules, in exactly the same way, and all men become sinners and unrighteous in Adam, and as such must die. The question about what is the special mark of the *Christian* is just not raised at all. What we are told is what it means for man as such that his objective relationship to Adam is subordinate to and dependent upon and included in his objective relationship to Christ. The question raised here—as distinct from vv. 1–11—concerns the relationship between Christ and all men.

Paul had obviously no intention of fathering an idle and arbitrary speculation when in this passage he passed on to this further account of the same subject. If we have understood the *dia touto* (therefore) of v. 12 rightly, his intention was rather to consolidate the special account he had already given of the relationship between Christ and faith, by placing it in this wider and more general context. Our standing as believers is as vv. 1–11 have described it, because our standing as men is as vv. 12–21 describe it. Our relationship to Christ as believers is based upon our prior relationship to him as Adam's children and heirs. For even when we were, in the words of vv. 1–11, weak, sinners, godless, and enemies, Christ died for us and so brought us into his kingdom and under his power.

We have come *to* Christ as believers and Christians, because we had already come *from* Christ, so that there was nothing else for us to do but believe in him. What is said in vv. 1–11 is not just "religious" truth that only applies to specially talented, specially qualified, or specially guided men; it is truth for *all* men, whether they know it or not, as surely as they are all Adam's children and heirs. The assurance of Christians, as it is described in vv. 1–11, has as its basis the fact that the Christian sphere is not limited to the "religious" sphere. What is *Christian* is secretly but fundamentally identical with what is *universally human*. Nothing in true human nature can ever be alien or irrelevant to the Christian; nothing in true human nature can ever attack or surpass or annul the objective reality of the Christian's union with Christ. Much in true human nature is unrelated to "religion," but nothing in true human nature is unrelated to the Christian faith. That means that we can understand true human nature only in the light of the Christian gospel that we believe. For Christ stands above and is first, and Adam stands below and is second. So it is Christ that reveals the true nature of man. Man's nature in Adam is not, as is usually assumed, his true and original nature; it is only truly human at all insofar as it reflects and corresponds to essential human nature as it is found in Christ. True human nature, therefore, can only be understood by Christians who look to Christ to discover the essential nature of man. Vv. 12–21 are revolutionary in their insistence that what is true of Christians must also be true of all men. That is a principle that has an incalculable significance for all our action and thought. To reject this passage as empty speculation is tantamount to denying that the human nature of Christ is the final revelation of the true nature of man. . . .

But how does this passage come to be so definite about its own interpretation of the true man? For it is dealing expressly with Adam and so with corrupt man, and it might seem questionable to base such definite statements about the true nature of man upon our knowledge of him. What is Paul's authority for basing a categorical conclusion about the structure of human nature upon nothing sounder than his knowledge of fallen man? We have seen that Paul dares to draw this conclusion because he sees Adam not in isolation but in his relationship to Christ. And for him Christ and Adam do not represent two conflicting interpretations of human nature. For in that case the doubt as to which was ultimately valid would still arise—and the tone of vv. 1–11 shows that Paul has no doubts at all. The answer is in vv. 13–14 and 20, where it is shown that the formal correspondence and identity between Adam and Christ is based upon their material disparity. In the encounter between them Christ has more right and power, and Adam less. It is only in this disparity of status and in this disproportion that they can be compared. Adam is subordinate to Christ, and not Christ to Adam. And if Adam is subordinate to Christ, then Adam represents true and genuine human nature insofar as he shows us the man in humanity and humanity in the man. Whatever else in his representation of human nature may have to be accounted for by its later corruption and ruin, this ordering principle at least belongs to its condition and character as created and untouched by sin. For the subordinate representation of human nature in Adam here corresponds to its primary representation in Christ. In Christ also, the man is in humanity and humanity is in the man. With one important difference: Adam is not God's Son become man, and so he cannot, like him, be man, and at the same time be *over* all men. Adam, as the one, can represent the many; he as man can represent humanity—but only as one among others. Thus he can represent all the others only in the same way that each of them can represent him. Adam has no essential priority of status over other men. He cannot be their lord and head; he cannot determine their life and their destiny. He can anticipate their life and destiny in himself, only insofar as he is the first man among many others, only insofar as he is *primus inter pares*. The *pollō mallon* (much more) of vv. 15–17 marks this difference. Where it is taken into account, what remains of the identity between Adam and Christ is the unity of the one and the many on both sides, of his deeds and their deeds, of his condition and theirs. In this unity Christ is, like Adam, man. In this unity of the one and the many Adam is the type and likeness of Christ, although formally he differs from Christ because he is not lord and head in this unity, and materially he differs from him, because his nature is perverted by sin. But this unity, as such, belongs not to the perversion of his nature but to its original constitution. And so Paul makes no arbitrary assertion, and he is not deceiving himself when he presupposes this unity as simply given even in Adam. He does so because he has found it given first and primarily in Christ.

Christ is not only God's Son; he is also a man who is not a sinner like Adam and all of us. He is true man in an absolute sense, and it is in his humanity that we have to recognize true human nature in the condition and character in which it was willed and created by God. To it there certainly belongs this unity of man and humanity. When we inquire about the true nature of man and seek an answer in terms of this unity, we are on firm ground, insofar as even sinful man, whom alone we know, reflects back, as far as this unity is concerned, the human nature of Christ and so has not ceased to be true man and has not ceased to show man's true nature to us.

4. NIEBUHR: HUMAN BEINGS AS CREATURES AND SINNERS

Exploring how it can be that persons are so radically capable of evil while yet remaining both human beings and God's good creatures, Reinhold Niebuhr develops a view of persons as finite individuals existing in dialectical tension between their own determinate limitedness and their

own capacities for self-transcendence. Insofar as the poles of this dialectic are simply a "given," they are God's creative gift, and good. Insofar as
persons must maintain the dialectic between these poles by their own
acts of will, they are self-constituting. Source: Reinhold Niebuhr, *The
Nature and Destiny of Man*, Vol. I (New York: Charles Scribner's Sons,
1949), pp. 169–70, 182–83, 258–60, 269–72, 274–76. Date of original publication: 1941.

Man as Creature

It is important to recognize how basic the Christian doctrine of the
goodness of creation is for a conception of man in which human finiteness is emphasized but not deprecated. In the biblical view the contrast
between the created world and the Creator, between its dependent and
insufficient existence and his freedom and self-sufficiency, is absolute.
But this contrast never means that the created world is evil by reason of
the particularization and individualization of its various types of existence. It is never a corruption of an original divine unity and eternity,
as in neo-Platonism; nor is it evil because of the desire and pain which
characterize all insufficient and dependent life, as in Buddhism.

The whole import of the Christian doctrine of creation for the
Christian view of man is really comprehended in the Christian concept of individuality. The individual is conceived of as a creature of
infinite possibilities which cannot be fulfilled within terms of this temporal existence. But his salvation never means the complete destruction of his creatureliness and absorption into the divine. On the
other hand, though finite individuality is never regarded as of itself
evil, its finiteness, including the finiteness of the mind, is never obscured. The self, even in the highest reaches of its self-consciousness,
is still the finite self, which must regard the pretensions of universality,
to which idealistic philosophies for instance tempt it, as a sin. It is always a self, anxious for its life and its universal perspectives qualified
by its "here and now" relation to a particular body. . . .

Man, being both free and bound, both limited and limitless, is anxious. Anxiety is the inevitable concomitant of the paradox of freedom
and finiteness in which man is involved. Anxiety is the internal precondition of sin. . . . Yet anxiety is not sin. It must be distinguished
from sin partly because it is its precondition and not its actuality, and
partly because it is the basis of all human creativity as well as the pre-

condition of sin. Man is anxious not only because his life is limited and dependent and yet not so limited that he does not know of his limitations. He is also anxious because he does not know the limits of his possibilities. He can do nothing and regard it perfectly done, because higher possibilities are revealed in each achievement. . . .

The ultimate proof of the freedom of the human spirit is its own recognition that its will is not free to choose between good and evil. For in the highest reaches of the freedom of the spirit, the self discovers in contemplation and retrospect that previous actions have invariably confused the ultimate reality and value, which the self as spirit senses, with the immediate necessities of the self. If the self assumes that because it realizes this fact in past actions it will be able to avoid the corruption in future actions, it will merely fall prey to the Pharisaic fallacy.

This difference between the self in contemplation and the self in action must not be regarded as synonymous with the distinction between the self as spirit and the self as natural vitality. To regard the two distinctions as identical is a plausible error, and one which lies at the root of all idealistic interpretations of man. But we have already discovered that the sins of the self in action are possible only because the freedom of spirit opens up the deterministic causal chains of the self in nature and tempts the self to assume dignities, to grasp after securities and to claim sanctities which do not belong to it. The contemplating self which becomes conscious of its sins does not therefore view some other empirical self which is not, properly speaking, its true self. There is only one self. Sometimes the self acts and sometimes it contemplates its actions. When it acts it falsely claims ultimate value for its relative necessities and falsely identifies its life with the claims of life *per se*. In contemplation it has a clearer view of the total human situation and becomes conscious, in some degree, of the confusion and dishonesty involved in its action. It must not be assumed, however, that the contemplating self is the universal self, judging the finite and empirical self. At its best the contemplating self is the finite self which has become conscious of its finiteness and its relation to God as the limit and the fulfillment of its finiteness. When the self in contemplation becomes contritely aware of its guilt in action it may transmute this realization into a higher degree of honesty in subsequent actions.

Repentance may lead to "fruits meet for repentance"; and differences between the moral quality in the lives of complacent and of contrite individuals are bound to be discovered by observers. But the self cannot make too much of them; for its real standard is not what others do or fail to do. Its real standard is its own essential self and this in turn has only God's will as norm. It must know that judged by that standard, the experience of contrition does not prevent the self from new dishonesties in subsequent actions. The self, even in contemplation, remains the finite self. In one moment it may measure its situation and discover its sin. In the next moment it will be betrayed by anxiety into sin. Even the distinction between contemplation and action must, therefore, not be taken too literally. For any contemplation which is concerned with the interests, hopes, fears and ambitions of this anxious finite self belongs properly in the field of action; for it is a preparation for a false identification of the immediate and the ultimate of which no action is free.

We cannot, therefore, escape the ultimate paradox that the final exercise of freedom in the transcendent human spirit is its recognition of the false use of that freedom in action. Man is most free in the discovery that he is not free. . . .

Essential Nature and Original Righteousness

It is impossible to do justice to the concept of the image of God and to the perfection of that image before the fall without making a distinction between the essential nature of man and the virtue of conformity to that nature. Nothing can change the essential nature and structure, just as blindness of the eye does not remove the eye from the human anatomy. Not even the destruction of the eye can change the fact that the human anatomy requires two eyes. On the other hand the freedom of man creates the possibility of actions which are contrary to and in defiance of the requirements of this essential nature. This fact justifies the distinction between the essential structure and nature, and the virtue of conformity to it. Man may lose this virtue and destroy the proper function of his nature but he can do so only by availing himself of one of the elements in that nature, namely his freedom. . . .

It is important to distinguish between the essential nature of man and the virtue and perfection which would represent the normal expression of that nature. The essential nature of man contains two elements; and there are correspondingly two elements in the original perfection of man. To the essential nature of man belong, on the one hand, all his natural endowments, and determinations, his physical and social impulses, his sexual and racial differentiations, in short his character as a creature imbedded in the natural order. On the other hand, his essential nature also includes the freedom of his spirit, his transcendence over natural process and finally his self-transcendence.

The virtue and perfection which corresponds to the first element of his nature is usually designated as the natural law. It is the law which defines the proper performance of his functions, the normal harmony of his impulses and the normal social relation between himself and his fellows within the limitations of the natural order. Since every natural function of man is qualified by his freedom and since a "law" defining normality is necessary only because of his freedom, there is always an element of confusion in thus outlining a law of nature. It has nevertheless a tentative validity; for it distinguishes the obvious requirements of his nature as a creature in the natural order from the special requirements of his nature as free spirit.

The virtues which correspond to the second element in his nature, that is, to the freedom of his spirit, are analogous to the "theological virtues" of Catholic thought, namely faith, hope and love. They must be analyzed at greater length presently. For the moment it is necessary to identify and validate them only provisionally as basic requirements of freedom. Faith in the providence of God is a necessity of freedom because, without it, the anxiety of freedom tempts man to seek a self-sufficiency and self-mastery incompatible with his dependence upon forces which he does not control. Hope is a particular form of that faith. It deals with the future as a realm where infinite possibilities are realized and which must be a realm of terror if it is not under the providence of God; for in that case it would stand under either a blind fate or pure caprice. The knowledge of God is thus not a supernatural grace which is a "further gift" beyond man's essential nature. It is the requirement of his nature as free spirit.

Love is both an independent requirement of this same freedom and a derivative of faith. Love is a requirement of freedom because the community to which man is impelled by his social nature is not possible to him merely upon the basis of his gregarious impulse. In his freedom and uniqueness each man stands outside of, and transcends, the cohesions of nature and the uniformities of mind which bind life to life. Since men are separated from one another by the uniqueness and individuality of each spirit, however closely they may be bound together by ties of nature, they cannot relate themselves to one another in terms which will do justice to both the bonds of nature and the freedom of their spirit if they are not related in terms of love. In love spirit meets spirit in the depth of the innermost essence of each. The cohesions of nature are qualified and transmuted by this relationship, for the other self ceases to be merely an object, serviceable to the self because of affinities of nature and reason. It is recognized as not merely object but as itself a subject, as a unique centre of life and purpose. This "I" and "Thou" relationship is impossible without the presupposition of faith for two reasons: (1) Without freedom from anxiety man is so enmeshed in the vicious circle of egocentricity, so concerned about himself, that he cannot release himself for the adventure of love. (2) Without relation to God, the world of freedom in which spirit must meet spirit is so obscured that human beings constantly sink to the level of things in the human imagination. The injunction, "love thy neighbor as thyself," is therefore properly preceded both by the commandment, "love the Lord thy God," and by the injunction, "be not anxious." . . .

This analysis of the matter leads to the conclusion that sin neither destroys the structure by virtue of which man is man nor yet eliminates the sense of obligation toward the essential nature of man, which is the remnant of his perfection. This sense of obligation is, in fact, the claim which the essential nature of man makes upon him in his present sinful state. The virtue which corresponds to the true nature of man therefore appears to sinful man in the form of law. . . .

Following St. Paul, Christian thought has consistently maintained that the law must be regarded, not simply as something which is given man either by revelation, or for that matter by the authority of society, but as written in the heart. This can only mean that the requirements of action, dictated by man's essential nature, are a part of his real self. They stand outside of the self in action; that is why they are "law," and appear in the guise of something imposed from without and are only the "form of knowledge and of truth" (Rom. 2:20). The particular content of the voice of conscience is of course conditioned by all the relativities of history. Men may be mistaken in their interpretation of what life is essentially; and conscience may be, in its very content, a vehicle of sin. Yet even in its content the universalities of conscience are at least as significant as its varieties and relativities. One must conclude that the real structure of life, the dependence of man upon his fellowmen for instance, which requires both organic and loving relations between them, asserts itself, in spite of all errors, against the confusion which human egotism and pride introduces into the relations of men.

If this analysis be correct it follows that if Protestantism was right in rejecting the Catholic doctrine that the fall had not altered man's essential nature because it had only destroyed a *donum supernaturale*, it was wrong in asserting that man's essential nature had been destroyed. The Catholic doctrine presumably saw an alteration only in the virtue and not in the structure of man. But its definition of that virtue, namely man's communion with God and intimate contact with him, contains by implication a part of the essential structure of man, namely his transcendent freedom, which can be tolerable and creative only when it has found its source, end and norm in the will of God. This structure of freedom is revealed in the very bondage of sin; for it is by this capacity for the eternal that man transmutes his finite self into infinite proportions. It is by this capacity that he is able both to sin and to have some knowledge of his sin.

5. RAHNER: PERSONS AS FREE AND RESPONSIBLE SUBJECTS

Recasting traditional themes in Roman Catholic theological anthropology in terms of a careful analysis of our most basic and general experience of ourselves, Rahner suggests a way to understand human nature in which our involvement in the physical world and our capacities both to transcend ourselves and to be held accountable for our behavior can all be held together. Source: Karl Rahner, *Foundations of Christian Faith*, trans. William V. Dych (New York: Crossroad, 1978), pp. 26, 28–38, 42–43.

Man as Person and Subject

There is no need to explain in any great detail that a notion of person and subject is of fundamental importance for the possibility of Christian revelation and the self-understanding of Christianity. A personal relationship to God, a genuinely dialogical history of salvation between God and man, the acceptance of one's own, unique, eternal salvation, the notion of responsibility before God and his judgment, all of these assertions of Christianity, however they are to be explained more precisely, imply that man is what we want to say here: person and subject. . . .

When we say that man is subject and person, this is not an assertion about a particular part of him which could be isolated, so that all other particular anthropologies could be excluded from it, and the assertion itself would then belong to just such a particular anthropology. The specific character of this experience and therefore the specific character of the concrete way in which it is had must be constantly kept in mind. Man can indeed overlook something which he is, or better: he can overlook the totality of what he is, and especially is. What he experiences he can also suppress. This suppression is meant here not in the sense of depth psychology, but in a much more general and at the same time more ordinary sense. One can overlook something, show himself uninterested and leave it alone, although it is part of him. He does not allow the original experience to surface. On the one hand we can talk about it only in words and concepts, and yet what is meant is not just what is contained in language as such. And it can even be the case that a person simply does not want to express in word and on the level of conceptual objectification such hidden and total experiences which are, as it were, silent and unobtrusive, or perhaps he cannot bring them to expression. . . .

In the fact that man raises analytical questions about himself and opens himself to the unlimited horizons of such questioning, he has already transcended himself and every conceivable element of such an analysis or of an empirical reconstruction of himself. In doing this he is affirming himself as more than the sum of such analyzable components of his reality. Precisely this consciousness of himself, this confrontation with the totality of all his conditions, and this very being-conditioned show him to be more than the sum of his factors. For a finite system of individual, distinguishable elements cannot have the kind of relationship to itself which man has to himself in the experience of his multiple conditioning and his reducibility. A finite system cannot confront itself in its totality. From its point of departure, which ultimately is imposed upon it, a finite system receives a relationship to a definite operation, although this might consist in maintaining the system itself, but it does not have a relationship to its own point of departure. It does not ask questions about itself. It is not a subject. The experience of radical questioning and man's ability to place himself in question are things which a finite system cannot accomplish.

It follows from our supposition, of course, that this standpoint outside of and above the system of empirical, individual and specifiable data may not be understood as an individual and separable element in the empirical reality of man. This is how the school theology likes to understand it when it speaks of spirit or of man's immortal soul as though what is meant by this were an element within the totality of man which can be encountered immediately and in itself, and distinguished empirically and in test-tube purity from the rest of him. This is understandable pedagogically, but ultimately it is a primitive conception. But if we do not go along with this primitive dualism, which comes ultimately from Greek anthropology and not from Christian anthropology, and instead realize that the one, single man as one has already confronted himself in a question which has already gone beyond every possible and empirical and partial answer, has gone beyond it not in its positive content but in the radical nature of the question, then we experience man as subject. He is experienced as the subjectivity of these multiple objectivities with which the empirical human sciences are concerned. On the one hand, man's ability to be related to himself, his "having to do with himself," is not and cannot be one element in him alongside of other elements. But it is, nevertheless and for this reason, a reality which constitutes the subjectivity of man as distinguished from his objectivity, which is the other aspect of him.

Being a person, then, means the self-possession of a subject as such in a conscious and free relationship to the totality of itself. This relationship is the condition of possibility and the antecedent horizon for the fact that in his individual empirical experiences and in his individual sciences man has to do with himself as one and as a whole.

169

Because man's having responsibility for the totality of himself is the condition of his empirical experience of self, it cannot be derived completely from this experience and its objectivities. Even when a man would want to shift all responsibility for himself away from himself as someone totally determined from without, and thus would want to explain himself away, *he* is the one who does this and does it knowingly and willingly. *He* is the one who encompasses the sum of all the possible elements of such an explanation, and thus *he* is the one who shows himself to be something other than the subsequent product of such individual elements. We can indeed speak of finite systems which are self-directing and so in a certain sense have a relationship to themselves. But such a self-directing system has only a limited possibility of self-regulation. This is an element in this system, and hence it cannot explain how man confronts himself in his totality and places himself in a question, and how he reflects upon the question of raising questions. . . .

Man as Transcendent Being

What is meant more precisely by the subjectivity which man experiences becomes clearer when we say that man is a transcendent being.

In spite of the finiteness of his system man is always present to himself in his entirety. He can place everything in question. In his openness to everything and anything, whatever can come to expression can be at least a question for him. In the fact that he affirms the possibility of a merely *finite* horizon of questioning, this possibility is already surpassed, and man shows himself to be a being with an *infinite* horizon. In the fact that he experiences his finiteness radically, he reaches beyond this finiteness and experiences himself as a transcendent being, as spirit. The infinite horizon of human questioning is experienced as a horizon which recedes further and further the more answers man can discover. . . .

Man is a transcendent being insofar as all of his knowledge and all of his conscious activity is grounded in a pre-apprehension *(Vorgriff)* of "being" as such, in an unthematic but ever-present knowledge of the infinity of reality (as we can put it provisionally and somewhat boldly). We are presupposing that this infinite pre-apprehension is not grounded by the fact that it can apprehend nothingness as such. We must make this presupposition because nothingness grounds nothing. Nothingness cannot be the term of this pre-apprehension, cannot be what draws and moves and sets in motion that reality which man experiences as his real life and not as nothingness. To be sure, a person also has the experience of emptiness, of inner fragility, and, if we want to call it so lest we make it innocuous, of the absurdity of what confronts him. But he also experiences hope, the movement towards liberating freedom, and the responsibility which imposes upon him real burdens and also blesses them.

But if a person experiences *both* things and nevertheless his experience is *one*, and in it all the individual movements and experiences are borne by an ultimate and primordial movement, and if he cannot be a gnostic who either recognizes two primordial realities or accepts a dualism in the ultimate and primordial ground of being, if he cannot accept this because it contradicts the unity of his experience, then only *one* possibility is left: a person can understand that absolute being establishes limits and boundaries outside of itself, and that it could will something that is limited. But logically and existentielly he cannot think that the movements of hope and the desire to reach out that he really experiences are only a charming and foolish illusion. He cannot think that the ultimate ground of everything is empty nothingness, provided he gives the term "nothingness" any meaning at all, and does not simply use it to signal that real and genuine existentiell[1] anxiety that he actually experiences.

Hence what grounds man's openness and his reaching out in the unlimited expanse of his transcendence cannot be nothingness, an absolutely empty void. For to assert that of a void would make absolutely no sense. But since on the other hand this pre-apprehension as merely a question is not self-explanatory, it must be understood as due to the working of that to which man is open, namely, being in an absolute sense. But the movement of transcendence is not the subject creating its own unlimited space as though it had absolute power over being, but it is the infinite horizon of being making itself manifest. Whenever man in his transcendence experiences himself as questioning, as dis-

---

1. [*Ed.*] This translates the German term *existentiell*, which refers to concretely experienced existence, as distinguished from *existential*, which refers to the ontological structures that underlie concrete existence. The distinction is based on the existentialist philosophy of Martin Heidegger.

quieted by the appearance of being, as open to something ineffable, he cannot understand himself as subject in the sense of an *absolute* subject, but only in the sense of one who receives being, ultimately only in the sense of grace. In this context "grace" means the freedom of the ground of being which gives being to man, a freedom which man experiences in his finiteness and contingency, and means as well what we call "grace" in a more strictly theological sense. . . .

It is self-evident that this transcendental experience of human transcendence is not the experience of some definite, particular objective thing which is experienced alongside of other objects. It is rather a basic mode of being which is prior to and permeates every objective experience. We must emphasize again and again that the transcendence meant here is not the thematically conceptualized "concept" of transcendence in which transcendence is reflected upon objectively. It is rather the a priori openness of the subject to being as such, which is present precisely when a person experiences himself as involved in the multiplicity of cares and concerns and fears and hopes of his everyday world. Real transcendence is always in the background, so to speak, in those origins of human life and human knowledge over which we have no control. This real transcendence is never captured by metaphysical reflection, and in its purity, that is, as not mediated objectively, it can be approached asymptotically at most, if at all, in mystical experience and perhaps in the experience of final loneliness in the face of death. Such an original experience of transcendence is something different from philosophical discussion about it, and precisely because it can usually be present only through the mediation of the categorical objectivity of man or of the world around him, this transcendental experience can easily be overlooked. It is present only as a secret ingredient, so to speak. But man is and remains a transcendent being, that is, he is that existent to whom the silent and uncontrollable infinity of reality is always present as mystery. This makes man totally open to this mystery and precisely in this way he becomes conscious of himself as person and as subject.

Man as Responsible and Free

By the fact that man in his transcendence exists as open and indetermined, he is at the same time responsible for himself. He is left to himself and placed in his own hands not only in his knowledge, but also in his *actions*. It is in being consigned to himself that he experiences himself as responsible and free. What was said earlier about the relationship between man's personhood and his origins within and his determination by the world is especially true here. In the first and original instance, man's responsibility and freedom are not a particular, empirical datum of human reality alongside of others. If an empirical psychology is able to find less freedom as it becomes more radical, that is perfectly consistent with its method.[2] The traditional scholastic psychology of the schools wants to discover freedom directly as an individual, concrete datum within the realm of human transcendentality and personhood, and this is indeed a good intention, but it is doing something which basically contradicts the essence of freedom. It is not surprising if it meets with contradiction in empirical psychology. Empirical psychology must always relate one phenomenon to another and so obviously cannot discover any freedom. Even when we say in our everyday affairs that in this and that we were free, and in something else presumably not, we are not dealing with one regional phenomenon alongside of others that can be located unambiguously in time and space. Rather we are dealing at most with the application and concretization of a transcendental experience of freedom, which is something quite different from that experience with which the particular sciences are concerned. . . .

Like subjectivity and personhood, so too responsibility and freedom are realities of transcendental experience, that is, they are experienced when a subject as such experiences himself, and hence precisely not when he is objectified in a subsequent scientific reflection. When the subject experiences himself as subject, and hence as the existent which through its transcendence has an original and indissoluble unity and self-presence before being, and when this subject experiences' his action as subjective action, although it cannot be made reflexive in the same way, then responsibility and freedom in an original sense are experienced in the depths of one's own existence. Corresponding to man's nature as a corporeal nature in the world, this freedom is always actualized in a multiplicity of concrete activities in time and space

---

2. [*Ed.*] Translation corrected.

which are also multiple, in a multiplicity of involvements, in history and also in society. All of this is self-evident: this free action is not something which would take place only in the hidden depths of a person, outside of the world and outside of history. But man's real freedom, therefore, still continues to be one freedom because it is a transcendental characteristic of the one subject as such. We can only say, then, that because and insofar as I experience myself as person and as subject, I also experience myself as free, as free in a freedom which does not refer primarily to an individual, isolated psychic occurrence, but in a freedom which refers to the subject as one and as a whole in the unity of its entire actualization of existence.

How this is actualized in time and space, over the length and breadth of an historical existence and in the concrete multiplicity of human life, this is a question which we cannot decide unambiguously. This freedom, then, is not a neutral power which one has and possesses as something different from himself. It is rather a fundamental characteristic of a personal existent, who experiences himself in what he has already done and is still to do in time as self-possession, as one who is responsible and has to give an account, and this includes the moment when a subjective and personal response to the infinite and the incomprehensible confronts this existence in his transcendence, and is either accepted or rejected. . . .

Man as Dependent

In spite of his free subjectivity, man experiences himself as being at the disposal of other things, a disposal over which he has no control. First of all, being constituted as transcendental subject, he is in the presence of being as mystery, a mystery which constantly reveals itself and at the same time conceals itself. We mentioned earlier that his transcendentality cannot be understood as that of an absolute subject which experiences and possesses what opens before it as something subject to its own power. His transcendentality is rather a relationship which does not establish itself by its own power, but is experienced as something which was established by and is at the disposal of another, and which is grounded in the abyss of ineffable mystery.

Beyond that, man always experiences himself both in his activity in the world and also in his theoretical, objective reflection as one to whom an historical situation in a world of things and of persons has been given in advance, given without his having chosen it for himself, although it is in and through it that he discovers and is conscious of transcendence. Man is always conscious of his historical limitations, his historical origins, and the contingency of his origins. But this places him in the quite specific situation which characterizes man's nature: insofar as he experiences his historical conditioning, he is already beyond it in a certain sense, but nevertheless he cannot really leave it behind. Being situated in this way between the finite and the infinite is what constitutes man, and is shown by the fact that it is in his infinite transcendence and in his freedom that man experiences himself as dependent and historically conditioned.

Man never establishes his own freedom in some absolute sense, in the sense of a freedom which could make complete use of the material which is given to him in his freedom, or could cast it off in an absolute self-sufficiency. He never realizes completely his possibilities in the world and in history. Nor can he distance himself from them and withdraw into the pure essence of a pseudo-subjectivity or pseudo-interiority in such a way that he could honestly say that he had become independent of the world and the history that was given him. In an ultimate and inescapable way, man even as doer and maker is still receiving and being made. What he experiences in himself is always a synthesis: of possibilities presented to his freedom and his free disposition of self, of what is himself and what is the other, of acting and suffering, of knowing and doing, and these elements are synthesized in a unity which cannot be completely and objectively analyzed. Therefore insofar as reflection can never control or master or grasp the totality of the ground from out of which and towards which the subject is actualizing himself, man is the unknown not only in this or that area of his concrete reality, but he is the subject whose origin and end remain hidden from himself. He comes to the real truth about himself precisely by the fact that he patiently endures and accepts this knowledge that his own reality is not in his own hands.

VII. SIN AND EVIL

1. AUGUSTINE: FREE WILL AND SIN

In a body of writing extending over three decades, Augustine gave classic expression to the Christian doctrine of sin. He did so in large measure by arguing against views which he judged to be contrary to basic Christian principles. First, he rejected Manichean dualism with its contention that evil is an ultimate power over against God on the grounds that God alone is ultimate and whatever is, is good. Evil, he concluded, results from sinful misuse of freedom. When Pelagius took this position to the extreme of saying that human beings are at all times free to sin or not to sin, Augustine replied that sin is universal and only through grace is one able to choose rightly. The first selection is from an anti-Manichean work, *On Free Will*, published in 395; the second from an anti-Pelagian treatise, *The Spirit and the Letter*, written in 412. Source: *Augustine: Earlier Writings*, trans. J. H. S. Burleigh (Philadelphia: Westminster Press, 1955), pp. 165–69; *Augustine: Later Works*, trans. John Burnaby (Philadelphia: Westminster Press, 1955), pp. 197–98, 236.

I

In our previous discussion it was made obvious, and was agreed by us both, that body occupies by nature a lower rank in the scale of being than does soul; and that therefore soul is a greater good than body. If, then, we find among the good things of the body some that a man can abuse, and yet cannot on that account say that they ought not to have been given, since we admit that they are good, it should not be matter for surprise if in the soul too there are some good things which may be abused, but which, because they are good, could only have been given by him from whom all good things come. You see of how much good a body is deprived if it has no hands, and yet a man makes a bad use of his hands who uses them to do cruel or base deeds. If you see a man without feet you will admit that, from the point of view of the wholeness of his body, a very great good is wanting. And yet you would not deny that a man makes a bad use of his feet who uses them to hurt another or to dishonor himself. With the eyes we see the light and distinguish the forms of bodies. Sight is the most splendid possession our bodies have, and for that reason the eyes are set in a place of great dignity. By the use of them we look after our safety and enjoy many other advantages in life. Yet many people use their eyes for many base purposes, compelling them to serve the interests of lust. You see how much good is lost to the human face if it has no eyes. Now who has given us eyes if not God, the bountiful giver of all good things? Just as you approve these good things which the body enjoys, and praise him who has given them, paying no attention to those who make a bad use of them; even so ought you to confess that free will, without which no one can live aright, is a good thing divinely bestowed, and that those are to be condemned who make a bad use of it, rather than to suggest that he who gave it ought not to have done so. . . .

Will is therefore an intermediate good when it cleaves to the unchangeable good as something that is common property and not its own private preserve; of the same nature, that is to say, as truth of which we have spoken a great deal, but nothing worthy of so great a theme; when will cleaves to this good, man attains the happy life. And the happy life, that is, the disposition of soul cleaving to the unchangeable good, is the proper and first good of man. All the virtues are there which no one can use badly. However great and important the virtues may be, we know well enough that they are not common property, but are the property of each individual man. Truth and wisdom are common to all, and all wise men are also happy by cleaving to truth. But one man does not become happy by another's happiness. If one man seeks to attain happiness by imitating another, he seeks his happiness where he sees the other found his, that is to say in unchangeable and common truth. No one is made prudent by the prudence of another, or courageous by his courage, or temperate by his temperance, or just by his justice. A man is made virtuous by regulating his soul according to the rules and guiding lights of the virtues which dwell indestructibly in the truth and wisdom that are the common property of all. For so the virtuous man whom he set before him for imitation has regulated his soul, giving it a fixed objective.

The will, therefore, which cleaves to the unchangeable good that is common to all, obtains man's first and best good things though it is itself only an intermediate good. But the will which turns from the unchangeable and common good and turns to its own private good or to anything exterior or inferior, sins. It turns to its private good, when it wills to be governed by its own authority; to what is exterior, when it is eager to know what belongs to others and not to itself; to inferior things, when it loves bodily pleasure. In these ways a man becomes proud, inquisitive, licentious, and is taken captive by another kind of life which, when compared with the life we have just described, is really death. And yet it is still governed and disposed by divine providence, which appoints for all things their proper places, and distributes to each man his due according to his deserts. So it happens that the good things sought by sinners cannot in any way be bad, nor can free will be bad, for we found that it was to be numbered among the intermediate goods. What is bad is its turning away from the unchangeable good and its turning to changeable goods. That "aversion" and "conversion" is voluntary and is not coerced. Therefore it is followed by the deserved and just penalty of unhappiness. . . .

II

All good is from God. Hence there is no natural existence which is not from God. Now that movement of "aversion," which we admit is sin, is a defective movement; and all defect comes from nothing. Observe where it belongs and you will have no doubt that it does not belong to God. Because that defective movement is voluntary, it is placed within our power. If you fear it, all you have to do is simply not to will it. If you do not will it, it will not exist. What can be more secure than to live a life where nothing can happen to you which you do not will. But since man cannot rise of his own free will as he fell by his own will spontaneously, let us hold with steadfast faith the right hand of God stretched out to us from above, even our Lord Jesus Christ. Let us wait for him with certain hope, and long for him with burning charity. . . .

But there is an opinion that calls for sharp and vehement resistance—I mean the belief that the power of the human will can of itself, without the help of God, either achieve perfect righteousness or advance steadily towards it. When we press upon those who so think the presumption of supposing this to happen without divine aid, they check themselves from venturing a statement which they see would be irreligious and intolerable. But they say that the reason why it does not happen without divine aid is that God has both created man in possession of a will that chooses freely, and teaches him by the gift of his commandments the right way of life; so that God's help consists in the removal by instruction of man's ignorance, so that he can know what is to be avoided in his actions and what is to be sought; and thus, by means of the power of free choice belonging to him by nature, he may enter upon the road pointed out to him, and by a life of self-control, justice and piety may merit attainment to the life which is both blessed and eternal.

Our own assertion, on the contrary, is this: that the human will is divinely assisted to do the right in such manner that, besides man's creation with the endowment of freedom to choose, and besides the teaching by which he is instructed how he ought to live, he receives the Holy Spirit, whereby there arises in his soul the delight in and the love of God, the supreme and changeless Good. This gift is his here and now, while he walks by faith, not yet by sight: that having this as earnest of God's free bounty, he may be fired in heart to cleave to his Creator, kindled in mind to come within the shining of the true light; and thus receive from the source of his being the only real well-being. Free choice alone, if the way of truth is hidden, avails for nothing but sin; and when the right action and the true aim has begun to appear clearly, there is still no doing, no devotion, no good life, unless it be also delighted in and loved. And that it may be loved, the love of God is shed abroad in our hearts, not by the free choice whose spring is in ourselves, but through the Holy Spirit which is given us. . . .

Do we then "make void" freedom of choice through grace? "God forbid! yea, we establish" freedom of choice (Rom. 3:31). As the law is not made void by faith, so freedom of choice is not made void but established by grace. Freedom of choice is necessary to the fulfilment of the law. But by the law comes the knowledge of sin; by faith comes the obtaining of grace against sin; by grace comes the healing of the soul from sin's sickness; by the healing of the soul comes freedom of choice; by freedom of choice comes the love of righteousness; by the love of righteousness comes the working of the law. And thus, as the law is not made void but established by faith, since faith obtains the grace whereby the law may be fulfilled, so freedom of choice is not made void but established by grace, since grace heals the will whereby righteousness may freely be loved. . . .

2. LUTHER: SIN AND GRACE

The Protestant Reformation brought a reaffirmation of the Augustinian position on sin and grace. Luther, for instance, argued that sin is so entrenched in human nature that the law cannot really guide one in the way of righteousness but can only serve to confirm one's sin. Justification is by grace through faith alone. In this selection from an early treatise, Luther shows how grace not only justifies but also sanctifies the sinner. Source: Martin Luther, *Against Latomus*, in *Luther's Works*, Vol. 32, trans. George Lindbeck (Philadelphia: Fortress Press, 1958), pp. 223–29. In this selection, Luther normally cites only biblical chapters; verse references have been added editorially without notation. Originally published in 1521.

The divine Scriptures deal with our sin in two ways: in one way, through the law of God, and in another way, through God's gospel. These are the two Testaments of God, which are ordained for our salvation so that we may be freed from sin. The law deals with sin only in order to reveal it, as Paul says in Rom. 3:20, "Through the law comes knowledge of sin." This knowledge teaches two things: the corruption of nature, and the wrath of God. Rom. 7:7 speaks of the first: "I should not have known that lust is sin if the law had not said, 'You shall not covet.'" For nature did not call this wanton itching sin, but rather its evil use on the bodies of others, as in debauchery, adultery, and fornication. Similarly, it does not call anger and avarice sin, but rather their expression in theft, fraud, slander, murder—and so also for other vices. As yet I do not know whether sin ever refers in Scripture to those works which we call sin, for it seems almost always to refer to the radical ferment which bears fruit in evil deeds and words. It is the law which reveals that what was before unknown and dead (as Rom. 5:13 says) is properly speaking sin, and that it is very much alive, though hidden under the false works of the hypocrites. Paul says that Scripture consigns all men to this sin (Gal. 3:22). Yet it can never remain hidden so that it does not produce its fruits (which are of different sorts in different people, for you are not able to indicate any single evil work to which you can consign all men, for there are many). Rom. 4:15 speaks of the second point: "The law brings wrath," because as is said in Gal. 3:10, "Cursed be everyone who does not abide by all things written in the book of the law, and do them." So also [it is said in] Rom. 5:12, "death through sin," and Rom. 6:23, "the wages of sin is death." Up to this point the light of the law instructs us, teaching us that we are under corruption and wrath, and designating all men as liars and sons of wrath. We would perhaps have disregarded corruption and been pleased with our evil unless this other evil, which is wrath, had refused to indulge our foolishness and had resisted it with terror and the danger of hell and death, so that we have but little peace in our wickedness. Plainly wrath is a greater evil for us than corruption, for we hate punishment more than guilt.

So the law reveals a twofold evil, [one] inward and [the other] outward. The first, which we inflict on ourselves, is sin and the corruption of nature; the second, which God inflicts, is wrath, death, and being accursed. These are, if you wish, guilt and penalty, but in using these terms we have talked far too poorly and coldly of guilt and penalty, inventing I know not what relations and imputations. In accordance with Scripture, we should speak fully and bluntly of sin—or guilt, or inward evil—as a universal corruption of nature in all its parts: an evil which inclines us to evil from our youth up, as is written in Gen. 6:5 and 8:21. So great is this wrath that there is nothing profitable in those things which seem good as, for instance, arts, talents, prudence, courage, chastity, and whatever natural, moral, and impressive goods there are. The common sense of all men can detect nothing wrong with these things, so that today even our theologians number them among the goods, attributing nothing evil to them, for although they do not merit the kingdom of heaven when they are present apart from grace, still, on the other hand, neither do they merit hell nor punishment. If they had not heard of the necessity of grace, our theologians would be ready to assert plainly that they can even merit heaven, for they suppose that these things lack nothing that the law requires, but only what grace supplies. . . .

It must be added that God himself does not deny that these [virtues] are good—for this cannot in fact be denied—but he rewards and bedecks them with temporal benefits, such as power, wealth, glory, fame, dignity, honor, enjoyment, and the like. Thus a covering—not merely of its own beauty, but of divine recompense—is added to this natural blindness which does not know the true good; thus it confidently and stubbornly maintains that it is good. This is the chief reason for the prophetic task, this is why all the prophets were killed, for they reviled these works and insisted on those which are more genuinely good. For prophecy was nothing else than the burnishing, activating—if I may speak thus—and application of the law; or, as is said in logic, the subsumption which declares whether any particular good work falls in the class of the truly or falsely good. . . .

Therefore it is only the law which shows that these [virtues] are evil—not, to be sure, in themselves, for they are the gifts of God, but because of that deeply hidden root of sin which is the cause of men being pleased with, relying, and glorying in these things which are not felt to be evil. This is now and always the innermost evil of sin, for trust, pleasure, and glorying must be in God alone, as Jer. 9:23 says: "Let not the wise man glory in his wisdom, let not the mighty man glory in his might, let not the rich man glory in his riches." All these are goods, but they are freely distributed among the evil more often than among the good, so that Ps. 73:2f. complains of the danger on account of this—his "steps had well nigh slipped." Yet as I said, all these fall under wrath and the curse, nor do they profit anyone, nor indeed, prepare a "congruence to grace," but rather fatten the heart so that it neither desires nor senses the necessity of grace, as says Ps. 119:70: "Their heart is curdled like milk." The Hebrew puts it better: "Their heart is gross like fat." These people are properly accused in Scripture of being godless, unbelieving, and stiff-necked, for they can neither restrain their unbridled inclination toward these apparently good things nor recognize in them the law and their sin. Through these things, they always suppose themselves to excel in obedience to God all others who are truly righteous. For them all preaching is vain; they are bloodthirsty and deceitful men (Ps. 5:6). In brief, they have fulfilled the law and do not need grace except in order to meet, as I said, a certain addition in the divine requirement. For them, Moses is veiled, nor can they bear his shining face.

In the midst of so much wisdom, goodness, righteousness, and religiousness, they will not to be evil, nor can they recognize that they are,

because they do not listen. You see, therefore, how incomparably the
law transcends natural reason, and how bottomless is the sin of which
it gives us knowledge. Therefore all are under wrath, since all are under sin.

The gospel, on the contrary, deals with sin so as to remove it, and
thus most beautifully follows the law. The law introduces us to sin and
overwhelms us with the knowledge of it. It does this so that we may
seek to be freed and to sigh after grace, for the gospel also teaches and
preaches two things, namely, the righteousness and the grace of God.
Through righteousness it heals the corruption of nature. This is done
by the true righteousness which is the gift of God, namely, faith in
Christ, as Rom. 3:21 says, "But now the righteousness of God has
been manifested apart from the law"; also in Rom. 5:1, "Since we are
justified by faith, we have peace, etc."; and Rom. 3:28, "For we hold
that a man is justified by faith." Almost always in Scripture, this righteousness which is contrary to sin refers to an innermost root whose
fruits are good works. The companion of this faith and righteousness is
grace or mercy, the good will [favor] of God, against wrath which is
the partner of sin, so that he who believes in Christ has a merciful
God. . . .

This grace truly produces peace of heart until finally a man is healed
from his corruption and feels he has a gracious God. It is this which
fattens the bones and gives joy, security, and fearlessness to the conscience so that one dares all, can do all and, in this trust in the grace of
God, laughs even at death. Hence, just as wrath is a greater evil than
the corruption of sin, so grace is a greater good than that health of
righteousness which we have said comes from faith. Everyone would
prefer—if that were possible—to be without the health of righteousness rather than the grace of God, for peace and the remission of sins
are properly attributed to the grace of God, while healing from corruption is ascribed to faith. Faith is the gift and inward good which purges
the sin to which it is opposed. It is that leaven which is described in the
gospel as wholly hidden under three measures of meal (Matt. 13:33).
The grace of God, on the other hand, is an outward good, God's favor,
the opposite of wrath. These two things are distinguished in Rom.
5:15: "For if many died through one man's trespass, much more have
the grace of God and the free gift in the grace of that one man Jesus

Christ abounded for many." He calls faith in Christ—which he more often calls a gift—the gift in the grace of one man, for it is given to us through the grace of Christ, because he alone among all men is beloved and accepted and has a kind and gentle God so that he might merit for us this gift and even this grace. . . .

We therefore have two goods of the gospel against the two evils of the law: the gift on account of sin, and grace on account of wrath. Now it follows that these two, wrath and grace, are so related—since they are outside us—that they are poured out upon the whole, so that he who is under wrath is wholly under the whole of wrath, while he who is under grace is wholly under the whole of grace, because wrath and grace have to do with persons. He whom God receives in grace, he completely receives, and he whom he favors, he completely favors. On the other hand, he is angry at the whole of him with whom he is angry. He does not divide this grace as gifts are divided, nor does he love the head and hate the foot, nor favor the soul and hate the body. However, he does give the soul what he does not give the body, and he gives the head what he does not give the foot. It is thus in the entirety of the church which stands under the same grace of God, as Rom. 5:2 says, "Through him we have obtained access to this grace in which we stand." He is diverse and multiform in his gifts. So also, conversely, he is unfavorable to the whole of the one to whom he is unfavorable, and yet he does not punish the whole. Rather, one man remains wholly under wrath through the sin of one member, while another remains wholly under grace through the one gift of one work. As was said, grace must be sharply distinguished from gifts, for only grace is life eternal (Rom. 6:23), and only wrath is eternal death.

Now we finally come to the point. A righteous and faithful man doubtless has both grace and the gift. Grace makes him wholly pleasing so that his person is wholly accepted, and there is no place for wrath in him any more, but the gift heals from sin and from all his corruption of body and soul. It is therefore most godless to say that one who is baptized is still in sin, or that all his sins are not fully forgiven. For what sin is there where God is favorable and wills not to know any sin, and where he wholly accepts and sanctifies the whole man? However, as you see, this must not be attributed to our purity, but solely to the grace of a favorable God. Everything is forgiven through grace, but as yet not everything is healed through the gift.

3. TENNANT: DIFFICULTIES IN THE CLASSIC DOCTRINE

The Enlightenment constituted a massive assault on traditional Christian belief, and nowhere was the effect more devastating than on the doctrine of the fall. It was considered by most "enlightened" thinkers to be both scientifically unsound, since there was no valid evidence that it actually occurred, and morally reprehensible, since it held persons accountable for an inherited imperfection. F. R. Tennant, a Cambridge philosopher and theologian writing in the early twentieth century, summarizes the major arguments against the traditional view. Source: F. R. Tennant, *The Origin and Propagation of Sin*, 2d ed. (Cambridge: Cambridge University Press, 1906), pp. 24–34.

There are difficulties connected with each of the constituent factors of the theory of the corruption of our nature by a fall; the conceptions, namely, of an original state of goodness, of the transition from it to the act of evil, of the derangement of the whole nature by an act, or even a course of sin, and of the hereditary transmission of a disturbance so acquired. The first three of these points have frequently been discussed, and therefore need not detain us long. The question of heredity, and the relation of the doctrine of transmitted sinfulness to the teachings of science, will exact a rather fuller notice.

(a) We have first to consider the conception of an original unfallen moral state which forms the basis upon which the whole structure of the ecclesiastical doctrines of the fall and original sin are grounded. . . .

It has already been hinted that the supposition of an original condition, such as the doctrine of the fall requires, is one which it becomes ever harder to retain. The very conception involves difficulties; and, apart from exegesis, the method by which it has been reached is unphilosophical. It results, in some of the forms in which it is met with, from referring back to the beginning of the human race a condition which the Christian revelation first made possible, and in all cases involves the assumption of a special creation of man as a being endowed from the first with a moral nature enabling him to discriminate between good and evil: a view the untenability of which will appear later.

It would scarcely be necessary, perhaps, even if there were now time, to call up the heavy fire of several natural sciences against this fundamental basis of the doctrine of the fall. The increased light which has been thrown upon the early history of mankind, not to speak of the continuity of the human species with those lower in the scale of animal life, compels us to entertain the conviction that what was once necessarily received as a genuine tradition is rather, transfigured and spiritualized, the product of primitive speculation on a matter beyond the reach of human memory. Literary criticism and historical exegesis, comparative religion and race-psychology, geology and anthropology all contribute materially to the cumulative evidence on this head.

(b) Even if the supposition of a state of original righteousness could be maintained it would be difficult to imagine how the transition from implanted goodness to actual sin could take its rise. The introduction of an external tempter from another world, a suggestion of somewhat late Jewish thought, possible only when early Hebrew demonology had proceeded to a relatively advanced stage of development, of course but shifts the difficulty further back, at the same time redoubling its intensity. And if we look for the cause of this transition, for the ultimate origin of sin, in fact, in the unfallen nature itself, we must ascribe to that nature something more than the mere possibility of evil, something more than the formal *liberum arbitrium*: something of solicitation from within. Whether the freedom ascribed to the will of unfallen Adam were that of perfect harmony with the will of God, or that of independence of all motives, or that of choice conditioned by motive and character, it is equally hard on the theory of an original balance or preestablished harmony of human nature to explain how sin could take its rise. It is the approach to evil, the indwelling propulsion to a wrong course which, on the theory that man was made at once an innocent and a moral being, precisely needs to be accounted for. If actual sin, in us, presupposes a sinful state, it is hard to see why the same inference should not equally apply to the case of the first man, whose *peccatum originans* has been held to be the cause of our *peccatum originatum*.

(c) Another difficulty is inherent in the premise of the ancient doc-

186

trine of original sin. It is not easy to understand how one act of sin, however momentous, could serve to dislocate at once the whole nature of man and to destroy the balance of all his faculties. Human experience furnishes no analogy to such disturbing action. The decisive single deeds which, we well know, can determine the after-course of a career and permanently blunt the sensibility of the moral faculty are not strictly parallel. For they are always but the final outcome and expression of gradually built-up character. . . . Nor is this objection much "less cogent than it seems" (Caird). For it is essential to the Augustinian theory of the origin of sin, or, more correctly, of human sinfulness, that the *peccatum originans* was in the strict sense a first sin. Writers such as Duns Scotus, who regarded Adam as having committed lighter offenses before the mortal sin which decided the fate of the race, rendering that great transgression possible; or Rupert of Deutz, who considered that Eve was already morally infected when she lent an ear to the serpent; or Jacob Boehme, who saw in Adam's "deep sleep" the beginning of his fall; nay, even Irenaeus and the Antiochenes, who taught that Adam, before the fall, was an *infans* or *nēpios*, are generally regarded by those who came under the mighty influence of St. Augustine to have been 'guilty of a tendency towards Pelagianizing. Adam's lapse was an initiative act; and though such acts, in the early years of life, are sometimes critical, surely the experience of all who have aided in the training of youth will testify that such cases are the exception, not the rule.

Thus at each step the old theory which traces human sinfulness to an original acquired defect of nature encounters difficulties when examined closely. Apart from its precariousness, if we may not say its untenability, from the point of view of empirical science, it is a nest of psychological and ethical inconsistencies. And to speak generally, these inconsistencies arise from the conception of man as a being created at once intelligent and elementarily moral, without the background of a past development, and as endowed with an implanted and unhindered aptitude for goodness. When we come to approach the whole problem from the standpoint which regards the very essence of man as a variable or flowing quantity, which finds it as impossible to define the concept of human nature as the psychologist, for instance, finds himself incapable of defining those of the self and personality except in relation to some specific purpose in his usage of them: which deems it as true to say that God is making man as that he has made him, and which looks for the origination of sin, not after man became the being he now is, but rather in the process of his becoming, we may hope to find that all these several obstacles will disappear.

(d) There remains now the difficulty of understanding how the results of the fall upon the nature of our first parents could be transmitted to their posterity by natural descent.

We encounter first, in this connection, the traducianist theory, of which there are several slightly divergent forms. This doctrine asserts that the soul of the child is generated from the souls of its parents. It seems to have been introduced into the Christian Church from the later Stoic philosophy by Tertullian. He presented it, however, in terms of a materialism so thinly veiled that, convenient as it would certainly have been for his purpose, St. Augustine shrank from definitely adopting it. Whether his doctrine of inherited sinfulness does not logically require some such view, as certain upholders of traducianism maintain, is, however, a debatable question. If it does, both fall together. For philosophy will not allow such notions as those which traducianism, when least materialistic, necessarily involves. If we may legitimately think of the soul as a substance, not only in the logical but also in the metaphysical sense of that word, we certainly cannot regard it as having extension in space. We cannot conceive of it as a matter-like entity capable of self-division and reproduction such as we attribute to a unicellular plant. We cannot endow it with a being prior to its activities without committing ourselves to belief in the actuality of the emptiest of all abstractions. Nor can we describe the soul in terms borrowed from biological science without depriving them of all their meaning. Its origin is rather to be conceived as gradual, and its existence as a matter of degree.

We may at once rule out of consideration all discussions of the merits of the rival theories of traducianism and creationism to be met with in manuals which treat the problem as a matter of exegesis and patristic opinion, and must bow to the authority of the psychologist and metaphysician. And if there is one point upon which all philosophers are in agreement, it is perhaps the impossibility of a materialistic metaphysics of mind. "No previous mental activity, or conscious state, can really be connected with the following activities and states as their progenitor, so as to explain the genesis of the latter in the same way in which the existence and action of the parents explain the origin of the offspring; or even in the same way as that in which the earlier forms of bodily development explain the origin of the later forms. . . . To speak of parents as transmitting their minds to their offspring, in part or in whole, is to use words that have no assignable meaning" (G. T. Ladd).

It is impossible to express what the traducianist theory states in terms of such conceptions of the mind's reality and identity, development, and relation to bodily organism, as may be derived from a scientific study of mental life. The only view of the origin of the soul which is consistent with the observed facts of experience and with the metaphysics which ethical theism can embrace is a form of creationism refined of the crudities incidental to its popular statement, such as is taught by Lotze. The soul, according to this philosopher, is, as it were, a "uniformly maintained act of God," begotten from himself when the organism with which it is destined to be associated has been prepared; [God] is the One which supplies underlying unity to the many, and they, despite that unity in him, when once arisen, are independent things.

It is therefore to be concluded that the organic unity of the race pertains directly only to the material side of our constitution. Heredity, in the strict sense of inheritance by birth or descent and not in that of appropriation of environment, cannot take place "in the region of the spiritual personality" (Charles Gore).

4. KIERKEGAARD: SIN AS DESPAIR

In the wake of Enlightenment criticism of the classic doctrine of sin, there were those who sought to recover its essential meaning while recognizing that certain of its features were no longer credible. The Danish theologian Søren Kierkegaard was one of these, dismissing the historicity of the fall yet taking the existential condition of sin with utmost seriousness. Source: Søren Kierkegaard, *The Sickness Unto Death*, trans. Howard V. and Edna H. Hong (Princeton: Princeton University Press, 1983), pp. 80–82. Written in 1848.

It was a very sound idea, one that came up so frequently in an older dogmatics, whereas a later dogmatics very frequently took exception to it because it did not have the understanding or the feeling for it—it was a very sound idea, even if at times it was misapplied: the idea that what makes sin so terrible is that it is before God. It was used to prove eternal punishment in hell. Later, as men became more shrewd, they said: Sin is sin; sin is no greater because it is against God or before God. Strange! Even lawyers speak of aggravated crimes; even lawyers make a distinction between a crime committed against a public official, for example, or against a private citizen, make a distinction between the punishment for a patricide and that for an ordinary murder.

No, the older dogmatics was right in maintaining that because sin is against God it is infinitely magnified. The error consisted in considering God as some externality and in seeming to assume that only occasionally did one sin against God. But God is not some externality in the sense that a policeman is. The point that must be observed is that the self has a conception of God and yet does not will as he wills, and thus is disobedient. Nor does one only occasionally sin before God, for every sin is before God, or, more correctly, what really makes human guilt into sin is that the guilty one has the consciousness of existing before God.

Despair is intensified in relation to the consciousness of the self, but the self is intensified in relation to the criterion for the self, infinitely when God is the criterion. In fact, the greater the conception of God, the more self there is; the more self, the greater the conception of God. Not until a self as this specific single individual is conscious of existing before God, not until then is it the infinite self, and this self sins before God. Thus, despite everything that can be said about it, the selfishness of paganism was not nearly so aggravated as is that of Christendom, inasmuch as there is selfishness here also, for the pagan did not have his self directly before God. The pagan and the natural man have the merely human self as their criterion. Therefore, from a higher point of view, it may be correct to regard paganism as immersed in sin, but the sin of paganism was essentially despairing ignorance of God, of existing before God; paganism is "to be without God in the world" (Eph. 2:12). Therefore, from another point of view, it is true that in the strictest sense the pagan did not sin, for he did not sin before God, and all sin is before God. Furthermore, in one sense it is also quite true that frequently a pagan is assisted in slipping blamelessly through the world simply because he is saved by his superficial Pelagian conception; but then his sin is something else, namely, his superficial Pelagian interpretation. On the other hand, it is certainly also the case that many a time, precisely by being strictly brought up in Christianity, a person has in a certain sense been plunged into sin because the whole Christian viewpoint was too earnest for him, especially in the early part of his life; but then again there is some help to him in this more profound conception of what sin is.

Sin is: before God in despair not to will to be oneself, or before God in despair to will to be oneself. Even though this definition may in other respects be conceded to have its merits (and of all of them, the most important is that it is the only scriptural definition, for scripture always defines sin as disobedience), is not this definition too spiritual? The first and foremost answer to that must be: A definition of sin can never be too spiritual (unless it becomes so spiritual that it abolishes sin), for sin is specifically a qualification of spirit. Furthermore, why is it assumed to be too spiritual? Because it does not mention murder, stealing, fornication, etc.? But does it not speak of these things? Are not they also self-willfulness against God, a disobedience that defies his commandments? On the other hand, if in considering sin we mention only such sins, we so easily forget that, humanly speaking, all such things may be quite in order up to a point, and yet one's whole life may be sin, the familiar kind of sin: the glittering vices, the self-willfulness that either in spiritlessness or with effrontery goes on being or wants to be ignorant of the human self's far, far deeper obligation in obedience to God with regard to its every clandestine desire and thought, with regard to its readiness to hear and understand and its willingness to follow every least hint from God as to his will for this self. The sins of the flesh are the self-willfulness of the lower self, but how often is not one devil driven out with the devil's help and the last condition becomes worse than the first. For this is how things go in the world: first a man sins out of frailty and weakness, and then—well, then he may learn to flee to God and be helped to faith, which saves from all sin, but this will not be discussed here—then he despairs over his weakness and becomes either a pharisee who in despair manages a sort of legal righteousness, or in despair he plunges into sin again.

Therefore, the definition embraces every imaginable and every actual form of sin; indeed, it rightly stresses the crucial point that sin is despair (for sin is not the turbulence of flesh and blood but is the spirit's consent to it) and is: before God. As a definition it is algebra; for me to begin to describe particular sins in this little book would be out of place, and, furthermore, the attempt might fail. The main point here is simply that the definition, like a net, embraces all forms. And this it does, as can be seen if it is tested by posing its opposite: faith, by which I steer in this whole book as by a trustworthy navigation guide. Faith is: that the self in being itself and in willing to be itself rests transparently in God.

Very often, however, it is overlooked that the opposite of sin is by no means virtue. In part, this is a pagan view, which is satisfied with a merely human criterion and simply does not know what sin is, that all sin is before God. No, *the opposite of sin is faith*, as it says in Romans 14:23: "whatever does not proceed from faith is sin." And this is one of the most decisive definitions for all Christianity—that the opposite of sin is not virtue but faith.

5. NIEBUHR: THE PRIDE OF POWER

The liberal theology which flourished in the late nineteenth and early twentieth centuries was not known for having a profound understanding of sin. It was basically Pelagian, assuming free choice and supposing that sin could be eradicated through education and moral suasion. Against this optimistic viewpoint, Reinhold Niebuhr mounted a devastating critique. Marshaling evidence from politics, sociology, and psychology—as well as traditional theological sources—he argued that sin is an "inevitable but not necessary" concomitant of the human condition. In this selection, he discusses the sin of pride, with particular attention to the pride of power. Source: Reinhold Niebuhr, *The Nature and Destiny of Man* (New York: Charles Scribner's Sons, 1949), Vol. 1, pp. 188–94. First published in 1941.

"Of the infinite desires of man," declares Bertrand Russell, "the chief are the desires for power and glory. They are not identical though closely allied." Mr. Russell is not quite clear about the relation of the two to each other, and the relation is, as a matter of fact, rather complex. There is a pride of power in which the human ego assumes its self-sufficiency and self-mastery and imagines itself secure against all vicissitudes. It does not recognize the contingent and dependent character of its life and believes itself to be the author of its own existence, the judge of its own values and the master of its own destiny. This proud pretension is present in an inchoate form in all human life but it rises to greater heights among those individuals and classes who have a more than ordinary degree of social power. Closely related to the pride which seems to rest upon the possession of either the ordinary or some extraordinary measure of human freedom and self-mastery, is the lust for power which has pride as its end. The ego does not feel secure and therefore grasps for more power in order to make itself secure. It does not regard itself as sufficiently significant or respected or feared and therefore seeks to enhance its position in nature and in society.

In the one case the ego seems unconscious of the finite and determinate character of its existence. In the other case the lust for power is prompted by a darkly conscious realization of its insecurity. The first form of the pride of power is particularly characteristic of individuals and groups whose position in society is, or seems to be, secure. In Biblical prophecy this security is declared to be bogus and those who rest in it are warned against an impending doom. . . .

In Ezekiel's prophecies of doom upon the nations of the earth, they are constantly accused of having foolishly overestimated their security, independence and self-mastery. Egypt, for instance, is accused of imagining herself the creator of the river Nile and saying, "My river is my own, I have made it for myself." In the doom which overtakes this pride the real source and end of life will be revealed: "They shall know that I am the Lord" (Ez. 30:8).

The second form of the pride of power is more obviously prompted by the sense of insecurity. It is the sin of those who, knowing themselves to be insecure, seek sufficient power to guarantee their security, inevitably of course at the expense of other life. It is particularly the sin of the advancing forces of human society in distinction to the established forces. Among those who are less obviously secure, either in terms of social recognition, or economic stability or even physical health, the temptation arises to overcome or to obscure insecurity by arrogating a greater degree of power to the self. Sometimes this lust for power expresses itself in terms of man's conquest of nature, in which the legitimate freedom and mastery of man in the world of nature is corrupted into a mere exploitation of nature. Man's sense of dependence upon nature and his reverent gratitude toward the miracle of nature's perennial abundance is destroyed by his arrogant sense of independence and his greedy effort to overcome the insecurity of nature's rhythms and seasons by garnering her stores with excessive zeal and beyond natural requirements. Greed is in short the expression of man's inordinate ambition to hide his insecurity in nature. It is perfectly described in Jesus' parable of the rich fool who assures himself: "Soul, thou hast much goods laid up for many years; take thine ease, eat, drink, and be merry." Significantly this false security is shattered by the prospect of death, a vicissitude of nature which greed cannot master. God said to the rich fool, "This night thy soul shall be required of thee" (Luke 12:19–20).

Greed as a form of the will-to-power has been a particularly flagrant sin in the modern era because modern technology has tempted contemporary man to overestimate the possibility and the value of eliminating his insecurity in nature. Greed has thus become the besetting sin of a bourgeois culture. This culture is constantly tempted to regard physical comfort and security as life's final good and to hope for its attainment to a degree which is beyond human possibilities. "Modern man," said a cynical doctor, "has forgotten that nature intends to kill man and will succeed in the end."

Since man's insecurity arises not merely from the vicissitudes of nature but from the uncertainties of society and history, it is natural that the ego should seek to overcome social as well as natural insecurity and should express the impulse of "power over men" as well as "power over matter." The peril of a competing human will is overcome by subordinating that will to the ego and by using the power of many subordinated wills to ward off the enmity which such subordination creates. The will-to-power is thus inevitably involved in the vicious circle of accentuating the insecurity which it intends to eliminate. "Woe to thee," declares the prophet Isaiah, "that spoilest, and thou wast not spoiled; and dealest treacherously, and they dealt not treacherously with thee! when thou shalt cease to spoil, thou shalt be spoiled" (Isa. 33:1). The will-to-power in short involves the ego in injustice. It seeks a security beyond the limits of human finiteness and this inordinate ambition arouses fears and enmities which the world of pure nature, with its competing impulses of survival, does not know.

The school of modern psychology which regards the will-to-power as the most dominant of human motives has not yet recognized how basically it is related to insecurity. Adler attributes it to specific forms of the sense of inferiority and therefore believes that a correct therapy can eliminate it. Karen Horney relates the will-to-power to a broader anxiety than the specific cases of the sense of inferiority which Adler enumerates. But she thinks that the will-to-power springs from the general insecurities of a competitive civilization and therefore holds out hope for its elimination in a co-operative society. This is still far short of the real truth. The truth is that man is tempted by the basic insecurity of human existence to make himself doubly secure and by the insignificance of his place in the total scheme of life to prove his significance. The will-to-power is in short both a direct form and an indirect instrument of the pride which Christianity regards as sin in its quintessential form.

We have provisionally distinguished between the pride which does not recognize human weakness and the pride which seeks power in order to overcome or obscure a recognized weakness; and we have sought to attribute the former to the more established and traditionally respected individuals and groups, while attributing the latter to the less secure, that is, to the advancing rather than established groups in society. This distinction is justified only if regarded as strictly provisional. The fact is that the proudest monarch and the most secure oligarch is driven to assert himself beyond measure partly by a sense of insecurity. This is partly due to the fact that the greater his power and glory, the more the common mortality of humankind appears to him in the guise of an incongruous fate. Thus the greatest monarchs of the ancient world, the Pharaohs of Egypt, exhausted the resources of their realm to build pyramids, which were intended to establish or to prove their immortality. A common mortal's fear of death is thus one prompting motive of the pretensions and ambitions of the greatest lords.

But furthermore, the more man establishes himself in power and glory, the greater is the fear of tumbling from his eminence, or losing his treasure, or being discovered in his pretension. Poverty is a peril to the wealthy but not to the poor. Obscurity is feared, not by those who are habituated to its twilight but by those who have become accustomed to public acclaim. Nor is this sense of insecurity of the powerful and the great to be wholly discounted as being concerned with mere vanities. Life's basic securities are involved in the secondary securities of power and glory. The tyrant fears not only the loss of his power but the possible loss of his life. The powerful nation, secure against its individual foes, must fear the possibility that its power may challenge its various foes to make common cause against it. The person accustomed to luxury and ease actually meets a greater danger to life and mere existence in the hardships of poverty than those who have been hardened by its rigors. The will-to-power is thus an expression of insecurity even when it has achieved ends which, from the perspective of an ordinary mortal, would seem to guarantee complete security. The fact that human ambitions know no limits must therefore be attributed not merely to the infinite capacities of the human imagination but to an uneasy recognition of man's finiteness, weakness and dependence, which become the more apparent the more we seek to obscure them, and which generate ultimate perils, the more immediate insecurities are eliminated. Thus man seeks to make himself God because he is betrayed by both his greatness and his weakness; and there is no level of greatness and power in which the lash of fear is not at least one strand in the whip of ambition.

6. RICOEUR: PARADOX OF THE
SERVILE WILL

Foremost among modern attempts to recover the original meaning of sin and evil has been the work of the French phenomenologist and philosopher of religion Paul Ricoeur. The concept toward which the primary symbols of evil tend, he maintains, is the "servile will"; yet since the ideas of free will and servitude are fundamentally incompatible, this concept can only be regarded as a paradox and approached indirectly through the symbols that have historically preceded it, namely, defilement, sin, and guilt. In this selection, he provides a summary of the argument, showing how each of the symbols recapitulates the meaning of the preceding ones at a higher level. Source: Paul Ricoeur, *The Symbolism of Evil*, trans. Emerson Buchanan (New York: Harper & Row, 1967), pp. 151–55. Published in French in 1960.

The concept toward which the whole series of the primary symbols of evil tends may be called the *servile will*. But that concept is not directly accessible; if one tries to give it an object, the object destroys itself, for it short-circuits the idea of will, which can only signify free choice, and so free will, always intact and young, always available— and the idea of servitude, that is to say, the unavailability of freedom to itself. *The concept of the servile will, then, cannot be represented as the concept of fallibility,* which we considered at the beginning of this work; for we should have to be able to think of free will and servitude as coinciding in the same existent. That is why the concept of the servile will must remain an indirect concept. . . .

[This concept,] to which the most differentiated, the most subtle, the most internalized experience of guilt draws near, was already aimed at by the most archaic experience of all, that of defilement. The final symbol indicates its limiting concept only by taking up into itself all the wealth of the prior symbols. Thus there is a *circular* relation among all the symbols: the last bring out the meaning of the preceding ones, but the first lend to the last all their power of symbolization.

It is possible to show this by going through the whole series of symbols in the opposite direction. It is remarkable, indeed, that guilt turns to its own account the symbolic language in which the experiences of defilement and sin took shape.

Guilt cannot, in fact, *express* itself except in the indirect language of "captivity" and "infection," inherited from the two prior stages. Thus both symbols are transposed "inward" to express a freedom that enslaves itself, affects itself, and infects itself by its own choice. Conversely, the symbolic and non-literal character of the captivity of sin and the infection of defilement become quite clear when these symbols are used to denote a dimension of freedom itself; then and only then do we know that they are symbols, when they reveal a situation that is centered in the relation of oneself to oneself. Why this recourse to the prior symbolism? Because the paradox of a captive free will— the paradox of a *servile will*—is insupportable for thought. That freedom must be delivered and that this deliverance is deliverance from self-enslavement cannot be said directly; yet it is the central theme of "salvation." . . .

This symbolism is central in the Jewish experience; but if it can be understood, that is because it belongs, at least as a lateral growth, to all cultures. The experience or the belief that furnishes the literal meaning may be manifold and varied, but the aim of the symbol remains the same. Thus the representation of demons as the origin of the state of *being bound*, among the Babylonians, furnishes the initial schema of possession; but this wholly corporeal possession can, in its turn, furnish the basic image through which the enslavement of free will is denoted. . . .

What assures us that the symbolism of the servile will, although still submerged in the letter of demonic representations, is already at work in the confession of the Babylonian suppliant is that the same symbolism of a man with his limbs bound appears again in writers who employed this symbol with a clear awareness that it was a symbol. Thus St. Paul knows that man is "inexcusable," although sin is said to "reign" in his members, "in his mortal body" (Rom. 6:12), and the body itself is called "body of sin" (Rom. 6:6) and the whole man a "servant of sin." . . .

The symbol of the enslaved body is the symbol of a sinful being who is at the same time *act* and *state*; that is to say, a sinful being in whom the very act of self-enslavement suppresses itself as "act" and relapses into a "state." The body is the symbol of this obliterated freedom, of a building from which the builder has withdrawn. In the language of St. Paul, the *act* is the "yielding" of the body to servitude (as you have yielded your members as servants), the state is the reign (let not sin therefore reign in your mortal bodies). A "yielding" *of* myself that is at the same time a "reign" *over* myself—there is the enigma of the servile will, of the will that makes itself a slave.

Finally, Plato himself, in spite of the Orphic myth of the soul exiled in a body that is its tomb, in spite of the temptation to harden the symbol of bodily captivity into a gnosis of the body as evil, in spite even of the guarantees that he gives to that gnosis for the future, knows perfectly well that the bodily captivity must not be taken literally, but as a sign of the servile will; the "prison" of the body is in the end only "the work of desire," and "he who co-operates most in putting on the chains is perhaps the chained man himself" *(Phaedo 82d–e)*. Thus, the captivity of the body and even the captivity of the soul in the body are the symbol of the evil that the soul inflicts on itself, the symbol of the affection of freedom by itself; the "loosing" of the soul assures us retrospectively that its "bonds" were the bonds of desire, active-passive fascination, autocaptivity; "to be lost" means the same thing.

The expression that we have just used—the affection of freedom by itself—helps us to understand how the most internalized guilt can recapitulate all the symbolism prior to it, including the symbolism of defilement; it turns it to its own account through the symbolism of captivity. I would even venture to say that defilement becomes a pure symbol when it no longer suggests a real stain at all, but only signifies the servile will. The symbolic sense of defilement is complete only at the end of all its repeated appearances.

7. FARRER: BEYOND AUGUSTINIAN THEODICY

From Augustine on, Christian theologians have tended to conceive of evil in anthropological terms, that is, as sin or punishment for sin. Modern science, however, has brought to light conditions of evil on a much broader scale. There is a corresponding need for theology to rethink the meaning of evil and, in particular, the relationship of natural evil to the good intention of God. Austin Farrer, a twentieth-century Anglican, provides an imaginative approach to this problem. Source: Austin Farrer, *Love Almighty and Ills Unlimited* (Garden City, N.Y.: Doubleday & Co., 1961), pp. 49–56.

In thinking of the world as a something which might be cured of its general evil, we are tempted to treat it as though it were a single system, from which external interferences might be banished, or internal incoherences eliminated; a beast with a thorn in its paw or a fault in its digestion; a car with nails through the tires or a misfit in the cylinders; even a molecule of some substance, broken down by external pressure or collapsing by some internal disintegration. But the world is not a system, it is an interaction of systems innumerable.

"Interaction" may be an awkward noun to describe the physical universe, but it has the merit of being a neutral one. It would sound better if we called it a society of systems; but the term would suggest a mutual regard and peaceful coexistence scarcely to be found. If we called it a battleground for the systems it contains, we should suggest a general hostility almost as false. We should not do justice to that degree of mutual adaptation, apart from which the several systems would neither have developed their existence, nor maintained it.

Nevertheless, in the many and various interactions of the world, there are innumerable misfits, vast damage to systems, huge destruction and waste. Why is it so, if God is wise and almighty? The question remains, and we will attack it forthwith. We will use two approaches in turn, value and possibility. First we will ask whether a more smoothly fitting world would be better; and second, whether it could exist.

First, then, do we even wish to see the world tamed to a universal harmony? Naturally, we should like it to provide a safer and less galling habitat for us men; but that is not the question. The present stage of our argument is not concerned with our special interests. Let us keep mankind out of the picture; let us contemplate the natural order as in itself splendid or mean, monotonous or various, vital or inert, boring or intriguing to the mental eye, whether of men or of angels.

Is it not plain, then, that the elimination of conflict between systems, if it could be achieved, would be achieved at a price? If the universe is to be, as it were, not a jungle of forces but a magically self-arranged garden; if the several systems are to occupy just so much free space each as they need, without crowding their neighbors; if none is ever to incorporate any part of another in itself, except in such fashion that it preserves or even enhances the self-being of that other; then what sort of a world shall we have? And do we welcome the prospect? Gone will be that enormous vitality of force, which makes every system or concentration of energy to radiate over the whole field of space, every living kind to propagate without restraint, and, in a word, every physical creature to absolutize itself, so far as in it lies, and to be the whole world, if it can. It cannot, admittedly; and why? Because of interference from a million rivals, all equally reckless in their own vitality. Eliminate the mutual interferences, and gone, equally, will be the drama of an existence continually at stake, of a being which has to be achieved and held, of the unexpected and the improvised.

Could we bring ourselves to wish these characteristics of the world away, supposing that we had the choice? Perhaps we might, if there were no other way of making the world safe or stable enough, to allow the emergence of any systems except the most rudimentary. But it is not so; in spite of the degree of chaos which actually prevails, there are intricacies of order in the minute, and sublimities of structure in the great, sufficient for our highest admiration, and beyond the reach of our minds. It seems mere greediness to wish for more; and having so much, can we wish that what we have should be rendered secure by being tamed, or unaggressive by being devitalized?

Even supposing that we should like to see physical nature thus transformed, it may still be that the transformation is impossible; otherwise put, that no such physical world could exist. The question of possibility was, indeed, the second point we proposed to consider; and it is surely the more important. Strictly speaking, it underlies the first point, the issue of valuation. We cannot sensibly discuss the value of an impossibility, nor continue to wish for what is seen to be absurd.

To proceed, then, to the question of what is possible, and what is not, in the way of physical nature. Could the world be physical, and yet be free from those often disastrous mutual interferences which ravage it? Evidently the first thing to get clear is what we mean by physicality. Only then can we pretend to judge whether it admits of separation from that accidentality and chaos which we are tempted to deplore.

Philosophers, when called upon to define the physical, are inclined to proceed cautiously and skeptically. Something, they say, makes itself known to us through the impressions we receive in our senses; and in forming an idea of this "something," we use certain mental pictures or diagrams. We do not know, in any absolute sense, what the physical thing is; we must be content to discover how it can most usefully be diagrammatized in our formulae.

Such an approach as this will be very proper in certain sorts of arguments; it is useless in theology. The theological question is not, how it is convenient for us to think; the question is, what God has made; not, what sorts of impressions physical realities make in us; but what sort of an existence they have or exercise; what sort of creatures in themselves they are, irrespective of whether we observe them.

Ancient theology spoke of God as the Father of all his creatures, not only of those among them that deserve to be called persons. And though we now restrict the range of divine fatherhood more narrowly, we need not forget the truth for which the wider usage stood. All creating is a sort of fathering. Where it is not the production of persons by the supreme person, it is nevertheless the production of individuals by the supreme individual. God's personal creatures share his spirituality and answer his speech. His physical creatures express his actuality, and mirror his vital force. They are action-systems, for to act is to be; they are what they do, or what they are apt to do. Their action is their own; for they cannot be themselves, except by acting of themselves. Physical things are physical agents. When God creates physical creatures, he lets loose physical forces; and until he dis-creates them again, they will do what they will do.

Every level of God's creation is run by the creatures composing it; but only the intelligent know (even in part) what they are running. The atomic world is run by the atomic energies. And it is a manifest absurdity to suppose that they can consider the whole, or even consider one another. They cannot consider anything; the principle of their action is simply that it should go on discharging itself.

The first and most elementary energies of the world, by their mutual action upon one another, constitute a diversified field of force which is both the space and matter of the universe. But for them, the higher systems with which alone we are directly acquainted would have nowhere to be, and nothing of which to consist. Whether there could have been a world sharing any of the characteristics we call physical, which was built on different foundations from these, is a question we are powerless to ask. It is true that our predecessors, both scientists and philosophers, conceived the elements of the world otherwise; supposed, for example, a system of passive atoms like minute billiard balls, scattered over a pre-existent space. But we, looking back on their world from our better knowledge, see it to have been not only false in fact but untenable in theory. So far as we can know, or even speculate, to consist of rudimentary interactive energies is to be a physical world, and to be a physical world is to consist of these.

The elementary energies are such rudiments of being, that we can scarcely attach value to them, or, if one is swallowed by another, think it a matter for tears; any more than we shall weep to see a little eddy in a running stream annexed by a neighboring eddy, or both of them lost in the main current of water. But creative skill has introduced higher forms of action, richer systems of being to organize the elements of the world. And these too, being real creatures of God, act of themselves, and from the principle of their own being; which is, to build and perfect and maintain their own organization, seizing on the matter which suits them, and resisting interferences. It is impossible to see how strife between them is to be avoided, if they are to run their own world in this active fashion. It is an old story, how trial and error, and the elimination of the unfit, have produced tolerable compromises between warring forms, and achieved an often precarious balance. This is God's masterpiece. Could it be improved upon in principle? Could we have a world in which unintelligent creatures were the real springs of action, and in which, nevertheless, they freely moved without ever one trampling another?

When we lament the mutual destructiveness of physical things, of what do we complain? Is it that unintelligent creatures are not like virtuous men, or indeed, better? Good men consider one another and, in Kant's pedantic phrase, never treat their fellows as mere means to the furtherance of their own purposes, but always at the same time as ends-in-themselves. Yet the best of men cannot extend such benevolence to all the sorts of creatures with which they share the field of space. Our stomachs ruthlessly destroy what they consume, and if we spare animals, we shall still butcher vegetables. Only pure spirits could be wholly non-destructive. How, then, should unintelligent bodily creatures be so?

But it may be that the standard by which we condemn physical nature is not that of rational benevolence, so much as that of mechanical perfection. Human engineers can construct quite extensive and elaborate systems, in which the parts are so adapted, that both waste and accident are virtually eliminated (except now and then). Why, then, we ask, has not the Creator engineered the Universe? Ah, but consider how utterly unlike to any mechanism of ours the Universal *machina* would have to be. The purpose of a machine is not that it should give the happiest scope possible to individual existences composing it. The purpose of a machine is to deliver the goods. What goods would a cosmic machine deliver, and to whom? Might the Creator have thought to glorify himself by constructing a cosmic gramophone, streamlined for the production of symphonic Alleluias? But that is not how, it seems, he thought to glorify himself; and he is wise.

The machines we make presuppose the matter out of which they are made. The matter has first to exist, by the free play of the energies composing it. That the matter itself should be mechanical, and the whole world from top to bottom a machine, is a senseless suggestion. Machines are certainly possible; bigger and bigger, better and better, machines. Machines are possible, as a special sort of order, artificially imposed on a careful selection from the wild variety of natural elements. Machines are possible, because men are actual, and because some men have turned engineers. God created the men, and he has at least permitted the machines. If he desires machines, this is how he makes them—by introducing into the world machine-making creatures. That God should create machines directly, or that he should weave the existing matter of the world into a single super-machine, is an idea as childish as that he once literally molded Adam from clay, like a potter making a pot. God does not make artificial arrangements, he calls creatures into being; and they act according to their kind, or according to their skill. For example, they may make machines.

If it were true that physical nature had to be redeemed by being mechanized, one can only suppose that God would usher into the world an engineer-messiah, to mechanize it. And he, no doubt, would need collaborators. As well, then, think of a messianic race, as of a messianic man. Here is a dream, indeed, for the prophets of space-conquest. Let man embrace the heavenly calling; let him harness the galaxies, control the traffic of the stars, and buffer celestial collisions. But let him not complain that God might have done the work for him by direct interference, and the use of heaven knows what invisible tools.

VIII. CHRIST AND SALVATION

1. THE NICENE CREED: *HOMOUSIOS* WITH THE FATHER

The first doctrinal statement to be adopted as common to the entire church, the Nicene Creed seeks to prohibit any watering down of the understanding that Christ is God—while simultaneously insisting that he is one who became incarnate, suffered, and died. Source: translation adapted from *Creeds of the Churches*, ed. John H. Leith (Garden City, N.Y.: Doubleday & Co., 1963), pp. 30–31. Date of original composition: 325.

We believe in one God, the Father All Governing, Creator of all things visible and invisible;

And in one Lord Jesus Christ, the Son of God, begotten of the Father as only begotten, that is, from the reality [or essence: *ousias*] of the Father, God from God, Light from Light, true God from true God, begotten not created, of the same reality [or same essence: *homoousias*] as the Father, through whom all things came into being, both in heaven and in earth; Who for us humans and for our salvation came down and was incarnate, becoming human. He suffered and the third day he rose, and ascended into the heavens. And he will come to judge both the living and the dead.

And [we believe] in the Holy Spirit.

But those who say, "once he was not," or "before he was begotten, he was not," or "he came to be out of nothing," or who assert that he, the Son of God, is of a different subsistence [*hupostasis*] or reality [or essence: *ousia*], or that he is created, or changeable, or mutable, the Catholic and Apostolic Church anathematizes them.

2. ATHANASIUS: TRULY HUMAN, TRULY GOD

Athanasius is generally recognized as the foremost interpreter of the Nicene position. In this selection from his *Orations Against the Arians*

205

he presents salvation as a key to understanding Christ as both God and human. Against the Arians, he argues that the Son may be distinct from the Father, receiving from the Father, without being inferior. The passage is also valuable for indicating the reasoning behind the problematic classical notion that God is "impassible," that is, beyond suffering and change. Source: Athanasius, "Orations Against the Arians: Book III," *The Christological Controversy*, trans. and ed. Richard A. Norris, Jr. (Philadelphia: Fortress Press, 1980), pp. 90–96. Date of original composition: ca. 358.

Who will not marvel at this? Who will not agree that it is truly something divine? If the works of the Logos' Godhead had not been done by means of the body, humanity would not have been divinized. Furthermore, if the properties of the flesh had not been reckoned to the Logos, humanity would not have been completely liberated from them. On the contrary, as I said above, they might have ceased for a brief space, but sin and corruption would have remained within humanity, just as they did in the case of human beings before Christ. What is more, this is apparent.

Many people, after all, have become holy and clean from all sin. Jeremiah was made holy even from the womb, and John, while still unborn, "leapt for joy" at the voice of Mary the mother of God. Nevertheless, "death reigned from Adam to Moses, even over those who had not sinned after the likeness of Adam's transgression" (Rom. 5:14), and in this way, human beings continued to be mortal and corruptible nonetheless, subject to the passions that belong to their nature.

Now that the Logos has become human and made the flesh his very own, these passions no longer affect the body because the Logos has come to dwell within it. In fact, the opposite is the case. The passions have been destroyed by him, and from now on human beings no longer continue as sinners and dead persons in accordance with the passions that are proper to them. Rather, they have risen from the dead in accordance with the power of the Logos, and they remain forever immortal and incorruptible.

This explains why he who supplies others with the origin of their being is himself said to have been born; his flesh was born of Mary the mother of God. The purpose of this is that we may have our origin relocated in him and that we may no longer return to earth because mere earth is what we are, but may be carried by him into the heavens because we are joined to the Logos who comes from heaven. In the same way, therefore, he has appropriately taken upon himself the other passions of the body too, in order that we may grasp eternal life no longer as human beings but as creatures belonging to the Logos, for we no longer die "in Adam" in accordance with our first origin. From now on, since our origin and all our fleshly weakness has been transferred to the Logos, we are being raised up from earth; the curse which sin occasioned has been removed through the agency of him who is in us and who "for our sakes became a curse" (Gal. 3:13). Just as we die in Adam because we are all from the earth, so "we are all made alive in Christ" because we are "reborn" from above "by water and the Spirit" (1 Cor. 15:22; John 3:5); the flesh is no longer earthly, but now it has been "logified" by the work of the divine Logos who on our account became flesh. . . .

So, then, let no one be scandalized by the human characteristics [of Christ]. Rather, let people see that the Logos himself is impassible by nature and that he nevertheless has these passions predicated of him in virtue of the flesh which he took on, since they are proper to the flesh and the body itself is proper to the Savior. Furthermore, he himself remains as he is—impassible in nature. He takes no hurt from these passions, but on the contrary destroys them and brings them to nothing. And human beings, because their own passions have been transferred to the impassible and abolished, are henceforth becoming impassible and free of them to all eternity. That is what John teaches when he says, "And know that he was manifested to take away our sins, and in him there is no sin" (1 John 3:5). . . .

We have necessarily begun by looking into these matters closely, so that if we see Christ acting or speaking in divine fashion through the instrumentality of his own body, we will know that he does these works because he is God; and again, so that if we see him speaking or suffering in the manner of a human being, we may not fail to understand that he became a human being by bearing flesh and that this is how he does and says these [human] things. If we recognize what is proper and peculiar to each, while at the same time perceiving and understanding that both sets of deeds come from one [agent], we believe rightly and shall never be led astray. But if anyone sees the things that are done divinely by the Logos and denies the body, or if anyone sees the things proper to the body and denies the enfleshed presence of the Logos or ascribes inferiority to the Logos because of his human characteristics—such a person . . . will consider the cross a scandal or, like a Gentile, will judge the preaching to be foolishness. These are the sorts of things that have happened to God's enemies the Arians. . . .

Consider these texts: "The Father loves the Son and has given everything into his hand" (John 3:35); "Everything has been handed over to me by my Father" (Matt. 11:27); "I can do no deed of myself, but I judge as I hear" (John 5:30). As many such passages as there are, they do not demonstrate that there was a time when the Son did not possess these privileges. How can it be the case that the one who is the sole essential Logos and Wisdom of the Father should fail to possess eternally what the Father possesses, especially when he also says, "Whatever things the Father possesses are mine" (John 16:15) and "The things which are mine belong to the Father" (John 17:10)? If the things which belong to the Father belong to the Son, while the Father possesses them eternally, it is plain that whatever the Son possesses, since it belongs to the Father, is in him eternally. Therefore, he did not make these statements because there was a time when these privileges were not his; he made them because even though the Son possesses eternally what he possesses, he nevertheless possesses them from the Father.

There is a danger here. Someone who sees the Son in full possession of whatever belongs to the Father may, by reason of the unalterable similarity—not to say identity—of the qualities he possesses, blaspheme by being led astray after the fashion of Sabellius. Such a person may conclude that the Son is identical with the Father. It was for the sake of avoiding this error that he said "was given me" and "I received" and "was handed over to me," for the sole purpose of showing that he is not the Father but the Logos of the Father and the eternal Son, who on account of his likeness to the Father has *eternally* whatever he possesses from the Father, and on account of his being Son has *from the Father* whatever he possesses eternally. . . .

The expressions "was given" and "was handed over" do not imply that there was a time when [the Son] did not have these things. This— and the like conclusion where all such expressions are concerned—we can gather from a similar passage. The Savior himself says, "As the Father possesses life in himself, in the same manner also he has given the Son to have life in himself" (John 5:26). By that phrase "he has given" he signifies that he is not himself the Father. When he says "in the same manner," he shows the Son's likeness of nature to the Father and the fact that he belongs to the Father. If there was a time when the Father did not possess life, obviously there was a time when the Son did not possess it either, for the Son possesses it "in the same manner" as the Father. If, however, it is irreligious to make this assertion, and, by contrast, is reverent to assert that the Father always possesses life, is it not absurd—when the Son states that he possesses life "in the same manner" as the Father—to assert that they possess it not "in the same manner" but differently? We conclude, rather, that the Logos is trustworthy and that everything he says he has received he possesses from the Father, though at the same time he possesses it eternally. Moreover, while the Father does not possess life from anyone, the Son possesses it from the Father.

It is like the case of radiance. Suppose that the radiance itself says, "The light has given me all places to illumine, and I illumine not from myself but as the light wills." In saying this, the radiance does not indicate that at one time it did not possess light but rather asserts, "I am proper to the light and everything which belongs to the light is mine." We ought to understand that this is so in the case of the Son, only more so, for when the Father has given everything to the Son, he still possesses everything in the Son, and when the Son possesses them, the Father still possesses them. The Son's deity is the deity of the Father, and in this way the Father carries out his providential care for all things in the Son.

3. THE CHALCEDONIAN DEFINITION: ONE PERSON, TWO NATURES

The culmination of a series of post-Nicene debates regarding the relation between the humanity and divinity in Christ, the Chalcedonian definition brought together the major theological traditions of the time in a carefully balanced statement. The definition has often been used as a positive, and even an exhaustive, account of the person of Christ. The proper function of the statement, however, may be more limited and negative: simply to mark the boundaries beyond which serious misunderstanding will occur. Source: translation adapted from *Documents of the Christian Church*, 2d ed., ed. Henry Bettenson (London: Oxford University Press, 1963), p. 73. Date of original composition: 451.

Therefore, following the holy Fathers, we all with one accord teach to acknowledge one and the same Son, our Lord Jesus Christ, at once complete in Godhead and complete in humanity, truly God and truly human, consisting also of a rational soul and body; of the same reality [or same essence] as the Father [*homoousion tō patri*] as regards his Godhead, and at the same time of the same reality [or same essence] as us [*homoousion hēmin*] as regards his humanity; like us in all respects, apart from sin; as regards his Godhead, begotten of the Father before the ages, but yet as regards his humanity begotten, for us and for our salvation, of Mary the Virgin, the God-bearer [*theotokos*]; one and the same Christ, Son, Lord, Only-begotten, recognized in two natures [*en duo phusein*], without confusion [*asugkhutōs*], without change [*atreptōs*], without division [*adiaretōs*], without separation [*achoristōs*]; the distinction of natures being in no way annulled by the union, but rather the characteristics of each nature being preserved and coming together to form one person [*prosōpon*] and subsistence [*hupostasis*], not as parted or separated into two persons [*prosōpa*], but one and the same Son and Only-begotten, God the Word, Lord Jesus Christ; even as the prophets from earliest times spoke of him, and our Lord Jesus Christ himself taught us, and the creed of the Fathers has handed down to us.

4. ANSELM: THE LOGIC OF ATONEMENT

In his highly influential treatise on salvation, Anselm asked why it was necessary for God to become human: *Cur Deus Homo*. His response established the framework for the "judicial" theory of atonement: only one who is both human and divine can accomplish the requisite payment or satisfaction. The discussion proceeds in the form of a dialogue between Anselm (A) and his conversation partner (B). Source: *Anselm of Canterbury*, ed. and trans. Jasper Hopkins and Herbert Richardson (Lewiston, N.Y.: Edwin Mellen Press, 1976), Vol. III. pp. 129–36. Date of original composition: 1098.

*How the life of Christ is paid to God for the sins of
men. The sense in which Christ ought, and the sense in
which he ought not, to have suffered.*

A. But tell me now what you think must still be resolved regarding
the problem you set forth at the beginning—because of which problem many other topics intruded themselves.

B. The crux of the problem was why God became a man in order to
save mankind through his death, although he was apparently able to
accomplish man's salvation in some other way. Responding to this
problem, you showed by many compelling reasons that the restoration
of human nature ought not to be left undone, and yet could not be
done unless man paid what he owed to God for his sin. This debt was
so great that only God was able to pay it, although only a man ought to
pay it; and, thus, the same [individual] who was divine was also human. Hence, it was necessary for God to assume a human nature into
a unity of person, so that the one who with respect to his nature ought
to make payment, but was unable to, would be the one who with respect to his person was able to. Next, you showed that that man who
was God had to be taken from a virgin by the person of the Son of God;
and you showed how he could be taken sinless from the sinful mass.
You proved very clearly that the life of this man was so sublime and so
precious that it can suffice to make payment for what is owed for the
sins of the whole world—and even for infinitely more [sins than
these]. Therefore, it now remains to show how his life is paid to God
for the sins of men.

A. If he allowed himself to be killed for the sake of justice, did he
not give his life for the honor of God?

B. Even though I do not see how he could reasonably have done
this—since he was able to keep justice unwaveringly and his life eternally—nevertheless, if I can understand a thing which I do not doubt,
I will admit that he freely gave to God, for God's honor, some such gift
to which whatever is not God is not comparable in value, and which
can make recompense for all the debts of all men.

A. Do you not realize that when he endured with patient kindness
the injuries, the abuses, the crucifixion among thieves—which were
all inflicted upon him (as I said above) for the sake of the justice which

he obediently kept—he gave men an example, in order that they would not, on account of any detriments they can experience, turn aside from the justice they owe to God? He would not at all have given this example if, as he was able to do, he had turned aside from the death that was inflicted upon him for such a reason.

B. It seems that it was not necessary for him to give this example, since we know that many people before his coming—and John the Baptist after his coming and before his death—sufficiently gave this example by bravely enduring death for the sake of the truth.

A. Except for him, no human being through his death ever gave to God what he was not necessarily going to lose at some time or other, or ever paid what he did not already owe. But that man freely offered to the Father what he was never going to lose as a result of any necessity; and he paid on behalf of sinners that which he did not already owe for himself. Therefore, it is much more the case that he gave an example, in order that no single human being would hesitate (when reason demands it) to render to God on behalf of himself that which one day he will summarily lose. For although he did not at all need to do so for himself, and although he was not at all compelled to do so for others to whom he owed only punishment, he gave with such great willingness so precious a life—indeed, his own self—i.e., so great a person.

B. You are coming very close to satisfying me. But bear with my asking a question which although you may think it foolish to ask, nevertheless I would not readily know what to answer if it were asked of me. You say that when he died, he gave what he was not obliged to. But no one will deny that when he gave this example in such a way, he did something better (and that his doing it was more pleasing to God) than if he had not done it. And no one will say that he was not obliged to do what he understood to be better and to be more pleasing to God. Therefore, how can we maintain that he did not owe to God the deed he performed—i.e., the deed he knew to be better and to be more pleasing to God—especially since a creature owes to God all that he is, all that he knows, and all that he can do?

A. Although a creature has nothing from himself, nevertheless when God grants him the right to do or not to do something, he gives him both prerogatives in such a way that although the one alternative is the better, neither alternative is definitely required. Rather, whether he does what is the better or whether he does the alternative, we say that he ought to do what he does. And if he does what is the better, he should have a reward, because he voluntarily gives what belongs to him. For example, although the state of virginity is better than the marital state, neither of these is definitely required of a man. Instead, we say both of him who prefers to marry and of him who prefers to keep his virginity that he ought to do what he does. For no one claims that virginity ought not to be chosen or that marriage ought not to be chosen. Rather, we say that before a man has decided upon either of these, he ought to do the one which he prefers; and if he keeps his virginity, he looks forward to a reward for the voluntary gift which he offers to God. Therefore, when you say that a creature owes to God what he knows to be the better and what he is able to do, then if you mean "[He owes it] as a debt" and do not add "provided God commands it," [your claim] is not in every case true. For, indeed, as I said, a man does not owe virginity as a debt; but if he prefers, he ought to marry.

Now, perhaps the word "ought" troubles you, and perhaps you cannot understand it apart from [its signifying] a debt. If so, then be aware that just as *ability* and *inability* and *necessity* are sometimes ascribed not because they are in the things to which they are ascribed but because they are in something else, so it also happens in the case of *ought to*. Indeed, when we say that the poor *ought* to receive alms from the rich, this statement means nothing other than that the rich ought to give alms to the poor. For this obligation ought to be exacted not of the poor but of the rich. We also say that God *ought* to rule over all things—not because he at all owes anything but because all things ought to be subject to him. And [we say that God] ought to do what he wills, since what he wills ought to occur. Likewise, when a creature wills to do what it is his prerogative to do or not to do, we say that he ought to do it, since what he wills ought to occur. Hence, when the Lord Jesus, as I said, willed to endure death: since it was his prerogative to undergo death or not to undergo death, he *ought* to have done what he did, because what he willed ought to have been done; and he *ought not* to have done it, because [he was] not [obliged to do it] out of debt.

Assuredly, the Lord Jesus was divine and human. Therefore, in accordance with his human nature (from the time that he was a man) he so received from his divine nature (which is different from his human nature) to have as his prerogative whatever-he-had that he was not obliged to give anything except what he willed to. And in accordance with his person he so possessed from himself what he possessed, and was so completely sufficient unto himself, that he was not obliged to make any recompense to anyone else and did not need to give anything in order to be recompensed.

B. I now see clearly that it was not in any respect out of debt that he gave himself over to death for the honor of God (as my argument seemed to show), and that nevertheless he ought to have done what he did.

A. Surely, that honor belongs to the whole Trinity. Therefore, since he himself is God—viz., the Son of God—he offered himself to himself (just as to the Father and the Holy Spirit) for his own honor. That is, [he offered] his humanity to his divinity, which is one and the same divinity common to the three persons. Nevertheless, in order to say more clearly what we mean, while still abiding within this truth, let us say (as is the custom) that the Son freely offered himself to the Father. For in this way we speak most fittingly. For by reference to one person [viz., the Father] we understand it to be God as a whole to whom the Son offered himself according to his humanity; and through the name "Father" and the name "Son," an enormous devotion is felt in the hearts of those listening when the Son is said to entreat the Father for us in this way.

B. I accept this most gladly.

How very reasonable it is that human salvation results from his death.

A. Let us see now, as best we can, how very reasonable it is that human salvation results from his death.

B. My mind strives toward this end. Now, although I think that I understand this point, I want you to produce the structure of the argument.

A. It is not necessary to discuss how great is the gift which the Son freely gave.

B. This is [already] sufficiently clear.

A. But you will not suppose that he who freely gives to God so great a gift ought to go unrewarded.

B. On the contrary, I recognize that it is necessary for the Father to reward the Son. Otherwise, the Father would seem to be either unjust, if he were unwilling [to give a reward], or powerless, if he were unable [to give a reward]. And both of these features are foreign to God.

A. One who rewards another either gives what the other does not already have or else remits what can be exacted from the other. Now, even before the Son performed so great a deed, everything that was the Father's was also the Son's; and the Son never owed anything that could be remitted. Therefore, what will be recompensed to one who needs nothing and to whom there is nothing that can be given or remitted?

B. On the one hand, I see the necessity for giving a reward—and, on the other, the impossibility thereof. For it is necessary that God pay what he owes; but there is not anything which he can pay.

A. If so great and so deserved a reward were not paid either to the Son or to someone else, then the Son would seem to have performed so great a deed in vain.

B. This is heinous to suppose.

A. Therefore, it is necessary that a reward be paid to someone else, since it cannot be paid to him.

B. This follows inescapably.

A. If the Son wanted to give to someone else that which is owed to himself, would the Father rightly be able either to prevent him or to withhold the reward from the one to whom the Son would give it?

B. Indeed, I think it both just and necessary that the reward be paid by the Father to the one to whom the Son wanted to give it. For the Son is permitted to bestow what is his own; and only to someone other than to the Son can the Father pay what he owes.

A. To whom will the Son more fittingly give the fruit and the recompense of his death than to those for whose salvation he became a man (as sound reasoning has taught us), and to whom (as we said), by dying, he gave an example of dying-for-the-sake-of-justice? Surely, they would imitate him in vain if they would not share in his merit. Or whom will he more justly make to be heirs of the reward he does not need, and heirs of his overflowing fulness, than his own kinsmen and brethren (whom—bound by such numerous and great debts—he sees languishing with need in the depth of miseries), so that what they owe for their sins may be forgiven them and what they lack on account of their sins may be given to them?

B. The world can hear of nothing more reasonable, nothing more kind, nothing more desirable. Indeed, I receive so much confidence from this thought that right now I cannot say with how much joy my heart exults. For it seems to me that God rejects no human being who approaches him under this name.

A. This is true—provided he approaches as he ought. Sacred Scripture everywhere teaches us how we are to approach the participation in such great grace and how we are to live under this grace. Sacred Scripture is founded upon the solid truth, as upon a firm foundation; and with God's help we have perceived this truth to some extent.

B. Truly, whatever is erected upon this foundation is established upon a solid rock.

A. I think that I have now to some extent satisfactorily answered your question—even though someone better than I can do this more fully, and even though the reasons for this matter are deeper and more numerous than my intelligence (or any mortal's intelligence) can comprehend. It is also clear that God did not at all need to do what we have been discussing; rather the immutable truth required it. For although on account of a unity of person God is said to have done the thing which that man did, nevertheless God did not need to come down from heaven in order to overcome the Devil. And [God did not need] to act against the Devil by means of justice in order to free man. Rather, God demanded of man that he overcome the Devil and that, having offended God by his sin, he make satisfaction by his justice. Indeed, God did not owe anything to the Devil except punishment; and man did not [owe the Devil anything] except to conquer him in return for having been conquered by him. But man owed to God, not to the Devil, whatever was required of him.

How great and how just the mercy of God is.

A. We have discovered that God's mercy—which, when we were examining God's justice and man's sin, seemed to you to perish—is so great and so harmonious with his justice that it cannot be conceived to be greater or more just. Indeed, what can be thought to be more merciful than for God the Father to say to a sinner, condemned to eternal

torments and having no way to redeem himself: "Receive my only begotten son and render him in place of yourself," and for the Son to say
"Take me and redeem yourself"? For the Father and the Son do make
these respective statements, as it were, when they call and draw us to
the Christian faith. And what is more just than that he to whom is
given a reward greater than every debt should forgive every debt if it is
presented to him with due affection?

5. SCHLEIERMACHER: THE WORK OF CHRIST

It is Schleiermacher who established the characteristically modern approach to Christology, namely, the tendency to understand Christ in
terms of his work, and his work in terms of the effect upon the believer's
experience. In this selection one may also observe Schleiermacher's concern to interpret the activity of Christ in such a way as to safeguard the
freedom and integrity of the individual believer. Source: Friedrich
Schleiermacher, *The Christian Faith*, § 100, ed. H. R. Mackintosh and
J. S. Stewart (Edinburgh: T. & T. Clark, 1928), pp. 425–28. Date of
original publication: 1830.

The Redeemer assumes believers into the power of his
God-consciousness, and this is his redemptive activity.

1. In virtue of the teleological character of Christian piety, both the
imperfect stage of the higher life, as also the challenge of it, appear in
our self-consciousness as facts due to our own individual action—
though we do not feel responsible for the latter in the same way as for
the former. In virtue, however, of the peculiar character of Christianity this challenge is also apprehended in our self-consciousness as the
act of the Redeemer. These two points of view can be reconciled only
by supposing that this challenge is the act of the Redeemer become our
own act. And this, accordingly, is the best way of expressing the
common element in the Christian consciousness of the divine grace.
Hence, from this point of view, the peculiar work of the Redeemer
would first be to evoke this act in us. But if we regard the matter more
closely, it is clear that what we have thus described is in every case an
act both of the Redeemer and of the redeemed. The original activity of
the Redeemer, therefore, which belongs to him alone, and which precedes all activity of our own in this challenge, would be that by means

of which he assumes us into this fellowship of his activity and his life. The continuance of that fellowship, accordingly, constitutes the essence of the state of grace; the new corporate life is the sphere within which Christ produces this act; in it is revealed the continuous activity of his sinless perfection.

But his act in us can never be anything but the act of his sinlessness and perfection as conditioned by the being of God in him. And so these too in addition must become ours, because otherwise it would not be his act that became ours. Now the individual life of each one of us is passed in the consciousness of sin and imperfection. Hence we can know the fellowship of the Redeemer only insofar as we are not conscious of our own individual life; as impulses flow to us from him, we find that in him from which everything proceeds to be the source of our activity also—a common possession, as it were. This too is the meaning of all those passages in Scripture which speak of Christ being and living in us, of being dead to sin, of putting off the old and putting on the new man. But Christ can only direct his God-consciousness against sin insofar as he enters into the corporate life of man and sympathetically shares the consciousness of sin, but shares it as something he is to overcome. This very consciousness of sin as something to be overcome becomes the principle of our activity in the action which he evokes in us. . . .

2. All Christ's activity, then, proceeds from the being of God in him. And we know no divine activity except that of creation, which includes that of preservation, or, conversely, that of preservation, which includes that of creation. So we shall have to regard Christ's activity too in the same way. We do not, however, exclude the soul of man from creation, in spite of the fact that the creation of such a free agent and the continued freedom of a being created in the context of a greater whole is something which we cannot expect to understand; all that we can do is to recognize the fact. The same is true of the creative activity of Christ, which is entirely concerned with the sphere of freedom. For his assumptive activity is a creative one, yet what it produces is altogether free. Now the being of God in him as an active principle is timeless and eternal, yet its expressions are all conditioned by the form of human life. It follows that he can influence what is free only in accordance with the manner in which it enters into his sphere of living

influence, and only in accordance with the nature of the free. The activity by which he assumes us into fellowship with him is, therefore, a creative production in us of the will to assume him into ourselves, or rather—since it is only receptiveness for his activity as involved in the impartation—only our assent to the influence of his activity. But it is a condition of that activity of the Redeemer that the individuals should enter the sphere of his historical influence, where they become aware of him in his self-revelation. Now this assent can only be conceived as conditioned by the consciousness of sin; yet it is not necessary that this should precede entrance into the sphere of the Redeemer. Rather it may just as well arise within that sphere as the effect of the Redeemer's self-revelation, as indeed it certainly does come to full clarity only as we contemplate his sinless perfection. Accordingly, the original activity of the Redeemer is best conceived as a pervasive influence which is received by its object in virtue of the free movement with which he turns himself to its attraction, just as we ascribe an attractive power to everyone to whose educative intellectual influence we gladly submit ourselves. Now, if every activity of the Redeemer proceeds from the being of God in him, and if in the formation of the Redeemer's person the only active power was the creative divine activity which established itself as the being of God in him, then also his every activity may be regarded as a continuation of that person-forming divine influence upon human nature. For the pervasive activity of Christ cannot establish itself in an individual without becoming person-forming in him too, for now all his activities are differently determined through the working of Christ in him, and even all impressions are differently received— which means that the personal self-consciousness too becomes altogether different. And just as creation is not concerned simply with individuals (as if each creation of an individual had been a special act), but it is the world that was created, and every individual as such was created only in and with the whole, for the rest not less than for itself, in the same way the activity of the Redeemer too is world-forming, and its object is human nature, in the totality of which the powerful God-consciousness is to be implanted as a new vital principle. He takes possession of the individuals relatively to the whole, wherever he finds those in whom his activity does not merely remain, but from whom, moving on, it can work upon others through the revelation of his life.

And thus the total effective influence of Christ is only the continuation of the creative divine activity out of which the person of Christ arose. For this, too, was directed towards human nature as a whole, in which that being of God was to exist, but in such a way that its effects are mediated through the life of Christ, as its most original organ, for all human nature that has already become personal in the natural sense, in proportion as it allows itself to be brought into spiritual touch with that life and its self-perpetuating organism. And this in order that the former personality may be slain and human nature, in vital fellowship with Christ, be formed into persons in the totality of that higher life.

Let us now look at the corporate life, or at the fellowship of the individual with the Redeemer. We may best describe its beginning, since it is conditioned by a free acceptance, by the term *calling*—the whole official activity of Christ began with just such a call. But the share of the Redeemer in the common life, viewed as continuing, we are fully justified in calling *soul-bestowal*, primarily with reference to the corporate life—as indeed the Church is called his body. In just the same way Christ is to be the soul also in the individual fellowship, and each individual the organism through which the soul works. The two things are related as in Christ the divine activity present in the act of union is related to that activity in the state of union, and as in God the activity of creation is related to that of preservation. Only that here it is still clearer how each moment of a common activity can be regarded also as a calling, and likewise how the calling proper can be regarded as soul-bestowal. But this formula, too, we shall employ in another place.

3. This exposition is based entirely on the inner experience of the believer; its only purpose is to describe and elucidate that experience. Naturally, therefore, it can make no claim to be a proof that things must have been so; in the sphere of experience such proof is only possible where mathematics can be used, which is certainly not the case here. Our purpose is simply to show that the perfect satisfaction to which we aspire can only be truly contained in the Christian's consciousness of his relation to Christ insofar as that consciousness expresses the kind of relation which has been described here. If this content be lacking in the Christian consciousness, then either the perfect satisfaction must come from some other quarter, or it does not ex-

ist at all, and we must be content with an indefinite appeasement of conscience, such as may be found without any Redeemer; and in that case there would be no special possession of divine grace in Christianity at all. Now these negations cannot be logically refuted; they can only be removed by actual facts: we must seek to bring doubters to the same experience as we have had.

6. BULTMANN: FAITH IN THE CROSS

Bultmann here defends his project of demythologizing the New Testament on the grounds that it is in fact the appropriate way of setting forth the radical challenge of the cross. The passage culminates in a particularly forceful statement of the conviction that soteriology must precede christology, that is, that a right understanding of Christ's "saving efficacy" must precede, and provide the way to, an understanding of who Christ is. Source: Rudolf Bultmann et al., *Kerygma and Myth: A Theological Debate*, ed. Hans Werner Bartsch (New York: Harper & Row, 1962), pp. 34–43. Published in German in 1948.

Now, it is beyond question that the New Testament presents the event of Jesus Christ in mythical terms. The problem is whether that is the only possible presentation. Or does the New Testament itself demand a restatement of the event of Jesus Christ in non-mythological terms? Now, it is clear from the outset that the event of Christ is of a wholly different order from the cult-myths of Greek or Hellenistic religion. Jesus Christ is certainly presented as the Son of God, a preexistent divine being, and therefore to that extent a mythical figure. But he is also a concrete figure of history—Jesus of Nazareth. His life is more than a mythical event; it is a human life which ended in the tragedy of crucifixion. We have here a unique combination of history and myth. The New Testament claims that this Jesus of history, whose father and mother were well known to his contemporaries (John 6:42) is at the same time the pre-existent Son of God, and side by side with the historical event of the crucifixion it sets the definitely non-historical event of the resurrection. This combination of myth and history presents a number of difficulties, as can be seen from certain inconsistencies in the New Testament material. The doctrine of Christ's preexistence as given by St. Paul and St. John is difficult to reconcile with the legend of the virgin birth in St. Matthew and St. Luke. On the one hand we hear that "he emptied himself, taking the form of a servant, being made in the likeness of men: and being found in fashion as a man . . ." (Phil. 2:7), and on the other hand we have the gospel portraits of a Jesus who manifests his divinity in his miracles, omniscience, and mysterious elusiveness, and the similar description of him in Acts as "Jesus of Nazareth, a man approved of God unto you by mighty works and wonders and signs" (Acts 2:22). On the one hand we have the resurrection as the exaltation of Jesus from the cross or grave, and on the other the legends of the empty tomb and the ascension.

We are compelled to ask whether all this mythological language is not simply an attempt to express the meaning of the historical figure of Jesus and the events of his life; in other words, the significance of these as a figure and event of salvation. If that be so, we can dispense with the objective form in which they are cast.

It is easy enough to deal with the doctrine of Christ's pre-existence and the legend of the virgin birth in this way. They are clearly attempts to explain the meaning of the person of Jesus for faith. The facts which historical criticism can verify cannot exhaust, indeed they cannot adequately indicate, all that Jesus means to me. How he actually originated matters little, indeed we can appreciate his significance only when we cease to worry about such questions. Our interest in the events of his life, and above all in the cross, is more than an academic concern with the history of the past. We can see meaning in them only when we ask what God is trying to say to each one of us through them. Again, the figure of Jesus cannot be understood simply from his context in human evolution or history. In mythological language, this means that he stems from eternity, his origin transcends both history and nature.

We shall not, however, pursue the examination of the particular incidents of his life any further. In the end the crux of the matter lies in the cross and resurrection. . . .

But what of the resurrection? Is it not a mythical event pure and simple? Obviously it is not an event of past history with a self-evident meaning. Can the resurrection narratives and every other mention of the resurrection in the New Testament be understood simply as an attempt to convey the meaning of the cross? Does the New Testament, in asserting that Jesus is risen from the dead, mean that his death is not just an ordinary human death, but the judgment and salvation of the world, depriving death of its power? Does it not express this truth in the affirmation that the Crucified was not holden of death, but rose from the dead?

Yes indeed: the cross and the resurrection form a single, indivisible cosmic event. "He was delivered up for our trespasses, and was raised for our justification" (Rom. 4:25). The cross is not an isolated event, as though it were the end of Jesus, which needed the resurrection subsequently to reverse it. When he suffered death, Jesus was already the Son of God, and his death by itself was the victory over the power of death. St. John brings this out most clearly by describing the passion of Jesus as the "hour" in which he is glorified, and by the double meaning he gives to the phrase "lifted up," applying it both to the cross and to Christ's exaltation into glory.

Cross and resurrection form a single, indivisible cosmic event which brings judgment to the world and opens up for men the possibility of authentic life. But if that be so, the resurrection cannot be a miraculous proof capable of demonstration and sufficient to convince the skeptic that the cross really has the cosmic and eschatological significance ascribed to it. . . .

It is however abundantly clear that the New Testament is interested in the resurrection of Christ simply and solely because it is the eschatological event *par excellence*. By it Christ abolished death and brought life and immortality to light (2 Tim. 1:10). This explains why St. Paul borrows Gnostic language to clarify the meaning of the resurrection. As in the death of Jesus all have died (2 Cor. 5:14 f.), so through his resurrection all have been raised from the dead, though naturally this event is spread over a long period of time (1 Cor. 15:21 f.). But St. Paul does not only say: "In Christ shall all be made alive"; he can also speak of rising again with Christ in the present tense, just as he speaks of our dying with him. Through the sacrament of baptism Christians participate not only in the death of Christ but also in his resurrection. It is not simply that we *shall* walk with him in newness of life and be united with him in his resurrection (Rom. 6:4 f.); we are doing so already here and now. "Even so reckon ye yourselves to be dead indeed unto sin, but alive unto God in Jesus Christ" (Rom. 6:11). . . .

In this way the resurrection is not a mythological event adduced in order to prove the saving efficacy of the cross, but an article of faith just as much as the meaning of the cross itself. Indeed, *faith in the resurrection is really the same thing as faith in the saving efficacy of the cross,* faith in the cross as the cross of Christ. Hence you cannot first believe in Christ and then in the strength of that faith believe in the cross. To believe in Christ means to believe in the cross as the cross of Christ. The saving efficacy of the cross is not derived from the fact that it is the cross of Christ: it is the cross of Christ because it has this saving efficacy. Without that efficacy it is the tragic end of a great man.

We are back again at the old question. How do we come to believe in the cross as the cross of Christ and as the eschatological event *par excellence?* How do we come to believe in the saving efficacy of the cross?

There is only one answer. This is the way in which the cross is proclaimed. It is always proclaimed together with the resurrection. Christ meets us in the preaching as one crucified and risen. He meets us in the word of preaching and nowhere else. The faith of Easter is just this—faith in the word of preaching.

It would be wrong at this point to raise again the problem of how this preaching arose historically, as though that could vindicate its truth. That would be to tie our faith in the word of God to the results of historical research. The word of preaching confronts us as the word of God. It is not for us to question its credentials. It is we who are questioned, we who are asked whether we will believe the word or reject it. But in answering this question, in accepting the word of preaching as the word of God and the death and resurrection of Christ as the eschatological event, we are given an opportunity of understanding ourselves. Faith and unbelief are never blind, arbitrary decisions. They offer us the alternative between accepting or rejecting that which alone can illuminate our understanding of ourselves.

The real Easter faith is faith in the word of preaching which brings illumination. If the event of Easter Day is in any sense an historical event additional to the event of the cross, it is nothing else than the rise of faith in the risen Lord, since it was this faith which led to the apostolic preaching. The resurrection itself is not an event of past history. All that historical criticism can establish is the fact that the first disciples came to believe in the resurrection. The historian can perhaps to some extent account for that faith from the personal intimacy which the disciples had enjoyed with Jesus during his earthly life, and so reduce the resurrection appearances to a series of subjective visions. But the historical problem is scarcely relevant to Christian belief in the resurrection. For the historical event of the rise of the Easter faith means for us what it meant for the first disciples—namely, the self-manifestation of the risen Lord, the act of God in which the redemptive event of the cross is completed.

We cannot buttress our own faith in the resurrection by that of the first disciples and so eliminate the element of risk which faith in the resurrection always involves. For the first disciples' faith in the resurrection is itself part and parcel of the eschatological event which is the article of faith.

In other words, the apostolic preaching which originated in the event of Easter Day is itself a part of the eschatological event of redemption. The death of Christ, which is both the judgment and the salvation of the world, inaugurates the "ministry of reconciliation" or "word of reconciliation" (2 Cor. 5:18 f.). This word supplements the cross and makes its saving efficacy intelligible by demanding faith and confronting men with the question whether they are willing to understand themselves as men who are crucified and risen with Christ. Through the word of preaching the cross and the resurrection are made present: the eschatological "now" is here, and the promise of Isa. 49:8 is fulfilled: "Behold, now is the acceptable time; behold, now is the day of salvation" (2 Cor. 6:2). That is why the apostolic preaching brings judgment. For some the apostle is "a saviour from death unto death" and for others a "saviour from life unto life" (2 Cor. 2:16). St. Paul is the agent through whom the resurrection life becomes effective in the faithful (2 Cor. 4:12). The promise of Jesus in the fourth gospel is eminently applicable to the preaching in which he is proclaimed: "Verily I say unto you, he that heareth my words and believeth on him that sent me, hath eternal life, and cometh not unto judgment, but hath passed out of death into life. . . . The hour cometh and now is, when the dead shall hear the voice of the Son of God; and they that hear shall live" (John 5:24 f.). In the word of preaching and there alone we meet the risen Lord. "So belief cometh of hearing, and hearing by the word of Christ" (Rom. 10:17).

225

7. BARTH: LORD AS SERVANT,
SERVANT AS LORD

Throughout his life Barth championed a radically christocentric theology. The accomplishment of his later work is to show that such a position is by no means incompatible with a remarkable amplitude of vision. Analogies have been suggested between Barth's mature writing style and the music of Mozart, his favorite composer; thus it may be useful to read the following pages with a particular eye toward balance, counterpoint, and the interweaving of themes. The selection provides an overview of the last completed volume of the *Church Dogmatics*, *The Doctrine of Reconciliation*. Source: Karl Barth, *Church Dogmatics*, Vol. 4/1, trans. G. W. Bromiley (Edinburgh: T. & T. Clark, 1956), pp. 128–37. Date of original publication: 1953.

If . . . we return to the being of Jesus Christ as we have briefly defined it, we find at once that there are three "christological" aspects in the narrower sense—aspects of his active person or his personal work which as such broaden into three perspectives for an understanding of the whole event of reconciliation.

The first is that in Jesus Christ we have to do with very God. The reconciliation of man with God takes place as God himself actively intervenes, himself taking in hand his cause with and against and for man, the cause of the covenant, and in such a way (this is what distinguishes the event of reconciliation from the general sway of the providence and universal rule of God) that he himself becomes man. God became man. That is what is, i.e., what has taken place, in Jesus Christ. He is very God acting for us men, God himself become man. He is the authentic revealer of God as himself God. Again, he is the effective proof of the power of God as himself God. Yet again, he is the fulfiller of the covenant as himself God. He is nothing less or other than God himself, but God as man. When we say God we say honor and glory and eternity and power, in short, a regnant freedom as it is proper to him who is distinct from and superior to everything else that is. When we say God we say the Creator and Lord of all things. And we can say all that without reservation or diminution of Jesus Christ—but in a way in which it can be said in relation to him, i.e., in which it corresponds to the Godhead of God active and revealed in him. No general idea of "Godhead" developed abstractly from such concepts must be allowed to intrude at this point. How the freedom of God is constituted, in what character he is the Creator and Lord of all things, distinct from and superior to them, in short, what is to be understood by "Godhead," is something which—watchful against all imported ideas, ready to correct them and perhaps to let them be reversed and renewed in the most astonishing way—we must always learn from Jesus Christ. He defines those concepts: they do not define him. When we start with the fact that he is very God we are forced to keep strictly to him in relation to what we mean by true "Godhead."

This means primarily that it is a matter of the Godhead, the honor and glory and eternity and omnipotence and freedom, the being as Creator and Lord, of the Father, Son and Holy Spirit. Jesus Christ is himself God as the Son of God the Father and with God the Father the source of the Holy Spirit, united in one essence with the Father by the Holy Spirit. That is how he is God. He is God as he takes part in the event which constitutes the divine being.

We must add at once that as this one who takes part in the divine being and event he became and is man. This means that we have to understand the very Godhead, that divine being and event and therefore himself as the one who takes part in it, in the light of the fact that it pleased God—and this is what corresponds outwardly to and reveals the inward divine being and event—himself to become man. In this way, in this condescension, he is the eternal Son of the eternal Father. This is the will of this Father, of this Son, and of the Holy Spirit who is the Spirit of the Father and the Son. This is how God is God, this is his freedom, this is his distinctness from and superiority to all other reality. It is with this meaning and purpose that he is the Creator and Lord of all things. It is as the eternal and almighty love, which he is actually and visibly in this action of condescension. This one, the one who loves in this way, is the true God. But this means that he is the one who as the Creator and Lord of all things is able and willing to make himself equal with the creature, himself to become a creature; the one whose eternity does not prevent but rather permits and commands him to be in time and himself to be temporal, whose omnipotence is so great that he can be weak and indeed impotent, as a man is weak and impotent. He is the one who in his freedom can and does in fact bind himself, in the same way as we all are bound. And we must go further: he, the true God, is the one whose Godhead is demonstrated and plainly consists in essence in the fact that, seeing he is free in his love, he is capable of and wills this condescension for the very reason that in man of all his creatures he has to do with the one that has fallen away from him, that has been unfaithful and hostile and antagonistic to him. He is God in that he takes this creature to himself, and that in such a way that he sets himself alongside this creature, making his own its penalty and loss and condemnation to nothingness. He is God in the fact that he can give himself up and does give himself up not merely to the creaturely limitation but to the suffering of the human creature, becoming one of these men, himself bearing the judgment under which they stand, willing to die and, in fact, dying the death which they have deserved. That is the nature and essence of the true God as he has intervened actively and manifestly in Jesus Christ. When we speak of Jesus Christ we mean the true God—he who seeks his divine glory and finds that glory, he whose glory obviously consists in the fact that because he is free in his love he can be and actually is lowly as well as exalted; he, the Lord, who is for us a servant, the servant of all servants. It is in the light of the fact of his humiliation that on this first aspect all the predicates of his Godhead, which is the true Godhead, must be filled out and interpreted. Their positive meaning is lit up only by this determination and limitation, only by the fact that in this act he is this God and therefore the true God, distinguished from all false gods by the fact that they are not capable of this act, that they have not in fact accomplished it, that their supposed glory and honor and eternity and omnipotence not only do not include but exclude their self-humiliation. False gods are all reflections of a false and all too human self-exaltation. They are all lords who cannot and will not be servants, who are therefore no true lords, whose being is not a truly divine being.

The second christological aspect is that in Jesus Christ we have to do with a true man. The reconciliation of the world with God takes place in the person of a man in whom, because he is also true God, the conversion of all men to God is an actual event. It is the person of a true man, like all other men in every respect, subjected without exception to all the limitations of the human situation. The conditions in which other men exist and their suffering are also his conditions and his suffering. That he is very God does not mean that he is partly God and only partly man. He is altogether man just as he is altogether God—altogether man in virtue of his true Godhead whose glory consists in his humiliation. That is how he is the reconciler between God and man. That is how God accomplishes in him the conversion of all men to himself. He is true man, and altogether man, for in him we have to do with the manifestation of the glory of the one who is true God and altogether God, and with the conversion to God of the one who is true man and altogether man. Here, too, there is no reservation and no diminution, which would be an immediate denial of the act of atonement made in him. Jesus Christ is man in a different way from what we are. That is why he is our mediator with God. But he is so in a complete equality of his manhood with ours. To say man is to say creature and sin, and this means limitation and suffering. Both these have to be said of Jesus Christ. Not, however, according to the standard of general concepts, but only with reference to him, only in correspondence with his true manhood. As in relation to his Godhead, so also in relation to his manhood, we must not allow any necessary idea of the human situation and its need to intervene. What his manhood is, and therefore true manhood, we cannot read into him from elsewhere, but must be told by him. But then we find that it is a matter of the manhood of the eternal Son of God. It is a matter of the real limitation and suffering of the man with whom the high God has ordained and elected and determined to be one, and has therefore humbled himself. In his limitation and suffering, this is the true man. And that means at once that he is the man exalted by God, lifted above his need and limitation and suffering. In virtue of the fact that he is one with God he is free man. He is a creature, but superior to his creatureliness. He is bound by sin, but quite free in relation to it because he is not bound to commit it. He is mortal, and has actually died as we must all die. But in dying he is superior to death, and at once and altogether rescued from it, so that (even as a man like us) he is triumphant and finally alive. As the true God, i.e., the God who humbles himself, Jesus Christ is this true man, i.e., the man who in all his creatureliness is exalted above his creatureliness. In this he is also exalted above us, because he is different from us, and is given the precedence in the ranks of our common humanity. But he does precede us. As God he was humbled to take our place, and as man he is exalted on our behalf. He is set at the side of God in the humanity which is ours. He is above us and opposed to us, but he is also for us. What has happened in him as the one true man is the conversion of all of us to God, the realization of true humanity. It is anticipated in him, but it is in fact accomplished and revealed. As in him God became like man, so too in him man has become like God. As in him God was bound, so too in him man is made free. As in him the Lord became a servant, so too in him the servant has become a Lord. That is the reconciliation in Jesus Christ in its second aspect. In him humanity is exalted humanity, just as Godhead is humiliated Godhead. And humanity is exalted in him by the humiliation of Godhead. We cannot regard the human being of Jesus Christ, we cannot—without denying or weakening them—interpret his predicates of liability to sin and suffering and death, in any other way than in the light of the liberation and exaltation accomplished in his unity with God. It is in its impotence that his being as man is omnipotent, in its temporality that it is eternal, in its shame that it is glorious, in its corruptibility that it is incorruptible, in its servitude that it is that of the Lord. In this way, therefore, it is his true being as man—true humanity. . . .

Insofar as he was and is and will be very man, the conversion of man to God took place in him, the turning and therefore the reconciliation of all men, the fulfilment of the covenant. And in the light of Jesus Christ the man who is still not free in relation to limitation and suffering, who is still not exalted, who is still lowly (lowly, as it were, *in abstracto*), can be understood only as false man—just as in the light of Jesus Christ the empty loveless gods which are incapable of condescension and self-humiliation can be understood only as false gods. . . .

The third christological aspect to which we must now turn is at once the simplest and the highest. It is the source of the two first, and it comprehends them both. As the God who humbles himself and therefore reconciles man with himself, and as the man exalted by God and therefore reconciled with him, as the one who is very God and very man in this concrete sense, Jesus Christ himself is one. He is the "God-man," that is, the Son of God who as such is this man, this man who as such is the Son of God. . . .

There can be no question of our trying to see a third thing in what we have called the third christological aspect. Everything that can be said materially concerning Jesus Christ and the reconciliation in him has been said exhaustively in the twofold fact—which cannot be further reduced conceptually but only brought together historically—that he is very God and very man, i.e., the Lord who became a servant and the servant who became Lord, the reconciling God and reconciled man. The third aspect can be only the viewing of this history in its unity and completeness, the viewing of Jesus Christ himself, in whom the two lines cross—in the sense that he himself is the subject of what takes place on these two lines. To that extent the reconciliation of the world with God and the conversion of the world to God took place in him. To that extent he himself, his existence, is this reconciliation. He himself is the mediator and pledge of the covenant. He is the mediator of it in that he fulfils it—from God to man and from man to God. He is the pledge of it in that in his existence he confirms and maintains and reveals it as an authentic witness—attesting himself, in that its fulfilment is present and shines out and avails and is effective in him. This is the new thing in the third christological aspect. Jesus Christ is the actuality of reconciliation, and as such the truth of it which speaks for itself. If we hear Jesus Christ, then whether we realize it or not we hear this truth. If we say Jesus Christ, then whether we realize it or not we express and repeat this truth: the truth of the grace in which God has turned to the world in him and which has come to the world in him; the truth of the living brackets which bring and hold together heaven and earth, God and all men, in him; the truth that God has bound himself to man and that man is bound to God. The one who bears this name is himself this truth in that he is himself this actuality. He attests what he is. He alone is the pledge of it because he alone is the mediator of it. He alone is the truth of it. But he is that truth, and therefore it speaks for itself in him. It is not in us. We cannot produce it ourselves. We cannot of ourselves attest it to ourselves or to others. But it encounters us majestically in him—the promise of the truth which avails for us as the atonement—of which it is the truth—took place for us and as ours, the truth which for that reason can and should be heard and accepted and appropriated by us, which we can and should accept as the truth which applies to us. It encounters us in him as the promise of our own future. It is he, and therefore the actuality of our reconciliation, who stands before us. It is to him, and therefore to the revelation of this actuality, that we move. He is the Word of God to men which speaks of God and man and therefore expresses and discloses and reveals God and ourselves—God in his actual relationship to us and us in our actual relationship to God. He is the Word of God by which he calls us in this relationship and therefore calls us to him and therefore calls us also to ourselves. He was and is the will of God to speak this word—this word of his act. And it is our destiny to hear this word, to live under and with and by this word. That is the third christological aspect. . . .

8. MOLTMANN: THE CRUCIFIED GOD

One of the foremost figures in contemporary theology, Jürgen Moltmann is perhaps best known as the author of *The Theology of Hope*. His subsequent work, *The Crucified God*, to which the present selection may serve as an introduction, speaks to those who reject the notion of God because of the reality of human suffering. Moltmann responds by pointing to the "passionate God" who is present to that suffering and who is found most fully revealed at the very moment of Christ's abandonment on the cross. Source: Jürgen Moltmann, "The 'Crucified God': God and the Trinity Today," in *New Questions on God*, ed. Johannes B. Metz (New York: Herder & Herder, 1972), pp. 31–35.

The Council of Nicaea rightly declared, in opposition to Arius, that God was not so changeable as his creature. This is not an absolute statement about God, but a comparative statement. God is not subject to compulsion by what is not divine. This does not mean, however, that God is not free to change himself or to be changed by something else. We cannot deduce from the relative statement of Nicaea that God is unchangeable that he is absolutely unchangeable.

The early Fathers insisted on God's inability to suffer in opposition to the Syrian Monophysite heresy. An essential inability to suffer was the only contrast to passive suffering recognized in the early Church. There is, however, a third form of suffering—active suffering, the suffering of love, a voluntary openness to the possibility of being affected by outside influences. If God were really incapable of suffering, he

232

would also be as incapable of loving as the God of Aristotle, who was loved by all, but could not love. Whoever is capable of love is also capable of suffering, because he is open to the suffering that love brings with it, although he is always able to surmount that suffering because of love. God does not suffer, like his creature, because his being is incomplete. He loves from the fullness of his being and suffers because of his full and free love.

The distinctions that have been made in theology between God's and man's being are externally important, but they tell us nothing about the inner relationship between God the Father and God the Son and therefore cannot be applied to the event of the cross which took place between God and God. Christian humanists also find this a profound *aporia*. In regarding Jesus as God's perfect man, and in taking his exemplary sinlessness as proof of his "permanently powerful consciousness of God," they interpret Jesus' death as the fulfilment of his obedience or faith, not as his being abandoned by God. God's incapacity, because of his divine nature, to suffer (*apatheia*) is replaced by the unshakeable steadfastness (*ataraxia*) of Jesus' consciousness of God. The ancient teaching that God is unchangeable is thus transferred to Jesus' "inner life," but the *aporia* is not overcome. Finally, atheistic humanists who are interested in Jesus but do not accept the existence of God find it impossible to think of Jesus as dying abandoned by God and therefore regard his cry to God from the cross as superfluous.

All Christian theologians of every period and inclination try to answer the question of Jesus' cry from the cross and to say, consciously or unconsciously, why God abandoned him. Atheists also attempt to answer this question in such a way that, by depriving it of its foundation, they can easily dismiss it. But Jesus' cry from the cross is greater than even the most convincing Christian answer. Theologians can only point to the coming of God, who is the only answer to this question.

Christians have to speak about God in the presence of Jesus' abandonment by God on the cross, which can provide the only complete justification of their theology. The cross is either the Christian end of all theology or it is the beginning of a specifically Christian theology. When theologians speak about God on the cross of Christ, this inevitably becomes a trinitarian debate about the "story of God" which is quite distinct from all monotheism, polytheism or pantheism. The

233

central position occupied by the crucified Christ is the specifically Christian element in the history of the world and the doctrine of the Trinity is the specifically Christian element in the doctrine of God. Both are very closely connected. "It is not the bare trinitarian formulas in the New Testament, but the constant testimony of the cross which provides the basis for Christian faith in the Trinity. The most concise expression of the Trinity is God's action on the cross, in which God allowed the Son to sacrifice himself through the Spirit" (B. Steffen).

It is informative to examine Paul's statements about Jesus' abandonment on the cross in this context. The Greek word for "abandon" (*paradidomi*) has a decidedly negative connotation in the gospel stories of the passion, meaning betray, deliver, "give up" and even kill. In Paul (Rom. 1:18ff.), this negative meaning of *paredōken* is apparent in his presentation of God's abandonment of ungodly men. Guilt and punishment are closely connected and men who abandon God are abandoned by him and "given" up to the way they have chosen for themselves—Jews to their law, Gentiles to the worship of their idols and both to death.

Paul introduced a new meaning into the term *paredōken* when he presented Jesus' abandonment by God not in the historical context of his life, but in the eschatological context of faith. God "did not spare his own Son, but gave him up for us all; will he not also give us all things with him?" (Rom. 8:32). In the historical abandonment of the crucified Christ by the Father, Paul perceived the eschatological abandonment or "giving up" of the Son by the Father for the sake of "ungodly" men who had abandoned and been abandoned by God. In stressing that God had given up "his own Son," Paul extended the abandonment of the Son to the Father, although not in the same way, as the Patripassian heretics had done, insisting that the Son's sufferings could be predicated of the Father. In the Pauline view, Jesus suffered death abandoned by God. The Father, on the other hand, suffered the death of his Son in the pain of his love. The Son was "given up" by the Father and the Father suffered his abandonment from the Son. Kazoh Kitamori has called this "the pain of God."

The death of the Son is different from this "pain of God" the Father, and for this reason it is not possible to speak, as the Theopaschites did, of the "death of God." If we are to understand the story of Jesus' death abandoned by God as an event taking place between the Father and the Son, we must speak in terms of the Trinity and leave the universal concept of God aside, at least to begin with. In Gal. 2:20, the word *paredōken* appears with Christ as the subject: ". . . the Son of God, who loved me and gave himself for me." According to this statement, then, it is not only the Father who gives the Son up, but the Son who gives himself up. This indicates that Jesus' will and that of the Father were the same at the point where Jesus was abandoned on the cross and they were completely separated. Paul himself interpreted Christ's being abandoned by God as love, and the same interpretation is found in John (John 3:16). The author of 1 John regarded this event of love on the cross as the very existence of God himself; "God is love" (1 John 4:16). This is why it was possible at a later period to speak, with reference to the cross, of *homoousia*, the Son and the Father being of one substance. In the cross, Jesus and his God are in the deepest sense separated by the Son's abandonment by the Father, yet at the same time they are in the most intimate sense united in this abandonment or "giving up." This is because this "giving up" proceeds from the event of the cross that takes place between the Father who abandons and the Son who is abandoned, and this "giving up" is none other than the Holy Spirit.

Any attempt to interpret the event of Jesus' crucifixion according to the doctrine of the two natures would result in a paradox, because of the concept of the one God and the one nature of God. On the cross, God calls to God and dies to God. Only in this place is God "dead" and yet not "dead." If all we have is the concept of one God, we are inevitably inclined to apply it to the Father and to relate the death exclusively to the human person of Jesus, so that the cross is "emptied" of its divinity. If, on the other hand, this concept of God is left aside, we have at once to speak of persons in the special relationship of this particular event, the Father as the one who abandons and "gives up" the Son, and the Son who is abandoned by the Father and who gives himself up. What proceeds from this event is the Spirit of abandonment and self-giving love who raises up abandoned men.

My interpretation of the death of Christ, then, is not as an event between God and man, but primarily as an event within the Trinity between Jesus and his Father, an event from which the Spirit proceeds.

This interpretation opens up a number of perspectives. In the first place, it is possible to understand the crucifixion of Christ non-theistically. Secondly, the old dichotomy between the universal nature of God and the inner triune nature of God is overcome and, thirdly, the distinction between the immanent and the "economic" Trinity becomes superfluous. It makes it necessary to speak about the Trinity in the context of the cross, and re-establishes it as a traditional doctrine. Seen in this light, this doctrine no longer has to be regarded as a divine mystery which is better venerated with silent respect than investigated too closely. It can be seen as the tersest way of expressing the story of Christ's passion. It preserves faith from monotheism and from atheism, because it keeps it close to the crucified Christ. It reveals the cross in God's being and God's being in the cross. The material principle of the trinitarian doctrine is the cross; the formal principle of the theology of the cross is the trinitarian doctrine. The unity of the Father, the Son and the Holy Spirit can be designated as "God." If we are to speak as Christians about God, then, we have to tell the story of Jesus as the story of God and to proclaim it as the historical event which took place between the Father, the Son and the Holy Spirit and which revealed who and what God is, not only for man, but in his very existence. This also means that God's being is historical and that he exists in history. The "story of God" then is the story of the history of man.

IX. THE CHURCH

1. CYPRIAN: THE UNITY OF THE CHURCH

The third-century bishop, Cyprian of Carthage, established the main lines of a Latin ecclesiology that prevailed for over a thousand years. Arguing against the Novatianist schism, he claimed that the unity of the church in Christ was passed on to Peter and the apostles and that it now resides in the collective episcopate, which is indivisible. Later his thought was modified into an argument for Roman primacy. Source: Cyprian, *On the Unity of the Catholic Church*, Chaps. 4–6, in *The Ante-Nicene Fathers* (New York: Christian Literature Co., 1886–97; reprint by Eerdmans), Vol. 5, pp. 422–23. Date of original composition: ca. 251.

If any one consider and examine these things, there is no need for lengthened discussion and arguments. There is easy proof for faith in a short summary of the truth. The Lord speaks to Peter, saying "I say unto thee, that thou art Peter; and upon this rock I will build my Church, and the gates of hell shall not prevail against it. And I will give unto thee the keys of the kingdom of heaven; and whatsoever thou shalt bind on earth shall be bound also in heaven, and whatsoever thou shalt loose on earth shall be loosed in heaven" (Matt. 16:18–19). And again to the same he says, after his resurrection, "Feed my sheep" (John 21:15). And although to all the apostles, after his resurrection, he gives an equal power, and says, "As the Father hath sent me, even so send I you: Receive ye the Holy Ghost: Whose soever sins ye remit, they shall be remitted unto him; and whose soever sins ye retain, they shall be retained" (John 20:21–23); yet, that he might set forth unity, he arranged by his authority the origin of that unity, as beginning from one. Assuredly the rest of the apostles were also the same as was Peter, endowed with a like partnership both of honor and power; but the beginning proceeds from unity. Which one Church, also, the Holy Spirit in the Song of Songs designated in the person of our Lord, and says, "My dove, my spotless one, is but one. She is the only one of her

237

mother, elect of her that bare her" (Cant. 6:9). Does he who does not hold this unity of the Church think that he holds the faith? Does he who strives against and resists the Church trust that he is in the Church, when moreover the blessed Apostle Paul teaches the same thing, and sets forth the sacrament of unity, saying, "There is one body and one spirit, one hope of your calling, one Lord, one faith, one baptism, one God" (Eph. 4:4)?

And this unity we ought firmly to hold and assert, especially those of us that are bishops who preside in the Church, that we may also prove the episcopate itself to be one and undivided. Let no one deceive the brotherhood by a falsehood: let no one corrupt the truth of the faith by perfidious prevarication. The episcopate is one, each part of which is held by each one for the whole. The Church also is one, which is spread abroad far and wide into a multitude by an increase of fruitfulness. As there are many rays of the sun, but one light; and many branches of a tree, but one strength based in its tenacious root; and since from one spring flow many streams, although the multiplicity seems diffused in the liberality of an overflowing abundance, yet the unity is still preserved in the source. Separate a ray of the sun from its body of light, its unity does not allow a division of light; break a branch from a tree—when broken, it will not be able to bud; cut off the stream from its fountain, and that which is cut off dries up. Thus also the Church, shone over with the light of the Lord, sheds forth her rays over the whole world, yet it is one light which is everywhere diffused, nor is the unity of the body separated. Her fruitful abundance spreads her branches over the whole world. She broadly expands her rivers, liberally flowing, yet her head is one, her source one; and she is one mother, plentiful in the results of fruitfulness: from her womb we are born, by her milk we are nourished, by her spirit we are animated.

The spouse of Christ cannot be adulterous; she is uncorrupted and pure. She knows one home; she guards with chaste modesty the sanctity of one couch. She keeps us for God. She appoints the sons whom she has born for the kingdom. Whoever is separated from the Church and is joined to an adulteress, is separated from the promises of the Church; nor can he who forsakes the Church of Christ attain to the rewards of Christ. He is a stranger; he is profane; he is an enemy. He can no longer have God for his Father, who has not the Church for his mother. If any one could escape who was outside the ark of Noah, then he also may escape who shall be outside of the Church. The Lord warns, saying, "He who is not with me is against me, and he who gathereth not with me scattereth" (Matt. 12:30). He who breaks the peace and the concord of Christ, does so in opposition to Christ; he who gathereth elsewhere than in the Church, scatters the Church of Christ. The Lord says, "I and the Father are one" (John 10:30), and again it is written of the Father, and of the Son, and of the Holy Spirit, "And these three are one" (1 John 5:7). And does any one believe that this unity which thus comes from the divine strength and coheres in celestial sacraments, can be divided in the Church, and can be separated by the parting asunder of opposing wills? He who does not hold this unity does not hold God's law, does not hold the faith of the Father and the Son, does not hold life and salvation.

2. THOMAS AQUINAS: THE SOUL
OF THE CHURCH

Thomas offers a brief exposition of the four classic marks of the church—one, holy, catholic, apostolic—arguing that the fundamental principle of the church is the Spirit as the "soul" animating its body. Thus a theological principle of unity replaces the juridical one, and an enduring metaphor is introduced into ecclesiological literature. Although an exposition of the Apostles' Creed, this treatise is profoundly biblical in its substance. Source: Thomas Aquinas, "Exposition on the Apostles' Creed," in St. Thomas Aquinas, *Theological Texts*, translated with notes and an introduction by Thomas Gilby (London: Oxford University Press, 1955), pp. 340–43. Date of original composition: mid-thirteenth century.

As in one single human being there is one soul and one body but many members, so the Catholic Church has one body but many members. The soul animating this body is the Holy Ghost. Hence the Creed, after bidding us believe in the Holy Ghost, adds, *the Holy Catholic Church*.

Church means congregation. Holy Church is the congregation of believers of which each Christian is a member: "Draw near to me, ye unlearned; and gather yourselves together into the house of discipline" (Ecclus. 51:23).

The Church has four marks, being *one, holy, catholic,* or *universal,* and *strong* or *lasting.* Heretics lack the first, for because they have invented a variety of sects and are split into factions they do not belong to the Church, which is *one:* "One is my dove; my perfect one is but one" (Cant. 6:9). This unity has a threefold cause; it comes from agreement of faith, of hope, of charity. Of faith, for all Christians who belong to the body of the Church believe the same truths: "Now I beseech you, brethren, by the name of our Lord Jesus Christ, that you all speak the same thing, and that there be no schisms among you" (1 Cor. 1:10). And again, "One Lord, one faith, one baptism" (Eph. 4:5). Unity of hope, for all are comforted by the same confidence of coming to life eternal: "One body and one spirit; as you are called in one hope of your redemption" (Eph. 4:4). Unity of charity, for all are bound together in the love of God and of one another: "The love which thou hast given me, I have given them; that they may be one, even as we are one" (John 17:22). The genuineness of this love is shown when the members of the Church care for one another and are compassionate together: "Doing the truth in charity, we may in all things grow up in him who is the head, even Christ; from whom the whole body, being compacted and fitly joined together by that which every joint supplieth, according to the effectual working in the measure of every part, maketh increase of the body unto the edifying of itself in love" (Eph. 4:15–16). According to the grace granted him, each should serve his neighbor: nobody should be despised, nobody should be treated as an outcast, for the Church is like the ark of Noah, outside of which nobody can be saved.

Then the Church is *holy:* "Know you not that you are the temple of God" (1 Cor. 3:16). A church when consecrated is washed—so are the faithful cleansed by the blood of Christ: "He hath loved us and washed us from our sins in his own blood" (Rev. 1:5). A church is anointed too—so also the faithful receive a spiritual unction for their sanctification, otherwise they would not be Christians. The Christ means the anointed one. And his unction is the grace of the Holy Spirit: "Now he that confirmeth you in Christ and hath anointed us is God, who also hath sealed us and given us the pledge of the Spirit in our hearts" (2 Cor. 1:21–22). Moreover, the Church is holy by the indwelling of the Blessed Trinity: "This is the place of awe, none other but the house of

God and the gate of heaven" (Gen. 28:17). There, also, is God invoked: "Thou, O Lord, art in the midst of us, and we are called by thy name; leave us not" (Jer. 14:9). So then, let us guard against defiling our soul with sin: "For if any man violate the temple of God, him shall God destroy" (1 Cor. 3:17).

The Church is *catholic*, that is, *universal*. First with regard to place: "We have received grace and apostleship for obedience to his faith, in all nations" (Rom. 1:5). Our Lord commanded us, "Go ye into the whole world and preach the gospel to every creature" (Mark 16:15). The Church has three parts, one on earth, a second in heaven, a third in purgatory. The Church is universal with regard to all conditions of human beings; nobody is rejected, whether they be masters or slaves, men or women: "There is neither Jew nor Greek, neither bond nor free, neither male nor female" (Gal. 3:28). It is universal in time, and those are wrong who allow it a limited span of time, for it began with Abel and will last even to the end of the world: "Behold, I am with you always, even to the consummation of the world" (Matt. 28:20). And even after, for the Church remains in heaven.

Fourthly, the Church is *firm*, solid as a house on massive foundations. The principal foundation is Christ himself: "For another foundation no man can lay but that which is laid, which is Christ Jesus" (1 Cor. 3:11). Secondary foundations are the Apostles and apostolic teaching: hence the Church is called *apostolic*: "The walls of the city had twelve foundations; and in them the names of the Apostles of the Lamb" (Rev. 21:14). Its strength is signified by Peter, or Rock, who is its crown. A building is strong when it can never be overthrown though it may be shaken. The Church can never be brought down. Indeed it grows under persecution, and those who attack it are destroyed: "Whosoever shall fall on this stone shall be broken; but on whomsoever it shall fall, it shall grind him to powder" (Matt. 21:44). Nor can the Church be destroyed by errors: "Men corrupted in mind, reprobate concerning the faith, but they shall proceed no farther, for their folly shall appear to all men" (2 Tim. 3:8–9). Nor by the temptations of demons, for the Church will stand, a secure place of refuge: "The name of the Lord is a strong tower" (Prov. 18:10). Though he strives to undermine it, the devil will never succeed: "The gates of hell shall not prevail" (Matt. 16:18). Only the Church of Peter, to whose lot fell all

Italy when the disciples were sent out to preach, has always stood fast in the faith. While the faith has disappeared or has partly decayed in other regions, the Church of Peter still flourishes in faith and free from heresy. This is not to be surprised at, for our Lord said to Peter, "I have prayed for thee that thy faith fail not, and thou, when thou are converted, confirm thy brethren" (Luke 22:32).

3. THE SECOND HELVETIC CONFESSION: CHRIST THE SOLE HEAD OF THE CHURCH

Although it was not commissioned by any church and was the work of a single hand, that of Heinrich Bullinger, the Second Helvetic Confession became the most widely received among Reformed creeds. Chapter 17 touches on all the major themes of classical Protestant ecclesiology in an irenic spirit, placing characteristically Calvinist stress upon Christ as the "sole head" of the ecclesial body, but adopting also Luther's designation of the church as a *congregatio fidelium*, an "assembly of the faithful." Source: *Reformed Confessions of the 16th Century*, ed. Arthur C. Cochrane (Philadelphia: Westminster Press, 1966), pp. 261–62, 263–66, 267–68. Date of original publication: 1566.

What Is the Church? The Church is an assembly of the faithful called or gathered out of the world; a communion, I say, of all saints, namely, of those who truly know and rightly worship and serve the true God in Christ the Savior, by the Word and Holy Spirit, and who by faith are partakers of all benefits which are freely offered through Christ. *Citizens of One Commonwealth.* They are all citizens of the one city, living under the same Lord, under the same laws, and in the same fellowship of all good things. For the apostle calls them "fellow citizens with the saints and members of the household of God" (Eph. 2:19), calling the faithful on earth saints (1 Cor. 1:2), who are sanctified by the blood of the Son of God. The article of the Creed, "I believe in the holy catholic Church, the communion of saints," is to be understood wholly as concerning these saints.

Only One Church for All Times. And since there is always but one God, and there is one mediator between God and men, Jesus the Messiah, and one shepherd of the whole flock, one head of this body, and, to conclude, one Spirit, one salvation, one faith, one Testament or covenant, it necessarily follows that there is only one Church. *The Catholic Church.* We, therefore, call this Church catholic because it is universal, scattered through all parts of the world, and extended unto all times, and is not limited to any times or places. Therefore, we condemn the Donatists who confined the Church to I know not what corners of Africa. Nor do we approve of the Roman clergy who have recently passed off only the Roman Church as Catholic.

Parts or Forms of the Church. The Church is divided into different parts or forms; not because it is divided or rent asunder in itself, but rather because it is distinguished by the diversity of the numbers that are in it. *Militant and Triumphant.* For the one is called the Church militant, the other the Church triumphant. The former still wages war on earth, and fights against the flesh, the world, and the prince of this world, the devil; against sin and death. But the latter, having been now discharged, triumphs in heaven immediately after having overcome all those things and rejoices before the Lord. Notwithstanding both have fellowship and union one with another. . . .

Christ the Sole Head of the Church. It is the head which has the preeminence in the body, and from it the whole body receives life; by its spirit the body is governed in all things; from it, also, the body receives increase, that it may grow up. Also, there is one head of the body, and it is suited to the body. Therefore the Church cannot have any other head besides Christ. For as the Church is a spiritual body, so it must have a spiritual head in harmony with itself. Neither can it be governed by any other spirit than by the Spirit of Christ. Wherefore Paul says: "He is the head of the body, the church; he is the beginning, the firstborn from the dead, that in everything he might be preeminent" (Col. 1:18). And in another place: "Christ is the head of the church, his body, and is himself its Savior" (Eph. 5:23). And again: he is "the head over all things for the church, which is his body, the fulness of him who fills all in all" (Eph. 1:22 f.). Also, "We are to grow up in every way into him who is the head, into Christ, from whom the whole body, joined and knit together, makes bodily growth" (Eph. 4:15 f.). And therefore we do not approve of the doctrine of the Roman clergy, who make their Pope at Rome the universal shepherd and supreme head of the Church militant here on earth, and so the very vicar of Jesus Christ, who has (as they say) all fullness of power and sovereign authority in the Church. *Christ the Only Pastor of the Church.* For we teach that Christ the Lord is, and remains the only universal pastor, and highest pontiff before God the Father; and that in the Church he himself performs all the duties of a bishop or pastor, even to the world's end; [*Vicar*] and therefore does not need a substitute for one who is absent. For Christ is present with his Church, and is its life-giving head. *No Primacy in the Church.* He has strictly forbidden his apostles and their successors to have any primacy and dominion in the Church. Who does not see, therefore, that whoever contradicts and opposes this plain truth is rather to be counted among the number of those whom Christ's apostles prophesied: Peter in 2 Peter, ch. 2, and Paul in Acts 20:2; 2 Cor. 11:2; 2 Thess., ch. 2, and also in other places?

No Disorder in the Church. However, by doing away with a Roman head we do not bring any confusion or disorder into the Church, since we teach that the government of the Church which the apostles handed down is sufficient to keep the Church in proper order. In the beginning when the Church was without any such Roman head as is now said to keep it in order, the Church was not disordered or in confusion. The Roman head does indeed preserve his tyranny and the corruption that has been brought into the Church, and meanwhile he hinders, resists, and with all the strength he can muster cuts off the proper reformation of the Church.

Dissensions and Strife in the Church. We are reproached because there have been manifold dissensions and strife in our churches since they separated themselves from the Church of Rome, and therefore cannot be true churches. As though there were never in the Church of Rome any sects, nor contentions and quarrels concerning religion, and indeed, carried on not so much in the schools as from pulpits in the midst of the people. We know, to be sure, that the apostle said: "God is not a God of confusion but of peace" (1 Cor. 14:33), and, "While there is jealousy and strife among you, are you not of the flesh?" Yet we cannot deny that God was in the apostolic Church and that it was a true Church, even though there were wranglings and dissensions in it. The apostle Paul reprehended Peter, an apostle (Gal. 2:11 ff.), and Barnabas dissented from Paul. Great contention arose in the Church of Antioch between them that preached the one Christ, as

Luke records in The Acts of the Apostles, ch. 15. And there have at all times been great contentions in the Church, and the most excellent teachers of the Church have differed among themselves about important matters without meanwhile the Church ceasing to be the Church because of these contentions. For thus it pleases God to use the dissensions that arise in the Church to the glory of his name, to illustrate the truth, and in order that those who are in the right might be manifest (1 Cor. 11:19).

Of the Notes or Signs of the True Church. Moreover, as we acknowledge no other head of the Church than Christ, so we do not acknowledge every church to be the true Church which vaunts herself to be such; but we teach that the true Church is that in which the signs or marks of the true Church are to be found, especially the lawful and sincere preaching of the Word of God as it was delivered to us in the books of the prophets and the apostles, which all lead us unto Christ, who said in the Gospel: "My sheep hear my voice, and I know them, and they follow me; and I give unto them eternal life. A stranger they do not follow, but they flee from him, for they do not know the voice of strangers" (John 10:5, 27, 28).

And those who are such in the Church have one faith and one spirit; and therefore they worship but one God, and him alone they worship in spirit and in truth, loving him alone with all their hearts and with all their strength, praying unto him alone through Jesus Christ, the only mediator and intercessor; and they do not seek righteousness and life outside Christ and faith in him. Because they acknowledge Christ the only head and foundation of the Church, and, resting on him, daily renew themselves by repentance, and patiently bear the cross laid upon them. Moreover, joined together with all the members of Christ by an unfeigned love, they show that they are Christ's disciples by persevering in the bond of peace and holy unity. At the same time they participate in the sacraments instituted by Christ, and delivered unto us by his apostles, using them in no other way than as they received them from the Lord. That saying of the apostle Paul is well known to all: "I received from the Lord what I also delivered to you" (1 Cor. 11:23 ff.). Accordingly, we condemn all such churches as strangers from the true Church of Christ, which are not such as we have heard they ought to be, no matter how much they brag of a succession of bishops, of unity, and of antiquity. Moreover, we have a charge from the apostles of Christ "to shun the worship of idols" (1 Cor. 10:14; 1 John 5:21), and "to come out of Babylon," and to have no fellowship with her, unless we want to be partakers with her of all God's plagues (Rev. 18:4; 2 Cor. 6:17).

Outside the Church of God There Is No Salvation. But we esteem fellowship with the true Church of Christ so highly that we deny that those can live before God who do not stand in fellowship with the true Church of God, but separate themselves from it. For as there was no salvation outside Noah's ark when the world perished in the flood; so we believe that there is no certain salvation outside Christ, who offers himself to be enjoyed by the elect in the Church; and hence we teach that those who wish to live ought not to be separated from the true Church of Christ.

The Church Is Not Bound to Its Signs. Nevertheless, by the signs [of the true church] mentioned above, we do not so narrowly restrict the Church as to teach that all those are outside the Church who either do not participate in the sacraments, at least not willingly and through contempt, but rather, being forced by necessity, unwillingly abstain from them or are deprived of them; or in whom faith sometimes fails, though it is not entirely extinguished and does not wholly cease; or in whom imperfections and errors due to weakness are found. For we know that God had some friends in the world outside the commonwealth of Israel. We know what befell the people of God in the captivity of Babylon, where they were deprived of their sacrifices for seventy years. We know what happened to St. Peter, who denied his master, and what is wont to happen daily to God's elect and faithful people who go astray and are weak. We know, moreover, what kind of churches the churches in Galatia and Corinth were in the apostles' time, in which the apostle found fault with many serious offenses; yet he calls them holy churches of Christ (1 Cor. 1:2, Gal. 1:2). . . .

The Unity of the Church Is Not in External Rites. Furthermore, we diligently teach that care is to be taken wherein the truth and unity of the Church chiefly lies, lest we rashly provoke and foster schisms in the Church. Unity consists not in outward rites and ceremonies, but rather in the truth and unity of the catholic faith. This catholic faith is not given to us by human laws, but by Holy Scriptures, of which the

246

Apostles' Creed is a compendium. And, therefore, we read in the ancient writers that there was a manifold diversity of rites, but that they were free, and no one ever thought that the unity of the Church was thereby dissolved. So we teach that the true harmony of the Church consists in doctrines and in the true and harmonious preaching of the Gospel of Christ, and in rites that have been expressly delivered by the Lord. And here we especially urge that saying of the apostle: "Let those of us who are perfect have this mind; and if in any thing you are otherwise minded, God will reveal that also to you. Nevertheless let us walk by the same rule according to what we have attained, and let us be of the same mind" (Phil. 3:15 f.).

4. SCHLEIERMACHER: THE FELLOWSHIP OF BELIEVERS

The first great post-Enlightenment ecclesiology attempts to show how and why the redemption accomplished in Jesus of Nazareth necessarily assumed a corporate form as its enduring historical embodiment. We offer here excerpts from the opening proposition in which Schleiermacher defines the church as "the fellowship of believers." In subsequent propositions, he locates the origin of the church in the "communication of the Holy Spirit," which he interprets nonsupernaturalistically. Source: Friedrich Schleiermacher, *The Christian Faith*, § 113, ed. H. R. Mackintosh and J. S. Stewart (Edinburgh: T. & T. Clark, 1928), pp. 525–28. Date of original publication: 1830.

All that comes to exist in the world through redemption
is embraced in the fellowship of believers, within which
all regenerate people are always found. This section,
therefore, contains the doctrine of the Christian
Church.

In reckoning the two expressions—the fellowship of believers and the Christian Church—as equivalent, our proposition seems to be in opposition to the Roman Symbol; but neither earlier versions of the latter nor the Nicene Creed know anything of using the two side by side yet with a distinction. What is evident is that fellowship may be taken in a narrower or a wider sense. For, if the regenerate find themselves already within it, they must have belonged to it even before regeneration, though obviously in a different sense from actual believers.

If this were not so, no accession to or extension of the Church could be imagined except by an absolute breach of continuity—that is, in a way unknown to history. But the truth is that the new life of each individual springs from that of the community, while the life of the community springs from no other individual life than that of the Redeemer. We must therefore hold that the totality of those who live in the state of sanctification is the inner fellowship; the totality of those on whom preparatory grace is at work is the outer fellowship, from which by regeneration members pass to the inner, and then keep helping to extend the wider circle. It would, however, be quite a novel and merely confusing use of terms to try to assign the two expressions in question respectively to the two forms of fellowship.

Further, no particular form of fellowship is here definitely asserted or excluded; every form, perfect and imperfect, that has ever been or that may yet appear, is included. This, and this only, is assumed, that wherever regenerate persons are within reach of each other, some kind of fellowship between them is bound to arise. For if they are in contact, their witness to the faith must in part overlap, and must necessarily involve mutual recognition and a common understanding as to their operation within the common area. What was stated at the beginning of our treatment of the consciousness of grace, namely, that it always proceeds from a common life, was meant exclusively in this far-reaching sense; but now that very statement finds for the first time its full explanation. For if, when regenerate, we did not find ourselves already within a common life, but had to set out to discover or constitute it, that would mean that just the most decisive of all the works of grace was not based on a life in common. . . .

The Christian self-consciousness expressed in our proposition is the general form, determined by our faith in Christ, taken by our fellow-feeling with human things and circumstances. This becomes all the clearer if we combine with it the corresponding negative expression. For if, leaving redemption out of account, the world is, relatively to humanity, the place of original perfection of men and things which yet has become the place of sin and evil; and if, with the appearance of Christ a new thing has entered the world, the antithesis of the old; it follows that only that part of the world which is united to the Christian Church is for us the place of attained perfection, or of the good, and

—relatively to quiescent self-consciousness—the place of blessedness. This is so, not in virtue of the original perfection of human nature and the natural order, though of course it is thus conditioned, but in virtue solely of the sinless perfection and blessedness which has come in with Christ and communicates itself through him. With this goes the converse; that the world, so far as it is outside this fellowship of Christ, is always, in spite of that original perfection, the place of evil and sin. No one, therefore, can be surprised to find at this point the proposition that salvation or blessedness cannot enter from without, but can be found within the Church only by being brought into existence there, the Church alone saves. For the rest, it is self-evident that the antithesis between what is realized in the world by redemption and all the rest of the world is acute in proportion to the completeness with which the peculiar dignity of Christ and the full content of redemption is apprehended. It disappears or loses itself in a vague distinction between better and worse only where the contrast between Christ and sinful man is similarly obliterated or toned down.

This, too, affords the best proof that our proposition is simply an utterance of the Christian self-consciousness. For if the Christian Church were in its essential nature an object of outward perception, that perception might be passed on without involving attachment to the fellowship. But the fact is that those who do not share our faith in Christ do not recognize the Christian fellowship in its antithesis to the world. Wherever the feeling of need of redemption is entirely suppressed, the Christian Church is misconstrued all round; and the two attitudes develop *pari passu*. With the first stirrings of preparatory grace in consciousness, there comes a presentiment of the divine origin of the Christian Church; and with a living faith in Christ awakens also a belief that the Kingdom of God is actually present in the fellowship of believers. On the other hand, an unalterable hostility to the Christian Church is symptomatic of the highest stage of insusceptibility to redemption; and this hostility hardly admits even of outward reverence for the person of Christ. But faith in the Christian Church as the Kingdom of God not only implies that it will ever endure in antithesis to the world, but also—the fellowship having grown to such dimensions out of small beginnings, and being inconceivable except as ever at work—contains the hope that the Church will increase and the world opposed to it decrease. For the incarnation of Christ means for human nature in general what regeneration is for the individual. And just as sanctification is the progressive domination of the various functions, coming with time to consist less and less of fragmentary details and more and more to be a whole, with all its parts integrally connected and lending mutual support, so too the fellowship organizes itself here also out of the separate redemptive activities and becomes more and more co-operative and interactive. This organization must increasingly overpower the unorganized mass to which it is opposed.

5. GUSTAFSON: THE CHURCH AS A HUMAN COMMUNITY

James Gustafson provides a good summary and reformulation of classic ecclesiological issues in the light of modern critical consciousness, interpreting the church as a human, historical, social community, yet seeking not to neglect its theological aspect as the redemptive action of God in history. Source: James M. Gustafson, *Treasure in Earthen Vessels: The Church as a Human Community* (New York: Harper & Brothers, 1961), pp. 100–102, 108–10.

The human studies have provided a framework in which to interpret not only the aspects of the life of the Church that it shares with all communities, but also its particularities and differentia. We have deliberately been as inclusive as possible in the social interpretation of the Church. In part this implies a critique of the theological reductionism that is characteristic of much of the contemporary interpretation of the Church, especially by professional theologians. By theological reductionism we mean the exclusive use of biblical and doctrinal language in the interpretation of the Church. Many make the explicit or tacit assumption that the Church is so absolutely unique in character that it can be understood only in its own private language. We have shown how the life of the Church can be understood in the language of social thought. Therefore questions arise. How can the same phenomenon, the Church, be understood from two radically diverse perspectives? Does the use of doctrinal language require inherently the exclusion of the language of social thought? Does a social interpretation of the Church necessarily exclude the more distinctively theological and doctrinal interpretation? If the two are not mutually exclusive, how can the significance of the social processes and elements be theologically understood? Since the center of our interpretation is social, the last question is most important for us.

The problem we have defined can be developed with reference to a particular aspect of the Church's life, namely, its existence as both a fellowship and an institution. The existence of both elements can be understood as social necessities on the one hand, or as God's ordering and gift on the other. The persisting institutional patterns of ministry, sacraments, and other forms of Church life are from a social point of view necessary developments in order to preserve the historical existence of the community, and particularly its special identity as a Christian community. From a theological point of view they can be understood as God's order for the Church. They have been instituted by God for the existence of his people; they are grounded in the New Testament account of what God has done for man. The fellowship of Christians in one spirit and mind can be understood in a double way as well. Socially it can be seen as a unity of common memory, loyalty, and meanings that are kept alive through the common life of the Church. Christians are united in the inner life of their common faith and commitment as well as by participation in the same institutions. Theologically this spiritual unity is interpreted as a gift of God in Jesus Christ. It is the unity of the body of which Christ is the head; it is the mark of the work of the Holy Spirit of God among his people.

The Church is both a fellowship and an institution. These two aspects of its life are necessary to each other and to the whole for the continuation of the Church and its social unity. We have seen how the objective expressions of the meanings of the Church (its institutional forms) are necessary to preserve the less institutionalized forms of common life and spirit. Its political structures, the Bible, the ministry, the sacraments, all make possible processes of life in which persons become identified with Jesus Christ, and with the common life of those who believe in him. The Bible is the most important objectification of the meaning of Jesus Christ and life in relation to him. Indeed, both the Old and New Testaments are expressions of the common life of a people who understand themselves and all events of history to be related to God. The Bible in its various types of literature carries in a relatively stable form the meanings that mark the Christian community in distinction from other human groups. It bears the possibility of those meanings becoming the center of life for individual persons, and remaining the center of life for the whole Church. It is not sufficient in and of itself, however, and therefore other institutional forms are necessary. The communication and interpretation of its meaning depend upon the existence of certain offices and rites. The ministry exists in part to make living and internal the meanings carried externally and objectively in the Bible. The Lord's Supper is a rite in which the significance of the death of Jesus Christ is remembered again. Liturgies as a whole carry out for each congregation and generation a pattern of meaning in which men can participate. . . .

A theological approach relates the life of the Church primarily to God; a social interpretation defines the processes and patterns with primary reference to their social function. The difference between them lies in *the understanding of that to which Church life is related,* or from which it has its source. . . .

The Christian understanding of the Church, then, breaks through the circle imposed by an exclusively social interpretation. It views human experience in the Church in the light of God's revelation and activity. The human agencies and processes whose function can be socially understood are mirrors in which God's presence is made known to man. They are God's creation, and a means of his redeeming work. . . . The affirmation that God acts in history means that in his power and good pleasure he chooses to use that which can be interpreted without reference to him as a means of ruling and making himself known. He uses the realm of the natural and the social as an agency or a mask for his presence and will toward men. The issue of causal relation is taken care of in the highly ambiguous language of God *acting in* history. . . . God uses human needs, for example, as a medium through which he gathers his people together, and through which his divine ministry becomes a ministry among men. Thus the commonplace, e.g., the American rural Protestant church supper, can be a human gathering and occasion through which God can act and speak. The patterns of political life in the churches can be the awesomely human social instruments through which God orders the common life of his people. They are the necessary instruments for the expression of this will and work in a given historical context. They are also the occasion for human pride and sin to take specific shape. The internalization processes are the human counterparts to the prior action of God's power and spirit, bringing men to a knowledge of Jesus Christ through the Church. Indeed, they may be the marks of the work of the Holy Spirit. The elements of faith and commitment are the human subjective counterparts to the divine initiative of grace. God initiates the covenant; God initiates personal faith. The actions characteristic of the Christian community are means of God's action, disclosing himself in worship, drawing men to himself in evangelism, and exercising his sovereignty in the world through the moral actions of men. The Bible testifies to this use of the human and the historical by God. . . . St. Paul says that we have our treasure in earthen vessels. . . .

Such an interpretation has a religious persuasiveness in spite of its ambiguities. It does not set the eternal over against the temporal, the abiding against the changing, the simple unity against the complex multiplicity. Rather it asserts that the one who is above history enters into history, and the eternal one is present in time. A social interpretation of the Church need not lead to religious uncertainty and despair. Christians can accept the human, social, and historical not merely in resignation to fate, but in the confidence that this realm is of significance to God and his activity. The problem of the believer, then, is not how to reconcile the social and historical character of the Church with a suprahistorical or even historical essence. This problem is avoided by not admitting its premise, namely, that a suprahistorical or essential nature of the Church is more real, purer, or of greater value than its changing social character. The issue is no longer the eternal absolute against the temporal relativity. Rather, Christians can affirm the historical community and participate in it in a clear and certain knowledge that its humanness is in the power of God. Precisely the natural community, the political community, the community of language, interpretation and understanding, the community of belief and action, is the Church, God's people.

6. PARIS: THE BLACK CHRISTIAN TRADITION

The social ethicist Peter Paris argues that the black church is nourished by an eschatological vision that funds its social and political struggles against the injustice of racism. As such it transcends the dichotomy

of the sacred and the secular, enabling an oppressed people both to survive and to resist. It is rooted in what Paris calls the "black Christian
tradition"—a nonracist appropriation of the Christian faith, which functions as a critical and prophetic principle within the black community
and beyond it. Source: Peter Paris, "The Social World of the Black
Church," *The Drew Gateway* 52/ 3 (Spring 1982): 1–2, 4–9.

Scholarly opinion on the relation of the black church to the American society can be classified in two ways: compensatory and political.
The former contends that black religion is basically an other-worldly
preoccupation seeking relief from the cruel realities of historical existence, while the latter views it as a dynamic agency for social change.
The one implies a passive disposition toward social injustice, while the
other infers an attitude of vigorous resistance.

Each of the above views is based on an inadequate understanding of
religion in general and of black American religion in particular. Every
religion is essentially related to history in two ways: a) to espouse a positive view of some distant future which serves as a lure for its adherents;
b) to exhibit the basic sociocultural forms and values relative to its
specific location. The former designates an eschatological vision of
the final end of humankind, while the latter expresses the nature and
meaning of historical experience. To deny either is to distort the nature of religion per se. Generalizations on the basis of one dimension
of religious experience at the expense of the other is the major error
implicit in both the compensatory and the political views of the black
churches.

Further, those who hold the compensatory position view the black
church as a pathological institution bent on leading its adherents away
from reality to some illusory, supra-historical ideal; hence, a repudiation of history. Correspondingly, those scholars who hold the political
view of the black churches see them as basically secular in nature since
they reduce religion to politics and deny thereby the reality of eternity
and of the sacred. . . .

The ensuing argument is rooted in the observation that the black
churches have always had a profound concern for the bitter and painful realities of black existence in America as well as for a bright and ra-
diant future (eschaton) free from any form of racial injustice. The
latter designates the locus of ultimate value where all people are in

harmony with the transcendent, holy and supreme God of the Judeo-Christian faith. Traditionally, the black churches have interpreted human life, including all of its suffering and pain, in accordance with that ultimate goal in which they have never lost faith. The convergence of that sacred principle with their efforts for improved temporal conditions reveals the integral relationship of religion and politics in the black churches. . . .

The growth of the black churches is both significant and inspirational. In its history lie the stories of countless men and women, often slaves and runaway slaves, frequently freed men of humble economic stature, completely lacking in social status. Under paralyzing conditions, both during and after slavery, a multiplicity of black churches emerged, some on the plantations, others in segregated quarters of urban centers, many along the back roads of southern and northern rural areas. In each case the black church was the primary community institution owned and controlled by blacks themselves.

Historically, the churches have performed the many and varied functions of governance within the black community. The importance of those functions cannot be overemphasized. Constrained in every dimension of their common life by the dehumanizing conditions of white racism, blacks made their churches agencies for teaching the race how to respond to racial hostility in creative and constructive ways. E. Franklin Frazier has described the internal activities of the black churches as forms of compensation for the denial of freedom in the larger society. He viewed the churches as crucial social institutions for the maintenance and enhancement of civility, self-respect, social order, and communal belonging (identity). This institution was broad and complex in both function and purpose. Frazier called this surrogate world, "a nation within a nation." . . .

C. Eric Lincoln's conclusions about the relation of the black church to the society are similar to [our] proposition offered above, namely, that the compensatory and social protest views belong together because the religious and the secular are integrally connected in the black churches. He argues that there has always been an integral relationship between the black churches and the black community. In fact, he claims that among black Americans there is no radical disjunction between the sacred and the secular spheres of human existence. The cleavage that characterizes so much of Protestantism simply does not exist. . . .

The black churches have a unique history in being the most important institutions embodying goals and purposes that pertain primarily to the welfare of black people. In America there have been no other enduring institutions with such purposes. Rather, white institutions have always aimed at the welfare of whites, even when they espoused causes that were seemingly focussed on the welfare of blacks. . . .

Further, the uniqueness of the black churches is seen in the fact that they are (as the literature constantly asserts) unequivocally "race institutions." . . . Racism and racial self-respect have been the two warring principles that caused the emergence of the black churches. While black churches have much in common with various churches of the economically underprivileged and socially impoverished, and while they minister to the peculiar needs of the race and strive for various forms of social amelioration, they cannot be understood completely by an appeal to social and economic forces. The churches of the lower classes tend (over time) to become middle class churches and thus become assimilated into the predominant values, customs, and practices of the so-called "mainline churches." That has not been the case with the black churches. Regardless of their socioeconomic class stratification, they never cease being black churches, victimized by racism, while, at the same time, embodying, nurturing, and promoting a radically different view of humanity which they consider to be theologically correct, biblically sound, and morally indisputable.

The tradition that has always been normative for both the black churches and the black community is not the so-called "Western Christian tradition" though that is an important source for it. More accurately, it is that tradition governed by the principle of nonracism, which we will call the "black Christian tradition."

Now, the terms "Western" and "black" designate two different but very significant modifications of Christianity. Each signifies a specifically different sociopolitical context in which the Christian religion has been appropriated and shaped. Since religious experience is always conditioned in important ways by its sociopolitical context, significant differences in the latter imply corresponding differences in the former.

The black Christian tradition became institutionalized in the independent black churches. Prior to their emergence, the desire and quest for freedom (together with their concomitant resistance to slavery and racism) had no enduring public form. The principle of freedom and equality of all persons under God is not an abstract idea but a normative condition of the black churches, wherein all can experience its reality. This institutionalization in the black churches gives it empirical status.

Out of the crucible of racial segregation, the black Christian tradition emerged as a nonracist appropriation of the Christian faith. As such, it represented the astounding transcendence of the human spirit over the conditions of racial oppression and their impact. But it also represented a principle of opposition to racism which radically challenged the latter in all spheres of its influence, social, religious, and moral. Thus, the black Christian tradition has been essentially prophetic, utilizing its powers to effect religious and moral reform in the society at large.

The black Christian tradition stands in opposition to the Western Christian tradition as represented in white American churches. It has always been the source of inspiration for black churches in their persistent attempts to reveal the fundamental depths of racism, i.e., that racial segregation and discrimination (not to mention slavery) are not merely social issues, but, rather, are rooted in a world view that is morally and religiously false. Accordingly, the black churches have revealed the self-contradictory nature of the race problem. Their basic source of authority has been that to which they have been unreservedly committed: a biblical anthropology that strongly affirms the equality of all persons under God regardless of race or any other natural quality. That doctrine has been the essence of the black Christian tradition and the most fundamental requirement of its churches. Its discovery soon revealed to blacks the basic contradiction implicit in the religion of white Americans. The contradiction between the biblical scriptures and the practices of the white churches has always been the strongest weapon the black churches have had in their struggle with their white counterparts. The black Christian tradition posited a fundamental moral and religious dilemma in the heart of white Christianity. The black church was born in opposition to that dilemma.

The moral and political significance of the black churches is derived from their common source of authority in the black Christian tradition. In that tradition the thought and practice of religion, politics, and morality are integrally related. The one always implies the other. Whenever they are isolated from one another the tradition itself is severely threatened. But, further, whenever individuals or groups betray the basic principles of that tradition, whether by direct assault or by some insidious compromise, the integrity of the entire black community is threatened, because the moral and political dimensions of the black Christian tradition are not only normative for the black churches but also the basic principle of meaning for the community at large. . . .

Thus, the moral and political character of the black churches is based on an authority that is not the controlled possession of the churches themselves. Rather, it transcends them as both lure and judge. In fact, the churches are either praised or blamed by the community at large in accordance with their faithfulness to that tradition. As we have observed, those that betray the tradition not only violate their own religious principle of authority but become vulnerable to the charge of forsaking the community's trust. Faithfulness to the principle of human equality under God and its implied opposition to racism determine the integrity of the churches and their relationship to the black community.

The black Christian tradition has been the lifeline of the black community. It alone has constituted the ground for their claims of humanity and, as such, has always placed blacks in opposition to the prevailing ethos of the larger American society. Apart from it, blacks would not have been able to survive the dehumanizing force of chattel slavery and its legacy of race oppression. As a creative and critical principle it has stimulated the interests and shaped the pursuits of countless artists, scholars, religionists, and reformers. Embodied in the communty's primary institutions, the churches, it has been the source of ultimate meaning for their varied social functions. The end of racism would surely imply the beginning of a new era for the tradition —an era in which the biblical understanding of humanity would continue to be proclaimed by the black church as normative for all people. But this proclamation would issue from a different vantage point. That is, the validity of the basic principle of the black Christian tradition would not be altered by the removal of the experiential condition of racism because blacks believe that the tradition itself is grounded in the eternal truth of God. Hence, it is no understatement to say that the thought and action of the black churches cannot be understood apart from this principle. It is to the black churches what the Protestant principle is to Protestantism: a prophetic principle of criticism. For the black churches every aspect of history must be related to it.

7. GUTIÉRREZ: SACRAMENT OF LIBERATION

The Peruvian priest Gustavo Gutiérrez starts with the new ecclesiology of the Second Vatican Council, but then broadens, deepens, and radicalizes it in unexpected directions, showing the profound significance for the Latin American situation of a theology that understands the church as the "sacrament" (the efficacious sign and manifestation) of God's salvific work construed as human-historical liberation. We are able to offer only a few selections from a book that has become a modern classic. Source: Gustavo Gutiérrez, A *Theology of Liberation: History, Politics and Salvation,* trans. Caridad Inda and John Eagleson (Maryknoll, N.Y.: Orbis Books, 1973; London: SCM Press, 1974), pp. 256–59, 260, 261, 267–69. Date of original publication: 1971.

The perspective we have indicated presupposes an "uncentering" of the Church, for the Church must cease considering itself as the exclusive place of salvation and orient itself towards a new and radical service of people. It also presupposes a new awareness that the action of Christ and his Spirit is the true hinge of the plan of salvation.

Indeed, the Church of the *first centuries* lived spontaneously in this way. Its minority status in society and the consequent pressure that the proximity of the non-Christian world exercised on it made it quite sensitive to the action of Christ beyond its frontiers, that is, to the totality of his redemptive work. This explains why, for example, the great Christian authors of that time affirmed without qualification the liberty of man in religious matters as a natural and human right and declared that the state is incompetent to intervene in this area. Because they had confidence in the possibility of salvation at work in every man, they saw liberty not so much as a risk of wandering from the path as the necessary condition for finding the path and arriving at a genuine encounter with the Lord.

The situation of the Christian community changed in *the fourth century.* Instead of being marginated and attacked, Christianity was now tolerated (Edict of Milan, 313 A.D.) and quickly became the religion of the Roman state (Decree of Thessalonica, 381 A.D.). The proclamation of the gospel message was then protected by the support of political authority, and the Christianization of the world of that time received a powerful impulse. This rapid advance of Christianity brought about a change in the manner of conceiving the relationship of mankind to salvation. It began to be thought that there were only two kinds of people: those who have accepted faith in Christ and those who have culpably rejected it. . . . The Church was regarded as the sole repository of religious truth. In a spontaneous and inevitable fashion there arose an ecclesiocentric perspective which centered more and more on the life and reflection of the Church—and continues to do so even up to the present time.

From that time on, therefore, there was a subtle displacement of religious liberty as "a human and natural right" of all men by "the liberty of the act of faith"; henceforth, the right of liberty in religious matters would be synonymous with the right not to be coerced by the forced imposition of the Christian faith. In a parallel fashion there occurred another important displacement: no longer was it a question of the "incompetence" of political power in religious matters; rather it was a question of the state's "tolerance"—which presupposed an "option" for the truth—toward religious error. The reason for these two displacements is the same: the position of strength of a Church which had begun to focus on itself, to ally itself with civil power, and to consider itself as the exclusive repository of salvific truth.

This condition of the Church began to change in the *modern period,* with the internal rupture of Christendom and the discovery of new peoples. But at the beginning of this period the ecclesiocentric perspective persisted, with a few exceptions. In the matter of religious liberty, which we have focused on here, it was the period of "religious tolerance": what Thomas Aquinas considered valid for the Jews was extended to the descendents of Christians who had "culpably" separated themselves from the Church. In the nineteenth century religious toleration gave rise to the by-product of the theory of the thesis and the hypothesis; this theory sought to respond to the ideas born in the French Revolution by giving a new impulse to the development of toleration.

But fundamentally the condition continued being the same: salvific truth could be found only in the Church. It is for this reason that "modern freedoms" endangered the eternal destiny of man.

The effects of the new historical situation in which the Church found itself began to be felt more strongly in the nineteenth century and even more so in recent decades. Vatican II did not hesitate to place itself in the line of a full affirmation of the universal will of salvation and to put an end to the anachronistic theological and pastoral consequences deduced from the ecclesiocentrism which we have already mentioned. This explains the change of attitude regarding religious liberty. The declaration dedicated to this subject tried to achieve a consensus by placing itself simply on the level of the dignity of the human person. But this position implies a change of position with regard to deep theological questions having to do with the role of the Church in the encounter between God and man.

We might speak here of a return to the posture of the Church in the first centuries. Without being inexact, however, this affirmation tends to schematize the process. There is never a pure and simple regression. The process which began in the fourth century was not simply an "accident." It was a long and laborious learning experience. And that experience forms part of the contemporary ecclesial consciousness; it is a factor which explains many phenomena today. It also cautions us against what might happen again. What was spontaneously and intuitively expressed in the first centuries must manifest itself today in a more reflective and critical fashion.

Thanks to the process which we have just reviewed, Vatican II was able to set forth the outlines of a new ecclesiological perspective. And it did this almost surprisingly by speaking of the Church as a *sacrament*. This is undoubtedly one of the most important and permanent contributions of the Council. The notion of sacrament enables us to think of the Church within the horizon of the salvific work and in terms radically different from those of the ecclesiocentric emphasis. The Council itself did not place itself totally in this line of thinking. Many of the texts still reveal the burden of a heavy heritage; they timidly point to a way out from this turning in of the Church on itself, without always accomplishing this. But what must be emphasized is that in the midst of the Council itself, over which hovered an ecclesiocentric perspective, new elements arose which allowed for a reflection which broke with this perspective and was more in accord with the real challenges to the Christian faith of today. . . .

To call the Church the "visible sacrament of this saving unity" (*Lumen gentium*, no. 9) is to define it in relation to the plan of salvation, whose fulfillment in history the Church reveals and signifies to men. A visible sign, the Church imparts to reality "union with God" and "the unity of all mankind" (*Lumen gentium*, no. 1). The Church can be understood only in relation to the reality which it announces to men. Its existence is not "for itself," but rather "for others." Its center is outside itself; it is in the work of Christ and his Spirit. It is constituted by the Spirit as "the universal sacrament of salvation" (*Lumen gentium*, no. 48); outside of the action of the Spirit which leads the universe and history towards its fullness in Christ, the Church is nothing. Even more, the Church does not authentically attain consciousness of itself except in the perception of this total presence of Christ and his Spirit in humanity. The mediation of the consciousness of the "other"—of the world in which this presence occurs—is the indispensable precondition of its own consciousness as community-sign. Any attempt to avoid this mediation can only lead the Church to a false perception of itself—to an ecclesiocentric consciousness. . . .

As a sacramental community, the Church should signify in its own internal structure the salvation whose fulfillment it announces. Its organization ought to serve this task. As a sign of the liberation of man and history, the Church itself in its concrete existence ought to be a place of liberation. A sign should be clear and understandable. If we conceive of the Church as a sacrament of the salvation of the world, then it has all the more obligation to manifest in its visible structures the message that it bears. Since the Church is not an end in itself, it finds its meaning in its capacity to signify the reality in function of which it exists. Outside of this reality the Church is nothing; because of it the Church is always provisional; and it is towards the fulfillment of this reality that the Church is oriented: this reality is the kingdom of God which has already begun in history. The break with an unjust social order and the search for new ecclesial structures—in which the most dynamic sectors of the Christian community are engaged—have their basis in this ecclesiological perspective. We are moving towards forms of presence and structure of the Church the radical newness of which can barely be discerned on the basis of our present experience. This trend, at its best and healthiest, is not a fad; nor is it due to professional nonconformists. Rather it has its roots in a profound fidelity to the Church as sacrament of the unity and salvation of mankind and in the conviction that its only support should be the Word which liberates. . . .

Within this framework the Latin American Church must make the prophetic *denunciation* of every dehumanizing situation, which is contrary to brotherhood, justice, and liberty. At the same time it must criticize every sacralization of oppressive structures to which the Church itself might have contributed. Its denunciation must be public, for its position in Latin American society is public. This denunciation may be one of the few voices—and at times the only one—which can be raised in the midst of a country submitted to repression. In this critical and creative confrontation of its faith with historical realities —a task whose roots must be in the hope in the future promised by God—the Church must go to the very causes of the situation and not be content with pointing out and attending to certain of its consequences. Indeed, one of the most subtle dangers threatening a "renewed" Church in Latin America is to allow itself to be assimilated into a society which seeks certain reforms without a comprehensive critique. It is the danger of becoming functional to the system all over again, only this time to a system which tries to modernize and to suppress the most outrageous injustices without effecting any deep changes. In Latin America this denunciation must represent a radical critique of the present order, which means that the Church must also criticize itself as an integral part of this order. This horizon will allow the Church to break out of its narrow enclosure of intraecclesial problems by placing these problems in their true context—the total society and the broad perspective of commitment in a world of revolutionary turmoil.

It has been pointed out, and rightly so, that this critical function of the Church runs the risk of remaining on a purely verbal and external level and that it should be backed up with clear actions and commitments. Prophetic denunciation can be made validly and truly only from within the heart of the struggle for a more human world. . . .

The denunciation, however, is achieved by confronting a given situation with the reality which is *announced*: the love of the Father which calls all men in Christ and through the action of the Spirit to union among themselves and communion with him. To announce the gospel is to proclaim that the love of God is present in the historical becoming of mankind. It is to make known that there is no human act which cannot in the last instance be defined in relation to Christ. To preach the good news is for the Church to be a sacrament of history, to fulfill its role as community—a sign of the convocation of all men by God. It is to announce the coming of the kingdom. The gospel message reveals, without any evasions, what is at the root of social injustice: the rupture of the brotherhood which is based on our sonship before the Father; the gospel reveals the fundamental alienation which lies below every other human alienation. In this way, evangelization is a powerful factor in personalization. Because of it men become aware of the profound meaning of their historical existence and live an active and creative hope in the fulfillment of the brotherhood that they seek with all their strength.

X. THE SACRAMENTS

1. CYRIL OF JERUSALEM: CHRISTIAN INITIATION

Cyril of Jerusalem's *Catechetical Lectures* provide us with unique insight into the baptismal rites of fourth-century Palestine. The last five lectures (the so-called mystagogical catechesis) were delivered to the newly baptized. Immediately before the excerpts printed here, Cyril describes how the candidates had assembled in the vestibule of the baptistry, and, facing west with outstretched hands, had renounced Satan and all his works. Then follow the stripping, anointing, and baptism proper; the sequence ended with a further anointing. It should be noted that both of baptism and of anointing it is said that the gift of the Holy Spirit is conveyed. Source: *St. Cyril of Jerusalem's Lectures on the Christian Sacraments,* ed. F. L. Cross, trans. R. W. Church (London: SPCK, 1951), pp. 59–67. The text of the translation has been slightly edited for purposes of stylistic consistency. Date of original composition: ca. 350.

I

Know ye not, that so many of us as were baptized into Jesus Christ, were baptized into his death? . . . For ye are not under the law, but under grace (Rom. 6:3, 14).

[You who have been renewed from oldness to newness, as soon as you entered the inner chamber, you] put off your garment; and this was an image of "putting off the old man with his deeds" (Col. 3:9). Having stripped yourselves, you were naked; in this also imitating Christ, who hung naked on the cross, and by his nakedness "spoiled principalities and powers, and openly triumphed over them on the tree" (Col. 2:15). For since the powers of the enemy made their lair in your members, you may no longer wear that old vestment; I do not at all mean this visible one, but that "old man, which is corrupt according to the deceitful lusts" (Eph. 4:22). May no soul which has once put him off, again put him on, but say with the spouse of Christ in the Song of Songs, "I have put off my coat, how shall I put it on?" (Cant. 5:3). O wondrous thing! You were naked in the sight of all, and were not ashamed; for truly you bore the likeness of the first-formed Adam, who was naked in the garden, and was not ashamed.

Then, when you were stripped, you were anointed with exorcized oil, from the very hairs of your head, to your feet, and were made partakers of the good olive-tree, Jesus Christ. For you were cut off from the wild olive-tree, and grafted into the good one, and were made to share the fatness of the true olive-tree. The exorcized oil therefore was a symbol of the participation of the fatness of Christ, the charm to drive away every trace of hostile influence. For as the breathing of the saints, and the invocation of the name of God, like fiercest flame, scorch and drive out evil spirits, so also this exorcized oil receives such virtue by the invocation of God and by prayer, as not only to burn and cleanse away the traces of sins, but also to chase away all the invisible powers of the evil one.

After these things, you were led to the holy pool of divine baptism, as Christ was carried from the cross to the sepulchre which is before our eyes. And each of you was asked whether he believed in the name of the Father, and of the Son, and of the Holy Spirit, and you made that saving confession, and descended three times into the water, and ascended again; here also covertly pointing by a figure at the three-days burial of Christ. For as our Savior passed three days and three nights in the heart of the earth, so you also in your first ascent out of the water, represented the first day of Christ in the earth, and by your descent, the night; for as he who is in the night, sees no more, but he who is in the day, remains in the light, so in descending, you saw nothing as in the night, but in ascending again, you were as in the day. And at the self-same moment, you died and were born; and that water of salvation was at once your grave and your mother. And what Solomon spoke of others will suit you also; for he said, "There is a time to bear and a time to die" (Eccles. 3:2); but to you, on the contrary, the time to die is also the time to be born; and one and the same season brings about both of these, and your birth went hand in hand with your death.

O strange and inconceivable thing! We did not really die, we were not really buried, we were not really crucified and raised again, but our imitation was but in a figure, while our salvation is in reality. Christ was actually crucified, and actually buried, and truly rose again; and all these things have been vouchsafed to us that we, by imitation communicating in his sufferings, might gain salvation in reality. O surpassing loving-kindness! Christ received the nails in his undefiled hands and feet, and endured anguish; while to me without suffering or toil, by the fellowship of his pain he vouchsafes salvation.

Let no one then suppose that baptism is merely the grace of remission of sins, or further, that of adoption; as John's baptism bestowed only the remission of sins. Nay we know full well, that as it purges our sins, and conveys to us the gift of the Holy Spirit, so also it is the counterpart of Christ's sufferings. For, for this cause Paul, just now read, cried aloud and says, "Know ye not that as many of us as were baptized into Christ Jesus, were baptized into his death? Therefore we are buried with him by baptism into death" (Rom. 6:3). These words he spoke to them who had settled with themselves that baptism ministers to us the remission of sins, and adoption, but not that further it has communion also in representation with Christ's true sufferings.

In order therefore that we may learn that whatsoever things Christ endured, he suffered them for us and our salvation, and that, in reality and not in appearance, we also are made partakers of his sufferings. Paul cried with all exactness of truth, "For if we have been planted together in the likeness of his death, we shall be also in the likeness of his resurrection" (Rom. 6:5). Well has he said, "planted together." For since the true vine was planted in this place, we also by partaking in the baptism of death, "have been planted together with him." And fix your mind with much attention on the words of the Apostle. He has not said, "For if we have been planted together in his death," but, "in the likeness of his death." For upon Christ death came in reality, for his soul was truly separated from his body, and his burial was true, for his holy body was wrapped in pure linen; and everything happened to him truly; but in your case only the likeness of death and sufferings, whereas of salvation, not the likeness, but the reality.

II

But ye have an unction from the Holy One, . . . that, when he shall appear, we may have confidence, and not be ashamed before him at his coming (1 John 2:20, 28).

Having been "baptized into Christ," and "put on Christ" (Gal. 3:27), you have been made conformable to the Son of God; for God having "predestinated us to the adoption of sons" (Eph. 1:5), made us "share the fashion of Christ's glorious body" (Phil. 3:21). Being therefore made "partakers of Christ" (Heb. 3:14), you are properly called Christs, and of you God said, "Touch not my Christs" (Ps. 105:15), or anointed. Now you were made Christs by receiving the emblem of the Holy Spirit; and all things were in a figure wrought in you, because you are figures of Christ. He also bathed himself in the river Jordan, and having imparted of the fragrance of his Godhead to the waters, he came up from them; and the Holy Spirit in substance lighted on him, like resting upon like. In the same manner to you also, after you had come up from the pool of the sacred streams, was given the unction, the emblem of that wherewith Christ was anointed; and this is the Holy Spirit of whom also the blessed Isaiah, in his prophecy respecting him, says in the person of the Lord, "The Spirit of the Lord is upon me, because he hath anointed me to preach glad tidings to the poor" (Isa. 61:1).

For Christ was not anointed by men with oil or material ointment, but the Father having appointed him to be the Savior of the whole world, anointed him with the Holy Spirit, as Peter says, "Jesus of Nazareth, whom God anointed with the Holy Spirit" (Acts 10:38). And David the prophet cried, saying, "Thy throne, O God, is for ever and ever; a sceptre of righteousness is the sceptre of thy kingdom; thou hast loved righteousness and hated iniquity; therefore God even thy God hath anointed thee with the oil of gladness above thy fellows" (Ps. 45:6–7). And as Christ was in truth crucified, and buried, and raised, and you in likeness are in baptism accounted worthy of being crucified, buried, and raised together with him, so is it with the unction also. As he was anointed with the spiritual oil of gladness, the Holy Spirit, who is so called, because he is the author of spiritual gladness, so you were anointed with ointment, having been made partakers and "fellows" of Christ.

But beware of supposing this to be plain ointment. For as the bread of the Eucharist, after the invocation of the Holy Spirit, is mere bread no longer, but the body of Christ, so also this holy ointment is no more simple ointment, nor (so to say) common, after the invocation, but the gift of Christ; and by the presence of his Godhead, it causes in us the Holy Spirit. It is symbolically applied to your forehead and your other senses; and while your body is anointed with visible ointment, your soul is sanctified by the Holy and life-giving Spirit.

And you were first anointed on your forehead, that you might be delivered from the shame, which the first man, when he had transgressed, bore about with him everywhere; and that "with open face ye might behold as in a glass the glory of the Lord" (2 Cor. 3:18). Then on your ears; that you might receive ears quick to hear the divine mysteries, of which Isaiah has said, "The Lord wakened mine ear to hear" (Isa. 50:4); and the Lord Jesus in the Gospel, "He that hath ears to hear let him hear" (Matt. 11:15). Then on your nostrils; that receiving the sacred ointment you may say, "We are to God a sweet savor of Christ, in them that are saved" (2 Cor. 2:15). Then on your breast; that having put on the breastplate of righteousness, you may stand against the wiles of the devil (Eph. 6:14). For as Christ after his baptism, and the descent of the Holy Spirit, went forth and vanquished the adversary, so likewise, having, after holy baptism and the mystical chrism, put on the whole armor of the Holy Spirit, do you stand against the power of the enemy, and vanquish it, saying, "I can do all things through Christ which strengtheneth me" (Phil. 4:13).

When you are counted worthy of this holy chrism, you are called Christians, verifying also the name by your new birth. For before you were vouchsafed this grace, you had properly no right to this title, but were advancing on your way towards being Christians.

Moreover, you should know that this chrism has its symbol in the old Scripture. For what time Moses imparted to his brother the command of God, and made him high priest, after bathing in water, he anointed him; and Aaron was called Christ or anointed, from the emblematical chrism. So also the high priest raising Solomon to the kingdom, anointed him after he had bathed in Gihon. To them, however, these things happened in a figure, but to you not in a figure, but in truth; because you were truly anointed by the Holy Spirit. Christ is the beginning of your salvation; he is truly the first fruit, and you the mass; but if the first fruit be holy, it is manifest that its holiness will pass to the mass also.

2. AMBROSE: THE EUCHARISTIC MIRACLE

Ambrose's treatise on the sacraments probably constitutes six lectures to the newly baptized. Though not strikingly original, it is of seminal importance for the eucharistic theology of the medieval period, especially in its clear expression of a miraculous change in the elements. The treatise, whose authenticity was once widely questioned but is now generally accepted, provides us with the earliest Latin text of the central part of the eucharistic prayer. Source: *St. Ambrose on the Sacraments and on the Mysteries*, ed. J. H. Strawley (London: SPCK, 1950), pp. 86–93. The text of the translation has been slightly edited for purposes of stylistic consistency. Date of original composition: ca. 391.

Who, then, is the author of the sacraments but the Lord Jesus? From heaven those sacraments came; for all counsel is from heaven. But it was truly a great and divine miracle that God "rained down manna" (Ex. 16:4) from heaven upon the people and the people ate without toiling.

You say perhaps, "My bread is of the usual kind." But that bread is bread before the words of the sacraments; when consecration has been added, from bread it becomes the flesh of Christ. Let us therefore prove this. How can that which is bread be the body of Christ? By consecration. But in what words and in whose language is the consecration? Those of the Lord Jesus. For all the other things which are said in the earlier parts of the service are said by the priest—praises are offered to God, prayer is asked for the people, for kings, and the rest; when it comes to the consecration of the venerable sacrament, the priest no longer uses his own language, but he uses the language of Christ. Therefore, the word of Christ consecrates this sacrament.

What is the word of Christ? That, to be sure, whereby all things are made. The Lord commanded, and the heaven was made; the Lord commanded, and the earth was made; the Lord commanded, and the seas were made; the Lord commanded, and every creature was produced. You see, therefore, how effective is the word of Christ. If, therefore, there is such power in the word of the Lord Jesus, that the things which were not began to be, how much more is it effective, that things previously existing should, without ceasing to exist, be changed into something else? The heaven was not, the sea was not, the earth was not; but hear David saying, "He spake, and they were made: he commanded, and they were created" (Ps. 33:9).

Therefore, that I may answer you, it was not the body of Christ before consecration; but after consecration, I tell you, it is now the body of Christ. "He spake," and it was made; "he commanded," and it was created. You yourself formerly existed, but you were an old creature; after you were consecrated, you began to be a new creature. Would you know how you are a new creature? "Everyone," it says, "in Christ is a new creature" (2 Cor. 5:17).

Hear, then, how the word of Christ is wont to change every creature, and changes, at will, the ordinances of nature. In what way? you ask. Hear; and, first of all, let us take an example from his generation. It is usual that a man is not generated save from a man and a woman and the use of marriage; but because the Lord willed it, because he chose this mystery, Christ was born of the Holy Spirit and the Virgin, that is, "the mediator between God and men, the man Christ Jesus" (1 Tim. 2:5). You see, then, that he was born contrary to the ordinances and course of nature; he was born as man from a virgin.

Hear another example. The people of the Jews were hard pressed by the Egyptians; they were shut in by the sea. At the divine command Moses touched the waters with his rod, and the wave divided, certainly not according to the use of its own nature, but according to the grace of the heavenly command. Hear another. The people thirsted, they came to the spring. The spring was bitter; holy Moses "cast wood" into the spring, and the spring which had been bitter was made sweet, that is, it changed the use of its nature, it received the sweetness of grace. Hear also a fourth example. "The axe head had fallen into the waters" (2 Kings 6:5); as iron it sank by its own use. Elisha "cast wood"; straightway "the iron rose," and "swam" upon the waters (2 Kings 6:6), certainly contrary to the use of iron, for the matter of iron is heavier than the element of water.

From all these examples, then, do you not understand how effectual is the heavenly word? If the heavenly word was effectual in the earthly spring, if it was effectual in other things, is it not effectual in the heavenly sacraments? Therefore you have learned that what was bread becomes the body of Christ, and that wine and water are put into the chalice, but become blood by the consecration of the heavenly word.

But perhaps you say, "I do not see the appearance of blood." But it has the likeness; for as you have taken "the likeness of the death" (Rom. 6:5), so also you drink the likeness of the precious blood, that there may be no shrinking from actual blood, and yet the price of redemption may effect its work. You have learned, therefore, that what you receive is the body of Christ.

Do you know that it is consecrated by heavenly words? Hear what the words are. The priest speaks. "Make for us," he says, "this oblation approved, ratified, reasonable, acceptable, seeing that it is the figure of the body and blood of our Lord Jesus Christ, who the day before he suffered 'took bread' in his holy hands, and 'looked up to heaven' to you, holy Father, almighty, everlasting God, and 'giving thanks, he blessed, brake,' and having broken, delivered it to his apostles and 'to his disciples, saying, take, and eat' ye all of this; for 'this is my body, which shall be broken for many.'

" 'Likewise also after supper,' the day before he suffered, he 'took the cup, looked up to heaven' to thee, holy Father, almighty, everlasting God, and 'giving thanks,' blessed it and delivered it to his apostles and to his disciples, 'saying, take, and drink ye all of this; for this is my blood'" (1 Cor. 11:23–26). Observe all those expressions. Those words are the Evangelists' up to "Take," whether the body or the blood. After that they are the words of Christ: "take, and drink ye all of this; for this is my blood." And observe them in detail.

"Who the day before he suffered," he says, "in his holy hands took bread." Before it is consecrated, it is bread, but when the words of Christ have been added, it is the body of Christ. Therefore hear him saying: "Take and eat ye all of it; for this is my body." And before the words of Christ it is a cup full of wine and water. When the words of Christ have operated, then and there it is made to be the blood of Christ which redeemed the people. Therefore, see in how many ways the word of Christ is mighty to change all things. There the Lord Jesus himself testifies to us that we receive his body and blood. Ought we to doubt of his trustworthiness and testimony?

Now come back with me to the point which I set out to prove. It is a great and awful thing that he rained manna on the Jews from heaven. But distinguish. What is greater, manna from heaven or the body of Christ? Certainly the body of Christ who is the maker of heaven. Then he who "ate manna died." Whosoever eats this body shall have remission of sins and "shall never die" (John 6:49).

Therefore when you receive, it is not superfluous that you say "Amen," already in spirit confessing that you receive the body of

Christ. The priest says to you, "The body of Christ." And you say, "Amen," that is, "True." What the tongue confesses let the heart hold fast.

But that you may know that this is a sacrament, it was prefigured beforehand. Then learn how great is the sacrament. See what he says: "As often as ye do this, so often will ye make a memorial of me until I come again" (1 Cor. 11:26).

And the priest says: "Therefore having in remembrance his most glorious passion and resurrection from the dead and ascension into heaven, we offer to thee this spotless offering, reasonable offering, unbloody offering, this holy bread and cup of eternal life: and we ask and pray that thou wouldst receive this oblation on thy altar on high by the hands of thy angels, as thou didst vouchsafe to receive the presents of thy righteous servant Abel, and the sacrifice of our patriarch Abraham, and that which the high priest Melchizedek offered to thee."

Therefore as often as you receive—what does the apostle say to you?—as often as we receive, "we show the Lord's death" (1 Cor. 11:26); if we show his death, we show remission of sins. If, as often as blood is poured forth, it is poured for remission of sins, I ought always to receive it, that my sins may always be forgiven me. I, who am always sinning, ought always to have a remedy.

3. LUTHER: BAPTISM AND FAITH

Luther's epoch-making treatise, *The Babylonian Captivity of the Church*, clarifies the impact which the doctrine of justification had upon medieval sacramental theology. Against the scholastics he argues that sin persists after baptism, and the treatise is remarkable for its depiction of the whole Christian life as a baptismal dying and rising again. Infant baptism is justified on the basis of the faith of the child's sponsors. Source: *Luther's Works*, Vol. 36, *Word and Sacrament II*, ed. A. B. Wentz (Philadelphia: Fortress Press, 1959), pp. 58–74. Date of original composition: 1520.

Now, the first thing to be considered about baptism is the divine promise, which says "He who believes and is baptized will be saved" (Mark 16:16). This promise must be set far above all the glitter of works, vows, religious orders, and whatever else man has introduced, for on it all our salvation depends. But we must so consider it as to exercise our faith in it, and have no doubt whatever that, once we have been baptized, we are saved. For unless faith is present or is conferred in baptism, baptism will profit us nothing; indeed, it will become a hindrance to us, not only at the moment when it is received, but throughout the rest of our lives. That kind of unbelief accuses God's promise of being a lie, and this is the greatest of all sins. If we set ourselves to this exercise of faith, we shall at once perceive how difficult it is to believe this promise of God. For our human weakness, conscious of its sins, finds nothing more difficult to believe than that it is saved or will be saved, and yet, unless it does believe this, it cannot be saved, because it does not believe the truth of God that promises salvation.

This message should have been impressed upon the people untiringly, and this promise should have been dinned into their ears without ceasing. Their baptism should have been called to their minds again and again, and their faith constantly awakened and nourished. For just as the truth of this divine promise, once pronounced over us, continues until death, so our faith in it ought never to cease, but to be nourished and strengthened until death by the continual remembrance of this promise made to us in baptism. . . .

The children of Israel, whenever they turned to repentance, remembered above all their exodus from Egypt, and remembering turned back to God who had brought them out. Moses impressed this memory and this protection upon them many times, and David afterwards did the same. How much more ought we to remember our exodus from Egypt, and by this remembrance turn back to him who led us through the washing of regeneration (Titus 3:5), remembrance of which is commended to us for this very reason! This can be done most fittingly if the sacraments—penance, baptism, and the bread—were all celebrated at the same service, and each one supplemented the other. . . .

All the sacraments were instituted to nourish faith. Yet these godless men pass over it so completely as even to assert that a man dare not be certain of the forgiveness of sins or the grace of the sacraments. With such wicked teaching they deluded the world, and not only take captive, but altogether destroy, the sacrament of baptism, in which the chief glory of our conscience consists. Meanwhile they madly rage against the miserable souls of men with their contritions, anxious confessions, circumstances, satisfactions, works, and endless other such absurdities. Therefore read with great caution the "Master of the Sentences" in his fourth book; better yet, despise him with all his commentators, who at their best write only of the "matter" and "form" of the sacraments; that is, they treat of the dead and death-dealing letter (II Cor. 3:6) of the sacraments, but leave untouched the spirit, life, and use, that is, the truth of the divine promise and our faith.

Beware, therefore, that the external pomp of works and the deceits of man-made ordinances do not deceive you, lest you wrong the divine truth and your faith. If you would be saved, you must begin with the faith of the sacraments, without any works whatever. The works will follow faith, but do not think too lightly of faith, for it is the most excellent and difficult of all works. Through it alone you will be saved, even if you should be compelled to do without any other works. For faith is a work of God, not of man, as Paul teaches (Eph. 2:8). The other works he works through us and with our help, but this one alone he works in us and without our help.

From this we can clearly see the difference in baptism between man who administers the sacrament and God who is its author. For man baptizes, and yet does not baptize. He baptizes in that he performs the work of immersing the person to be baptized; he does not baptize, because in so doing he acts not on his own authority but in God's stead. . . .

This will put an end to that idle dispute about the "form" of baptism, as they term the words which are used. The Greeks say: "May the servant of Christ be baptized," while the Latins say: "I baptize." Others again, adhering rigidly to their pedantry, condemn the use of the words, "I baptize you in the name of Jesus Christ," although it is certain the apostles used this formula in baptizing, as we read in the Acts of the Apostles (2:38; 10:48; 19:5); they would allow no other form to be valid than this: "I baptize you in the name of the Father, and of the Son, and of the Holy Spirit. Amen." But their contention is in vain, for they bring no proof, but merely assert their own dreams. Baptism truly saves in whatever way it is administered, if only it is administered not in the name of man, but in the name of the Lord. Indeed, I have no doubt that if anyone receives baptism in the name of the Lord, even if the wicked minister should not give it in the name of the Lord, he would yet be truly baptized in the name of the Lord. For the power of baptism depends not so much on the faith or use of the one who confers it as on the faith or use of the one who receives it. . . .

The second part of baptism is the sign, or sacrament, which is that immersion in water from which it derives its name, for the Greek *baptizo* means "I immerse," and *baptisma* means "immersion." For, as has been said, along with the divine promises signs have also been given to picture that which the words signify, or as they now say, that which the sacrament "effectively signifies." We shall see how much truth there is in this.

A great majority have supposed that there is some hidden spiritual power in the sacraments, but that grace is given by God alone, who according to his covenant is present in the sacraments which he has instituted. Yet all are agreed that the sacraments are "effective signs" of grace, and they reach this conclusion by this one argument: if the sacraments of the New Law were mere signs, there would be no apparent reason why they should surpass those of the Old Law. Hence they have been driven to attribute such great powers to the sacraments of the New Law that they think the sacraments benefit even those who are in mortal sin; neither faith nor grace are required—it is sufficient that no obstacle be set in the way, that is, no actual intention to sin again.

Such views, however, must be carefully avoided and shunned, because they are godless and infidel, contrary to faith and inconsistent with the nature of the sacraments. For it is an error to hold that the sacraments of the New Law differ from those of the Old Law in the effectiveness of their signs. For in this respect they are the same. The same God who now saves us by baptism and the bread, saved Abel by his sacrifice, Noah by the rainbow, Abraham by circumcision, and all the others by their respective signs. So far as the signs are concerned, there is no difference between a sacrament of the Old Law and one of the New, provided that by the Old Law you mean that which God did among the patriarchs and other fathers in the days of the Law. But those signs which were given to the patriarchs and fathers must be clearly distinguished from the legal symbols [*figurae*] which Moses instituted in his law, such as the priestly usages concerning vestments, vessels, foods, houses, and the like. . . .

The difference, then, between the legal symbols and the new and old signs is that the legal symbols do not have attached to them any word of promise requiring faith. Hence they are not signs of justification, for they are not sacraments of the faith that alone justifies, but only sacraments of works. Their whole power and nature consisted in works, not in faith. Whoever performed them fulfilled them, even if he did it without faith. But our signs or sacraments, as well as those of the fathers, have attached to them a word of promise which requires faith, and they cannot be fulfilled by any other work. Hence they are signs or sacraments of justification, for they are sacraments of justifying faith and not of works. Their whole efficacy, therefore, consists in faith itself, not in the doing of a work. Whoever believes them, fulfills them, even if he should not do a single work. . . .

Baptism, then, signifies two things—death and resurrection, that is, full and complete justification. When the minister immerses the child in the water it signifies death, and when he draws it forth again it signifies life. Thus Paul expounds it in Rom. 6:4, "We were buried therefore with Christ by baptism into death, so that as Christ was raised from the dead by the glory of the Father, we too might walk in newness of life." This death and resurrection we call the new creation, regeneration, and spiritual birth. This should not be understood only allegorically as the death of sin and the life of grace, as many understand it, but as actual death and resurrection. For baptism is not a false sign. Neither does sin completely die, nor grace completely rise, until the sinful body that we carry about in this life is destroyed, as the Apostle says in the same passage (Rom. 6:6–7). For as long as we are in the flesh, the desires of the flesh stir and are stirred. For this reason, as soon as we begin to believe, we also begin to die to this world and live to God in the life to come; so that faith is truly a death and a resurrection, that is, it is that spiritual baptism into which we are submerged and from which we rise.

It is therefore indeed correct to say that baptism is a washing away of sins, but the expression is too mild and weak to bring out the full significance of baptism, which is rather a symbol of death and resurrection. . . . For as long as we live we are continually doing that which baptism signifies, that is, we die and rise again. We die, not only mentally and spiritually by renouncing the sins and vanities of this world, but in very truth we begin to leave this bodily life and to lay hold on the life to come, so that there is, as they say, a "real" and bodily passing out of this world unto the Father.

We must therefore beware of those who have reduced the power of baptism to such small and slender dimensions that, while they say grace is indeed inpoured by it, they maintain that afterwards it is poured out again through sin, and that then one must reach heaven by another way, as if baptism had now become entirely useless. Do not hold such a view, but understand that this is the significance of baptism, that through it you die and live again. . . . Baptism swallowed up your whole body and gave it forth again; in the same way that which baptism signifies should swallow up your whole life, body and soul, and give it forth again at the last day, clad in the robe of glory and immortality.

In contradiction to what has been said, some might cite the baptism of infants who do not comprehend the promise of God and cannot have the faith of baptism; so that therefore either faith is not necessary or else infant baptism is without effect. Here I say what all say: Infants are aided by the faith of others, namely, those who bring them for baptism. For the Word of God is powerful enough, when uttered, to change even a godless heart, which is no less unresponsive and helpless than any infant. So through the prayer of the believing church which presents it, a prayer to which all things are possible (Mark 9:23), the infant is changed, cleansed, and renewed by inpoured faith. Nor should I doubt that even a godless adult could be changed, in any of the sacraments, if the same church prayed for and presented him, as we read of the paralytic in the Gospel, who was healed through the faith of others (Mark 2:3–12). I should be ready to admit that in this sense the sacraments of the New Law are efficacious in conferring grace, not only to those who do not, but even to those who do most obstinately present an obstacle. What obstacle cannot be removed by the faith of the church and the prayer of faith? Do we not believe that Stephen converted Paul the Apostle by this power? (Acts 7:58—8:1). But then the sacraments do what they do not by their own power, but by the power of faith, without which they do nothing at all, as I have said.

4. KANT: SACRAMENTS AND THE MORAL COMMUNITY

Towards the end of his remarkably productive philosophical career, Immanuel Kant found himself embroiled in theological controversy and under threat of official censorship. Written against this background, *Religion within the Limits of Reason Alone* is his most sustained attempt to construe Christian teaching from the standpoint of rational philosophical ethics. His greatest difficulty lies with the problem of divine forgiveness, which is in severe tension with his account of absolute freedom, the individual's self-making by means of his or her own moral actions. This leads Kant to challenge the intelligibility of the very concept, "means of grace," as a fruitful source of self-deception. Source: Immanuel Kant, *Religion within the Limits of Reason Alone*, trans. Theodore M. Greene and Hoyt H. Hudson (New York: Harper & Row, 1960), pp. 180–90. Date of original publication: 1793.

The true (moral) service of God, which the faithful must render as subjects belonging to his kingdom but no less as citizens thereof (under laws of freedom), is itself, indeed, like the kingdom, invisible, *i.e.*, *a service of the heart* (in spirit and in truth). It can consist solely in the disposition of obedience to all true duties as divine commands, not in actions directed exclusively to God. Yet for man the invisible needs to be represented through the visible (the sensuous); yea, what is more, it needs to be accompanied by the visible in the interest of practicability and, though it is intellectual, must be made, as it were (according to a certain analogy), perceptual. This is a means of simply picturing to ourselves our duty in the service of God, a means which, although really indispensable, is extremely liable to the danger of misconstruction; for, through an *illusion* that steals over us, it is easily held to be the *service of God* itself, and is, indeed, commonly thus spoken of.

This alleged service of God, when brought back to its spirit and its true meaning, namely, to a disposition dedicating itself to the kingdom of God within us and without us, can be divided, even by reason, into four observances of duty; and certain corresponding rites, which do not stand in a necessary relation to these observances, have yet been associated with them, because the rites are deemed to serve as schemata for the duties and thus, for ages past, have been regarded as useful means

279

for sensuously awakening and sustaining our attention to the true service of God. They base themselves, one and all, upon the intention to further the morally good and are: (1) (private prayer)—firmly to establish this goodness *in ourselves*, and repeatedly to awaken the disposition of goodness in the heart; (2) (church-going)—the *spreading abroad* of goodness through public assembly on days legally dedicated thereto, in order that religious doctrines and wishes (together with corresponding dispositions) may be expressed there and thus be generally shared; (3) (in the Christian religion, baptism)—the *propagation* of goodness in posterity through the reception of newly entering members into the fellowship of faith, as a duty; also their instruction in such goodness; (4) (communion)—the *maintenance of this fellowship* through a repeated public formality which makes enduring the union of these members into an ethical body and this, indeed, according to the principle of the mutual equality of their rights and joint participation in all the fruits of moral goodness. . . . [Kant treats of (1) private prayer and (2) church going.]

3. The ceremonial *initiation*, taking place but once, into the church-community, that is, one's first acceptance *as a member of a church* (in the Christian church through *baptism*) is a highly significant ceremony which lays a grave obligation either upon the initiate, if he is in a position himself to confess his faith, or upon the witnesses who pledge themselves to take care of his education in this faith. This aims at something holy (the development of a man into a citizen in a divine state) but this act performed by others is not in itself holy or productive of holiness and receptivity for the divine grace in this individual; hence it is no *means of grace*, however exaggerated the esteem in which it was held in the early Greek church, where it was believed capable, in an instant, of washing away all sins—and here this illusion publicly revealed its affinity to an almost more than heathenish superstition.

4. The oft-repeated ceremony (*communion*) of a *renewal, continuation, and propagation of this churchly community* under laws of *equality*, a ceremony which indeed can be performed, after the example of the founder of such a church (and, at the same time, in memory of him), through the formality of a common partaking at the same table,

280

contains within itself something great, expanding the narrow, selfish, and unsociable cast of mind among men, especially in matters of religion, toward the idea of a cosmopolitan *moral community*; and it is a good means of enlivening a community to the moral disposition of brotherly love which it represents. But to assert that God has attached special favors to the celebration of this solemnity, and to incorporate among the articles of faith the proposition that this ceremony, which is after all but a churchly act, is, in addition, a *means of grace*—this is a religious illusion which can do naught but work counter to the spirit of religion. *Clericalism* in general would therefore be the dominion of the clergy over men's hearts, usurped by dint of arrogating to themselves the prestige attached to exclusive possession of means of grace.

All such artificial self-deceptions in religious matters have a common basis. Among the three divine moral attributes, holiness, mercy, and justice, man habitually turns directly to the second in order thus to avoid the forbidding condition of conforming to the requirements of the first. It is tedious to be a good *servant* (here one is forever hearing only about one's duties); man would therefore rather be a *favorite*, where much is overlooked or else, when duty has been too grossly violated, everything is atoned for through the agency of some one or other favored in the highest degree—man, meanwhile, remaining the servile knave he ever was. But in order to satisfy himself, with some color of truth, concerning the feasibility of this intention of his, he has the habit of transferring his concept of a man (including his faults) to the Godhead; and just as, even in the best *ruler of our race*, legislative rigor, beneficent grace, and scrupulous justice do not (as they should) operate separately, each by itself, to produce a moral effect upon the actions of the subject, but *mingle* with one another in the thinking of the human ruler when he is making his decisions, so that one need only seek to circumvent one of these attributes, the fallible wisdom of the human will, in order to determine the other two to compliance; even so does man hope to accomplish the same thing with God by applying himself solely to his *grace*. . . .

To this end man busies himself with every conceivable formality, designed to indicate how greatly he *respects* the divine commands, in order that it may not be necessary for him to *obey* them; and, that his idle wishes may serve also to make good the disobedience of these commands, he cries: "Lord, Lord," so as not to have to "do the will of his heavenly Father" (Matt. 7:21). Thus he comes to conceive of the ceremonies, wherein certain means are used to quicken truly practical dispositions, as in themselves means of grace; he even proclaims the belief, that they are such, to be itself an essential part of religion (the common man actually regards it as the whole of religion); and he leaves it to all-gracious Providence to make a better man of him, while he busies himself with *piety* (a passive respect for the law of God) rather than with *virtue* (the application of one's own powers in discharging the duty which one respects)—and, after all, it is only the latter, *combined with the former*, that can give us the idea which one intends by the word *godliness* (true *religious disposition*).

When the illusion of this supposed favorite of heaven mounts to the point where he fanatically imagines that he feels special works of grace within himself (or even where he actually presumes to be confident of a fancied occult *intercourse* with God), virtue comes at last actually to arouse his loathing, and becomes for him an object of contempt. Hence it is no wonder that the complaint is made publicly, that religion still contributes so little to men's improvement, and that the inner light ("under a bushel," Matt. 5:15) of these favored ones does not shine forth outwardly in good works also, yea, (as, in view of their pretensions, one could rightly demand) *preeminently*, above other men of native honesty who, in brief, take religion unto themselves not as a substitute for, but as a furtherance of, the virtuous disposition which shows itself through actions, in a good course of life. Yet the teacher of the Gospel has himself put into our hands these external evidences of outer experience as a touchstone, [by telling us that] we can know men by their fruits and that every man can know himself. But thus far we do not see that those who, in their own opinion, are extraordinarily favored (the chosen ones) surpass in the very least the naturally honest man, who can be relied upon in social intercourse, in business, or in trouble; on the contrary, taken as a whole, the chosen ones can scarcely abide comparison with him, which proves that the right course is not to go from grace to virtue but rather to progress from virtue to pardoning grace.

5. SCHMEMANN: CHRIST OUR EUCHARIST

Alexander Schmemann, a leading Russian Orthodox theologian, played a crucial role in interpreting Eastern Orthodox liturgy to the West from 1960 onward. The volume from which the following extracts are reproduced circulated originally as a study guide for a conference of the World Christian Student Federation. His work shows the influence of exposure to the liturgical movement, and also knowledge of Roman Catholic–Protestant controversy on the Eucharist. The basic thought which is developed is that the eucharistic sacrament is not a specialized cult performed by the community, or by such as are aesthetically and liturgically minded, but is the natural activity by which the church is constituted as the church. Schmemann's exposition follows the order of the orthodox Eucharist, which had in its essentials reached its present structure by the ninth century. Source: Alexander Schmemann, *The World as Sacrament* (London: Darton, Longman & Todd, 1966), pp. 29–55.

The liturgy of the Eucharist is best understood as a journey or procession. It is the journey of the Church into the dimension of the kingdom. We use this word "dimension" because it seems the best way to indicate the manner of our sacramental entrance into the risen life of Christ. . . .

The early Christians realized that in order to become the temple of the Holy Spirit, they must *ascend to heaven* where Christ has ascended. They realized also that this ascension was the very condition of their mission in the world, of their ministry to the world. For there —in heaven—they were immersed in the new life of the Kingdom; and when after this "liturgy of ascension," they returned into the world, their faces reflected the light, the "joy and peace" of that Kingdom and they were truly its witnesses. . . .

The Orthodox liturgy begins with the solemn doxology: "Blessed is the Kingdom of the Father, the Son and the Holy Spirit, now and ever, and unto ages on ages." From the beginning the destination is announced: the journey is to the Kingdom. This is where we are going—and not symbolically, but really. In the language of the Bible, which is *the* language of the Church, to bless the Kingdom is not simply to acclaim it. It is to declare it to be the goal, the end of all our desires and interests, of our whole life, the supreme and ultimate value of all that exists. To bless is to accept in love, and to move towards what is loved and accepted. The Church thus is the assembly, the gathering of those to whom the ultimate destination of all life has been revealed and who have accepted it. . . .

The next act of the liturgy is the *entrance:* the coming of the celebrant to the altar. It has been given all possible symbolical explanations, but it is not a "symbol." It is the very movement of the Church as *passage* from the old into the new, from "this world" into the "world to come" and, as such, it is the essential movement of the liturgical "journey." In "this world" there is no altar and the temple has been destroyed. For the only altar is Christ himself, his humanity—which he has assumed and deified and made the temple of God, the altar of his presence. And Christ has ascended into heaven. The altar, thus, is the sign that in Christ we have been given access to heaven, that the Church is the "passage" to heaven, the *entrance* into the heavenly sanctuary, and that only by "entering," by ascending to heaven does the Church fulfill itself, become what it is. And so, the *entrance* at the Eucharist, this approach of the celebrant—and in him, of the whole Church—to the altar is not a symbol. It is the crucial and decisive act in which the true dimensions of the sacrament are revealed and established. It is not "grace" that comes down; it is the Church that enters into "grace," and grace means the new being, the Kingdom, the world to come. And as the celebrant approaches the altar, the Church intones the hymn which the angels eternally sing at the throne of God: Holy God, Holy Mighty, Holy Immortal. . . .

Now, for the first time since the eucharistic journey began, the celebrant turns back and faces the people. Up to this moment he was the one who led the Church in its ascension, but now the movement has reached its goal. And the priest whose liturgy, whose unique function and obedience in the Church is to re-present, to make present the priesthood of Christ himself, says to the people: "Peace be with you." . . .

It is within this peace—"which passeth all understanding"—that now begins the liturgy of the Word. Western Christians are so accustomed to distinguishing the Word from the sacrament that it may be difficult for them to understand that in the Orthodox perspective the liturgy of the Word is as sacramental as the sacrament is "evangelical."

The sacrament is a manifestation of the Word. And unless the false dichotomy between Word and sacrament is overcome, the true meaning of both Word and sacrament, and especially the true meaning of Christian "sacramentalism" cannot be grasped in all their wonderful implications. The proclamation of the Word is a sacramental act par excellence because it is a transforming act. It transforms the human words of the Gospel into the Word of God and the manifestation of the Kingdom. And it transforms the man who hears the Word into a receptacle of the Word and a temple of the Spirit. . . . .

Bread and wine: to understand their initial and eternal meaning in the Eucharist, we must forget for a time the endless controversies which little by little transformed them into "elements" of an almost abstract theological speculation. It is indeed one of the main defects of sacramental theology that instead of following the order of the eucharistic journey with its progressive revelation of meaning, theologians applied to the Eucharist a set of abstract questions in order to squeeze it into their own intellectual framework. In this approach what virtually disappeared from the sphere of theological interest and investigation was liturgy itself and what remained were isolated "moments," "formulas" and "conditions of validity." What disappeared was the Eucharist as one organic, all-embracing and all-transforming act of the whole Church and what remained were: "essential" and "nonessential" parts, "elements," "consecration," etc. Thus, for example, to explain and define the meaning of the Eucharist the way certain theology does it, there is no need for the word "eucharist"; it becomes irrelevant. And yet for the early Fathers it was the key word giving unity and meaning to all the "elements" of the liturgy. The Fathers called "eucharist" the bread and wine of the offering, and their offering and consecration, and finally, communion. All this was *Eucharist* and all this could be understood only within the Eucharist.

As we proceed further in the eucharistic liturgy, the time has come now to offer to God the totality of all our lives, of ourselves, of the world in which we live. This is the first meaning of our bringing to the altar the elements of our food. For we already know that food is life, that it is the very principle of life and that the whole world has been created as food for man. We also know that to offer this food, this world, this life to God is the initial "eucharistic" function of man, his very fulfilment as man. We know that we were created as *celebrants* of the sacrament of life, of its transformation into life in God, communion with God. We know that real life is "eucharist," a movement of love and adoration towards God, the movement in which alone the meaning and the value of all that exists can be revealed and fulfilled. We know that we have lost this eucharistic life and, finally, we know that in Christ, the new Adam, the perfect man, this eucharistic life was restored to man. For he himself was the perfect Eucharist; he offered himself in total obedience, love and thanksgiving to God. God was his very life. And he gave this perfect and eucharistic life to us. In him God became our life.

And thus this offering to God of bread and wine, of the food that we must eat in order to live, is our offering to him of ourselves, of our life and of the whole world. . . . But we do it *in Christ* and in *remembrance of him*. We do it in Christ because he has already offered all that is to be offered to God. He has performed once and for all this Eucharist and nothing has been left unoffered. In him was *life*—and this life of all of us, he gave to God. The Church is all those who have been accepted into the eucharistic life of Christ. And we do it in *remembrance of him* because, as we offer again and again our life and our world to God, we discover each time that there is nothing else to be offered but Christ himself—the life of the world, the fullness of all that exists. . . .

"Let us lift up our hearts," says the celebrant, and the people answer: "We have lifted them up to the Lord." The Eucharist is an *anaphora*, the "lifting up" of our offering, and, of ourselves. . . . The Eucharist has so often been explained with reference to the gifts alone: What "happens" to bread and wine, and why, and when does it happen? But we must understand that what "happens" to bread and wine, happens *because* something has, first of all, happened to us, to the Church. It is because we have "constituted" the Church, and this means we have followed Christ in his ascension; because he has accepted us at his table in his Kingdom; because, in terms of theology, we have entered the eschaton, and are now standing beyond time and space; it is because all this has first happened to us that something will happen to bread and wine. . . . This beginning of eucharistic prayer is usually termed the "Preface." And although this preface belongs to all known eucharistic rites, not much attention was given to it in the development of eucharistic theology. A "preface" is something that does not really belong to the body of a book. And theologians neglected it because they were anxious to come to the real "problems": those of consecration, the change of the elements, sacrifice, and other matters. It is here that we find the main "defect" of Christian theology; the theology of the Eucharist ceased to be eucharistic and thus took away the eucharistic spirit from the whole understanding of sacrament, from the very life of the Church. The long controversy about the words of institution and the invocation of the Holy Spirit (*epiclesis*) that went on for centuries between the East and the West is a very good example of this "noneucharistic" stage in the history of sacramental theology.

But we must understand that it is precisely this *preface*—this act, these words, this movement of thanksgiving—that really "makes possible" all that follows. . . . It is indeed the *preface* to the world to come, the door into the Kingdom: and this we confess and proclaim when, speaking of the Kingdom *which is to come*, we affirm that God *has already endowed us with it*. This future has been given to us in the past that it may constitute the very *present*, the life itself, now, of the Church. . . .

And thus the preface fulfills itself in the Sanctus—the Holy, Holy, Holy of the eternal doxology, which is the secret essence of all that exists: "Heaven and earth are full of thy glory." We had to ascend to heaven in Christ to see and to understand the creation in its real being as glorification of God, as that *response* to divine love in which alone creation becomes what God wants it to be: thanksgiving, Eucharist, adoration. . . .

Up to this point the Eucharist was our ascension in Christ, our entrance in him into the "world to come." And now, in this eucharistic offering in Christ of all things to the One to whom they belong and in whom alone they really exist—now this movement of ascension has reached its *end*. We are at the paschal table of the Kingdom. What we have offered—our food, our life, ourselves, and the whole world—we offered in Christ and as Christ because he himself has assumed our life and is our life. And now all this is given back to us as the gift of new life and therefore—necessarily—as *food*.

"This is my body, this is my blood. Take, eat, drink. . . ." And generations upon generations of theologians ask the same questions. How is this possible? How does this happen? And what exactly does happen in this transformation? And when exactly? And what is the cause? No answer seems to be satisfactory. Symbol? But what is a symbol? Substance, accidents? Yet one immediately feels that something is lacking in all these theories, in which the Sacrament is reduced to the categories of time, substance, and causality, the very categories of "this world."

Something is lacking because the theologian thinks of the sacrament and forgets the liturgy. As a good scientist he first isolates the object of his study, reduces it to one moment, to one "phenomenon"—and then, proceeding from the general to the particular, from the known to the unknown, he gives a definition, which in fact raises more questions than it answers. But throughout our study the main point has been that the whole liturgy is *sacramental*, that is, one transforming act and one ascending movement. And the very goal of this movement of ascension is to take us out of "this world" and to make us partakers of the *world to come*. . . .

But this is not an "other" world, different from the one God has created and given to us. It is our same world, *already* perfected in Christ, but *not yet* in us. It is our same world redeemed and restored in which Christ "fills all things with himself." And since God has created the world as food for us and has given us food as means of communion with him, as life in him—the new food of the new life which we receive from God in his Kingdom *is Christ himself*. . . . There and only there can we confess with St. Basil that "this bread is in very truth the precious body of our Lord, this wine the precious blood of Christ." What is "supernatural" here, in *this world*, is revealed as "natural" there. And it is always in order to lead us "there" and to make us what we are that the Church fulfills itself in liturgy.

It is the Holy Spirit who *manifests* the bread as the body and the wine as the blood of Christ. The Orthodox Church has always insisted that the *transformation (metabole)* of the eucharistic elements is performed by the *epiclesis*—the invocation of the Holy Spirit—and not by the words of institution. This doctrine, however, was often misunderstood by the Orthodox themselves. Its point is not to replace one "causality"—the words of institution—by another, a different "formula." It is to reveal the eschatological character of the sacrament. The Holy Spirit comes on the "last and great day" of Pentecost. He manifests the world to come. He inaugurates the Kingdom. He always takes us *beyond*. To be in the Spirit means to be in heaven, for the Kingdom of God is "joy and peace in the Holy Spirit." And thus in the Eucharist it is he who *seals* and *confirms* our ascension into heaven, who transforms the Church into the body of Christ and—therefore—*manifests* the elements of our offering as *communion in the Holy Spirit*. This is the consecration.

But before we can partake of the heavenly food there remains one last, essential and necessary act: the *intercession*. To be in Christ means to be like him, to make ours the very movement of his life. And as he "ever liveth to make intercession" for all "that come unto God by him" (Heb. 7:25), so we cannot help accepting his intercession as our own. The Church is not a society for escape—corporately or individually—from this world to taste of the mystical bliss of eternity. Communion is not a "mystical experience": we drink of the chalice of Christ, and he gave himself for the life of the world. The bread on the paten and the wine in the chalice are to remind us of the incarnation of the Son of God, of the cross and death. And thus it is the very joy of the Kingdom that makes us *remember* the world and pray for it. . . .

And now the time has come for us to *return into the world*. "Let us depart in peace," says the celebrant as he leaves the altar, and this is the last *commandment* of the liturgy. . . . And it is as witnesses of this Light, as witnesses of the Spirit, that we must "go forth" and begin the neverending mission of the Church. Eucharist was the *end* of the journey, the end of time. And now it is again the *beginning*, and things that were impossible are again revealed to us as possible. The time of the world has become the time of the Church, the time of salvation and redemption. And God has made us *competent*, as Paul Claudel has said; competent to be his witnesses, to fulfill what he has done and is ever doing. This is the meaning of the Eucharist; this is why the mission of the Church begins in the liturgy of ascension, for it alone makes possible the liturgy of mission.

6. RAHNER: THE SELF-COMMUNICATION OF GOD

Rahner has consistently attempted to unite traditional Roman Catholic sacramental theology to a philosophical account of human freedom and responsibility. This has involved interpreting the essentially objective mode of working of the sacraments, *ex opere operato* ("by the act done"), and the personal response of the believer, *opus operantis* ("the act of the doer"). A sacrament is final and certain as part of God's word to humanity in the history of salvation; but it is not magic, because it requires the free response of the person. In the passage which follows, the word "existentiell" is used to refer to the free and personal appropriation by a subject. Source: Karl Rahner, *Foundations of Christian Faith: An Introduction to the Idea of Christianity*, trans. William V. Dych (New York: Crossroad, 1978), pp. 411–15, 427–28.

The history of salvation and grace has its roots in the essence of man which has been divinized by God's self-communication. We are not people who have nothing to do with God, who do not receive grace and in whom the event of God's self-communication does not take place until we receive the sacraments. Wherever a person accepts his life and opens himself to God's incomprehensibility and lets himself fall into it, and hence wherever he appropriates his supernatural transcendentality in interpersonal communication, in love, in fidelity, and in a task which opens him even to the inner-worldly future of man [as an individual] and of the human race, there is taking place the history of the salvation and the revelation of the very God who communicates himself to man, and whose communication is mediated by the whole length and breadth and depth of human life.

What we call church and what we call the explicit and official history of salvation, and hence also what we call the sacraments, are only especially prominent, historically manifest and clearly tangible events in a history of salvation which is identical with the life of man as a whole. As the universal and collective history of the salvation of all mankind, this salvation history has entered into its final, eschatological and irreversible phase through Jesus Christ. Through Jesus Christ the drama and the dialogue between God and his world has entered into a phase which already implies God's irreversible triumph, and which also makes this victory in the crucified and risen Jesus Christ historically tangible. The all-encompassing word of God has been proclaimed in such a way that its victory and God's "yes" can no longer be undone by man's "no."

This also becomes effective in the *individual* history of the salvation of an individual. And wherever the finality and the invincibility of God's offer of himself becomes manifest in the concrete in the life of an individual through the church which is the basic sacrament of salvation, we call this a Christian sacrament. As the ongoing presence of Jesus Christ in time and space, as the fruit of salvation which can no longer perish, and as the means of salvation by which God offers his salvation to an individual in a tangible way and in the historical and social dimension, the church is the basic sacrament. This means that the church is a *sign* of salvation, and is not simply salvation itself. But insofar as the church is the continuation of God's self-offer in Jesus Christ in whom he has the final, victorious and salvific word in the dialogue between God and the world, the church is an *efficacious* sign. And to this extent the church is what is called *opus operatum* as applied to the individual sacraments. In Jesus Christ and in his presence, that is, in the church, God offers himself to man in such a way that by God's act of grace this offer continues to be definitively bound up with the acceptance of this offer by the history of the world's freedom. From this perspective the church is the sign and the historical manifestation of the victorious success of God's self-communication. It is not just the sign of an offer which is still open, the sign merely of God's question to his creatures, a question about which we would not know how it will be answered by the world. It is rather the sign of a question which itself, looked at from the totality of human history, effects and brings with it a positive answer without prejudice to man's freedom. And to this extent the church is a sign, but it is the sign of an *efficacious* and successful grace for the world, and it is the basic sacrament in this radical sense. . . .

In his own individual history of salvation, the history which he can survey, an individual is free and he has no *certain* knowledge of a victorious conclusion to his *own* history of God's grace. If we can put it this way, the individual is still running "out in the open" towards the mystery of God's election. As an individual he cannot apply to himself with theoretical certainty what we said about the basic eschatological situation of the history of the salvation of the world as a whole, the history which has been founded in Christ, although he grasps this basic eschatological situation in the firm *hope* that it is also true for him. He is still on his way to meet God's history, and he does not know reflexively how God will judge the secret depths of his own freedom. In our Christian faith and in the collective hope which this implies, we can and indeed we have to say that the world as a whole is redeemed, that the drama of salvation history as a whole will reach a positive conclusion, and that God has already overcome the world's sinful rejection through Jesus Christ, the crucified and risen one. And to this extent of course the individual sacrament encounters the individual person with this eschatological finality and certainty.

Because God has offered himself unambiguously to the world in history, and because Christ with his life, his death and his resurrection is promised to the individual as his own destiny, God's offer of his grace to us has an absolute unconditionality and certainty which is effected by the word of God itself. To this extent we say that a sacrament is an *opus operatum*: as the unambiguous and efficacious word of God it causes of itself. But insofar as this sacrament is offered to a person in his individual and still open salvation history, *he* cannot say with absolute, theoretical certainty that he accepts with the same absolute certainty the word and the offer which comes to him from God with absolute certainty. But as the Council of Trent says, not only is he given the power of a "most firm hope," but he is also obliged to have it, for the grace of God which comes to him in the sacraments has already mysteriously outstripped the possibility in him of a rejection of this grace. Prescinding here from sacraments which are administered to those who have not come of age, as the irrevocable and absolute word of the offer of God's grace the *opus operatum* encounters the still open word of an individual who responds with a "yes" or a "no," and this is the *opus operantis*. And insofar as the *opus operatum* of the sacraments encounters the *opus operantis* of the believer or the person who accepts God's act, it is clear that sacraments are only efficacious in faith, hope and love. Hence they have nothing to do with magic rites. They are not magic because they do not coerce God, and because they are God's free act upon us. Moreover, they have nothing to do with magic because they are efficacious only to the extent that they encounter man's openness and freedom. If a person responds to God's offer with an acceptance, he has to profess, of course, that this acceptance of his also takes place by the power of God's grace.

This statement does not deny that in individual instances of personally unenlightened people a concrete Christian can misunderstand the sacraments in a magical way and also does in fact misunderstand them. Such a person misunderstands them if he thinks that the sacraments do not address the freedom of his faith and his love, or if he thinks that they exist in order to relieve him of his ultimate and personal decision in faith, hope and love. Sacraments are nothing else but God's efficacious word to man, the word in which God offers himself to man and thereby liberates man's freedom to accept God's self-communication by his own act. . . .

It should have become clear by now that the individual sacraments do have common aspects. There is present in all of the sacraments the efficacious word of God and, when they are not only received validly but also fruitfully, as theology says, there is also present man's response, and indeed not only in the depths of his free and graced being, but also in his historical and social dimension. Hence a sacrament is a tangible word and a tangible response. It comes from God and from man. And since, however much man is a being of word and of language, he is also a being of gesture, of symbol and of action, the sacraments, which ultimately can be brought under the common definition of an *efficacious word of God*, also contain in themselves forms other than words in various ways and in various intensities. These forms are cultic rites: being baptized with water, eating, anointing and the laying on of hands. But according to the Catholic understanding these elements do not belong necessarily to the essence of the sacrament; this is seen in the fact that in matrimony as a sacrament and in the church's word of reconciliation to a sinner the efficacious word of Christ is present basically only in a human word. To this extent it is theologically legitimate to understand the sacraments as the most radical and most intensive instance of God's word as a word of the church when this word represents an absolute involvement of the church and is what is called *opus operatum*.

It is to be taken for granted that the whole dialectic between a person as an individual and as a member of the church is also found in the sacraments. All of the sacraments have a quite specific ecclesiological meaning, and they always relate a person to the church. The sacraments are not only something which is administered by the church, but they are also and really the self-actualization of the church, and indeed both in the one who administers the sacrament and in the one who receives it. And at the same time they represent the most individual, historical and salvific results for the individual in his individual history of salvation, although they take place in the church. This also includes the Eucharist, which is received by the individual. . . .

Obviously we also have in the sacraments the dialectical unity, relationship and non-identity between the individual person as an individual and as a member of the community. It is precisely in a sacramental word, where the church addresses God's word to an individual in his quite concrete salvific situation, that the individual precisely as individual is addressed by the word of God in a way which is not found in the general word of preaching even in a really existentiell sermon. On the other hand this individual precisely as individual is called through the sacraments by the church, which makes demands upon a person as a person of the church and as a member of the community. For the church does not merely give and administer the sacraments, but rather in giving and administering them it also actualizes its own essence as the ongoing presence of eschatologically victorious grace. And for this reason every sacrament has its own quite special ecclesiological and ecclesial aspect. Every sacrament is really an event in the relationship between the individual and the church, and the individual receives a quite definite place in the church and a quite definite function in the church. He is incorporated into the church by baptism; he is reconciled again with the church's community of grace by the sacrament of penance; or as a member of the holy people of God and of the altar community of Christ he concelebrates the deepest mystery of the church in the Eucharist. In this mystery the church really exists in the fullest sense, exists as the presence of its dying, crucified and risen Lord, so that Christ himself is present in the midst of the altar community.

XI. THE SPIRIT AND THE CHRISTIAN LIFE

1. ISAAC OF SYRIA: DIRECTIONS ON SPIRITUAL TRAINING

Born in Nineveh in the mid-sixth century, Isaac of Syria represents the ideal pattern of Eastern monasticism, moving from the common life of a cenobitic monastery to the solitary vigil of a hermit. In time, however, he was prevailed upon to administer the church of Nineveh, though the call of solitude soon lured him back to the desert. His writings, which have reached us in Syriac and Arabic, all have the touch of firsthand experience. Source: *Early Fathers from the Philokalia*, trans. E. Kadloubovsky and G. E. H. Palmer (London: Faber & Faber, 1954), pp. 183–87.

1. Fear of God is the beginning of virtue; it is the offspring of faith and is sown in the heart, when the mind is withdrawn from worldly distractions in order to collect its wandering thoughts into meditation about the future restoration.

2. In order to lay the foundation of virtue, it is best for man to keep removed from worldly affairs and to abide in the law, which illumines the holy paths of righteousness, as the Holy Spirit has shown through the singer of Psalms (Ps. 23:3; 119:35).

3. The beginning of the path of life is always to be instructing one's mind in the Words of God and to spend one's life in poverty. Filling oneself with the one helps to gain perfection in the other. If you fill yourself with study of the Words of God, this helps towards progress in poverty; and progress in non-acquisitiveness gives you leisure to make progress in study of the Words of God. So the two combine to help the speedy building of the whole edifice of virtues.

4. No one can approach God without withdrawing from the world. By withdrawal I do not mean change of physical dwelling place, but withdrawal from worldly affairs. The virtue of withdrawal from the world consists in not occupying your mind with the world.

5. When grace increases in a man, then fear of death on the path of the righteousness he desires (or in the face of obstacles on this path) becomes of no account for him. Then he finds in his soul many reasons why, for fear of God, he should be ready to suffer afflictions as being something necessary. Then all things unpleasant to the body, and apt to cause it suffering, are as nothing in a man's eyes, compared with his hopes in the future. But when grace grows less in a man, all that happens in him and with him is the reverse; then, owing to investigation (which can be based only on the tangible), knowledge becomes for him more important than faith, trust in God is not present in all he does, and divine providence in relation to man is understood differently. Such a man is for ever subject to fears, through the wiles of those who lurk to shoot privily at him with their arrows (Ps. 11:2).

6. A doubting heart makes the soul timid; whereas faith can make the will firm, even if the body's members are cut off. In the measure that love of the flesh has the upper hand in you, you cannot be daring and fearless amid the many battles waged around the object of your love.

7. Not he is chaste in whom shameful thoughts stop in time of struggle, work and endeavor, but he who by the trueness of his heart makes chaste the vision of his mind, not letting it stretch out towards unseemly thoughts. And while the honesty of his conscience testifies, in what his eyes see, that he is true (to the law of purity), pudency hangs like a veil in the secret place of thoughts, and his innocence, like a chaste virgin, is kept inviolate for Christ by faith.

8. To drive away the wrong tendencies previously acquired by the soul, nothing is more helpful than immersing oneself in love of studying the divine Scriptures, and understanding the depths of the thoughts they contain. When thoughts become immersed in the delight of fathoming the hidden wisdom of the words, a man leaves the world behind and forgets all that is therein, in proportion to the enlightenment he draws from the words. But even when the mind floats only on the surface of the waters of the divine Scriptures and cannot penetrate to the very depths of the thoughts contained therein, even then the very fact that he is occupied with zeal to understand the Scriptures is enough firmly to pinion his thoughts in ideas of the miraculous alone, and to prevent them from seeking after the material and the carnal.

9. In everything you meet with in the Scriptures, strive to find the purpose of the word, to penetrate into the depth of the thought of the saints and to understand it more exactly. Those whose life is guided by divine grace towards enlightenment, always feel as though some inner ray of light travels over the written lines and allows the mind to discern from the bare words what is said with great thought for the instruction of the soul.

10. If a man reads lines of great meaning without going deeply into them, his heart remains poor (it gets no food); and the holy force which, through wondrous understanding of the soul, gives most sweet food to the heart, grows dim in him.

11. Each thing is usually attracted to its like. So the soul, being endowed with the spirit, ardently attracts to itself the content of a saying, as soon as it hears words which contain hidden spiritual force. Not every man is moved to wonder by what is said spiritually and possesses great spiritual force concealed in it. Words which speak of virtue require a heart not occupied with the earth; and in a man whose mind is burdened with temporal cares, virtue does not awake thought to love it and seek to possess it.

12. Renunciation of matter by one's being precedes union with God, although, through the dispensation of grace, the latter is in some found to precede the former. The order normal for dispensation differs from the order general among men. But you should preserve the general order. If grace comes first in you, that is its own affair; if it does not come first, you too must climb to the summit of the spiritual tower by the way of all men.

13. The insatiability of the soul in acquiring virtue turns to its use a part of the visible (sensory) desires of the body with which it is joined. Each thing is made good by measure. Without measure even things deemed excellent become harmful.

14. Do you wish to commune with God in your mind?—Strive to be merciful. To the spiritual love which imprints the invisible image (of God in oneself), there is no other path than that a man should first of all begin to be merciful in the measure that our heavenly Father is merciful, as the Lord said (Luke 6:36).

15. A word not made good by action is like an artist who makes pictures of water on walls, yet cannot quench his thirst with it. When a

man speaks of virtue from his own experience, it is the same as giving to another money earned by his own labors. And if a man sows teaching into the ears of his listeners from what he himself has gained, he opens his lips with confidence, saying to his spiritual children as the aged Jacob said to the chaste Joseph: "I give to thee Sicima, a select portion above thy brethren, which I took out of the hand of the Amorites with my sword and bow" (Gen. 48:22).

16. Someone said with perfect truth that fear of death afflicts a man, whose conscience condemns him; but a man who bears good testimony in himself desires death as much as he desires life.

17. If something has become deeply united with your soul, you should not only regard it as your possession in this life, but believe that it will accompany you into the life to come. If it is something good, rejoice and give thanks to God in your mind; if it is something bad, grieve and sigh, and strive to free yourself from it while you are still in the body.

18. Always keep in your mind the grievous afflictions of those stricken with sorrow and tribulations, that you may render due thanks for the small and insignificant adversities, which may happen to you, and be able to bear them with joy.

19. In times of cooling and laziness, imagine in your heart those past times when you were full of zeal and solicitude in all things, even the smallest; remember your past efforts and the energy with which you opposed those who wished to obstruct your progress. These recollections will reawaken your soul from its deep sleep, will invest it anew with the fire of zeal, will raise it, as it were, from the dead and will make it engage in an ardent struggle against the devil and sin, thus returning to its former rank.

20. The activity of cross-bearing is of two kinds: one consists in enduring bodily afflictions (bodily privations, inevitable in struggling with passions), and is called activity proper; the other consists in subtle doing of the mind, meditation on God, abiding in prayer, and so on, and is called contemplation. The first purifies the passionate part of the soul, the other brings light to its mental part. Every man who, before perfecting his training in the first activity, passes to the second, being attracted to its delights, not to speak of his own laziness, becomes

overtaken by wrath for not having first mortified his "members which are upon the earth" (Col. 3:5), that is, for not having overcome the impotence of thoughts by patient exercise in the activity of bearing the cross, and for presuming to let his mind dream of the cross's glory. This is the meaning of the saying of the saints of old that, if a man's mind conceives an intention to climb on to the cross, before his senses are cured of their sickness and have achieved a state of serenity, he is overtaken by the wrath of God. A man whose mind is defiled of shameful passions, who is quick to fill it with fantasies, has an interdiction set on his lips, because, without first purifying his mind by suffering, without conquering carnal lusts, he puts his trust on what his ear has heard and what is written in ink, and has forged ahead on a path shrouded in darkness, when his eyes are blind.

21. Imagine virtue as the body, contemplation as the soul, and the two together as forming one perfect man, whose two parts—the senses and the mind—are made one by the spirit. Just as it is impossible for a soul to manifest its being before the forming of the body, with its members, has been completed; so too is it impossible for a soul to reach contemplation without active work in virtue.

22. When you hear that it is necessary to withdraw from the world, to leave the world, to purify yourself from all that belongs to the world, you must first learn and understand the term *world*, not in its everyday meaning, but in its purely inward significance. When you understand what it means and the different things that this term includes, you will be able to learn about your soul—how far removed it is from the world and what is mixed with it that is of the world. "World" is a collective name, embracing what are called passions. When we want to speak of passions collectively, we call them "the world"; when we want to distinguish between them according to their different names, we call them passions.

23. When you have learned what the world means, then, by discerning all that is implied in this term, you will also learn what ties you to the world and in what you are freed from it. I will say, more briefly, that the world is carnal life and minding of the flesh. Therefore a man is seen to be free of the world inasmuch as he has wrenched himself free of this.

2. THOMAS AQUINAS: ACTION
AND CONTEMPLATION

Writing in the thirteenth century, Thomas proved most notable in allowing the Western awakening to Aristotle to structure our appreciation of Christian teaching. In the first of two selections from the *Summa Theologica*, he offers a corrective to the perennial tendency of persons to reduce the Christian life to a code of conduct. In the second selection, he weighs the relative importance of a contemplative life over against a life of action. The structure of his argument follows the form of scholastic disputations. Source: Thomas Aquinas, *Summa Theologica* 1a2ae. 106,1 (Blackfriars ed., Vol. 30, trans. Cornelius Ernst [London: Eyre & Spottiswoode, 1972], pp. 3–7); 2a2ae. 182,4 (Blackfriars ed., Vol. 46, trans. Jordan Aumann [London: Eyre & Spottiswoode, 1966], pp. 79–83). Date of original composition: 1266 ff.

Is the New Law a Written Law?

1. It seems that the new law is a written law. For the new law is the Gospel itself. But the Gospel is written down: "These things are written so that you may believe" (John 20:31). Therefore the new law is a written law.

2. The inward law is the natural law; as Paul says, "They do by nature what is contained in the law, having what is required by the law written in their hearts" (cf. Rom. 2:14–15). Therefore if the law of the Gospel were within, it would not differ from the natural law.

3. The law of the Gospel belongs properly to those who are in the state of the New Covenant. But the inward law is the common possession of those who are in the Old Covenant as well as those who are in the New; for the divine wisdom "passes among every people into holy souls, and makes them friends of God and prophets" (Wisd. 7:27). Therefore the new law is not an inward law.

On the other hand, the new law is the law of the New Covenant. But the law of the New Covenant is inwardly implanted in the heart. For Paul quotes the authoritative text of Jeremiah, "Behold the days will come, says the Lord, and I will bring to fulfilment a new covenant for the house of Israel and the house of Judah"; and the text goes on to explain this covenant by saying, "For this is the covenant that I will set up with the house of Israel: I will put my laws in their minds and write them upon their hearts" (Heb. 8:10, quoting Jer. 31:33). Therefore the new law is an inward law.

Reply: As Aristotle says, "It is plain that each thing can be identified with its predominant characteristic" (*Ethics* 9.8). Now it is the grace of the Holy Spirit, given through faith in Christ, which is predominant in the law of the New Covenant, and that in which its whole power consists. So before all else the new law is the very grace of the Holy Spirit, given to those who believe in Christ. This is quite clear from Paul's words, "What then becomes of your boasting? It is excluded. By what law? That of works? No, but by the law of faith" (Rom. 3:27); for he calls the very grace of faith *law*. And still more clearly he says later, "The law of the Spirit of life in Christ Jesus has set me free from the law of sin and death" (Rom. 8:2). So too Augustine says that "As the law of works was written on tables of stone, so the law of faith is written in the hearts of the faithful." And elsewhere in the same book he says, "What are the laws of God written by God himself in our hearts, if not the very presence of the Holy Spirit?" (*De Spiritu et Littera* 21, 24).

There do however belong to the new law certain elements which in a way dispose us for the grace of the Holy Spirit, and some which are concerned with its exercise. These may be considered secondary in the new law, and Christ's faithful had to be instructed about them both orally and in writing, both as regards matters of faith and as regards actions. Hence the new law is first and foremost an inward law, and secondarily a written law.

Hence: 1. There is nothing in the written text of the Gospel except what is concerned with the grace of the Holy Spirit, either by disposing us for it or by providing directions for the exercise of this grace. Thus as regards our minds, we are disposed by faith, through which the grace of the Holy Spirit is bestowed; here belongs everything in the Gospel which is concerned to manifest Christ's divinity or his humanity. As regards our attitudes and attachments, again, the Gospel contains teaching about the contempt of the world, by which man becomes open to the grace of the Holy Spirit; for "the world"—that is, lovers of the world—"cannot receive the Holy Spirit" (John 14:17). On the other hand, the grace of the Spirit is exercised in virtuous actions, to which the scriptures of the New Covenant exhort us in all sorts of ways.

2. Something can be inward to man in two ways. Firstly, with reference to human nature; in this sense the natural law is inward to man. Secondly, something may be inward to man as though added on to nature by the gift of grace. It is in this sense that the new law is inward to man; it not only points out to him what he should do, but assists him actually to do it.

3. No one has ever had the grace of the Holy Spirit except by faith in Christ, whether this faith be explicit or implicit. Now by faith in Christ man belongs to the New Covenant. Hence anyone who received the law of grace inwardly by this very fact belonged to the New Covenant.

Whether the Active Life Precedes the Contemplative Life

1. It seems that the active life does not precede the contemplative life, for the contemplative life directly engages the love of God, and the active life the love of neighbor. The love of God precedes the love of neighbor, since the neighbor is loved because of God. Therefore it seems that the contemplative life also precedes the active life.

2. Further, Gregory says, "It should be observed that while the proper order of life is to proceed from action to contemplation, it is sometimes useful for the soul to turn from the contemplative to the active life" (*Homil. In Ezech.* 2, hom. 2). Therefore the active life does not come before the contemplative life in every respect.

3. Further, it would seem that there is not necessarily any order between things that are proper to different subjects. Now the active and contemplative life are proper to different persons, for Gregory says, "Frequently those who could contemplate God in leisure have been overwhelmed by the pressure of work; and frequently those who could live well when occupied with human affairs have perished by the sword of their leisure" (*Moralia* 6.37). Therefore the active life is not prior to the contemplative.

On the other hand, Gregory says, "The active life precedes the contemplative life in time, because from good works one is led to contemplation" (*Homil. In Ezech.* 1, hom. 3).

Reply: One thing can precede another in two ways. First, of its nature, and in this way the contemplative life precedes the active life, since it deals with things that are prior and more excellent; and hence it moves and directs the active life. For the higher reason, which is used in contemplation, is compared to the lower reason, which is used in action, as the husband to the wife, who should be ruled by him, as Augustine says (De Trinitate 12.3,7,12).

Secondly, one thing can precede another as regards us, i.e., it comes first in the order of generation. In this way the active life precedes the contemplative life, because it disposes for the contemplative life, as stated above. In the order of generation the disposition precedes the form, though absolutely speaking and by its nature the form is prior.

Hence: 1. The contemplative life is not directed to any love of God whatever, but to perfect love. But the active life is necessary for any love of neighbor. Hence, Gregory says, "Those who do not neglect to do the good they are able, can enter heaven without the contemplative life; but those who neglect to do the good they could do, cannot enter without the active life" (Homil. In Ezech. 1, hom. 3). From this it is clear that the active life precedes the contemplative life, as that which is common to all precedes that which is proper to the perfect.

2. A person progresses from the active to the contemplative way of life according to the order of generation, whereas his return to the active life from the contemplative is by way of direction, in that the active life is guided by the contemplative; even thus habit is acquired by repeated acts and then by the habit acquired one acts yet more perfectly, as Aristotle says (Ethics 2.1).

3. Those who are more prone to yield to their passions because of their impulse to activity are, simply speaking, more suited for the active life because of a spirit of restlessness. Thus, Gregory says that "Some are so restless that when they have a rest from labor, they labor all the more, because the more time they have for thought, the more they suffer from agitation of spirit" (Moralia 6.37).

Others, however, have a naturally pure and calm spirit, which makes them suited for contemplation; and if they were to dedicate themselves entirely to action, it would be harmful to them. Hence, Gregory says that "Some men are of such a tranquil spirit that if they were to engage in any hard work, they would succumb at the very outset." But then he adds, "Frequently love impels slothful spirits to labor and fear holds restless souls in contemplation" (ibid.). Consequently, those who are more suited for the active life can prepare themselves for the contemplative life by the works of the active life, while those who are more suited for the contemplative life can undertake the works of the active life so as to become even readier for contemplation.

3. JOHN OF THE CROSS AND TERESA OF AVILA: THE MYSTICAL WAY

These two sixteenth-century mystics stand as twin beacons in the history of Christian teaching on life with God. Although much older than John, Teresa had a capacity to guide and to inspire others that found its fruition in John's systematic penetration into the stages of growth in the life of the Spirit. As Castilian Carmelites, they contributed mightily to the reform of their order during Europe's century of reform. The first selection is from John's *Ascent of Mount Carmel*, Chaps. 8–9 (written in 1579–81); the second from Teresa's *Life*, Chap. 22 (written in 1565). Sources: *The Collected Works of St. John of the Cross*, trans. K. Kavanaugh and O. Rodriguez (Washington, D.C.: Institute of Carmelite Studies, 1973), pp. 125–29; and *The Collected Works of St. Teresa of Avila*, trans. K. Kavanaugh and O. Rodriguez (Washington, D.C.: Institute of Carmelite Studies, 1976), Vol. 1, pp. 144–47.

I

[John of the Cross in this passage discusses "the direction of the self to God through faith," and in particular "the purification of what is contrary to faith so that the soul by 'straitening' itself may enter upon the narrow path of obscure contemplation."]

Before dealing with faith, the proper and adequate means of union with God, we should prove how nothing created or imagined can serve the intellect as a proper means for union with God, and how all that can be grasped by the intellect would serve as an obstacle rather than a means, if a person were to become attached to it.

This chapter will contain a general proof of this; afterwards we shall discuss in particular the knowledge which the intellect can receive through the interior or exterior senses. We shall also deal with the difficulty and harm occasioned by these exterior and interior ideas, for due to them the intellect does not advance with the support of faith, which is the proper means.

Let it be recalled, then, that according to a philosophical axiom all means must be proportionate to their end. That is, they must manifest a certain accord with and likeness to the end—of such a degree that they would be sufficient for the attainment of the desired goal.

For example, if a man wants to reach a city, he must necessarily take the road, the means, that leads to the city.

As another example: If fire is to be united with a log of wood, it is necessary for heat, the means, to prepare the log first with a certain likeness and proportion to the fire. This is done by communicating to the wood a particular amount of heat. Now if anyone wanted to prepare the log by an inadequate means, such as air, water, or earth, there would be no possibility of union between the log and the fire, just as it would be impossible to reach the city without taking the proper road that connects with it.

If the intellect, then, is to reach union with God in this life, insofar as is possible, it must take that means which bears a proximate likeness to God and unites with him.

It is noteworthy that among all creatures both superior and inferior none bears a likeness to God's being or unites proximately with him. Though truly, as theologians say, all creatures carry with them a certain relationship to God and a trace of him (greater or less according to the perfection of their being), yet God has no relation or essential likeness to them. Rather the difference which lies between his divine being and their being is infinite. Consequently, intellectual comprehension of God through heavenly or earthly creatures is impossible, since there is no proportion of likeness.

David proclaims in reference to heavenly creatures: "There is none among the gods like you, O Lord!" (Ps. 86:8), thereby calling the angels and saints gods. And elsewhere he declares: "O God, your way is in the holy place, what great God is there like our God?" (Ps. 77:13). This was equivalent to saying that the way of approach to you, O God, is a holy way, namely, purity of faith. For what god can be great enough (that is, what angel so elevated in being, or saint in glory) to serve as an adequate and sufficient approach to you?

David also proclaims of earthly and heavenly things: "The Lord is high up and looks at low things, and the high things he knows from afar" (Ps. 138:6). In other words: high in his own being, he looks at the being of objects here below as exceedingly low in comparison with his

305

high being; and the high things, the heavenly creatures, he knows to be far distant from his own being.

Thus, no creature can serve the intellect as a proportionate means to the attainment of God.

Nothing which could possibly be imagined or comprehended in this life can be a proximate means of union with God.

In our natural way of knowing, the intellect can only grasp an object through the forms and phantasms of things perceived by the bodily senses. Since these objects cannot serve as a means, the intellect cannot profit from its natural knowing.

As for the supernatural way of knowing, the intellect according to the possibilities of its ordinary power is neither capable nor prepared, while in the prison of the body, for the reception of the clear knowledge of God. Such knowledge does not belong to this state, since death is a necessary condition for possessing it.

God told Moses, who had asked for this clear knowledge, that no one would be able to see him: "No man shall see me and remain alive" (Ex. 33:20). St. John exclaims: "No man has ever seen God nor anything like him" (John 1:18). And St. Paul with Isaiah says: "Eye has not seen, nor ear heard, nor has it entered into the heart of man" (1 Cor. 2:9; Isa. 64:4). This is why Moses, as affirmed in the Acts of the Apostles, dared not look at the bush while God was present, because, in conformity with his feelings about God, he thought his intellect was powerless to look fittingly upon him (Acts 7:30–32). It is told of our father Elijah that on the mount he covered his face (blinded his intellect) in the presence of God (1 Kings 19:11–13). He did this because he did not dare, in his lowliness, to gaze on something so lofty, and he realized that anything he might behold or understand particularly would be far distant from God and most unlike him.

In this mortal life no supernatural knowledge or apprehension can serve as a proximate means for the high union with God through love. Everything the intellect can understand, the will experience, and the imagination picture is most unlike and disproportioned to God, as we have said.

Isaiah brought this out admirably in a noteworthy passage: "To what have you been able to liken God? Or what image will you fashion like to him? Will the ironsmith by chance be able to cast a statue? Or will the goldsmith be able to mold him out of gold, or the silversmith with plates of silver?" (Isa. 40:18–19).

The ironsmith signifies the intellect whose work is to form the concept by removing the iron of sensible species and phantasms.

The goldsmith symbolizes the will which is capable of receiving the figure and form of delight caused by the gold of love.

The silversmith, who was unable to fashion him from plates of silver, typifies both the memory and the imagination. The concepts and images which these powers mold and construct can easily be likened to plates of silver.

It is as if Isaiah had said that the intellect will not be able through its ideas to understand anything like God, nor the will experience a delight and sweetness resembling him, nor the memory place in the phantasy remembrances and images representing him.

Manifestly, then, none of these ideas can serve the intellect as a proximate means leading to God. In order to draw nearer the divine ray the intellect must advance by unknowing rather than by the desire to know, and by blinding itself and remaining in darkness rather than by opening its eyes.

Contemplation, consequently, by which the intellect has a higher knowledge of God, is called mystical theology, meaning the secret wisdom of God. For this wisdom is secret to the very intellect that receives it. St. Dionysius on this account refers to contemplation as a ray of darkness. The prophet Baruch declares of this wisdom: "There is no one who knows its way or can think of its paths" (Bar. 3:23). To reach union with God the intellect must obviously blind itself to all the paths along which it can travel. Aristotle teaches that just as the sun is total darkness to the eyes of a bat, so the brightest light in God is complete darkness to our intellect. And he teaches in addition that the loftier and clearer the things of God are in themselves, the more unknown and obscure they are to us. The Apostle also affirms this teaching: That which is highest in God is least known by men (Rom. 11:33).

We would never finish if we continued to quote passages and present arguments as proof that there is no ladder among all created, knowable things by which the intellect can reach this high Lord. Rather, it should be known that if the intellect did desire to use all or any of these objects as a proximate means to this union, they would be not merely

307

an encumbrance to it, but also an occasion of many errors and deceptions in the ascent of this mount.

We can gather from what has been said that to be prepared for this divine union the intellect must be cleansed and emptied of everything relating to sense, divested and liberated of everything clearly apprehensible, inwardly pacified and silenced, and supported by faith alone, which is the only proximate and proportionate means to union with God. For the likeness between faith and God is so close that no other difference exists than that between believing in God and seeing him. Just as God is infinite, faith proposes him to us as infinite; as there are three persons in the one God, it presents him to us in this way; and as God is darkness to our intellect, so does faith dazzle and blind us. Only by means of faith, in divine light exceeding all understanding, does God manifest himself to the soul. The more intense a man's faith, the closer is his union with God.

St. Paul indicated in the passage cited above: "He who would be united with God must believe" (Heb. 11:6). This means that a man must walk by faith in his journey to God. The intellect must be blind and dark, and abide in faith alone, because it is joined with God under this cloud. And as David proclaims, God is hidden under the cloud: "He set darkness under his feet. And he rose above the cherubim and flew upon the wings of the wind. He made darkness and the dark water his hiding place" (Ps. 18:9–11).

II

[Teresa in this chapter considers "how safe a path it is for contemplatives not to raise the spirit to high things unless the Lord raises it and how the humanity of Christ must be the means to the most sublime contemplation."]

There is one thing I want to say that in my opinion is important. If your reverence thinks it is good, it can be used for giving advice since it could happen that you will have need of it. In some books written on prayer it is said that even though the soul cannot reach this state of prayer by itself, since the work is an entirely supernatural one that the Lord effects in the soul, it will be able to help itself by lifting the spirit above all creatures and humbly raising it up, and that the soul can do this after having passed many years in the purgative life while it is advancing in the illuminative. . . . They give strong advice to rid oneself of all corporeal images and to approach contemplation of the divinity. They say that in the case of those who are advancing, these corporeal images, even when referring to the humanity of Christ, are an obstacle or impediment to the most perfect contemplation. In support of this theory they quote what the Lord said to the apostles about the coming of the Holy Spirit—I mean at the time of his ascension. They think that since this work is entirely spiritual, any corporeal thing can hinder or impede it, that one should try to think of God in a general way, that he is everywhere, and that we are immersed in him.

This is good, it seems to me, sometimes; but to withdraw completely from Christ or that this divine body be counted in a balance with our own miseries or with all creation, I cannot endure. May it please his majesty that I be able to explain myself.

I am not contradicting this theory; those who hold it are learned and spiritual men and they know what they are saying, and God leads souls by many paths and ways. I want to speak now of the way he led my soul—I'm not considering other ways—and of the danger I found myself in for wanting to put into practice what I was reading. I really believe that anyone who reaches the experience of union without passing beyond—I mean to raptures and visions and other favors God grants to souls—will think what is said in these books is the best practice, as I did. But if I should have kept to that practice, I believe I would never have arrived at where I am now because in my opinion the practice is a mistaken one. Now it could be that I am the mistaken one, but I'll speak of what happened to me.

I had no master and was reading these books in which I thought I was gradually coming to understand something. (And afterward I understood that if the Lord didn't show me, I was able to learn little from books, because there was nothing I understood until his majesty gave me understanding through experience, nor did I know what I was doing.) As a result, when I began to experience something of a supernatural prayer, I mean of the prayer of quiet, I strove to turn aside from everything corporeal, although I did not dare lift up the soul—since I was always so wretched, I saw that doing so would be boldness. But it seemed to me that I felt the presence of God, as was so, and I strove to recollect myself in his presence. This is a pleasing prayer, if God helps in it, and the delight is great. Since I felt that benefit and consolation, there was no one who could have made me return to the humanity of Christ; as a matter of fact, I thought the humanity was an impediment. O Lord of my soul and my good, Jesus Christ crucified! At no time do I recall this opinion I had without feeling pain; it seems to me I became a dreadful traitor—although in ignorance.

I had been so devoted all my life to Christ (for I held this opinion toward the end, that is, just before the Lord granted me these favors of raptures and visions, and I didn't remain long in so extreme a practice of it); and thus I always returned to my custom of rejoicing in this Lord, especially when I received Communion. I wanted to keep ever before my eyes a painting or image of him since I was unable to keep him engraved in my soul as I desired. Is it possible, my Lord, that it entered my mind for even an hour that you would be an impediment to my greater good? Where have all my blessings come from but from you? I don't want to think I was at fault in this, because it deeply saddens me—and certainly it was ignorance. Thus you desired, in your goodness, to remedy the matter by sending me someone who would draw me away from this error—and afterward by letting me see you so many times, as I shall explain later on—so that I would understand more clearly how great the error is, and tell many persons what I just said, and put it in writing here.

In my opinion this practice is why many souls, when they reach the prayer of union, do not advance further or attain a very great freedom of spirit. It seems to me there are two reasons on which I can base my thinking. Perhaps I'm saying nothing, but what I'm about to say I've seen through experience. My soul was in a very bad state until the Lord gave it light. All its consolations were coming in small portions, and, once they were passed, it didn't then have the companionship of Christ to help in trials and temptations. The first reason is lack of humility in such persons; so small is this lack and so hidden and concealed that it goes unnoticed. Who is so proud and miserable—as I am—that he will not, after having labored the whole of life with as many penances, prayers, and persecutions as can be imagined, feel greatly enriched and well paid when the Lord allows him to remain at the foot of the cross with St. John? Not to feel greatly enriched by this could happen only to stupid persons like myself, for in every way I was losing when I should have been gaining.

If our nature or health doesn't allow us to think always about the passion, since to do so would be arduous, who will prevent us from being with him in his risen state? We have him so near in the blessed sacrament, where he is already glorified and where we don't have to gaze upon him as being so tired and worn out, bleeding, wearied by his journeys, persecuted by those for whom he did so much good, and not believed in by the apostles. Certainly there is no one who can endure thinking all the time about the many trials he suffered. Behold him here without suffering, full of glory, before ascending into heaven, strengthening some, encouraging others, our companion in the most blessed sacrament; it doesn't seem it was in his power to leave us for a moment. And what a pity it was for me to have left you, my Lord, under the pretext of serving you more! When I was offending you I didn't know you; but how, once knowing you, did I think I could gain more by this path! Oh, what a bad road I was following, Lord! Now it seems to me I was walking on no path until you brought me back, for in seeing you at my side I saw all blessings. There is no trial that it wasn't good for me to suffer once I looked at you as you were, standing before the judges. Whoever lives in the presence of so good a friend and excellent a leader, who went ahead of us to be the first to suffer, can endure all things. The Lord helps us, strengthens us, and never fails; he is a true friend. And I see clearly, and I saw afterward, that God desires that if we are going to please him and receive his great favors, we must do so through the most sacred humanity of Christ, in whom he takes his delight. Many, many times have I perceived this truth through experience. The Lord has told it to me. I have definitely seen that we must enter by this gate if we desire his sovereign majesty to show us great secrets.

Thus your reverence and lordship should desire no other path even if you are at the summit of contemplation; on this road you walk safely. This Lord of ours is the one through whom all blessings come to us. He will teach us these things. In beholding his life we find that he is the best example. What more do we desire than to have such a good friend at our side, who will not abandon us in our labors and tribulations, as friends in the world do? Blessed is he who truly loves him and always keeps him at his side! Let us consider the glorious St. Paul: it doesn't seem that any other name fell from his lips than that of Jesus, as coming from one who kept the Lord close to his heart. Once I had come to understand this truth, I carefully considered the lives of some of the saints, the great contemplatives, and found that they hadn't taken any other path: St. Francis demonstrates this through the stigmata; St. Anthony of Padua, with the infant; St. Bernard found his delight in the humanity; St. Catherine of Sienna—and many others about whom your reverence knows more than I.

This practice of turning aside from corporeal things must be good, certainly, since such spiritual persons advise it. But, in my opinion, the soul should be very advanced because until then it is clear that the Creator must be sought through creatures. Everthing depends on the favor the Lord grants to each soul; this is not what I'm concerned with. What I wanted to explain was that the most sacred humanity of Christ must not be counted in a balance with other corporeal things. And may this point be well understood, for I should like to know how to explain myself.

4. LAW: CALL TO A DEVOUT
AND HOLY LIFE

The Reformation, while critical of monasticism, did not signal an end to the type of spirituality nurtured there. William Law reflects in his writings the influence of the *devotio moderna*: Johann Tauler, Jan van Ruysbroeck, and Thomas à Kempis, as well as the German mystic, Jakob Boehme. Although Law was a nonjuring Anglican, his writings nonetheless have a flavor we associate with Quakers, while his spiritual masters include the Desert Fathers. Source: William Law, *A Serious Call to a Devout and Holy Life*, Chap. 4 (New York: Paulist Press, 1978), pp. 75–79. Date of original publication: 1729.

Having in the first chapter stated the general nature of devotion and shown that it implies not any form of prayer but a certain form of life that is offered to God not at any particular times or places, but everywhere and in everything, I shall now descend to some particulars and show how we are to devote our labor and employment, our time and fortunes, unto God.

As a good Christian should consider every place as holy because God is there, so he should look upon every part of his life as a matter of holiness because it is to be offered unto God.

The profession of a clergyman is a holy profession because it is a ministration in holy things, an attendance at the altar. But worldly business is to be made holy unto the Lord by being done as a service to him and in conformity to his divine will.

For as all men and all things in the world as truly belong unto God as any places, things, or persons that are devoted to divine service, so all things are to be used, and all persons are to act in their several states and employments, for the glory of God.

Men of worldly business therefore must not look upon themselves as at liberty to live to themselves, to sacrifice to their own humors and tempers because their employment is of a worldly nature. But they must consider that as the world and all worldly professions as truly belong to God as persons and things that are devoted to the altar, so it is as much the duty of men in worldly business to live wholly unto God as 'tis the duty of those who are devoted to divine service.

As the whole world is God's, so the whole world is to act for God. As all men have the same relation to God, as all men have all their powers and faculties from God, so all men are obliged to act for God with all their powers and faculties.

As all things are God's, so all things are to be used and regarded as the things of God. For men to abuse things on earth and live to themselves is the same rebellion against God as for angels to abuse things in heaven, because God is just the same Lord of all on earth as he is the Lord of all in heaven.

Things may and must differ in their use, but yet they are all to be used according to the will of God.

Men may and must differ in their employments, but yet they must all act for the same ends, as dutiful servants of God in the right and pious performance of their several callings.

Clergymen must live wholly unto God in one particular way, that is, in the exercise of holy office, in the ministration of prayers and sacraments, and a zealous distribution of spiritual goods.

But men of other employments are in their particular ways as much obliged to act as the servants of God and live wholly unto him in their several callings.

This is the only difference between clergymen and people of other callings.

When it can be shown that men might be vain, covetous, sensual, worldly minded, or proud in the exercise of their worldly business, then it will be allowable for clergymen to indulge the same tempers in their sacred profession. For though these tempers are most odious and most criminal in clergymen, who besides their baptismal vow have a second time devoted themselves to God to be his servants, not in the common offices of human life, but in the spiritual service of the most holy sacred things, and who are therefore to keep themselves as separate and different from the common life of other men as a church or an altar is to be kept separate from houses and tables of common use; yet as all Christians are by their baptism devoted to God and made professors of holiness, so are they all in their several callings to live as holy and heavenly persons, doing everything in their common life only in such a manner as it may be received by God as a service done to him. For things spiritual and temporal, sacred and common, must like men and angels, like heaven and earth, all conspire in the glory of God.

As there is but one God and Father of us all, whose glory gives light and life to everything that lives, whose presence fills all places, whose power supports all beings, whose providence ruleth all events, so everything that lives whether in heaven or earth, whether they be thrones or principalities, men or angels, they must all with one spirit live wholly to the praise and glory of this one God and Father of them all. Angels as angels in their heavenly ministrations, but men as men, women as women, bishops as bishops, priests as priests, and deacons as deacons, some with things spiritual, and some with things temporal, offering to God the daily sacrifice of a reasonable life, wise actions, purity of heart, and heavenly affections.

This is the common business of all persons in this world. It is not left to any women in the world to trifle away their time in the follies and impertinencies of a fashionable life, nor to any men to resign themselves up to worldly cares and concerns; it is not left to the rich to gratify their passions in the indulgencies and pride of life, nor to the poor to vex and torment their hearts with the poverty of their state; but men and women, rich and poor, must with bishops and priests walk before God in the same wise and holy spirit, in the same denial of all vain tempers and in the same discipline and care of their souls, not only because they have all the same rational nature and are servants of the same God, but because they all want the same holiness to make them fit for the same happiness to which they are all called. It is therefore absolutely necessary for all Christians, whether men or women, to consider themselves as persons that are devoted to holiness, and so order their common ways of life by such rules of reason and piety as may turn it into continual service unto almighty God.

Now to make our labor or employment an acceptable service unto God, we must carry it on with the same spirit and temper that is required in giving of alms, or any work of piety. For, if "whether we eat or drink, or whatsoever we do, we must do all to the glory of God" (1 Cor. 10:31); if "we are to use this world as if we used it not"; if "we are to present our bodies a living sacrifice, holy, acceptable to God" (Rom. 12:1); if "we are to live by faith, and not by sight," and to "have our conversation in heaven"; then it is necessary that the common way of our life in every state be made to glorify God by such tempers as make our prayers and adorations acceptable to him. For if we are worldly or earthly minded in our employments, if they are carried on with vain desires and covetous tempers only to satisfy ourselves, we can no more be said to live to the glory of God than gluttons and drunkards can be said to eat and drink to the glory of God.

As the glory of God is one and the same thing, so whatever we do suitable to it must be done with one and the same spirit. That same state and temper of mind which makes our alms and devotions acceptable must also make our labor or employment a proper offering unto God. If a man labors to be rich and pursues his business that he may raise himself to a state of figure and glory in the world, he is no longer serving God in his employment; he is acting under other masters and has no more title to a reward from God than he that gives alms that he may be seen, or prays that he may be heard of men. For vain and earthly desires are no more allowable in our employments than in our alms and devotions. For these tempers of worldly pride and vainglory are not only evil when they mix with our good works, but they have the same evil nature and make us odious to God when they enter into the common business of our employment. If it were allowable to indulge covetous or vain passions in our worldly employment, it would then be allowable to be vainglorious in our devotions. But as our alms and devotions are not an acceptable service but when they proceed from a heart truly devoted to God, so our common employment cannot be reckoned a service to him but when it is performed with the same temper and piety of heart.

Most of the employments of life are in their own nature lawful, and all those that are so may be made a substantial part of our duty to God if we engage in them only so far, and for such ends, as are suitable to beings that are to live above the world. This is the only measure of our application to any worldly business, let it be what it will, where it will, it must have no more of our hands, our hearts, or our time than is consistent with a hearty, daily, careful preparation of ourselves for another life. For as all Christians, as such, have renounced this world to prepare themselves by daily devotion and universal holiness for an eternal state of quite another nature, they must look upon worldly employments as upon worldly wants and bodily infirmities, things not to be desired, but only to be endured and suffered till death and the resurrection has carried us to an eternal state of real happiness.

Now he that does not look at the things of this life in this degree of littleness cannot be said either to feel or believe the greatest truths of Christianity. For if he thinks anything great or important in human business, can he be said to feel or believe those scriptures which represent this life and the greatest things of life as bubbles, vapors, dreams, and shadows?

If he thinks figure and show and worldly glory to be any proper happiness of a Christian, how can he be said to feel or believe this doctrine, "Blessed are ye when men shall hate you, and when they shall separate you from their company, and shall reproach you, and cast out your name as evil for the son of man's sake"? For surely if there was any real happiness in figure and show and worldly glory, if these things deserved our thoughts and care, it could not be matter of the highest joy when we are torn from them by persecutions and sufferings. If, therefore, a man will so live as to show that he feels and believes the most fundamental doctrines of Christianity, he must live above the world. This is the temper that must enable him to do the business of life and yet live wholly unto God and to go through some worldly employment with a heavenly mind. And it is as necessary that people live in their employments with this temper as it is necessary that their employment itself be lawful.

5. RAUSCHENBUSCH: THEOLOGY AND THE SOCIAL GOSPEL

Alongside the more personal modes of embodying the Christian life, there have been frequent attempts to organize society in accordance with Christian principles. The impetus for social change was particularly strong in nineteenth- and early twentieth-century America, where it produced the Social Gospel movement. Walter Rauschenbusch, whose ministry began in the Hell's Kitchen section of New York and culminated in a major work of systematic theology, was the leading spokesman for this movement; the kingdom of God was its central symbol. Source: Walter Rauschenbusch, A *Theology for the Social Gospel* (Nashville: Abingdon Press, 1945), Chap. 13, pp. 131, 133–37, 142–43. Originally published in 1917.

If theology is to offer an adequate doctrinal basis for the social gospel, it must not only make room for the doctrine of the kingdom of God, but give it a central place and revise all other doctrines so that they will articulate organically with it. . . .

To those whose minds live in the social gospel, the kingdom of God is a dear truth, the marrow of the gospel, just as the incarnation was to Athanasius, justification by faith alone to Luther, and the sovereignty of God to Jonathan Edwards. It was just as dear to Jesus. He too lived in it, and from it looked out on the world and the work he had to do. . . .

The distinctive ethical principles of Jesus were the direct outgrowth of his conception of the kingdom of God. When the latter disappeared from theology, the former disappeared from ethics. Only persons having the substance of the kingdom ideal in their minds, seem to be able to get relish out of the ethics of Jesus. Only those church bodies which have been in opposition to organized society and have looked for a better city with its foundations in heaven, have taken the Sermon on the Mount seriously. . . .

The kingdom ideal is the test and corrective of the influence of the Church. When the kingdom ideal disappeared, the conscience of the Church was muffled. It became possible for the missionary expansion of Christianity to halt for centuries without creating any sense of shortcoming. It became possible for the most unjust social conditions to fasten themselves on Christian nations without awakening any consciousness that the purpose of Christ was being defied and beaten back. The practical undertakings of the Church remained within narrow lines, and the theological thought of the Church was necessarily confined in a similar way. The claims of the Church were allowed to stand in theology with no conditions and obligation to test and balance them. If the kingdom had stood as the purpose for which the Church exists, the Church could not have fallen into such corruption and sloth. Theology bears part of the guilt for the pride, the greed, and the ambition of the Church.

The kingdom ideal contains the revolutionary force of Christianity. When this ideal faded out of the systematic thought of the Church, it became a conservative social influence and increased the weight of the other stationary forces in society. If the kingdom of God had remained part of the theological and Christian consciousness, the Church could not, down to our times, have been salaried by autocratic class governments to keep the democratic and economic impulses of the people under check.

Reversely, the movements for democracy and social justice were left without a religious backing for lack of the kingdom idea. The kingdom of God as the fellowship of righteousness, would be advanced by the abolition of industrial slavery and the disappearance of the slums of civilization; the Church would only indirectly gain through such social changes. Even today many Christians cannot see any religious importance in social justice and fraternity because it does not increase the number of conversions nor fill the churches. Thus the practical conception of salvation, which is the effective theology of the common man and minister, has been cut back and crippled for lack of the kingdom ideal. . . .

When the doctrine of the kingdom of God is lacking in theology, the salvation of the individual is seen in its relation to the Church and to the future life, but not in its relation to the task of saving the social order. Theology has left this important point in a condition so hazy and muddled that it has taken us almost a generation to see that the salvation of the individual and the redemption of the social order are closely related, and how. . . .

The kingdom of God is humanity organized according to the will of God. Interpreting it through the consciousness of Jesus we may affirm these convictions about the ethical relations within the kingdom: (a) Since Christ revealed the divine worth of life and personality, and since his salvation seeks the restoration and fulfillment of even the least, it follows that the kingdom of God, at every stage of human development, tends toward a social order which will best guarantee to all personalities their freest and highest development. This involves the redemption of social life from the cramping influence of religious bigotry, from the repression of self-assertion in the relation of upper and lower classes, and from all forms of slavery in which human beings are treated as mere means to serve the ends of others. (b) Since love is the supreme law of Christ, the kingdom of God implies a progressive reign of love in human affairs. We can see its advance wherever the free will of love supersedes the use of force and legal coercion as a regulative of the social order. This involves the redemption of society from political autocracies and economic oligarchies; the substitution of redemptive for vindictive penology; the abolition of constraint through hunger as part of the industrial system; and the abolition of war as the supreme expression of hate and the completest cessation of freedom. (c) The highest expression of love is the free surrender of what is truly our own, life, property, and rights. A much lower but perhaps more decisive expression of love is the surrender of any opportunity to exploit men. No social group or organization can claim to be clearly within the kingdom of God which drains others for its own ease, and resists the effort to abate this fundamental evil. This involves the redemption of society from private property in the natural resources of the earth, and from any condition in industry which makes monopoly profits possible. (d) The reign of love tends toward the progressive unity of mankind, but with the maintenance of individual liberty and the opportunity of nations to work out their own national peculiarities and ideals.

6. WILLIAMS: CHRISTIAN SPIRITUALITY

Currently a lecturer in divinity at Cambridge, Rowan Williams writes in that ecumenical spirit characteristic of our times, yet displays a rare grasp of history and sensitivity to diverse social contexts, which allows him to recover much in our shared traditions that we might be tempted to dismiss as *passé*. Source: Rowan Williams, *Christian Spirituality* (Atlanta: John Knox Press, 1980), pp. 176–79.

Why conclude an essay such as this one with John of the Cross? Christian spirituality did not come to the end of its development in 1591, and it seems to beg a serious question if we suggest that everything of real significance had been said by the end of the sixteenth century. That is nonsense, and I have no intention of implying any such view. But what I have sought to show is that St. John sums up, in very many respects, those classical themes of Christian spirituality, of the *distinctively* Christian understanding of spiritual maturation, without which there can be no fruitful new exploration and articulation of the tradition. John gives exceptionally strong expression to the Christian suspicion of conceptual neatness, of private revelation and religious experience uncontrolled by reference to the givenness of Christ's cross, of infantile dependence on forms and words and images; he accepts the fact that there is a draining and crucifying conflict at the center of Christian living and refuses to countenance any joy or celebration which has not faced this conflict and endured it. He and Luther are, among the great writers of the Christian past, the most poignantly aware of the ways in which spirituality can be an escape from Christ. For both of them, as for so many others, the test of honesty is whether a man or woman has looked into the darkness in which Christianity has its roots, the darkness of God being killed by his creatures, of God himself breaking and reshaping all religious language by manifesting his activity in vulnerability, failure and contradiction.

The late Cornelius Ernst, O.P., argued in two very important papers in *New Blackfriars* (October and November 1969) on "World Religions and Christian Theology" that the "genetic moment" of Christian experience, the fundamental novelty of understanding which gives Christianity its identity, "is at once an experience of the creatively new become manifest in human articulation, and an experience of an ultimate source, the hidden God, *Deus absconditus* who has made his transcendence known in the darkness of a death. If the experience were not *both at once*, it would split apart into an insipid humanism of progress (or a revolutionary arrogance), or an esoteric mystique of world abnegation." This I believe to be the heart of classical Christian spirituality; and these pages have been written out of the conviction that, if we want to discover what Christian identity means historically, we must look at this area of reflection and interrogation that we call "spirituality" at least as much as we look at the systematic theology which is properly inseparable from it. It is here that we see most clearly the tension in Christian experience between the affirmation of the human and contingent and the devastating rejection of creaturely mediation. On the one hand: the Word is flesh and is communicated in flesh—in historical tradition, in personal human encounter, in material sacrament. The Word re-forms the possibilities of human existence and calls us to the creation of new humanity in the public, the social and historical, world—to the transformation of behavior and relationship, knowing God in acting and making. On the other hand: the Word made flesh is recognized as such in the great crisis and resolution of crucifixion and resurrection. The Word is rejected and crucified by the world; only when we see that there is no place for the Word in the world do we see that he is *God's* word, the Word of the hidden, transcendent creator. And *then*, only then, can we see, hear, experience (what you will) the newness of that creative God, resurrection and grace, new life out of the ultimate negation and despair. To believe in the newness and the transformation without the rejection and dark is, as Fr. Ernst says, insipid and in danger of being cheap; not to believe in it at all is to look for an escape out of this messy world into pure and clear vision, the peace of final negativity. But Christian peace is the peace between the Father and his Son Jesus, person and person together, encounter and gift; it is a peace which *includes* the moment of hopelessness and emptiness, the moment of the cross, and weaves it into life. "It is the passage," writes Fr. Ernst in another work, "through ultimate negation into the blessed peace beyond the Cross in the exchange of love of Jesus and the Father, the exchange which Christian tradition has called the Holy Spirit. And it is a passage as real as God and as man, as real as Jesus."

321

Christianity begins in contradictions, in the painful effort to live with the baffling plurality and diversity of God's manifested life—law and gospel, judgment and grace, the crucified Son crying to the Father. Christian experience does not simply move from one level to the next and stay there, but is drawn again and again to the central and fruitful darkness of the cross. But in this constant movement outwards in affirmation and inwards to emptiness, there *is* life and growth. The end is not yet; the frustrated longing for homecoming, for the journey's end, is unavoidable. Yet we can perhaps begin to see, through all the cost and difficulty, how we are entering more deeply into a divine life which is itself diverse and moving—Father and Son eternally brought to each other in Spirit. To discover in our "emptying" and crucifying the "emptying" of Jesus on his cross is to find God there, and so to know that God is not destroyed or divided by the intolerable contradictions of human suffering. He is one in the Spirit, and in that same Spirit *includes* us and our experience, setting us within his own life in the place where Jesus his firstborn stands, as sharers by grace in that eternal loving relation, men and women made whole in him. In the middle of the fire we are healed and restored—though never taken out of it. As Augustine wrote, it is at night that his voice is heard. To want to escape the "night" and the costly struggles with doubt and vacuity is to seek another God from the one who speaks in and as Jesus crucified. *Crux probat omnia.* There is no other touchstone. "I decided to know nothing among you except Jesus Christ and him crucified . . . that your faith might not rest in the wisdom of men but in the power of God" (1 Cor. 2:2, 5).

XII. THE KINGDOM OF GOD AND LIFE EVERLASTING

1. IRENAEUS: NEW HEAVENS AND
A NEW EARTH

In Irenaeus, the first great postbiblical theologian, the enthusiasm of biblical eschatology still echoes. His thought is set within an elaborate scheme according to which, during the thousand years' reign of the antichrist, the souls of the just would remain in "the invisible place allotted to them by God," until, ensuing upon the final victory of Christ, the general resurrection of the dead would occur—a physical resurrection in which the new flesh would be identical with the old, and the saints would receive the "inheritance" of "new heavens and a new earth." This rich and literal imagery has reverberated in Christian eschatological speculation ever since. Source: Irenaeus, *Against Heresies*, Book 5, Chaps. 32–33, 36, trans. and ed. Cyril C. Richardson in *Early Christian Fathers* (*LCC*, Vol. 1; Philadelphia: Westminster Press, 1953), pp. 391–93, 396–97. Date of original composition: ca. 182–88.

Since the opinions of some have been affected by the discourses of the heretics, and they are ignorant of the dispensations of God, and the mystery of the resurrection of the just and the kingdom which is the beginning of incorruption, by which kingdom those who are worthy will gradually be accustomed to receive [the fullness of] God, it is necessary to speak about these things. For the righteous must first rise again at the appearance of God to receive in this created order, then made new, the promise of the inheritance which God promised to the fathers, and will reign in this order. After this will come the judgment. It is just that in the same order in which they labored and were afflicted, and tried by all kinds of suffering, they should receive the fruits of [their suffering]—that in the same order in which they were put to death for the love of God they should again be made alive—and that in the same order in which they suffered bondage they should reign. For God is rich in all things, and all things are his. It is right, therefore, for this created order to be restored to its pristine state, and to serve the just without restraint. The apostle made this clear in the Epistle to the Romans, saying: "For the expectation of the creature awaits the revelation of the sons of God. For the creature was subject to vanity, not willingly, but because of him who subjected it in hope; for the creature itself shall be freed from the servitude of corruption into the freedom of the glory of the sons of God" (Rom. 8:19–21)

So, then, God's promise which he promised to Abraham remains firm. . . . If, then, God promised him the inheritance of the [promised] land, but in all his sojourning there he did not receive it, it must be that he will receive it with his seed, that is, with those who fear God and believe in him, at the resurrection of the just. For his seed is the Church, which receives through the Lord adoption to God. . . .

Because of this, when [the Lord] came to his Passion, that he might declare to Abraham and those with him the glad tidings of the opening of the inheritance, after he had given thanks as he held the cup, and had drunk of it, and given to the disciples, he said to them: "Drink of this, all of you. For this is my blood of the new covenant, which is shed for many for the remission of sins. For I say to you, that I will not drink of the produce of this vine, until that day when I shall drink it with you new in the kingdom of my Father" (Matt. 26:27–29). Then he himself will renew the inheritance of the land, and will re-establish the mystery of the glory of the sons, as David said, "He who renewed the face of the earth" (Ps. 104:30). He promised that he would drink of the produce of the vine with his disciples, thus showing both the inheritance of the earth, in which the new produce of the vine is drunk, and the physical resurrection of his disciples. For the new flesh that rises again is the same that has received the new cup. For he cannot be understood as drinking the produce of the vine when established on high with his own, somewhere above the heavens, nor again are they who drink it without flesh, for it belongs to flesh and not to spirit to receive the drink of the vine. . . .

Since men are real, they must have a real existence, not passing away into things which are not, but advancing [to a new stage] among things that are. Neither the substance nor the essence of the created order vanishes away, for he is true and faithful who established it, but the pattern of this world passes away, that is, the things in which the transgression took place, since in them man has grown old. Therefore God, foreknowing all things, made this pattern of things temporary, as I showed in the book before this, pointing out as far as I could the reason for the creation of the temporal universe. But when this pattern has passed away, and man is made new, and flourishes in incorruption, so that he can no longer grow old, then there will be new heavens and a new earth. In this new order man will always remain new, in converse with God. . . .

John therefore predicted precisely the first resurrection of the just, and [their] inheritance of the earth in the kingdom (Rev., ch. 20), and the prophets prophesied about this in agreement with each other. The Lord also taught thus, promising that he would enjoy the new mixture of the chalice with [his] disciples in the kingdom. The apostle also confessed that the creature would be free from the bondage of corruption into the freedom of the glory of the sons of God. In all and through all these things the same God the Father is manifest, who formed man, and promised to the fathers the inheritance of the earth, who brings this [promise] forth at the resurrection of the just, and fulfills the promises in the kingdom of his Son, afterwards bestowing with paternal love those things which eye has not seen, nor ear heard, nor have they entered into the heart of man (1 Cor. 2:9). Then there is one Son, who accomplished the Father's will, and one human race, in which the mysteries of God are accomplished, which angels long to behold (1 Peter 1:12). For they cannot search out the wisdom of God, by which what he had fashioned is perfected by being conformed and incorporated with the Son—or how that his offspring, the first-begotten Word, could descend into his creature, that is, into what he had fashioned, and be contained within it—and that the creature again should lay hold on the Word and should ascend to him, passing beyond the angels, and be made [anew] according to the image and likeness of God.

2. ORIGEN: THE CONSUMMATION OF ALL THINGS

This selection contains Origen's theology of the final end of history and the world. It explains briefly his famous doctrine of *apokatastasis ton panton*, "the restitution of all things," the final state when God will be all in all. His spiritual interpretation contrasts sharply with Irenaeus's literalism. Source: Origen, *On First Principles*, Book 3, Chap. 6, Secs. 1, 3–5, translated with an introduction and notes by G. W. Butterworth (London: SPCK, 1936), pp. 245–51. Date of original composition: ca. 219–25.

In regard to the end and consummation of all things, . . . we call to mind a few further points, since the course of our inquiry has brought us again to this topic. The highest good, towards which all rational nature is progressing, and which is also called the end of all things, is defined by very many even among philosophers in the following way, namely, that the highest good is to become as far as possible like God. But this definition is not so much, I think, a discovery of their own, as something taken by them out of the divine books. For Moses, before all others, points to it when in recording the first creation of man he says, "And God said, Let us make man in our own image and likeness" (Gen. 1:26). Then he adds afterwards, "And God made man; in the image of God made he him; male and female made he them, and he blessed them" (Gen. 1:27, 28).

Now the fact that he said, "He made him in the image of God," and was silent about the likeness, points to nothing else but this, that man received the honor of God's image in his first creation, whereas the perfection of God's likeness was reserved for him at the consummation. The purpose of this was that man should acquire it for himself by his own earnest efforts to imitate God, so that while the possibility of attaining perfection was given to him in the beginning through the honor of the "image," he should in the end through the accomplishment of these works obtain for himself the perfect "likeness." . . .

Now I myself think that when it is said that God is "all in all," it means that he is also all things in each individual person. And he will be all things in each person in such a way that everything which the rational mind, when purified from all the dregs of its vices and utterly cleared from every cloud of wickedness, can feel or understand or think will be all God and that the mind will no longer be conscious of anything besides or other than God, but will think God and see God and hold God and God will be the mode and measure of its every movement; and in this way God will be all to it. For there will no longer be any contrast of good and evil, since evil nowhere exists; for

God, whom evil never approaches, is then all things to it; nor will one who is always in the good and to whom God is all things desire any longer to eat of the tree of the knowledge of good and evil (Gen. 2:17). If then the end is renewed after the pattern of the origin and the issue of things made to resemble their beginning and that condition restored which rational nature once enjoyed when it had no need to eat of the tree of the knowledge of good and evil, so that all consciousness of evil has departed and given place to what is sincere and pure and he alone who is the one good God becomes all things to the soul and he himself is all things not in some few or in many things but in all things, when there is nowhere any death, nowhere any sting of death (1 Cor. 15:55–56), nowhere any evil at all, then truly God will be all in all. But some think that this perfection and blessedness of rational natures can only remain in the condition which we have described above, that is, the condition in which all things possess God and God is all things to them, if they are in no way impeded by union with a bodily nature. Otherwise, if there were any intermingling of a material substance, they consider that the glory of the highest blessedness would be prevented. . . .

But now, since we find the apostle Paul making mention of a "spiritual body" (1 Cor. 15:44), let us inquire to the best of our ability what sort of idea we ought to form from this passage about such a body. So far then as our understanding can grasp it, we believe that the quality of a spiritual body is something such as will make a fitting habitation not only for all saints and perfected souls but also for that "whole creation" which is to be "delivered from the bondage of corruption" (Rom. 8:21). Of this body the same apostle has also said that "we have a house not made with hands, eternal in the heavens" (2 Cor. 5:1), that is, in the dwelling-places of the blest. From this statement we may then form a conjecture of what great purity, what extreme fineness, what great glory is that quality of that body, by comparing it with those bodies which, although heavenly and most splendid, are yet made with hands and visible. For of that body it is said that it is a house not made with hands but "eternal in the heavens." Now since "the things which are seen are temporal, but the things which are not seen are eternal" (2 Cor. 4:18), all those bodies which we see whether on earth or in the heavens, which are capable of being seen and are made with hands and not eternal, are very greatly surpassed in excellence by that which is neither visible nor made with hands but is eternal.

From this comparison we may gain an idea how great is the beauty, how great the splendor and how great the brightness of a spiritual body, and how true is the saying that "eye hath not seen nor ear heard, nor hath it entered into the heart of man to conceive what things God hath prepared for them that love him" (1 Cor. 2:9). But we must not doubt that the nature of this present body of ours may, through the will of God who made it what it is, be developed by its Creator into the quality of that exceedingly refined and pure and splendid body, according as the condition of things shall require and the merits of the rational being shall demand. Finally, when the world was in need of variety and diversity, matter lent itself to the fashioning of the diverse aspects and classes of things in wholly obedient service to the maker, as to its Lord and Creator, that from it he might produce the diverse forms of things heavenly and earthly. But when events have begun to hasten towards the ideal of all being one as the Father is one with the Son (see John 17:21, 10:30), we are bound to believe as a logical consequence that where all are one there will no longer be any diversity.

It is on this account, moreover, that the last enemy, who is called death, is said to be destroyed (see 1Cor. 15:26); in order, namely, that there may be no longer any sadness when there is no death nor diversity when there is no enemy. For the destruction of the last enemy must be understood in this way, not that its substance which was made by God shall perish, but that the hostile purpose and will which proceeded not from God but from itself will come to an end. It will be destroyed, therefore, not in the sense of ceasing to exist, but of being no longer an enemy and no longer death. For to the Almighty nothing is impossible (see Job 42:2), nor is anything beyond the reach of cure by its Maker; for it was on this account that he made all things, that they might exist, and those things which were made in order to exist cannot cease to exist. Consequently they will suffer change and difference of such a kind as to be placed in a better or worse position in accordance with their merits; but things which were made by God for the purpose of permanent existence cannot suffer a destruction of their substance. Those things which in the opinion of the common people are believed to perish have not really perished, as the principles of our faith and of the truth alike agree.

Our flesh indeed is considered by the uneducated and by unbelievers to perish so completely after death that nothing whatever of its substance is left. We, however, who believe in its resurrection, know that death only causes a change in it and that its substance certainly persists and is restored to life again at a definite time by the will of its Creator and once more undergoes a transformation; so that what was at first flesh, "of the earth" (1 Cor. 15:47), and was then dissolved through death and again made "dust and ashes" (Gen. 18:27)—for "dust thou art," it is written, "and unto dust shalt thou return" (Gen. 3:19)—is raised again from the earth and afterwards, as the merits of the "indwelling soul" shall demand, advances to the glory of a "spiritual body" (1 Cor. 15:44).

3. AUGUSTINE: THE ETERNAL HAPPINESS OF THE SAINTS

The concluding book of Augustine's classic rendering of salvation history treats as a whole the end of the city of God, including such topics as the eternal happiness of the saints, the resurrection of the body, and the immortal and fully spiritual condition of the body. It includes some rather imaginative speculation on what persons in such a state of eternal felicity would do. Source: Augustine, *The City of God*, Book 22, Chap. 30, in *Fathers of the Church: Writings of Saint Augustine*, Vol. 8, trans. G. G. Walsh and D. J. Honan (Washington, D.C.: Catholic University of America Press, 1954), pp. 505–11. Date of original composition: 413–26.

Who can measure the happiness of heaven, where no evil at all can touch us, no good will be out of reach; where life is to be one long laud extolling God, who will be all in all; where there will be no weariness to call for rest, no need to call for toil, no place for any energy but praise. Of this I am assured whenever I read or hear the sacred song: "Blessed are they that dwell in thy house, O Lord: they shall praise thee forever and ever" (Ps. 84:4). Every fiber and organ of our imperishable body will play its part in the praising of God. On earth these varied organs have each a special function, but, in heaven, function will be swallowed up in felicity, in the perfect certainty of an untroubled everlastingness of joy. Even those muted notes in the diapason of the human organ, which I mentioned earlier, will swell into a great hymn of praise to the supreme artist who has fashioned us, within and without, in every fiber, and who, by this and every other element of a magnificent and marvelous order, will ravish our minds with spiritual beauty.

These movements of our bodies will be of such unimaginable beauty that I dare not say more than this: There will be such poise, such grace, such beauty as become a place where nothing unbecoming can be found. Wherever the spirit wills, there, in a flash, will the body be. Nor will the spirit ever will anything unbecoming either to itself or to the body.

In heaven, all glory will be true glory, since no one could ever err in praising too little or too much. True honor will never be denied where due, never be given where undeserved, and, since none but the worthy are permitted there, no one will unworthily ambition glory. Perfect peace will reign, since nothing in ourselves or in any others could disturb this peace. The promised reward of virtue will be the best and the greatest of all possible prizes—the very giver of virtue himself, for that is what the prophet meant: "I will be your God and you shall be my people" (Lev. 26:12). God will be the source of every satisfaction, more than any heart can rightly crave, more than life and health, food and wealth, glory and honor, peace and every good—so that God, as St. Paul said, "may be all in all" (1 Cor. 15:28). He will be the consummation of all our desiring—the object of our unending vision, of our unlessening love, of our unwearying praise. And in this gift of vision, this response of love, this paean of praise, all alike will share, as all will share in everlasting life.

But, now, who can imagine, let alone describe, the ranks upon ranks of rewarded saints, to be graded, undoubtedly, according to their variously merited honor and glory. Yet, there will be no envy of the lower for the higher, as there is no envy of angel for archangel—for this is one of the great blessednesses of this blessed city. The less rewarded will be linked in perfect peace with the more highly favored, but lower could not more long for higher than a finger, in the ordered integration of a body, could want to be an eye. The less endowed will have the high endowment of longing for nothing loftier than their lower gifts.

The souls in bliss will still possess the freedom of will, though sin will have no power to tempt them. They will be more free than ever —so free, in fact, from all delight in sinning as to find, in not sinning, an unfailing source of joy. By the freedom which was given to the first man, who was constituted in rectitude, he could choose either to sin or not to sin; in eternity, freedom is that more potent freedom which makes all sin impossible. Such freedom, of course, is a gift of God, beyond the power of nature to achieve. For, it is one thing to be God, another to be a sharer in the divine nature. God, by his nature, cannot sin, but a mere sharer in his nature must receive from God such immunity from sin. It was proper that, in the process of divine endowment, the first step should be a freedom not to sin, and the last a freedom even from the power to sin. The first gift made merit possible; the second is a part of man's reward. Our nature, when it was free to sin, did sin. It took a greater grace to lead us to that larger liberty which frees us from the very power to sin. Just as the immortality that Adam lost by his sin was, at first, a mere possibility of avoiding death, but, in heaven, becomes the impossibility of death, so free will was, at first, a mere possibility of avoiding sin, but, in heaven, becomes an utter inability to sin.

Our will will be as ineradicably rooted in rectitude and love as in beatitude. It is true that, with Adam's sin, we lost our right to grace and glory, but, with our right, we did not lose our longing to be happy. And, as for freedom, can we think that God himself, who certainly cannot sin, is therefore without freedom? The conclusion is that, in the everlasting city, there will remain in each and all of us an inalienable freedom of the will, emancipating us from every evil and filling us with every good, rejoicing in the inexhaustible beatitude of everlasting happiness, unclouded by the memory of any sin or of sanction suffered, yet with no forgetfulness of our redemption nor any loss of gratitude for our Redeemer.

The memory of our previous miseries will be a matter of purely mental contemplation, with no renewal of any feelings connected with these experiences—much as learned doctors know by science many of those bodily maladies which, by suffering, they have no sensible experience. All ills, in fact, can be forgotten in the double way in which we learn them, namely, notionally and experientially. It is one thing to be a philosopher, learning by ethical analysis the nature of each and every vice, and another to be a scoundrel, learning his lessons from a dissolute life. So, too, the student who becomes a doctor forgets in a way different from that of a patient who has suffered disease. The one forgets by giving up his practice; the patient, by being freed from pains. Now, it is into this second kind of oblivion that the previous miseries of the saints will fall, for not a trace of any sensible experience of suffering will remain.

However, in virtue of the vigor of their minds, they will have not merely a notional remembrance of their own past but also a knowledge of the unending torments of the damned. For, if they had no kind of memory of past miseries, how could the psalmist have said: "The mercies of the Lord they will sing forever?" (Ps. 89:1). And, surely, in all that city, nothing will be lovelier than this song in praise of the grace of Christ by whose blood all there were saved.

Heaven, too, will be the fulfillment of that sabbath rest foretold in the command: "Be still and see that I am God" (Ps. 46:10). This, indeed, will be that ultimate sabbath that has no evening and which the Lord foreshadowed in the account of his creation: "And God rested on the seventh day from all his work which he had done. And he blessed the seventh day and sanctified it: because in it he had rested from all his work which God created and made" (Gen. 2:2–3). And we ourselves will be a "seventh day" when we shall be filled with his blessing and remade by his sanctification. In the stillness of that rest we shall see that he is the God whose divinity we ambitioned for ourselves when we listened to the seducer's words, "You shall be as Gods" (Gen. 3:5), and so fell away from him, the true God who would have given us a divinity by participation that could never be gained by desertion. For, where did the doing without God end but in the undoing of man through the anger of God?

Only when we are remade by God and perfected by a greater grace shall we have the eternal stillness of that rest in which we shall see that he is God. Then only shall we be filled with him when he will be all in all. For, although our good works are, in reality, his, they will be put to our account as payment for this sabbath peace, so long as we do not claim them as our own; but, if we do, they will be reckoned as servile and out of place on the sabbath, as the text reminds us: "The seventh day . . . is the rest of the Lord. . . . Thou shalt not do any work therein" (Deut. 5:14). In this connection, too, God has reminded us, through the prophet Ezechiel: "I gave them my sabbaths, to be a sign between me and them, that they might know that I am the Lord that sanctifies them" (Ezech. 20:12). It is this truth that we shall realize perfectly when we shall be perfectly at rest and shall perfectly see that it is he who is God.

There is a clear indication of this final sabbath if we take the seven ages of world history as being "days" and calculate in accordance with the data furnished by the Scriptures. The first age or day is that from Adam to the flood; the second, from the flood to Abraham. (These two "days" were not identical in length of time, but in each there were ten generations.) Then follow the three ages, each consisting of fourteen generations, as recorded in the Gospel of St. Matthew: the first, from Abraham to David; the second, from David to the transmigration to Babylon; the third, from then to Christ's nativity in the flesh. Thus, we have five ages. The sixth is the one in which we now are. It is an age not to be measured by any precise number of generations, since we are told: "It is not for you to know the times or dates which the Father has fixed by his own authority" (Acts 1:7). After this "day," God will rest on the "seventh day," in the sense that God will make us, who are to be this seventh day, rest in him.

There is no need here to speak in detail of each of these seven "days." Suffice it to say that this "seventh day" will be our sabbath and that it will end in no evening, but only in the Lord's day—that eighth and eternal day which dawned when Christ's resurrection heralded an eternal rest both for the spirit and for the body. On that day we shall rest and see, see and love, love and praise—for this is to be the end without the end of all our living, that kingdom without end, the real goal of our present life.

4. SCHLEIERMACHER: THE CONSUMMATION OF THE CHURCH AND PERSONAL SURVIVAL

Schleiermacher deals with eschatology or the doctrine of last things as a set of topics of least significance because they seem quite remote from the sphere of the inner life and its immediate religious feelings. He discusses them as "prophetic doctrines," which must be interpreted in nonliteral fashion. Our excerpts are from the three introductory propositions to this discussion. Source: Friedrich Schleiermacher, *The Christian Faith*, §§ 157–59, ed. H. R. Mackintosh and J. S. Stewart (Edinburgh: T. & T. Clark, 1928), pp. 696–707. Date of original publication: 1830.

*Since the Church cannot attain to its consummation
in the course of human life on earth, the representation
of its consummated state is directly useful only as a
pattern to which we have to approximate.*

Strictly speaking . . . from our point of view we can have no doctrine
of the consummation of the Church, for our Christian consciousness
has absolutely nothing to say regarding a condition so entirely outside
our ken. We have recognized Christ as the end of prophecy; which implies that even the Church does not acknowledge any gift of the Spirit
enabling her to form a prophetic picture of a future on which (since it
lies altogether beyond human experience) our action can exert no
influence whatever; indeed, in the absence of all analogy we could
hardly understand the picture aright or retain it securely. None the
less, these prophetic pictures fill a great place in the Church, and it is
incumbent on us, before pronouncing for their exclusion from this exposition, to inquire as to their source. In the first place, reference must
be made to the New Testament predictions of the consummation of
the Church, all of which we certainly must trace back to prophetic ut-
terances of Christ. Now if these are to be treated by the rules of art, and
yet not to be made doctrines proper, but only propositions which we
receive on testimony, yet which do not stand in so intimate a relation
with our faith as do similar propositions regarding the person of the Redeemer, we shall hardly be able to give them a place in our dogmatic,
or at least only insofar as they concern the Redeemer and our relation
to him. While, however, these propositions are not doctrines of faith,
since their content (as transcending our faculties of apprehension) is
not a description of our actual consciousness, the matter takes on another aspect if, abstracting from the fact that they transcend our present
conditions, we concentrate on the point that they must contain no reference to anything in our present state due to the influences of the
world. That these influences may be restrained, in a higher degree
than the mere co-operation of individuals could secure, is the constant
object of our prayers; and the consummated Church is accordingly the
sphere where such prayer is answered in full measure. Hence this idea
of the consummation of the Church is rooted in our Christian consciousness as representing the unbroken fellowship of human nature
with Christ under conditions wholly unknown and only faintly imag-

inable, but the only fellowship which can be conceived as wholly free from all that springs from the conflict of flesh and spirit.

As the belief in the immutability of the union of the divine essence with human nature in the person of Christ contains in itself also the belief in the persistence of human personality, this produces in the Christian the impulse to form a conception of the state that succeeds death.

. . . This belief naturally is accompanied by a desire to form and keep clear ideas as to the condition of personality after death. But it is wholly impossible for us to claim that in this we shall definitely succeed. The question as to the conditions of existence after death (and a knowledge of them must form the basis of any clear conception) is a purely cosmological question; and space and spatialities are so closely connected with times and seasons that equally with these they lie outside the range of those communications which the Redeemer had to make to us. Hence all the indications he gives are either purely figurative, or otherwise so indefinite in tenor that nothing can be gathered from them more than what for every Christian is so much the essential thing in every conception he may form of existence after death, that without it such existence would be mere perdition—namely, the persistent union of believers with the Redeemer. Similarly, what the Apostles say on the subject is said merely by way of dim presentiment, and with the confession that definite knowledge is lacking. True, then, as it may be that each moment of our present life is intrinsically more perfect and wise the more completely and clearly it embraces both past and future, we should not seek to determine our purposes by picturing to ourselves the form of our future life. . . .

The solution of these two problems, to represent the Church in its consummation and the state of souls in the future life, is attempted in the ecclesiastical doctrines of the last things; but to these doctrines we cannot ascribe the same value as to the doctrines already handled.

The phrase, "the last things," which has been somewhat generally accepted, has a look of strangeness which is more concealed by the word "eschatology"; for the term "things" threatens to carry us quite away from the domain of the inner life, with which we alone are concerned. This of itself indicates that something is being attempted here which cannot be secured by doctrines proper in our sense of the word. The terms have this in common, that if the beginning of a wholly new and ever-enduring spiritual form of life be represented as from our point of view "the last thing," that endless duration appears merely as the end of a time-life which, as contrasted therewith, is almost a vanishing quantity. This can only be justified by bringing in the idea of retribution, and that idea accordingly becomes dominant. On the other hand, if the same endless duration be regarded as the further development of the new life begun here, the brief time-life appears rather as its preparatory and introductory first stage. The former view, insisting on the idea of retribution, appeals for support chiefly to those passages in which Christ represents himself as one to whom judgment has been committed; the latter, based on the idea of development, to passages in which he says that he is come to save. Indisputably this latter view is more closely akin to the premonition of personal survival as that is demonstrably present in the Christian consciousness; on the other hand, the former is more in harmony with the idea of the consummation of the Church, an idea which, in order to find a point of attachment in our present life as a whole, insists on the exclusion of all that can be called "world" even from the Church's environment. Thus doctrines of the last things have connections equally with both these problems; each doctrine relates to both. If we tried to form a Christian idea of a state subsequent to this life, and it failed to agree with our idea of the consummation of the Church, we could not believe that it really expressed the absolutely final stage; we should have to suppose that there still remained a further development, in which the Church would be perfected. Conversely, if we viewed the consummation of the Church as arriving within the present course of human affairs, we should have to add something in thought for the state after death, in order to give it a content of its own; the material for this, however, could not be drawn from our Christian consciousness, for its contents are all of the other kind. Hence it was in the nature of the case that both elements should be thus conjoined—the consummation of the Church (which we cannot regard as possible in this life) being placed in that future life of which we cannot but form a conception, and the idea of that life (based as it must be on fellowship with Christ) being filled out with content from the perfected state of the Church. It must be so, if the new form of life is decisively to transcend the present.

At the same time we are not in a position to exhibit the confluence of the two factors, or to guarantee it. The consummated Church cannot be thought of as analogous to the Church militant; nor do we know whether into the future life we ought to project the idea of an interdependent common life and work, to which no proper goal can be assigned. On the other hand, if we seek to conceive the future life by analogy with the present, as an ascending development, we cannot but have doubts whether any such development is possible in the consummated Church. Thus the solution of one problem seems never exactly to fit the other. We encounter the same difficulty if we keep to the indications of Scripture. There much is said by way of representing the consummated Church; but it is not so said that we can affirm with certainty that it ought to be dated subsequently to the end of all earthly things (John 6:53–58, Acts 1:6–7, Eph. 4); and for that reason from of yore many Christians have actually expected the consummation of the Church here on earth. Other passages are meant rather to describe the life after death (1 Cor. 15:23f., Phil. 3:21), but whether they are also a representation of the consummated Church may be doubted. . . .

Under the circumstances, an exact construction of these paragraphs in a closely knit context is not to be thought of. We must be content to assume their sense as generally acknowledged, and let the facts prove that in their regard matters really are as I have indicated. This means exhibiting the two points—personal survival and the consummation of the Church—in their relation to each other, in a picture appealing to the sensuous imagination. Hence, in the first place, the survival of personality, above all, as the abolition of death, is represented under the figure of *the resurrection of the flesh*. The consummation of the Church, on the other hand, is represented in a twofold manner—first, as conditioned by the fact that no further influence upon the Church can now be exerted by those who form no part of the Church, it is introduced in its character as the separation of believers from unbelievers, by the *last judgment*. But as excluding (in contrast to the Church militant) all the activities of sin and all imperfection in believers, it is represented as *eternal blessedness*. Since the survival of personality, and therefore also the resurrection of the flesh, had to be taken as applying to the whole human race, and some mode of existence had to be found for those separated from believers, over against eternal blessedness stands (also introduced by the last judgment) the eternal damnation of the unbelieving. It is clear that, as this last pictorial representation is not an anticipation of any object of our future experience, it cannot be given the form of a special doctrine; all we can do is to treat it as the shadow of eternal blessedness or the darker side of judgment. These separate pictures fit together into a single imaginative picture, for this reason that the new form of existence is conditional on the *return of Christ*, to which everything which belongs to the completion of his work must be related.

5. BULTMANN: JESUS CHRIST AS THE ESCHATOLOGICAL EVENT

Bultmann stresses that Christianity is essentially an eschatological faith, not reducible to ethics and morality, and he provides a strictly existentialist interpretation of the meaning of eschatology. Source: Rudolf Bultmann, *History and Eschatology*, (Edinburgh: Edinburgh University Press, 1957), pp. 151–55. These were the Gifford Lectures delivered in 1955.

[The Christian] message knows itself to be legitimated by the revelation of the grace of God in Jesus Christ. According to the New Testament, *Jesus Christ is the eschatological event*, the action of God by which God has set an end to the old world. In the preaching of the Christian Church the eschatological event will ever again become present and does become present ever and again in faith. The old world has reached its end for the believer; he is "a new creature in Christ." For the old world has reached its end with the fact that he himself as "the old man" has reached his end and is now "a new man," a free man.

It is the paradox of the Christian message that the eschatological event, according to Paul and John, is not to be understood as a dramatic cosmic catastrophe but as happening within history, beginning with the appearance of Jesus Christ and in continuity with this occurring again and again in history, but not as the kind of historical development which can be confirmed by any historian. It becomes an event repeatedly in preaching and faith. Jesus Christ is the eschatological event not as an established fact of past time but as repeatedly present, as addressing you and me here and now in preaching.

Preaching is address, and as address it demands answer, *decision.* This decision is obviously something other than the decisions in responsibility over against the future which are demanded in every present moment. For in the decision of faith I do not decide on a responsible action, but on a new understanding of myself as free from myself by the grace of God and as endowed with my new self, and this is at the same time the decision to accept a new life grounded in the grace of God. In making this decision I also decide on a new understanding of my responsible acting. This does not mean that the responsible decision demanded by the historical moment is taken away from me by faith, but it does mean that all responsible decisions are born of love. For love consists in unreservedly being for one's neighbor, and this is possible only for the man who has become free from himself.

It is the paradox of Christian being that the believer is taken out of the world and exists, so to speak, as unworldly and that at the same time he remains within the world, within his historicity. To be historical means to live from the future. The believer too lives from the future; first because his faith and his freedom can never be possession; as belonging to the eschatological event they can never become facts of past time but are reality only over and over again as event; secondly because the believer remains within history. In principle, the future always offers to man the gift of freedom; Christian faith is the power to grasp this gift. The freedom of man from himself is always realized in the freedom of historical decisions.

The paradox of Christ as the historical Jesus and the ever-present Lord and the paradox of the Christian as an eschatological and historical being is excellently described by Erich Frank: ". . . to the Christians the advent of Christ was not an event in that temporal process which we mean by history today. It was an event in the history of salvation, in the realm of eternity, an eschatological moment in which rather this profane history of the world came to its end. And in an analogous way, history comes to its end in the religious experience of any

Christian 'who is in Christ.' In his faith he is already above time and history. For although the advent of Christ is an historical event which happened 'once' in the past, it is, at the same time, an eternal event which occurs again and again in the soul of any Christian in whose soul Christ is born, suffers, dies and is raised up to eternal life. In his faith the Christian is a contemporary of Christ, and time and the world's history are overcome. The advent of Christ is an event in the realm of eternity which is incommensurable with historical time. But it is the trial of the Christian that although in the spirit he is above time and world, in the flesh he remains in this world, subject to time; and the evils of history, in which he is engulfed, go on. . . . But the process of history has gained a new meaning as the pressure and friction operate under which the Christian has to refine his soul and under which, alone, he can fulfill his true destiny. History and the world do not change, but man's attitude to the world changes."

In the New Testament the eschatological character of the Christian existence is sometimes called "sonship." F. Gogarten says: "Sonship is not something like an habitus or a quality, but it must be grasped ever and again in the decisions of life. For it is that towards which the present temporal history tends, and therefore it happens within this history and nowhere else." Christian faith just "by reason of the radical eschatological character of the salvation believed in never takes man out of his concrete worldly existence. On the contrary, faith calls him into it with unique sobriety. . . . For the salvation of man happens only within it and nowhere else."

We have no time to describe how Reinhold Niebuhr in his stimulating book *Faith and History* (1949) endeavors to explain the relation between faith and history in a similar way. Nor have we time to dispute with H. Butterfield's thought, developed in his book *Christianity and History*. Although I do not think he has clearly seen the problem of historicism and the nature of historicity, his book contains many important statements. And I agree with him when he says: "Every instant is eschatological." I would prefer, however, to say: every instant has the possibility of being an eschatological instant and in Christian faith this possibility is realized.

The paradox that Christian existence is at the same time an eschatological unworldly being and an historical being is analogous with the

Lutheran statement *simul iustus, simul peccator.* In faith the Christian has the standpoint above history which Jaspers like many others has endeavored to find, but without losing his historicity. His unworldliness is not a quality, but it may be called *aliena* (foreign), as his righteousness, his *iustitia* is called by Luther *aliena.*

We started our lectures with the question of meaning in history, raised by the problem of historicism. We have seen that man cannot answer this question as the question of the meaning in history in its totality. For man does not stand outside history. But now we can say: *the meaning in history lies always in the present,* and when the present is conceived as the eschatological present by Christian faith the meaning in history is realized. Man who complains: "I cannot see meaning in history, and therefore my life, interwoven in history, is meaningless," is to be admonished: do not look around yourself into universal history, you must look into your own personal history. Always in your present lies the meaning in history, and you cannot see it as a spectator, but only in your responsible decisions. In every moment slumbers the possibility of being the eschatological moment. You must awaken it.

6. TILLICH: *KAIROS*

Tillich made a major contribution to the interpretation of the kingdom of God through his philosophy of history. He used the biblical concept of the *kairos,* defined as that moment in time when the eternal breaks into history, as a summons to his contemporaries in the Germany of the 1930s to rise to the challenge of that special moment of destiny in history. Source: Paul Tillich, *The Protestant Era,* trans. James Luther Adams (Chicago: University of Chicago Press, 1948), pp. 33, 35–38. From the essay, "Kairos," originally published in 1922.

It was a fine feeling that made the spirit of the Greek language signify *chronos,* "formal time," with a different word from *kairos,* "the right time," the moment rich in content and significance. And it is no accident that this word found its most pregnant and most frequent usage when the Greek language became the vessel for the dynamic spirit of Judaism and primitive Christianity—in the New Testament. His "kairos" had not yet come, is said of Jesus; and then it had once at some time or other come, *en kairo,* in the moment of the fulness of time.

341

Time is an empty form only for abstract, objective reflection, a form that can receive any kind of content; but to him who is conscious of an ongoing creative life it is laden with tensions, with possibilities and impossibilities, it is qualitative and full of significance. Not everything is possible at every time, not everything is true at every time, nor is everything demanded at every moment. Various "rulers," that is different cosmic powers, rule at different times, and the "ruler," conquering all the other angels and powers, reigns in the time that is full of destiny and tension between the Resurrection and the Second Coming, in the "present time," which in its essence is different from every other time of the past. In this tremendous, most profoundly stirred consciousness of history is rooted the idea of the kairos; and from this beginning it will be molded into a conception purposely adapted to a philosophy of history. . . .

The first great philosophy of history was born out of a keen sense of duality and conflict. The struggle between light and darkness, between good and evil, is its essence. World history is the effect of this conflict; in history the entirely new occurs, the unique, the absolutely decisive; defeats may be suffered on the way, but in the end comes the victory of the light. Thus did Zarathustra, the Persian prophet, interpret history. Jewish prophecy brought into this picture the ethical drive of its God of justice. The epochs of the struggle are the epochs of history. History is determined by supra-historical events. The most important period is the final one, that of the struggle for the ultimate decision, an epoch beyond which no new epoch can be imagined. This type of historical consciousness thinks in conceptions of an absolute character: the absolute opposition between light and darkness, between good and evil; the final decision; the unconditional "No" and the unconditional "Yes" which are struggling with each other. It is an attitude toward history which is moved by a tremendous spiritual tension and by an ultimate responsibility on the part of the individual. This is the great, early expression of man's historical consciousness: the philosophy of history expressed in absolute terms.

It can take on two basic forms. The first form of the absolute philosophy of history is defined by a tense feeling that the end of time is near: the Kingdom of God is at hand, the time of decision is imminent, the great, the real kairos is appearing which will transform everything. This is the revolutionary-absolute type. It sees the goal of history in the "kingdom from above" or in the victory of reason within this world. In both cases an absolute "No" is pronounced upon all the past, and an absolute "Yes" is pronounced upon the future. This interpretation of history is fundamental for all strong historical consciousness, as is the interpretation in which the conception of the kairos was first grasped.

The second form of the absolute philosophy of history can be called a conservative transformation of the revolutionary form as it was achieved by Augustine in his struggle against the chiliastic revivals of the early Christian belief in the imminent coming of the Kingdom of God in history. The background of this type is the same as that of the revolutionary type: the vision of a struggle between two forces in all epochs of history. But, according to the conservative type, the decisive event has already happened. The new is victoriously established in history, although it is still attacked by the forces of darkness. The church in its hierarchical structure represents this new reality. There are still improvements, partial defeats, and partial victories to be expected and, of course, the final catastrophe, in which the evil is destroyed and history will come to an end. But nothing really new can be expected within history. A conservative attitude toward the given is demanded.

The dangerous element in both forms of the absolute philosophy of history, in the conservative as well as in the revolutionary form, is the fact that a special historical reality is set up as absolute, whether it be an existing church or the expected rational society. This, of course, brings a continuous tension into the historical consciousness; but, at the same time, it depreciates all other historical realities. In the Augustinian interpretation, which in principle corresponds with the inner feeling and self-consciousness of all predominantly sacramental churches, only the history of a special church is, in the strict sense, significant for the philosophy of history. Her inner conflicts and their resolution, her fights against external enemies—these are the viewpoints under which all other events are envisaged and estimated. The fight for God and against the world, which is the present historical task, means, in practice, a fight for the church, for a pure doctrine, for a hierarchy. Against this ecclesiastical interpretation of history we must conceive of the kairos in universal terms, and we must not limit it to the past but raise it to a general principle of history, to a principle that is also relevant to the present.

Again and again sectarian revolutionary impulses have opposed the ecclesiastical-conservative mentality, in religious or in secular terms. Whether the great revolution is thought of as from beyond and is expected through the action of God exclusively, or as prepared for by human action, or as being a creation of the human spirit and an act of political revolution; whether the utopias are based on ideas of natural law, such as democracy, socialism, and anarchism (heirs of the religious utopias) or on a transcendent myth, the consciousness of the kairos is equally strong and equally unconditional in all of them. But, in contrast to the conservative interpretation, the kairos in this view lies in the present: "The kingdom is at hand." This excitement, however, about the present and the exclusive orientation toward the future in the revolutionary movements blinds them with respect to the past. The sects are opposed to the ecclesiastical traditions, the *bourgeoisie* destroys the aristocratic forms of life, socialism fights against the bourgeois heritage. The history of the past disappears in the dynamic thrust toward the future. This is the reason why a strong historical consciousness has often accompanied ignorance about past history—for instance, in the proletarian masses—and this is the reason why, on the other hand, a tremendous amount of historical knowledge has not overcome an attitude of detachment and misapprehension with respect to the present moment of history, for instance, in the bourgeois historians of the last decades (in contrast to the great bourgeois historians of the eighteenth century, with their revolutionary visions). For these scholars history was an object of causal explanation or of exact descriptions, but it did not concern them existentially. It was not a place of actual decisions (in spite of their great achievements in historical research). But oppressed and ignorant people, and those few from the educated classes who identified themselves with the people, created the revolutionary-absolute interpretation of history. So it was in early Christianity, in most of the medieval sects, and in our own period. But the lack of a sense of tradition was also the reason for the strong elements of utopianism in all these movements. Their ignorance of the past betrayed them into the feeling that the period of perfection had already started, that the absolute transformation was only a matter of days or of a few years, and that they were its representatives and bearers.

Both forms of an absolute philosophy of history are judged by the absolute itself. The unconditional cannot be identified with any given reality, whether past or future; there is no absolute church, there is no absolute kingdom of reason and justice in history. A conditional reality set up as something unconditional, a finite reality to which divine predicates are attributed, is antidivine; it is an "idol." This prophetic criticism, launched in the name of the unconditional, breaks the absolute church and the absolute society; conservative ecclesiasticism and revolutionary utopianism are alike idolatry.

This is the message of the so-called "theology of crisis," represented by Karl Barth in his powerful commentary on Paul's Epistle to the Romans. No finite reality can claim an absolute status. Everything conditioned is judged by the unconditional in terms of "Yes" and "No." There is a permanent crisis going on in history, a crisis in the double sense of the Greek word: judgment and separation. No moment of history is without this tension, the tension between the unconditional and the conditional. The crisis is permanent. The kairos is always given. But there are no outstanding moments in history with respect to the manifestation of the unconditional (except the *one* moment which is called "Jesus Christ" and which has a supra-historical character). History as such loses its absolute significance; hence it loses the tremendous weight it has in the revolutionary interpretations of history. From the absolute point of view, history becomes indifferent. A third type of absolute philosophy of history appears in this doctrine of "crisis," the "indifference" type. It is indifferent to the special heights and depths of the historical process. A kind of "divine humor" toward history is praised, reminding one of romantic irony or of Luther's understanding of history as the realm of God's strange acting. In this attitude the concept of crisis has no actuality; it remains abstract, beyond every special criticism and judgment. But this is not the way in which the crisis can be effective and the negative can be overcome. The latter is possible only by a new creation. Not negation but affirmation conquers the negative. The appearance of the new is the concrete crisis of the old, the historical judgment against it. The new creation may be worse than the old one which is brought into crisis by it; and, whether better or worse, it is subjected to judgment itself. But in the special historical moment it is *en kairo* ("at the right time") while the old creation is not. In this way history receives the weight and seriousness which belong to it. The absolute—to vary a famous saying of Hegel—is not so impotent as to remain in separation from the relative. It appears in the relative as judgment and creation.

7. PANNENBERG: ESCHATOLOGY AND THE EXPERIENCE OF MEANING

Pannenberg seeks to transcend the existentialist view of eschatology, which limits its meaning to religious experience or existential decisions. The idea of the kingdom of God is concerned with a real future of history and humanity, and not just with the interior spiritual life of individuals. Source: Wolfhart Pannenberg, *The Idea of God and Human Freedom*, trans. R. A. Wilson (Philadelphia: Westminster Press, 1973), pp. 196–99. From the essay "Eschatology and the Experience of Meaning," a lecture delivered to the Congress on the Future of Religion, in 1972.

The Christian hope is directed towards the coming of the kingdom of God and towards participation in the new life it brings. All other "last things" in Christian tradition are related to this, particularly the resurrection of the dead and the judgment of the world. What kind of future is this? The concern is everywhere, even in the expectation of an end of the present world and a new creation with man, the future of man.

This can be demonstrated in the first instance by looking at the central conception of the kingdom of God. This is a kingdom of peace and righteousness, such as Isaiah (2:1–5) expects in the coming messianic kingdom, which will bring to reality the righteous will of God expressed in the God-given law of Israel. The book of Daniel associates the fulfilment of this hope of political salvation with the expectation of direct rule by God himself, by contrast to the kingdoms of the world, based upon human rule. Consequently, in the book of Daniel (7:13) the kingdom of God is symbolized by the figure of a human being, while the nature of the kingdoms of the world is expressed in animal symbols: not until the kingdom of God comes will there be a basis for a truly human society. Of course peace and justice are goals which every political order seeks to bring about. But under the ordinances of human rule these goals are constantly perverted into their opposite. This is why the rule of God himself is necessary, so that both the righteousness of God, and with it man's social being, can be brought to reality. But to bring to reality the righteousness of God requires a revision of the present unjust relationships amongst men, in which violence and deceit so often triumph. If the righteousness of God is to be realized not merely in a future generation, but in all men, it requires some form of compensation in the world to come, a judgment of the dead, and for this the resurrection of the dead is necessary. Finally, the perfect society of the kingdom of God also requires a change in the natural conditions of existence; it requires a new heaven and a new earth.

Thus the eschatological conceptions of early Judaism, which were taken over as such by primitive Christianity, were directly concerned with the future of mankind. Do they consist of prophecies of particular individual happenings which are to come about at some time in the course of events, preceded and followed by a period of time? In my opinion this is to misunderstand the meaning of the eschatological prophecies of the future. They are of course concerned with a real future, but in a different sense from predictions on the basis of natural laws, forecasts of political developments or the intuitive foreknowledge of contingent future events. The eschatological prophecies of the future formulate the conditions of the final realization of man's humanity as a consequence of the establishment of the righteousness of God, which is essential to man's being as such. The realization of man's being as such requires a community in which everyone has his own proper place, so that in it the conflicts between the individual and society, between individual interests and the interests of society, are overcome. If the unity of man's being as an individual and a member of society is an indispensable condition for the realization of his humanity, it is not sufficient for a balance to be struck in some future order of society between the individual and society, even if this could be supposed possible under the present conditions of human existence, where the common interest must be discerned and furthered by individuals who repeatedly do so from the point of view of their private interests. But even if it were possible to establish the unity of men's individual and common interests in a future society, how then would people of previous generations participate in the destiny of man realized in such a future society? The possibility of all human individuals participating in the perfect society in which the destiny of mankind is realized is unimaginable without a resurrection of the dead. And for everyone to participate in the life of the society in the way appropriate to him is inconceivable unless a balance is struck by a judgment of the world which takes place beyond and outside it. Thus the association of judgment, the resurrection of the dead and the realization of a perfect society in the concept of the end of the world and of history, as they have existed hitherto, is in accordance with the idea of the consummation of man's destiny in the unity of its individual and social aspects.

If, then, the statements of early Jewish eschatology concerning the future are intended to formulate the conditions for the realization of man's destiny in the unity of its individual and social aspects, then in the future of the kingdom of God we are concerned with the true and essential future of man. The eschatological statements concerning the future tell us nothing of the happenings by which, in the material course of events, this essential future of human nature is to be realized. The eschatological hope leaves such questions open. In particular, no answer is given to the question of the relationship between the idea of a new creation of the natural world, as the condition of the realization of human nature, and the physical processes with which we are familiar. Are these processes to come to an end, and are they to be replaced by something quite different? Do these physical processes continue, or will they lead beyond the stage which the realization of human nature has at present reached? Must we suppose a "curvature" of time, analogous to the "curvature" of the dimension of space in the theory of relativity? All of these ideas are worth discussion. They are mentioned here only to show that the conceptions found in eschatological statements concerning the end of the world, in the sense of the future of human nature, relieve theology of any need to settle for any one particular conception of the end of the world. But they do not mean that the eschatological future ceases to have any connection with real time, or does not differ from the present and the past.

Does this interpretation of the eschatological conceptions developed in the biblical traditions amount to an anthropological reinterpretation of the eschatological language of the Bible? This would be so only if it could be shown that historically the statements concerned did not have the function here attributed to them. Of course the eschatological conceptions in the scriptures are not formulated as conditions for the realization of human nature. The way they are formulated does not exclude the anthropological perspectives of our own age. But may not the perspectives of a later period reveal something in traditional texts which has hitherto lain unnoticed? Only when the statements of tradition are so forced that they are made to say something different from what can be shown to be present in them, can we properly say their meaning has been altered.

8. MOLTMANN: THE RESURRECTION AS HOPE

Along with Pannenberg, Jürgen Moltmann has been a major force in the mid-twentieth-century revival of interest in eschatology. In the conclusion to his Ingersoll Lecture, he offers a brief statement of the central thesis of the "theology of hope," accenting futurity, newness, and freedom anchored in the resurrection of Jesus of Nazareth. Source: Jürgen Moltmann, "Resurrection as Hope," *Religion, Revolution, and the Future* (New York: Charles Scribner's Sons, 1969), pp. 60–62. The lecture was given at Harvard Divinity School in 1967.

In a time when God was questioned, the Christian faith saw, in Jesus, God's incarnation. Not the resurrection, but the incarnation; not Easter, but Christmas stood at the center. In a time when man began to regard himself as questionable, faith saw in Jesus the true man, the creative archetype of the divine man. Today the future is becoming more and more the pressing question for a mankind that is now able to destroy itself. Thus Christian faith discovers today in God the power of a future that stems itself against the destruction of the world. The God of the exodus and of the resurrection is the "God of hope" rather than the "God above" or the "ground of being." He is in history "the coming God," as the Old Testament prophets said, who announces his coming in his promises and his lowly Messiah. He is "the absolute future" (Karl Rahner) or, figuratively, the Lord of the future, who says, "Behold, I make all things new."

If we simultaneously begin to think of God and future, faith and hope, we move in a new way close to the primitive Christian Easter message. We are able to understand it again eschatologically. We can recognize in the inexplicable *novum* of Christ the anticipation and the incarnation of the ultimately or universally new, which in the coming of the recreating God can be hoped for. God is the power of the future. God is the power of the new. Jesus himself has been translated into the future of the new. He represents this future and at the same time mediates it. Following the emphasis on divine Sonship and the emphasis on true humanity, the old titles for Jesus, "Messiah" and *ho erchomenos,* the "coming one," seem quite timely again. In him, who from cross, God-forsakenness, and hell was raised, we become certain of a future which will conquer God-forsakenness and hell. But this is not everything: The fulfillment of the resurrection hope must now be joined with the expectation of a future which has not existed before, with the expectation of the presence of the God who announces himself in Word and Spirit. The ultimately new lies in the promise: "He will dwell with them, and they shall be his people" (Rev. 21:3). The resurrection hope can fulfill itself only in the future of God in which God is really God and will be "all in all" (1 Cor. 15:28).

The hope for such a presence of God can be fulfilled, however, only if the negatives of death, suffering, tears, guilt, and evil have disappeared from reality, that is, in a new creation, which, figuratively speaking, is no longer a mixture of day and night, earth and sea, and in which, ontologically speaking, being and nonbeing are no longer intertwined. The hope for the future, in which God is God and a new creation his dwelling place, the expectation of that home of identity in which man is at one with God, nature, and himself radically anew confronts the unfulfilled present with the theodicy question. Where freedom has come near, the chains begin to hurt. Where life is close, death becomes deadly. Where God proclaims his presence, the God-forsakenness of the world turns into suffering. Thus the theodicy question, born of suffering and pain, negatively mirrors the positive hope for God's future. We begin to suffer from the conditions of our world if we begin to love the world. And we begin to love the world if we are able to discover hope for it. And we discover hope for this world if we hear the promise of a future which stands against frustration, transiency, and death. To be sure, we can find certainty only in complete uncertainty. To be sure, we can hope for God only in the pain of the open theodicy question. But it does not take more . . . to make man immortal.

XIII. THE RELIGIONS

1. JUSTIN MARTYR: IN DEFENSE
OF CHRISTIANITY

A philosopher who had come to realize that unaided reason cannot attain truth about God, Justin argued in relation to both Jews and Greeks that God is fully revealed only in Jesus Christ, the incarnation of the Logos. In the first selection, from his *Dialogue with Trypho*, the argument centers on the interpretation of Jewish scriptures. The second selection, from his *Second Apology*, acknowledges the wisdom of Greek thinkers, notably Plato, while the third selection, from the *Hortatory Address to the Greeks*, mounts an argument against Greek thought similar to that against the Jews. Source: Justin Martyr, *Dialogue with Trypho*, Chaps. 10–13; *Second Apology*, Chap. 13; *Hortatory Address to the Greeks*, Chaps. 20, 22–23, in *The Ante-Nicene Fathers* (New York: Christian Literature Co., 1886–97; reprinted 1960 by Eerdmans), Vol. 1, pp. 192–93, 199–200, 281–82. Date of original composition: ca. 155–65.

I

"Is there any other matter, my friends, in which we are blamed, than this, that we live not after the law, and are not circumcised in the flesh as your forefathers were, and do not observe sabbaths as you do? Are our lives and customs also slandered among you? And I ask this: have you also believed concerning us, that we eat men; and that after the feast, having extinguished the lights, we engage in promiscuous concubinage? Or do you condemn us in this alone, that we adhere to such tenets, and believe in an opinion, untrue, as you think?"

"This is what we are amazed at," said Trypho, "but those things about which the multitude speak are not worthy of belief; for they are most repugnant to human nature. Moreover, I am aware that your precepts in the so-called Gospel are so wonderful and so great, that I suspect no one can keep them; for I have carefully read them. But this is what we are most at a loss about: that you, professing to be pious, and supposing yourselves better than others, are not in any particular

351

separated from them, and do not alter your mode of living from the nations, in that you observe no festivals or sabbaths, and do not have the rite of circumcision; and further, resting your hopes on a man that was crucified, you yet expect to obtain some good thing from God, while you do not obey his commandments. Have you not read, that that soul shall be cut off from his people who shall not have been circumcised on the eighth day? And this has been ordained for strangers and for slaves equally. But you, despising this covenant rashly, reject the consequent duties, and attempt to persuade yourselves that you know God, when, however, you perform none of those things which they do who fear God. If, therefore, you can defend yourself on these points, and make it manifest in what way you hope for anything whatsoever, even though you do not observe the law, this we would very gladly hear from you, and we shall make other similar investigations." . . .

"There will be no other God, O Trypho, nor was there from eternity any other existing" (I thus addressed him), "but he who made and disposed all this universe. Nor do we think that there is one God for us, another for you, but that he alone is God who led your fathers out from Egypt with a strong hand and a high arm. Nor have we trusted in any other (for there is no other), but in him in whom you also have trusted, the God of Abraham, and of Isaac, and of Jacob. But we do not trust through Moses or through the law; for then we would do the same as yourselves. But now—for I have read that there shall be a final law, and a covenant, the chiefest of all, which it is now incumbent on all men to observe, as many as are seeking after the inheritance of God. For the law promulgated on Horeb is now old, and belongs to yourselves alone; but *this* is for all universally. Now, law placed against law has abrogated that which is before it, and a covenant which comes after in like manner has put an end to the previous one; and an eternal and final law—namely, Christ—has been given us, and the covenant is trustworthy, after which there shall be no law, no commandment, no ordinance. Have you not read this which Isaiah says: 'Hearken unto me, hearken unto me, my people; and, ye kings, give ear unto me: for a law shall go forth from me, and my judgment shall be for a light to the nations. My righteousness approaches swiftly, and my salvation shall go forth, and nations shall trust in mine arm?' (Isa. 51:4–5). And by Jeremiah, concerning this same new covenant, he thus speaks: 'Behold, the days come, saith the Lord, that I will make a new covenant with the house of Israel and with the house of Judah; not according to the covenant which I made with their fathers, in the day that I took them by the hand, to bring them out of the land of Egypt' (Jer. 31:31–32). If, therefore, God proclaimed a new covenant which was to be instituted, and this for a light of the nations, we see and are persuaded that men approach God, leaving their idols and other unrighteousness, through the name of him who was crucified, Jesus Christ, and abide by their confession even unto death, and maintain piety. Moreover, by the works and by the attendant miracles, it is possible for all to understand that he is the new law, and the new covenant, and the expectation of those who out of every people wait for the good things of God. For the true spiritual Israel, and descendants of Judah, Jacob, Isaac, and Abraham (who in uncircumcision was approved of and blessed by God on account of his faith, and called the father of many nations), are we who have been led to God through this crucified Christ, as shall be demonstrated while we proceed." . . .

I also adduced another passage in which Isaiah exclaims: "'Hear my words, and your soul shall live; and I will make an everlasting covenant with you, even the sure mercies of David. Behold, I have given him for a witness to the people: nations which know not thee shall call on thee; peoples who know not thee shall escape to thee, because of thy God, the Holy One of Israel; for he has glorified thee' (Isa. 55:3ff.). This same law you have despised, and his new holy covenant you have slighted; and now you neither receive it, nor repent of your evil deeds. 'For your ears are closed, your eyes are blinded, and the heart is hardened,' Jeremiah has cried; yet not even then do you listen. The Lawgiver is present, yet you do not see him; to the poor the Gospel is preached, the blind see, yet you do not understand. You have now need of a second circumcision, though you glory greatly in the flesh. The new law requires you to keep perpetual sabbath, and you, because you are idle for one day, suppose you are pious, not discerning why this has been commanded you: and if you eat unleavened bread, you say the will of God has been fulfilled. The Lord our God does not take pleasure in such observances: if there is any perjured person or a thief among you, let him cease to be so; if any adulterer, let him repent; then he has kept the sweet and true sabbaths of God. If any one has impure hands, let him wash and be pure.

"For Isaiah did not send you to a bath, there to wash away murder and other sins, which not even all the water of the sea were sufficient to purge; but, as might have been expected, this was that saving bath of the olden time which followed those who repented, and who no longer were purified by the blood of goats and of sheep, or by the ashes of an heifer, or by the offerings of fine flour, but by faith through the blood of Christ, and through his death, who died for this very reason. . . ." [There follows a quotation from Isaiah 52–54.]

II

For I myself, when I discovered the wicked disguise which the evil spirits had thrown around the divine doctrines of the Christians, to turn aside others from joining them, laughed both at those who framed these falsehoods, and at the disguise itself, and at popular opinion; and I confess that I boast and with all my strength strive to be found a Christian; not because the teachings of Plato are different from those of Christ, but because they are not in all respects similar, as neither are those of the others, Stoics, and poets, and historians. For each man spoke well in proportion to the share he had of the spermatic word, seeing what was related to it. But they who contradict themselves on the more important points appear not to have possessed the heavenly wisdom, and the knowledge which cannot be spoken against. Whatever things were rightly said among all men, are the property of us Christians. For next to God, we worship and love the Word who is from the unbegotten and ineffable God, since also he became man for our sakes, that, becoming a partaker of our sufferings, he might also bring us healing. For all the writers were able to see realities darkly through the sowing of the implanted word that was in them. For the seed and imitation imparted according to capacity is one thing, and quite another is the thing itself, of which there is the participation and imitation according to the grace which is from him. . . .

III

But Plato, though he accepted, as is likely, the doctrine of Moses and the other prophets regarding one only God, which he learned while in Egypt, yet fearing, on account of what had befallen Socrates, lest he also should raise up some Anytus of Meletus against himself, who should accuse him before the Athenians, and say, "Plato is doing harm, and making himself mischievously busy, not acknowledging the gods recognized by the state"; in fear of the hemlock juice, contrives an elaborate and ambiguous discourse concerning the gods, furnishing by his treatise gods to those who wish them, and none for those who are differently disposed, as may readily be seen from his own statements. For when he has laid down that everything that is made is mortal, he afterwards says that the gods were made. If, then, he would have God and matter to be the origin of all things, manifestly it is inevitably necessary to say that the gods were made of matter; but if of matter, out of which he said that evil also had its origin, he leaves right-thinking persons to consider what kind of beings the gods should be thought who are produced out of matter. For, for this very reason did he say that matter was eternal, that he might not seem to say that God is the creator of evil. And regarding the gods who were made by God, there is no doubt he said this: "Gods of gods, of whom I am the creator." And he manifestly held the correct opinion concerning the really existing God. For having heard in Egypt that God had said to Moses, when he was about to send him to the Hebrews, "I am that I am," he understood that God had not mentioned to him his own proper name. . . .

Plato accordingly having learned this in Egypt, and being greatly taken with what was said about one God, did indeed consider it unsafe to mention the name of Moses, on account of his teaching the doctrine of one only God, for he dreaded the Areopagus; but what is very well expressed by him in his elaborate treatise, the *Timaeus*, he has written in exact correspondence with what Moses said regarding God, though he has done so, not as if he had learned it from him, but as if he were expressing his own opinion. For he said, "In my opinion, then, we must first define what that is which exists eternally, and has no generation, and what that is which is always being generated, but never really is." Does not this, ye men of Greece, seem to those who are able to understand the matter to be one and the same thing, saving only the difference of the article? For Moses said, "*He* who is," and Plato, "that which is." But either of the expressions seems to apply to the ever-existent God. For he is the only one who eternally exists, and has no generation. What, then, that other thing is which is contrasted with the ever-existent, and of which he said, "And what that is which is always being generated, but never really is," we must attentively consider. For we shall find him clearly and evidently saying that he who is unbegotten is eternal, but that those that are begotten and made are generated and perish—as he said of the same class, "god of gods, of whom I am maker"—for he speaks in the following words: "In my opinion, then, we must first define what that is which is always existent and has no birth, and what that is which is always being generated but never really is. The former, indeed, which is apprehended by reflection combined with reason, always exists in the same way; while the latter, on the other hand, is conjectured by opinion formed by the perception of the senses unaided by reason, since it never really is, but is coming into being and perishing." These expressions declare to those who can rightly understand them the death and destruction of the gods that have been brought into being. And I think it necessary to attend to this also, that Plato never names him the creator, but the fashioner of the gods, although, in the opinion of Plato, there is considerable difference between the two. For the creator creates the creature by his own capability and power, being in need of nothing else; but the fashioner frames his production when he has received from matter the capability for his work. . . .

But, perhaps, some who are unwilling to abandon the doctrines of polytheism, will say that to these fashioned gods the maker said, "Since ye have been produced, ye are not immortal, nor at all imperishable; yet shall ye not perish nor succumb to the fatality of death, because you have obtained my will, which is a still greater and mightier bond." Here Plato, through fear of the adherents of polytheism, introduces his "maker" uttering words which contradict himself. For having formerly stated that he said that everything which is produced is perishable, he now introduces him saying the very opposite; and he does not see that it is thus absolutely impossible for him to escape the charge of falsehood. For he either at first uttered what is false when he said that everything which is produced is perishable, or now, when he propounds the very opposite to what he had formerly said. For if, according to his former definition, it is absolutely necessary that every created thing be perishable, how can he consistently make that possible which is absolutely impossible? So that Plato seems to grant an empty and impossible prerogative to his "maker," when he propounds that those who were once perishable because made from matter should again, by his intervention, become imperishable and enduring. For it is quite natural that the power of matter, which, according to Plato's opinion, is uncreated, and contemporary and coeval with the maker, should resist his will. For he who has not created has no power, in respect of that which is uncreated, so that it is not possible that it (matter), being free, be controlled by any external necessity. Wherefore Plato himself, in consideration of this, has written thus: "It is necessary to affirm that God cannot suffer violence."

2. TROELTSCH: THE ABSOLUTENESS AND RELATIVITY OF CHRISTIANITY

Nineteenth-century Protestant theology tended to conceive of Christianity under the category of religion and to view it as the most perfect form of religion. In an earlier work, Ernst Troeltsch espouses this viewpoint, arguing that the absoluteness of Christianity could be historically demonstrated, but in this essay written near the end of his life he concludes that Christianity along with all other religions is culturally relative. Source: Ernst Troeltsch, "Christianity Among World Religions," in *Christian Thought: Its History and Application*, ed. Baron F. von Hugel (London: University of London Press, 1923), pp. 9–27.

In my book on *The Absolute Validity of Christianity*,[1] . . . I believed that I could . . . determine two . . . concepts, both of which claimed to establish the ultimate validity of the Christian revelation in opposition to the relativities revealed by the study of history.

The first of these concepts was the theory that the truth of Christianity is guaranteed by miracles. In our times we are no longer primarily concerned here with miracles in the external world, i.e., with the so-called "nature-miracles," involving an infringement of natural law, but with the miracles of interior conversion and the attainment of a higher quality of life through communion with Jesus and his community. In this connection, it is claimed, an entirely different type of causation comes into operation from that which is operative anywhere else in the world. The Christian life may indeed be compared to an island in the midst of the stream of history, exposed to all the storms of secu-

1. [*Ed.*] This work, published in German in 1902, has appeared in English as *The Absoluteness of Christianity*, trans. David Reid (Richmond: John Knox Press, 1971).

lar life, and lured by all its wiles, yet constituting, in reality, a stronghold of experience of quite another order. The absolute validity of Christianity rests upon the absoluteness of God himself, who is made manifest here directly in miracles but who manifested himself beyond this island only as a *causa remota*—as the ground of the inter-connection of all relative things. In this way both a natural and a supernatural theology are possible, the latter resting upon the new birth and experience of the inner man, whilst natural theology is based upon the facts and forces of the external world. This theory is simply a restatement of the old miracle apologetic in the more intimate and spiritual form which it acquired under the influence of Methodism and Pietism.

The second fundamental concept of theology, which I have called the concept of evolution, presents a considerable contrast to the first. Its most important exponent is Hegel. According to this view Christianity is simply the perfected expression of religion as such. In the universal process of the unfolding of Spirit, the fundamental impulse towards salvation and communion with God overcomes all the limitations of sense experience, of the natural order, of mythological form, until it attains perfect expression in Christianity, and enters into combination with the loftiest and most spiritual of all philosophies, namely, that of Platonism. Christianity, it is maintained, is not *a particular* religion, it is *religion*. It is no isolated manifestation of Spirit, but the flower of spiritual life itself. . . .

I found myself obliged to dismiss both these views as untenable. The former I rejected on the ground that an inward miracle, though it is indeed a powerful psychical upheaval, is not a miracle in the strict sense of the term. . . .

If, however, we turn this reason to the second view, we find the difficulties to be different, indeed, but no less formidable. The actual history of religion knows nothing of the common character of all religions, or of their natural upward trend towards Christianity. It perceives a sharp distinction between the great world-religions and the national religions of heathen tribes, and further discovers certain irresolvable contradictions between these world-religions themselves which render their ultimate fusion and reconciliation in Christianity highly improbable, either in theory or in practice. Moreover, Christianity is itself a theoretical abstraction. It presents no historical uniformity, but displays a different character in every age, and is, besides, split up into many different denominations, hence it can in no wise be represented as the finally attained unity and explanation of all that has gone before, such as religious speculation seeks. It is rather a particular, independent, historical principle, containing, similarly to the other principles, very diverse possibilities and tendencies.

This leads us finally to a conception which has, I think, obtained less recognition in other countries than in Germany—I mean the conception which dominates the whole sphere of history, viz., individuality. History cannot be regarded as a process in which a universal and everywhere similar principle is confined and obscured. Nor is it a continual mixing and remixing of elemental psychical powers, which indicate a general trend of things towards a rational end or goal of evolution. It is rather an immeasurable, incomparable profusion of always-new, unique, and hence individual tendencies, welling up from undiscovered depths, and coming to light in each case in unsuspected places and under different circumstances. . . .

What, then, is the solution? This is the question which I attempted to answer in my book. . . . It is quite possible, I maintained, that there is an element of truth in every religion, but that this is combined with innumerable transitory, individual features. This element of truth can only be disentangled through strife and disruption, and it should be our constant endeavor to assist in this process of disentanglement. The recognition of this truth is, however, an intuition which . . . can only be confirmed retrospectively and indirectly by its practical fruits, and by the light that it sheds upon all the problems of life. . . .

I believed that I had discovered such a foundation for Christianity in the terms in which its claim to ultimate validity finds instinctive and immediate expression; in other words, in its faith in revelation and in the kind of claim it makes to truth. I thought it necessary to compare it from this point of view with other religions, whose belief in revelation and claim to validity were in every case of quite a different kind. If we examine any of the great world religions we shall find that all of them, Judaism, Islam, Zoroastrianism, Buddhism, Christianity, even Confucianism, indeed claim absolute validity, but quite naively. . . . The differences they exhibit in their naive claims to absolute validity indicate the varying degree of such absolute validity as they really mean and intend within their own minds. This seemed to me to be nearly the most important point in every comparison between the religions, and the one which furnished the most searching test of the character of the dogmatic contents to be compared. . . .

Now, the naive claim to absolute validity made by Christianity is of quite a different kind. All limitation to a particular race or nation is excluded on principle, and this exclusion illustrates the purely human character of its religious ideal, which appeals only to the simplest, the most general, the most personal and spiritual needs of mankind. . . . The naive claim to absolute validity of Christianity. . . is indeed a corollary of its belief in a revelation within the depths of the soul, awakening men to a new and higher quality of life, breaking down the barriers which the sense of guilt would otherwise set up, and making a final breach with the egoism obstinately centered in the individual self. It is from this point of view that its claim to absolute validity, following as it does from the content of its religious ideal, appears to be vindicated. It possesses the highest claim to universality of all the religions, for this its claim is based upon the deepest foundations, the nature of God and of man. . . .

Such was the conclusion I reached in the book which I wrote some twenty years ago, and, from the practical standpoint at least, it contains nothing that I wish to withdraw. From the point of view of theory, on the other hand, there are a number of points which I should wish to modify today, and these modifications are, of course, not without some practical effects.

My scruples arise from the fact that, whilst the significance for history of the concept of individuality impresses me more forcibly every day, I no longer believe this to be so easily reconcilable with that of supreme validity. The further investigations, especially into the history of Christianity, of which I have given the results in my *Social Teachings* . . . have shown me how thoroughly individual is historical Christianity after all, and how invariably its various phases and denominations have been due to varying circumstances and conditions of life. . . . On the other hand, a study of the non-Christian religions convinced me more and more that their naive claims to absolute validity are also genuinely such. . . .

The subject to which I devoted most attention, however, was that of the relation of individual historical facts to standards of value within the entire domain of history in connection with the development of political, social, ethical, aesthetic, and scientific ideas. . . . I encountered the same difficulties in each of these provinces—they were not confined to religion. Indeed, even the validity of science and logic seemed to exhibit, under different skies and upon different soil, strong individual differences present even in their deepest and innermost rudiments. What was really common to mankind, and universally valid for it, seemed, in spite of a general kinship and capacity for mutual understanding, to be at bottom exceedingly little, and to belong more to the province of material goods than to the ideal values of civilization.

The effect of these discoveries upon the conclusions reached in my earlier book was as follows:

The individual character of European civilization, and of the Christian religion which it is intimately connected with, receives now much greater emphasis, whilst the somewhat rationalistic concept of validity, and specifically of *supreme validity*, falls considerably into the background. It is impossible to deny facts or to resist the decrees of fate. And it is historical facts that have welded Christianity into the closest connection with the civilizations of Greece, Rome and Northern Europe. All our thoughts and feelings are impregnated with Christian motives and Christian presuppositions; and, conversely, our whole Christianity is indissolubly bound up with elements of the ancient and modern civilizations of Europe. From being a Jewish sect Christianity has become the religion of all Europe. It stands or falls with European civilization; whilst, on its own part, it has entirely lost its Oriental character and has become hellenized and westernized. . . .

Its primary claim to validity is thus the fact that only through it have we become what we are, and that only in it can we preserve the religious forces that we need. Apart from it we lapse either into a self-destructive titanic attitude, or into effeminate trifling, or into crude brutality. And at the same time our life is a consistent compromise as little unsatisfactory as we can manage between its lofty spirituality and our practical everyday needs—a compromise that has to be renewed at every fresh ascent and every bend of the road. This tension is characteristic of our form of human life and rouses us to many an heroic endeavor, though it may also lead us into the most terrible mendacity and crime. Thus we are, and thus we shall remain, as long as we survive. . . .

But this does not preclude the possibility that other racial groups, living under entirely different cultural conditions, may experience their contact with the Divine Life in quite a different way, and may themselves also possess a religion which has grown up with them, and from which they cannot sever themselves so long as they remain what they are. . . .

3. BARTH: CRITIQUE OF CHRISTIANITY AS A RELIGION

The most radical theological response to Troeltsch and the tradition of reflection culminating with him was that of Barth. He recognized that Christianity empirically is a religion but argued that this only means it shares the problematic of all religions. All religion expresses unbelief, and in and of itself religion possesses no truth. The sole basis of "religious truth" is the self-revelation of God and the justification of the sinner, which is an event of pure grace. Source: Karl Barth, *Church Dogmatics*, Vol. 1/2, *The Doctrine of the Word of God*, trans. G. T. Thomson and Harold Knight (Edinburgh: T. & T. Clark, 1956), pp. 280, 297–98, 299–300, 309–10, 325–27, 338, 353–54. Published in German in 1932.

A theological evaluation of religion and religions must be characterized primarily by the great cautiousness and charity of its assessment and judgments. It will observe and understand and take man in all seriousness as the subject of religion. But it will not be man apart from God, in a human *per se*. It will be man for whom (whether he knows it or not) Jesus Christ was born, died, and rose again. It will be man who (whether he has already heard it or not) is intended in the Word of God. It will be man who (whether he is aware of it or not) has in Christ his Lord. It will always understand religion as a vital utterance and activity of this man. It will not ascribe to this life-utterance and activity of his a unique "nature," the so-called "nature of religion," which it can then use as a gauge to weigh and balance one human thing against another, distinguishing the "higher" religion from the "lower," the "living" from the "decomposed," the "ponderable" from the "imponderable." It will not omit to do this from carelessness or indifference towards the manifoldness with which we have to do in this human sphere, nor because a prior definition of the "nature" of the phenomena in this sphere is either impossible or in itself irrelevant, but because what we have to know of the nature of religion from the standpoint of God's revelation does not allow us to make any but the most incidental use of an immanent definition of the nature of religion. It is not, then, that this "revealed" nature of religion is not fitted in either form or content to differentiate between the good and the bad, the true and the false in the religious world. Revelation singles out the Church as the *locus* of true religion. But this does not mean that the Christian religion as such is the fulfilled nature of human religion. It does not mean that the Christian religion is the true religion, fundamentally superior to all other religions. We can never stress too much the connection between the truth of the Christian religion and the grace of revelation. We have to give particular emphasis to the fact that through grace the Church lives by grace, and to that extent it is the *locus* of true religion. And if this is so, the Church will as little boast of its "nature," i.e., the perfection in which it fulfils the "nature" of religion, as it can attribute that nature to other religions. We cannot differentiate and separate the Church from other religions on the basis of a general concept of the nature of religion. . . .

We begin by stating that religion is unbelief. It is a concern, indeed, we must say that it is the one great concern, of godless man. . . .

Where we want what is wanted in religion, i.e., justification and sanctification as our own work, we do not find ourselves—and it does not matter whether the thought and representation of God has a primary or only a secondary importance—on the direct way to God, who can then bring us to our goal at some higher stage on the way. On the contrary, we lock the door against God, we alienate ourselves from him, we come into direct opposition to him. God in his revelation will not allow man to try to come to terms with life, to justify and sanctify himself. God in his revelation, God in Jesus Christ, is the one who takes on himself the sin of the world, who wills that all our care should be cast upon him, because he careth for us. . . .

It is the characteristically pious element in the pious effort to reconcile him to us which must be an abomination to God, whether idolatry is regarded as its presupposition or its result, or perhaps as both. Not by any continuing along this way, but only by radically breaking away from it, can we come, not to our own goal but to God's goal, which is the direct opposite of our goal. . . .

Religion is never true in itself and as such. The revelation of God denies that any religion is true, i.e., that it is in truth the knowledge and worship of God and the reconciliation of man with God. For as the self-offering and self-manifestation of God, as the work of peace which God himself has concluded between himself and man, revelation is the truth beside which there is no other truth, over against which there is only lying and wrong. If by the concept of a "true religion" we mean truth which belongs to religion in itself and as such, it is just as unattainable as a "good man," if by goodness we mean something which man can achieve on his own initiative. No religion is true. It can only become true, i.e., according to that which it purports to be and for which it is upheld. And it can become true only in the way in which man is justified, from without; i.e., not of its own nature and being but only in virtue of a reckoning and adopting and separating which are foreign to its own nature and being, which are quite inconceivable from its own standpoint, which come to it quite apart from any qualifications or merits. Like justified man, true religion is a creature of grace. But grace is the revelation of God. No religion can stand before it as true religion. No man is righteous in its presence. It subjects us all to the judgment of death. But it can also call dead men to life and sinners to repentance. And similarly in the wider sphere where it shows all religion to be false, it can also create true religion. The abolishing of religion by revelation need not mean only its negation: the judgment that religion is unbelief. Religion can just as well be exalted in revelation, even though the judgment still stands. It can be upheld by it and concealed in it. It can be justified by it, and—we must at once add—sanctified. Revelation can adopt religion and mark it off as true religion. And it not only can. How do we come to assert that it can, if it has not already done so? There is a true religion: just as there are justified sinners. If we abide strictly by that analogy—and we are dealing not merely with an analogy, but in a comprehensive sense with the thing itself—we need have no hesitation in saying that the Christian religion is the true religion.

In our discussion of "religion as unbelief" we did not consider the distinction between Christian and non-Christian religion. Our intention was that whatever we said about the other religions affected the Christian similarly. In the framework of that discussion we could not speak in any special way about Christianity. We could not give it any special or assured place in face of that judgment. Therefore the discussion cannot be understood as a preliminary polemic against the non-Christian religions, with a view to the ultimate assertion that the Christian religion is the true religion. If this were the case our task now would be to prove that, as distinct from the non-Christian religions, the Christian is not guilty of idolatry and self-righteousness, that it is not therefore unbelief but faith, and therefore true religion; or, which comes to the same thing, that it is no religion at all, but as against all religions, including their mystical and atheistical self-criticism, it is in itself the true and holy and as such the unspotted and incontestable form of fellowship between God and man. To enter on this path would be to deny the very thing we have to affirm. If the statement is to have any content we can dare to state that the Christian religion is the true one only as we listen to the divine revelation. But a statement which we dare to make as we listen to the divine revelation can only be a statement of faith. And a statement of faith is necessarily a statement which is thought and expressed in faith and from faith, i.e., in recognition and respect of what we are told by revelation. Its explicit and implicit content is unreservedly conditioned by what we are told. But that is certainly not the case if we try to reach the statement that the Christian religion is the true religion by a road which begins by leaving behind the judgment of revelation, that religion is unbelief, as a matter which does not apply to us Christians but only to others, the non-Christians, thus enabling us to separate and differentiate ourselves from them with the help of this judgment. On the contrary, it is our business as Christians to apply this judgment first and most acutely to ourselves: and to others, the non-Christians, only insofar as we recognize ourselves in them, i.e., only as we see in them the truth of this judgment of revelation which concerns us, in the solidarity, therefore, in which, anticipating them in both repentance and hope, we accept this judgment to participate in the promise of revelation. At the end of the road we have to tread there is, of course, the promise to those who accept God's judgment, who let themselves be led beyond their unbelief. There is faith in this promise, and, in this faith, the presence and reality of the grace of God, which, of course, differentiates our religion, the Christian, from all others as the true religion. This exalted goal cannot be reached except by this humble road. And it would not be a truly humble road if we tried to tread it except in the consciousness that any "attaining" here can consist only in the utterly humble and thankful adoption of something which we would not attain if it were not already attained in God's revelation before we set out on the road.

We must insist, therefore, that at the beginning of a knowledge of truth of the Christian religion there stands the recognition that this religion, too, stands under the judgment that religion is unbelief, and that it is not acquitted by any inward worthiness, but only by the grace of God, proclaimed and effectual in his revelation. But concretely this judgment affects the whole practice of our faith: our Christian conceptions of God and the things of God, our Christian theology, our Christian worship, our forms of Christian fellowship and order, our Christian morals, poetry, and art, our attempts to give individual and social form to the Christian life, our Christian strategy and tactics in the interest of our Christian cause, in short our Christianity, to the extent that it is *our* Christianity, the human work which we undertake and adjust to all kinds of near and remote aims and which as such is seen to be on the same level as the human work in other religions. . . .

We cannot expect that at a fourth or fifth or sixth stage the history of Christianity will be anything but a history of the distress which Christianity creates for itself. May it not lack in future reformation, i.e., expressions of warning and promise deriving from Holy Scripture! But before the end of all things we cannot expect that the Christian will not always show himself an enemy of grace, in spite of all intervening restraints.

Notwithstanding the contradiction and therefore our own existence, we can and must perceive that for our part we and our contradiction against grace stand under the even more powerful contradiction of grace itself. We can and must—in faith. To believe means, in the knowledge of our sin to rely upon the righteousness of God which makes an infinite satisfaction for our sin. Concretely, it means, in the knowledge of our contradiction against grace to cleave to the grace of

God which infinitely contradicts this contradiction. In this knowledge of grace, in the knowledge that it is the justification of the ungodly, that it is grace for the enemies of grace, the Christian faith attains to its knowledge of the truth of the Christian religion. There can be no more question of any immanent rightness or holiness of this particular religion as the ground and content of the truth of it than there can be of any other religion claiming to be the true religion in virtue of its inherent advantages. The Christian cannot avoid abandoning any such claim. He cannot avoid confessing that he is a sinner even in his best actions as a Christian. And that is not, of course, the ground, but the symptom of the truth of the Christian religion. The abandoning and confessing means that the Christian Church is the place where, confronted with the revelation and grace of God, by grace men live by grace. . . .

There is, of course, one fact which powerfully and decisively confirms the assertion, depriving it of its arbitrary character and giving to it a necessity which is absolute. But to discern this fact, our first task—and again and again we shall have to return to this "first"—must be to ignore the whole realm of "facts" which we and other human observers as such can discern and assess. For the fact about which we are speaking stands in the same relationship to this realm as does the sun to the earth. That the sun lights up this part of the earth and not that means for the earth no less than this, that day rules in the one part and night in the other. Yet the earth is the same in both places. In neither place is there anything in the earth itself to dispose it for the day. Apart from the sun, it would everywhere be enwrapped in eternal night. The fact that it is partly in the day does not derive in any sense from the nature of the particular part as such. Now it is in exactly the same way that the light of the righteousness and judgment of God falls upon the world of man's religion, upon one part of that world, upon the Christian religion, so that that religion is not in the night but in the day, it is not perverted but straight, it is not false religion but true. Taken by itself, it is still human religion and therefore unbelief, like all other religions. Neither in the root nor in the crown of this particular tree, neither at the source nor at the outflow of this particular stream, neither on the surface nor in the depth of this particular part of humanity can we point to anything that makes it suitable for the day of divine righteousness and judgment. If the Christian religion is the right and true religion the reason for it does not reside in facts which might point to itself or its own adherents, but in the fact which as the righteousness and the judgment of God confronts it as it does all other religions, characterizing and differentiating it and not one of the others as the right and true religion.

4. PANNENBERG: CHRISTIANITY IN THE HISTORY OF RELIGIONS

Pannenberg has renewed earlier theological attempts to integrate Christian affirmations with the totality of human knowledge. This requires viewing Christianity again as one religion among others. To the extent that a tradition absolutizes its origins and truth claims, it blocks itself from being enriched and transformed through its contacts with other traditions. Christianity's "superiority" consists in its greater readiness to learn from other traditions and thereby to be changed through its interaction with them. Source: Wolfhart Pannenberg, "Toward a Theology of the History of Religions," in *Basic Questions in Theology*, Vol. 2, trans. George H. Kehm (Philadelphia: Fortress Press, 1971), pp. 92–96, 110–15. A revised version of a lecture delivered in 1962.

The religions of mankind have as little unity at the outset as mankind itself. The different religious traditions seem rather to have had a multiplicity of different starting points among the different tribes and peoples. In another sense, these independently originated religious traditions had a universal character from early on, namely, as ascriptions of universal meaning to existence. Such an intended universalism stands in contrast to the actual pluralism of religious origins. But this conflict becomes conscious only to the extent that communication develops between the individual groups. A common history of religions arises only when suitable conditions bring about a competition between the different religions stemming from a collision between their competing intentions of universal meaning, and proceeds hand in hand with the onset of the political and economic integration of man. One can begin to speak of a global process of integration for the first time in relation to the history of Christian missions and the Islamic conquests. Christian missionary activity especially, which proceeded apace with the expansion of Western civilization and technology in the last century, drew together the different, more or less isolated religious traditions into a world history of religion. . . .

Up to now, the inevitable religious conflicts have been concealed by a tendency toward relativizing every kind of religious faith as a result of a secular understanding of human existence. But this secular under-standing of human existence which has brought about an unheard of homogenization among the various cultures is in itself, once again, a product of Christianity. Thus, by means of its thrust toward a universal mission, Christianity has become the ferment for the rise of a common religious situation of the whole of mankind. And only in relation to this is it possible to speak of a general religious history of mankind. The unity of the history of religions is therefore not to be found in their be-ginnings, but rather in their end. . . .

In this connection, the history of Christianity is of special interest in the history of religions on account of its specific contribution to the rise of a worldwide religious situation. The rise of Christianity as a religion already presupposes the religious and cultural unification of the an-cient Mediterranean region by Hellenism. Christianity, as could be shown in detail, took possession of the heritage of this whole, complex cultural and religious world. Thus, the process which was bringing about the fusion of the cultures of the ancient Mediterranean world temporally as well as substantively paved the way for the ascent of Christianity as a world religion, and in this double sense constitutes its historical footing.

This provides a point of entry for a presentation of the unity of the history of religions as a unity that proceeds from the processes of histor-ical interaction between the different religions. It is not necessary to take as such a point the obscure, scarcely discoverable beginnings of religion. The path to the religious unity of mankind can be attacked from many points of departure, but the critical process of integration begins in the comparatively bright light of historical knowledge, with the religions of the ancient Mediterranean world and of the Near East, with the Egyptians and in the Tigris-Euphrates valley, with the Per-sians and their Indian kin who then went their own way for quite a while. The overlapping and coalescence of the most varied religious traditions is evidenced with particular intensity in the history of Israel and then of the Greeks—and more than ever in primitive Christianity, in which the Jewish and Greek heritages were united, and in the expansion of Christianity throughout the ancient religious world, which was saturated with Hellenism. The process of religious integration was at first interrupted by the rise of Islam at the borders of the Christian world, only then to maintain a development that was nonetheless in many respects parallel to it. This process advanced farther in the outreach of the Christian missionary movement beyond the Hellenistic realm, especially by the conversion of the Slavic and Germanic peoples to the Christian faith, and then by the colonization of America, and finally by encountering the religions of the Far East and the illiterate cultures of Africa and Australia, which at that time along with their histories entered the stream of the world history of religion which the Christian mission had mediated. Finally, in this century, the diffusion of the secular culture of the West altered the traditional form of the Christian mission itself after this had led—not to the conversion of man, of course, but in another sense—to a common religious situation characterized, on the one hand, by the confrontation of all the religious traditions of mankind with the Christian tradition, and, on the other, by the secularized form of human existence in industrialized society.

It is possible in such a way to trace how the unity of the history of religions takes shape in the history of particular religions, and how therein—this has still to be shown—the unity of the divine reality itself is operative, upon whose appearance the religions depend. This path of a progressive religious integration of mankind—in ever new surges, even if not without interruptions, defeats, and new splits—is possible because from the very beginning different peoples understood their gods as powers determining the totality of reality. Only because of this can the controversy between the religions about the nature of reality arise, the result of which is the progressive unification of the history of religions, even if in a plurality of differently articulated religious perspectives. . . .

I return here once more to the question of the reality-reference of religious experiences. The result of our study has been that this question cannot be settled by merely psychological investigation. Nor can it be decided yet on the basis of the formal structure of human existence, but rather only in men's association with the transcendent mystery that is always presupposed in the structure of human existence and which proves in the actual course of life whether it is sustaining or not, powerful or impotent, reality or nonentity. The reality of the gods—and of God—is at stake in the process of the history of religions in which gods collapse and newly arise. Therefore, an interpretation of religious experiences and concepts will be able to do justice to them only on the condition that it does not construe the religious life as, on the one hand, a mere epiphenomenon of profane—psychological or social—processes or, on the other hand, as an expression of a divine presence that is independent of the history of its appearances. The religious event moves between these alternatives because the reality of the gods is itself risked or even made debatable in the history of religions. The individual religious appearances are to be understood as arguments in this controversy, arguments—more or less strong—for the reality of the power of the divine mystery. This applies not only to the individual religious happening, but also to religious transformations. Even the transformations of religious ideas, rites, and institutions in the course of their history—for instance, the transformations of a divine figure or of a cult—should not be viewed entirely as functions of political or social upheavals. It is just the transformations of religious phenomena that become intelligible only as the expression in men's existence—no matter in what form—of the presupposed divine mystery *in its debatability*. Naturally, political or social changes play a great role in this since the religious life indeed concerns the understanding of the whole of reality and what makes its wholeness possible. And political and social relations and changes are of considerable importance for the whole of human experience of existence. But they themselves are not unqualifiedly this whole. They may provide the *occasion* for religious transformations—which, moreover, they could never provide were they merely profane states of affairs. However, political and social changes can hardly ever automatically produce religious transformations; rather, they signify a challenge whose mastery or non-mastery remains a matter of the inner strength, the inner health and adaptability of the religious tradition itself at that time.

The result of such reflections is that the history of religions is not adequately understood when it is taken as only a history of the representations and behavior of specific men and groups which in themselves might also be described in purely profane categories. More appropriate to its content is a history of religions understood as the history of the appearing of the divine mystery presupposed in the structure of human existence, whose reality and peculiar character, however, are themselves at stake in the process of this history.

Clearly, this mode of observation requires no dogmatic assertion of the reality of God. But in spite of this does it not concern a *theology* of the history of religions? Certainly not in the sense of deriving from the history of religions propositions of one sort or another by means of an undiscussable, presupposed standpoint of faith. But "theology of the history of religions" is a more appropriate expression for the mode of observation only prepared for here, since the reality of God (or of the gods) is precisely the object of its occupation with the history of religions. . . .

The notion of understanding the history of religions as the history of the appearances of the divine mystery indeed did not arise by chance. If this perspective, as I hope, comes closer than others to the logic of the essential content of the phenomena of the history of religions, it is nevertheless not *produced* by these phenomena; rather, it is this perspective that first allows the phenomena to be discovered. And reducing it to its proper *concept* could hardly be accomplished without commitment to the God of the Bible and his eschatological revelation in Jesus Christ. For if the processes of religious transformation are to be thought of as the history of appearances of the divine, then it is certainly necessary to have an understanding of God that lies beyond the scope of the thought of almost all the religions under investigation as to their changes, so far as just these remain closed to the process of their own transformation. If it is impossible for a religion that is oriented toward the primordial and archetypal to acknowledge the changes in its contents, then the understanding of such changes manifestly requires a vantage point beyond the sphere of this ban.

In contradistinction to other peoples and their religions, Israel, in the light of its particular experience of God, learned to understand the reality of human existence as a history moving toward a goal which had not yet appeared. A painful process of historical experience opened the way for the radical reorientation involved in this knowledge. If in the early period of the monarchy Israel still relied upon the redemptive facts of the past, which it had to thank for the foundation of its independent national existence—the gift of the land and the election of Zion along with the Davidic dynasty—so it was by the loss of these saving endowments that its hope was turned completely toward a future, definitive redemptive act of Yahweh. Thereby it came to interpret world history as the path through the present misery to that salvation which was still to appear; as the manner in which the God of the future salvation was already powerful in the present. Nevertheless, Israel continued to seek the fundamental revelation of its God in the events of the past, in the giving of the law at Sinai, and not in the future of God's reign. It was Jesus who first turned this relationship around, departing from the religious traditions of his people where it seemed necessary to do so for the sake of the coming reign of God. This reign was no longer expected as the complete dominance of traditional norms and conceptions of salvation—as the ultimate realization of all that had been included in the election of Zion, or as the delivery of men to their destinies corresponding to their attitude toward the law of God handed down by the tradition. Understood in this way, the coming of God would only be the full realization of a principle already given elsewhere. Thus, who or what God is could not be understood from the side of God's coming. The message of Jesus brought about this change, however, so that now trust in the coming God was to be the sole decisive factor for the salvation or doom of the individual regardless of how his behavior might have appeared from the standpoint of the other traditions of Israel. Certainly when Jesus spoke of "God" he meant the God of Israel. But he did not think of God's future as fixed by the religious traditions of the Israelitic people, as those who adhered to the piety of the law did. Rather, this future compelled him to do the reverse: to criticize the established and the traditional, and to make a life in love the determining basis of life in the present.

The God of the coming kingdom is thereby understood not only as the author of historical change—as was already the case in ancient Israel—but also as the power for altering his own previous manifestations. As the power to be conceived from the standpoint of its futurity, from the side of its future coming, he can no longer be superseded by any other future or any new experience of God, but instead new happenings of the divine mystery will be only further manifestations of himself in new forms of appearance. . . .

The history of Christianity is burdened by a great many dogmatic finitizations which lose sight of the provisionality and historical mutability of all forms of Christian life and thought. The hierarchical structure of the church and its dogmas especially try to secure a false ultimacy that misplaces its true ultimacy—which is to be found in the historical openness made possible by Jesus. Nevertheless, in the origin of the Christian tradition which remains its norm—with Jesus' message of the coming of God and with the appearance of the divine mystery in his resurrection from the dead—the critical element of historical change in the light of the still-open eschatological future gained entrance into the substance of the Christian religion itself.

As the power of the future, the God of the coming reign of God proclaimed by Jesus already anticipates all later epochs of the history of the church and of the non-Christian religions. From this standpoint, the history of religions even beyond the time of the public ministry of Jesus presents itself as a history of the appearance of the God who revealed himself through Jesus.

But even looking back at it from the standpoint of Jesus, the history of religions permits of being understood as the appearance of the God revealed by him. The alien religions cannot be adequately interpreted as mere fabrications of man's strivings after the true God. Ultimately, they have to do with the same divine reality as the message of Jesus. To be sure, one may observe in the religions man's peculiar resistance to the infinity (non-finitude) of the divine mystery. The forms of religious finitization that result from this, images of God and the cult, may be described, with Paul, as a radical confusion of the infinite with the form of the finite. The deepest reason for this might be found once again in the temporality of the religious attitude. The non-Christian religions perceived the appearance of the divine mystery only in a fragmentary way because they were closed to their own transformation, to their own history. Insofar as the process of religious transformation —described by the historian of religion—takes place behind the backs of the religions, they exemplify in ever new ways the fixation of the infinite God onto the finite medium of its appearance at some time, a fixation over which the infinity of God prevails by means of this process of transformation.

5. COBB: BEYOND DIALOGUE

Following an analysis of traditional and modern Christian attitudes toward other religions, ranging from persecution to dialogue, John Cobb proposes that the time has come to move "beyond dialogue" to mutual transformation and a possible convergence of the religions. In the book from which these selections are drawn, Cobb focuses on the relationship between Christianity and Mahayana Buddhism, with which he has had extensive personal contact, arguing that Christianity can be transformed by incorporating the truth contained in the Buddhist understanding of ultimate reality as Nirvana or "emptiness," while Buddhism can be transformed by incorporating the truth revealed in Jesus as the Christ. Source: John B. Cobb, Jr., *Beyond Dialogue: Toward a Mutual Transformation of Christianity and Buddhism* (Philadelphia: Fortress Press, 1982), pp. 47-52, 141-43.

Authentic dialogue will necessarily carry us beyond itself. That is, authentic dialogue changes its participants in such a way that new developments beyond dialogue must follow. A statement of how Christians enter dialogue and what kind of outcome they might expect from it will clarify this point.

Although dialogue has its place in all human relationships, the most important dialogues will be those with communities which are most impressive in their attainment of understanding, insight, distinctive experience, community life, or character. It is these from which Christians have most to learn, whether they are religious or not and regardless of how different they are from Christianity. It is these also toward which traditional forms of witness are least likely to be effective. And, indeed, conversion of members of these communities, if it involves their abandonment of those virtues which are distinctive to them, is a doubtful gain. If the conversion of all Jews to Christianity meant the obliteration of Judaism, the world would be a poorer place.

Dialogue with representatives of such groups would be first and foremost for our own sake as Christians. We would hope to enrich our lives and purify our faith by learning from them. We would of course also offer what we believed to be true and valuable in our own tradi-

375

tion. It would be important to us to display its importance in such a way as to challenge our dialogue partners to grow.

But this dialogue, if it succeeds, passes quickly beyond dialogue. It realizes what is sometimes spoken of as the "risk" of dialogue. That risk is that in the process of listening one will be forced to change in a more than superficial way. Christian dialogue theory is ambiguous with respect to its desire to impose that risk on the partner. It denies the intention to convert, and yet witnesses to Christian truth with the intention that it be heard in all its transformative power. Official dialogue theory has thus far had almost nothing to say about the desirability of fundamental change on the part of the Christian participants, although as we have seen, participants in dialogue are moving vigorously to change this situation.

Beyond dialogue, I suggest, lies the aim of mutual transformation. One may, if one wishes, speak of this as simply another stage of dialogue. However, once a Christian has learned something of first importance from the partner, much of the work of internalizing and integrating this new understanding may better be done in solitude or with other Christians rather than in further conversation. Only when some significant progress has been made in this work will it be important to meet again to take up the dialogue at that new place to which the participants have come.

There is an acute question as to whether one can both play a representative role and also allow oneself to be significantly transformed through dialogue. The transformation that happens to the individuals involved may raise keen suspicions among those whom they initially represented. But changes among leaders, if they are truly leaders, can and do at times affect the communities which they lead. Changes in Catholic and Jewish leaders resulting from dialogue can alter Catholic-Jewish relations at many levels over a period of time. If Christian dialogue with Jews alters the formulations of Christology by those Christians who participate, and if this is truly a representative and influential group of Christians, the implicit anti-Judaism of much of our Christological work may be overcome, and in time preaching and Christian education may be affected. This is a legitimate goal for dialogue and for what lies beyond dialogue.

The emphasis thus far is upon the transformation of Christians and, through Christian individuals, of Christianity. To follow the previous example, it is not clear that Christians can offer much to Jews except apologies until Christianity has been freed of its anti-Judaism. Sensitization to the manifold dimensions and depths of anti-Judaism can be gained by Christians through dialogue with Jews, but the transformation of Christian teaching and practice must be the work of Christians beyond dialogue. The Christianity that would emerge from such a transformation could approach Jews in a quite new way. Its witness to Jesus as the Christ might even be convincing! Perhaps Jews could some day be encouraged to reintegrate into their own history the story of Jesus, and perhaps that would prove an event of transforming significance in the inner history of Judaism. But Christians are not in a position to speak thus to Jews until our own transformation has advanced a long way. The Christian purpose in the dialogue with Jews must be to change Christianity.

What is involved in drawing two communities together is not only a matter of adjustment of doctrine. H. Richard Niebuhr rightly pointed out that what is involved includes the transformation of their respective historical memories. Writing in 1941, Niebuhr focused on the divisions within Christianity and how they might be overcome. He said:

> There will be no union of Catholics and Protestants until through the common memory of Jesus Christ the former repent of the sin of Peter and the latter of the sin of Luther, until Protestants acknowledge Thomas Aquinas as one of their fathers, the Inquisition as their own sin and Ignatius Loyola as one of their own Reformers, until Catholics have canonized Luther and Calvin, done repentance for Protestant nationalism, and appropriated Schleiermacher and Barth as their theologians.

Niebuhr would no doubt be astounded at how far, at least from the Catholic side, there has been movement in the direction he pointed, beginning with the Second Vatican Council. What once appeared more as an eschatological dream is being concretely realized, and indeed as Niebuhr foresaw, Protestants and Catholics now work together as Christians out of our common history. . . .

In this book I wish to treat a more difficult example, that of Mahayana Buddhism. I believe the pattern here should be similar. At present we are not in a position to offer much to thoughtful Buddhists. The reason is different. Anti-Buddhism is not built into our traditions, and

377

our crimes against Buddhists are not comparable to those against Jews. But Buddhists have a depth of insight into the nature of reality which we lack. As long as a Buddhist's becoming Christian entails abandoning that insight, conversion is not a serious possibility, and it is certainly not a desirable goal of the Christian mission. Until we can share that insight and transform our understanding of our own faith through it, we will have little to say that can or should command Buddhist attention. Hence our present need is to learn through dialogue, and then beyond dialogue to rethink our beliefs. But our purpose in all this cannot be only our own edification and improvement. It must be also to help Buddhists.

We may quite properly say that our concern for the Buddhists is that they become better Buddhists. But as in the preceding case, that can easily be misunderstood. We believe that Buddhists lack something of supreme importance when they do not incorporate Jesus Christ into their Buddhism. We believe they will be better Buddhists when they have done so.

To think of the transformation of Christianity by Buddhism must involve, as in the case of Judaism, the incorporation into our effective memories of Buddhist history. That process has begun. Gautama, at least, is a figure of human history revered also by many Christians. But that is just a beginning. The story of the Buddhist saints and the expansion of Buddhism throughout East Asia is not yet a part of the effective historical memory of Christians. And the history of what took place in Palestine remains outside the effective historical memory of Buddhists. If Buddhism and Christianity are to grow together, both must cultivate a global memory. Since both understand themselves as universal religious traditions, this must be at the same time the road to their own inner fulfillment.

But in the Christian approach to Buddhism the incorporation of historical memories does not suffice. Through their history Buddhists have gained an understanding and experience of reality that is deeper than history. Until Christians have come to appreciate and in some measure to share that understanding and experience, the celebration of Buddhist saints will not do much to bridge the gap.

In these reflections we go beyond the antithesis of all religious traditions moving toward Christianity or each making its permanent separate contribution to the history of salvation. A Christianity which has been transformed by the incorporation of the Buddhist insight into the nature of reality will be a very different Christianity from any we now know. A Buddhism that has incorporated Jesus Christ will be a very different Buddhism from any we now know. That will not obliterate the difference between the two traditions, but it will provide a new basis for fresh dialogue and fresh transformation. The lines that now sharply divide us will increasingly blur. . . .

[Christianity and Buddhism transformed in the ways indicated clearly would] be far closer than any now existing forms of Christianity and Buddhism. Yet there would continue to be differences rooted in the profoundly different roads they have traveled. To what extent these differences would disappear as each appropriated more fully the history and truth of the other, only time can tell. It is not clear that this would matter very much. From the Christian point of view, if Buddhists realize the rich meaning of faith in Jesus Christ, there is no reason to hope that they would also become like us in those many ways that are determined by our dominantly Western historical experience. Why should they become Roman Catholics, Southern Baptists, Missouri Synod Lutherans, members of the United Church of Christ in Japan or join the nonchurch Christian movement there? Similarly, if Christians can realize the truth of the Buddhist doctrine of Nirvana, no essential Buddhist concern is served by the Easternization of Christianity in ways that are only accidentally related to that realization. A Buddhized Christianity and a Christianized Buddhism may continue to enrich each other and human culture generally through their differences.

This vision clearly has implications for the Christian mission. I suggest that in relation to other religious ways today this has two main features neither of which has been prominent in missiology in the past. First, it is the mission of Christianity to *become* a universal faith in the sense of taking into itself the alien truths that others have realized. This is no mere matter of addition. It is instead a matter of creative transformation. An untransformed Christianity, that is, a Christianity limited to its own parochial traditions, cannot fulfill its mission of realizing the universal meaning of Jesus Christ. It can only continue to offer its fragment alongside the offerings of other traditions. When it appeals for total commitment to so fragmentary a realization of Christ, it is idolatrous. When, to avoid idolatry, it asks for only fragmentary commitment to the fragment of truth it offers, it ceases to express the ultimacy of the claim of Christ and continues its inevitable decay. Only as, in faithfulness to Christ, it opens itself to transformation can it ask people to participate wholeheartedly. Thus the most pressing Christian mission is the mission of self-transformation.

Second, it is the mission of a self-transforming Christianity to invite other religious traditions to undergo self-transformation as well. There is nothing wrong with opening our doors to individual converts from other traditions. Indeed, if we begin seriously to undergo self-transformation we will need the help of those who have known other truths from within other traditions. But more important than the conversion of individual Buddhists, Hindus, or Muslims is the conversion of Buddhism, Hinduism, and Islam. I have tried to indicate what that might mean in the case of Mahayana Buddhism. Equally concrete descriptions are possible in other cases. Our mission is to display the universal meaning of Christ freed from our past compulsion to contradict the truths known in other traditions. As long as we present Christ as the opponent of something that others know to be true, they will not be open to hearing what Christ has to say to them. But once we allow Christ to speak apart from the impediments we have placed in the way, Christ will carry out the authentic Christian mission. Christ as Truth will transform the truths of all other traditions even as they transform ours.

XIV. THE CHRISTIAN PARADIGM: ALTERNATIVE VISIONS

1. NIEBUHR: RADICAL MONOTHEISM

More than any other twentieth-century theologian, H. Richard Niebuhr stressed both the universality of the one God and the relativity of all historical manifestations of God and expressions of faith in God. Thus "radical monotheism" sets the appropriate context for dealing with issues of pluralism, relativity, and new understandings of the relationship of God and the world that comprise the theological task in our time. Source: H. Richard Niebuhr, *Radical Monotheism and Western Culture* (New York: Harper & Row, 1960), pp. 31–34.

There is a third form of human faith with which we are acquainted in the West, more as hope than as datum, more perhaps as a possibility than as an actuality, yet also as an actuality that has modified at certain emergent periods our natural social faith and our polytheism. In all the times and areas of our Western history this faith has struggled with its rivals, without becoming triumphant save in passing moments and in the clarified intervals of personal existence. We look back longingly at times to some past age when, we think, confidence in the One God was the pervasive faith of men; for instance, to early Christianity, or to the church society of the Middle Ages, or to early Protestantism, or to Puritan New England, or to the pious nineteenth century. But when we study these periods we invariably find in them a mixture of the faith in the One God with social faith and polytheism; and when we examine our longings we often discover that what we yearn for is the security of the closed society with its social confidence and social loyalty. It is very questionable, despite many protestations to the contrary, despite the prevalence of self-pity among some modern men because "God is dead," that anyone has ever yearned for radical faith in the One God.

We shall call this third form of faith radical monotheism. We must try to describe it formally, in abstract fashion, though the form does not appear in our history or in our contemporary life otherwise than as embodied and expressed in the concreteness of communal and personal, of religious and moral existence.

For radical monotheism the value-center is neither closed society nor the principle of such a society but the principle of being itself; its reference is to no one reality among the many but to One beyond all the many, whence all the many derive their being, and by participation in which they exist. As faith, it is reliance on the source of all being for the significance of the self and of all that exists. It is the assurance that because I am, I am valued, and because you are, you are beloved, and because whatever is has being, therefore it is worthy of love. It is the confidence that whatever is, is good, because it exists as one thing among the many which all have their origin and their being, in the One—the principle of being which is also the principle of value. In him we live and move and have our being not only as existent but as worthy of existence and worthy in existence. It is not a relation to any finite, natural or supernatural, value-center that confers value on self and some of its companions in being, but it is value relation to the One to whom all being is related. Monotheism is less than radical if it makes a distinction between the principle of being and the principle of value; so that while all being is acknowledged as absolutely dependent for existence on the One, only some beings are valued as having worth for it; or if, speaking in religious language, the Creator and the God of grace are not identified.

Radical monotheism is not in the first instance a theory about being and then a faith, as though the faith orientation toward the principle of being as value-center needed to be preceded by an ontology that established the unity of the realm of being and its source in a single power beyond it. It is not at all evident that the One beyond the many, whether made known in revelation or always present to man in hiddenness, is principle of being before it is principle of value. Believing man does not say first, "I believe in a creative principle," and then, "I believe that the principle is gracious, that is, good toward what issues from it." He rather says, "I believe in God the Father, Almighty Maker of heaven and earth." This is a primary statement, a point of departure and not a deduction. In it the principle of being is identified with the principle of value and the principle of value with the principle of being. Neither is it evident, despite our intellectualist bias toward identifying ourselves with our reason, that the self is more itself as reasoning self than as faithful self, concerned about value. It is the "I" that reasons and the "I" that believes; it is present in its believing as in its reasoning. Yet the believing self must reason; there is always a reasoning in faith so that rational efforts to understand the One beyond the many are characteristic of radical monotheism. Only, the orientation of faith toward the One does not wait on the development of theory.

As faith reliance, radical monotheism depends absolutely and assuredly for the worth of the self on the same principle by which it has being; and since that principle is the same by which all things exist it accepts the value of whatever is. As faith loyalty, it is directed toward the principle and the realm of being as the cause for the sake of which it lives. Such loyalty on the one hand is claimed by the greatness and inclusiveness of the objective cause; on the other hand it is given in commitment, since loyalty is the response of a self and not the compulsive reaction of a thing. The cause also has a certain duality. On the one hand it is the principle of being itself; on the other, it is the realm of being. Whether to emphasize the one or the other may be unimportant, since the principle of being has a cause, namely, the realm of being, so that loyalty to the principle of being must include loyalty to its cause; loyalty to the realm of being, on the other hand, implies keeping faith with the principle by virtue of which it is, and is one realm.

The counterpart, then, of universal faith assurance is universal loyalty. Such universal loyalty cannot be loyalty to loyalty, as Royce would have it, but is loyalty to all existents as bound together by a loyalty that is not only resident in them but transcends them. It is not only their loyalty to each other that makes them one realm of being, but the loyalty that comes from beyond them, that originates and maintains them in their particularity and their unity. Hence universal loyalty expresses itself as loyalty to each particular existent in the community of being and to the universal community. Universal loyalty does not express itself as loyalty to the loyal but to whatever is; not as reverence for the reverent but as reverence for being; not as the affirmation of world affirmers but as world affirmation. Such loyalty gives form to morality, since all moral laws and ends receive their form, though not their immediate content, from the form of faith reliance and faith loyalty. Love of the neighbor is required in every morality formed by a faith; but in polytheistic faith the neighbor is defined as the one who is near me in my interest group, *when* he is near me in that passing association. In henotheistic social faith my neighbor is my fellow in the closed society. Hence in both instances the counterpart of the law of neighbor-love is the requirement to hate the enemy. But in radical monotheism my neighbor is my companion in being; though he is my enemy in some less than universal context the requirement is to love him. To give to everyone his due is required in every context; but what is due to him depends on the relation in which he is known to stand.

2. CONE: THE SOCIAL CONTEXT
OF THEOLOGY

The selection from James Cone powerfully illustrates contemporary awareness of the ways ideology and interests influence all reflection, including theological. Cone's indictment of "white American theology," and his brief exposition of the ways that "black religious thought" differs, show one kind of pluralism currently emerging. Source: James H. Cone, *God of the Oppressed* (New York: Seabury Press, 1975), pp. 45–46, 52–56.

The dialectic of theology and social existence is particularly obvious in its white American branch when that theology is related to the people of African descent on the American continent. While some white theologians in the twentieth century have emphasized the relativity of faith in history, they have seldom applied this insight to the problem of the color line. Because the conceptual framework of their consciousness has been shaped already by white sociopolitical interests, their exposition of the problem of faith and history is limited to defending the intellectual status of religious assertions against erosion by historical criticism. Even a casual look at the contemporary discussion of the problem of faith in the context of the historical-critical method reveals that such problems are unique to oppressors as they seek to reconcile traditional theology with modern scientific thinking about history.

It is not that the problem of faith and history is unimportant. Rather, its importance, as defined by white theologians, is limited to their social interests. Although oppressed blacks are interested in faith as they struggle in history, the shape of the faith-history problem in contemporary American theology did not arise from the social existence of black people. On the contrary, its character was shaped by those who, sharing the consciousness of the Enlightenment, failed to question the consequences of the so-called enlightened view as reflected in the colonization and slavery of that period.

Perhaps it is true to say, as does Van Harvey, that the Enlightenment created a "revolution in the consciousness of Western man"; but not all people are Western and not all people in the West experienced the Enlightenment in the same way. For black and red peoples in North America, the spirit of the Enlightenment was socially and politically demonic, becoming a pseudo-intellectual basis for their enslavement or extermination.

Through an examination of the contemporary white theological scene, it is clear that the children of the Enlightenment have simply accepted the issues passed on by their grandparents. Although the historical events of the twentieth century have virtually destroyed the nineteenth-century confidence in the goodness of humanity and the inevitable progress of history, twentieth-century white theologians are still secure in their assumption that important theological issues emerge, primarily if not exclusively, out of the white experience. Despite the sit-ins and pray-ins, the civil rights movement and black power, Martin Luther King and Stokely Carmichael, white theologians still continue their business as usual. These theologians fail to realize that such a procedure is just as racist and oppressive against black people as Billy Graham's White House sermons. This is so because the black judgment on this matter is that those who are not for us must be against us. . . .

Because white theologians live in a society that is racist, the oppression of black people does not occupy an important item on their theological agenda. Again as Karl Marx put it: "It is not consciousness that determines life, but life that determines consciousness." Because white theologians are well fed and speak for a people who control the means of production, the problem of hunger is not a theological issue for them. That is why they spend more time debating the relation between the Jesus of history and the Christ of faith than probing the depths of Jesus' command to feed the poor. It is theologically much more comfortable to write essays and books about the authenticity or non-authenticity of this or that word of Jesus than it is to hear his Word of liberation, calling the humiliated into existence for freedom. To hear Jesus' Word of liberation requires a radical decision, not just about my self-understanding (although that is definitely included, as Rudolf Bultmann clearly demonstrated) but about *practice,* a decision that defines theology as a weapon in the struggle of the little ones for liberation.

The history of white American theology illustrates the concept of the *social a priori* asserted by Werner Stark and the other sociologists of knowledge whom we discussed earlier. The social environment functions as a "mental grid," deciding what will be considered as relevant data in a given inquiry. For example, because white theologians are not the sons and daughters of black slaves but the descendants of white slave masters, their theological grid automatically excludes from the field of perception the data of Richard Allen, Henry H. Garnet, and Nathaniel Paul, David Walker, and Henry M. Turner. This same axiological grid accounts for the absence of the apocalyptic expectations of the spirituals among the so-called "hope theologians"; and the same explanation can be given why the white existentialists do not say anything about absurdity in the blues. . . .

The mental grid influences not only what books theologians read when doing their research, but also which aspects of personal experience will shape theological style and methodology. Again it is obvious that because white theologians were not enslaved and lynched and are not ghettoized because of color, they do not think that color is an important point of departure for theological discourse. Color is not *universal* they say, moving on to what they regard as the more important problems of theological scholarship. Universalism is a social product and it remains such even (especially!) when it is legitimated in pious or scholarly language. The only way people can enhance their vision of the universal is to break out of their cultural and political boxes and encounter another reality. They must be challenged to take seriously another value system. That is, instead of studying only Jonathan Edwards, they must also examine the reality of David Walker. Here truth is expanded beyond the limitations of white culture.

Like white American theology, black thought on Christianity has been influenced by its social context. But unlike white theologians, who spoke to and for the culture of the ruling class, black people's religious ideas were shaped by the cultural and political existence of the victims in North America. Unlike Europeans who immigrated to this land to escape from tyranny, Africans came in chains to serve a nation of tyrants. It was the slave experience that shaped our idea of this land. And this difference in social existence between Europeans and Africans must be recognized, if we are to understand correctly the contrast in the form and content of black and white theology.

What then is the form and content of black religious thought when viewed in the light of their social situation? Briefly, *the form of black religious thought is expressed in the style of story and its content is liberation.* Black theology, then, is the story of black people's struggle for liberation in an extreme situation of oppression. Consequently there is no sharp distinction between thought and practice, worship and theology, because black theological reflections about God occurred in the black struggle of freedom.

White theologians built logical systems; black folks told tales. Whites debated the validity of infant baptism or the issue of predestination and free will; blacks recited biblical stories about God leading the Israelites from Egyptian bondage, Joshua and the battle of Jericho, and the Hebrew children in the fiery furnace. White theologians argued about the general status of religious assertions in view of the development of science generally and Darwin's *Origin of Species* in particular; blacks were more concerned about their status in American society and its relation to the biblical claim that Jesus came to set the captives free. White thought on the Christian view of salvation was largely "spiritual" and sometimes "rational," but usually separated from the concrete struggle of freedom in this world. Black thought was largely eschatological and never abstract, but usually related to their struggle against earthly oppression.

The difference in the form of black and white religious thought is, on the one hand, *sociological.* Since blacks were slaves and had to work from sun-up to nightfall, they did not have time for the art of philosophical and theological discourse. They, therefore, did not know about the systems of Augustine, Calvin, or Edwards. And if Ernst Bloch is correct in his contention that "need is the mother of thought," then it can be said that black slaves did not *need* to know about Anselm's ontological argument, Descartes's *Cogito, ergo sum,* and Kant's *Ding an sich.* Such were not their philosophical and theological problems as defined by their social reality. Blacks did not ask whether God existed or whether divine existence can be rationally demonstrated. Divine existence was taken for granted, because God was the point of departure of their faith. The divine question which they addressed was whether or not God was with them in their struggle for liberation. . . .

The difference between black and white thought is also *theological.* Black people did not devise various philosophical arguments for God's existence, because the God of black experience was not a metaphysical idea. He was the God of history, the Liberator of the oppressed from bondage. Jesus was not an abstract Word of God, but God's Word made flesh who came to set the prisoner free. He was the "Lamb of God" that was born in Bethlehem and was slain on Golgotha's hill. He was also "the Risen Lord" and "the King of Kings." He was their Alpha and Omega, the One who had come to make the first last and the last first.

While white preachers and theologians often defined Jesus Christ as a spiritual Savior, the deliverer of people from sin and guilt, black preachers were unquestionably historical. They viewed God as the Liberator in history. That was why the black Church was involved in the abolitionist movement in the nineteenth century and the civil rights movement in the twentieth. Black preachers reasoned that if God delivered Israel from Pharaoh's army and Daniel from the lion's den, then he will deliver black people from American slavery and oppression. So the content of their thought was liberation and they communicated that message through preaching, singing, and praying, telling their story of how "we shall overcome."

3. GUTIÉRREZ: ORTHOPRAXIS, NOT ORTHODOXY

From the perspective of Latin American theology, Gutiérrez presses another indictment of traditional theology, this time for its preoccupation with thought over action and otherworldly salvation over the alleviation of oppression in this world. The turn to the self in nineteenth-century theology now takes the form of a turn to the global human community. Source: Gustavo Gutiérrez, A *Theology of Liberation: History, Politics and Salvation*, trans. Caridad Inda and John Eagleson (Maryknoll, N.Y.: Orbis Books, 1973), pp. 6–11. Date of original publication: 1971.

For various reasons the existential and active aspects of the Christian life have recently been stressed in a different way than in the immediate past.

In the first place, *charity* has been fruitfully rediscovered as the center of the Christian life. This has led to a more biblical view of the faith as an act of trust, a going out of one's self, a commitment to God and neighbor, a relationship with others. It is in this sense that St. Paul tells us that faith works through charity: love is the nourishment and the fullness of faith, the gift of one's self to the Other, and invariably to others. This is the foundation of the *praxis* of the Christian, of his active presence in history. According to the Bible, faith is the total response of man to God, who saves through love. In this light, the understanding of the faith appears as the understanding not of the simple affirmation—almost memorization—of truths, but of a commitment, an overall attitude, a particular posture toward life.

In a parallel development, Christian *spirituality* has seen a significant evolution. In the early centuries of the Church there emerged the primacy, almost exclusiveness, of a certain kind of contemplative life, hermitical, monastic, characterized by withdrawal from the world, and presented as the model way to sanctity. About the twelfth century the possibility of sharing contemplation by means of preaching and other forms of apostolic activity began to be considered. This point of view was exemplified in the mixed life (contemplative and active) of the mendicant orders and was expressed in the formula: *contemplata aliis tradere* ("to transmit to others the fruits of contemplation"). Viewed historically this stage can be considered as a transition to Ignatian spirituality, which sought a difficult but fruitful synthesis between contemplation and action: *in actione contemplativus* ("contemplative in action"). This process, strengthened in recent years by the search for a spirituality of the laity, culminates today in the studies on the religious value of the profane and in the spirituality of the activity of the Christian in the world.

Moreover, today there is a greater sensitivity to the *anthropological aspects* of revelation. The Word about God is at the same time a promise to the world. In revealing God to us, the Gospel message reveals us to ourselves in our situation before the Lord and with other men. The God of Christian revelation is a God made man, hence the famous comment of Karl Barth regarding Christian anthropocentrism: "Man is the measure of all things, since God became man." All this has caused the revaluation of the presence and the activity of man in the world, especially in relation to other men. On this subject Congar writes: "Seen as a whole, the direction of theological thinking has been characterized by a transference away from attention to the being *per se* of supernatural realities, and toward attention to their relationship with man, with the world, and with the problems and the affirmations of all those who for us represent the *Others*." There is no *horizontalism* in this approach. It is simply a question of the rediscovery of the indissoluble unity of man and God.

On the other hand, *the very life of the Church* appears ever more clearly as a *locus theologicus*. Regarding the participation of Christians in the important social movements of their time, Chenu wrote insightfully more than thirty years ago: "They are active *loci theologici* for the doctrines of grace, the Incarnation, and the redemption, as expressly promulgated and described in detail by the papal encyclicals. They are poor theologians who, wrapped up in their manuscripts and scholastic disputations, are not open to these amazing events, not only in the pious fervor of their hearts but formally in their science; there is a theological datum and an extremely fruitful one, in the *presence* of the Spirit." The so-called "new theology" attempted to adopt this posture some decades ago. The fact that the life of the Church is a source for all theological analysis has been recalled to mind often since then. The Word of God gathers and is incarnated in the community of faith, which gives itself to the service of all men.

Vatican Council II has strongly reaffirmed the idea of a Church of service and not of power. This is a Church which is not centered upon itself and which does not "find itself" except when it "loses itself," when it lives "the joys and the hopes, the griefs and the anxieties of men of this age" (*Gaudium et spes*, no. 1). All of these trends provide a new focus for seeing the presence and activity of the Church in the world as a starting point for theological reflection.

What since John XXIII and Vatican Council II began to be called a theology of the *signs of the times* can be characterized along the same lines, although this takes a step beyond narrow ecclesial limits. It must not be forgotten that the signs of the times are not only a call to intellectual analysis. They are above all a call to pastoral activity, to commitment, and to service. Studying the signs of the times includes both dimensions. Therefore, *Gaudium et spes*, no. 44, points out that discerning the signs of the times is the responsibility of every Christian, especially pastors and theologians, to hear, distinguish, and interpret the many voices of our age, and to judge them in the light of the divine Word. In this way, revealed truths can always be more deeply penetrated, better understood, and set forth to greater advantage. Attributing this role to every member of the People of God and singling out the pastors—charged with guiding the activity of the Church—highlights the call to commitment which the signs of the times imply. Necessarily connected with this consideration, the function of theologians will be to afford greater clarity regarding this commitment by means of intellectual analysis. (It is interesting to note that the inclusion of theologians in the above-mentioned text met opposition during the conciliar debates.)

Another factor, this time of a *philosophical* nature, reinforces the importance of human action as the point of departure for all reflection. The philosophical issues of our times are characterized by new relationships of man with nature, born of advances in science and technology. These new bonds affect the awareness man has of himself and of his active relationships with others.

Maurice Blondel, moving away from an empty and fruitless spirituality and attempting to make philosophical speculation more concrete and alive, presented it as a critical reflection on action. This reflection attempts to understand the internal logic of an action through which man seeks fulfillment by constantly transcending himself. Blondel thus contributed to the elaboration of a new *apologetics* and became one of the most important thinkers of contemporary theology, including the most recent trends.

To these factors can be added the influence of *Marxist thought*, focusing on praxis and geared to the transformation of the world. The Marxist influence began to be felt in the middle of the nineteenth century, but in recent times its cultural impact has become greater. Many agree with Sartre that "Marxism, as the formal framework of all contemporary philosophical thought, cannot be superseded." Be that as it may, contemporary theology does in fact find itself in direct and fruitful confrontation with Marxism, and it is to a large extent due to Marxism's influence that theological thought, searching for its own sources, has begun to reflect on the meaning of the transformation of this world and the action of man in history. Further, this confrontation helps theology to perceive what its efforts at understanding the faith receive from the historical praxis of man in history as well as what its own reflection might mean for the transformation of the world.

Finally, the rediscovery of the *eschatological dimension* in theology has also led us to consider the central role of historical praxis. Indeed, if human history is above all else an opening to the future, then it is a task, a political occupation, through which man orients and opens himself to the gift which gives history its transcendent meaning: the full and definitive encounter with the Lord and with other men. "To do the truth," as the Gospel says, thus acquires a precise and concrete meaning in terms of the importance of action in Christian life. Faith in a God who loves us and calls us to the gift of full communion with him and brotherhood among men not only is not foreign to the transformation of the world; it leads necessarily to the building up of that brotherhood and communion in history. Moreover, only by doing this truth will our faith be "veri-fied," in the etymological sense of the word. From this notion has recently been derived the term *orthopraxis*, which still disturbs the sensitivities of some. The intention, however, is not to deny the meaning of *orthodoxy*, understood as a proclamation of and reflection on statements considered to be true. Rather, the goal is to balance and even to reject the primacy and almost exclusiveness which doctrine has enjoyed in Christian life and above all to modify the emphasis, often obsessive, upon the attainment of an orthodoxy which is often nothing more than fidelity to an obsolete tradition or a debatable interpretation. In a more positive vein, the intention is to recognize the work and importance of concrete behavior, of deeds, of action, of praxis in the Christian life. "And this, it seems to me, has been the greatest transformation which has taken place in the Christian conception of existence," said Edward Schillebeeckx in an interview. "It is evident that thought is also necessary for action. But the Church has for centuries devoted her attention to formulating truths and meanwhile did almost nothing to better the world. In other words, the Church focused on orthodoxy and left orthopraxis in the hands of nonmembers and nonbelievers."

In the last analysis, this concern for praxis seeks to avoid the practices which gave rise to Bernanos' sarcastic remark: "God does not choose the same men to keep his word as to fulfill it."

4. RUETHER: THE PROPHETIC, ICONOCLASTIC CHRIST

Several notes join in the selections from Rosemary Ruether: the overturning of all conventional hierarchies as the heart of the gospel, the assertion that such a gospel speaks especially to women, for they are among the despised and outcast peoples, an emphasis on the future rather than the past as the time of salvific transformation, and a holistic insistence —the new order is *all* downtrodden people, women *and* men. Source: Rosemary Radford Ruether, *To Change the World: Christology and Cultural Criticism* (New York: Crossroad, 1981), pp. 14–15, 53–56.

Of all Jesus' sayings, the one that most probably comes down to us close to its original form is the Lord's Prayer. Here the word "heaven" is used as a symbol for the dwelling-place of God. But there is not the slightest notion that the kingdom means that we, human beings, are going to dwell in heaven. Rather, the kingdom means that the conditions of heaven will come down and reign here on earth. The kingdom, for whose coming Jesus taught us to pray, is defined quite simply as "God's will done on earth." God's will done on earth means the fulfilment of people's basic human physical and social needs: daily bread, remission of debts, which includes both the wrongs that we have done others, and also the financial indebtedness that holds the poor in bondage to the rich, avoidance of the temptations that lead us to oppress one another, even in God's name, and, finally, deliverance from evil. There is nothing to suggest that his vision includes conquest of death. The kingdom means conquest of human historical evil: the setting up of proper conditions of human life with God and one another here on earth within the limits of mortal existence.

Jesus' originality does not lie in his spiritualization of the kingdom, but rather in the fact that he saw the true fulfilment of its earthly hopes in a more radical way than many of his contemporaries. He did not see the struggle against injustice and oppression primarily as a holy war against the Romans. This does not mean that deliverance from oppression did not include deliverance from the Romans. But Jesus looked deeper than the oppression of Israel by Rome to the fundamental roots of oppression itself. He sees this as the love of prestige, power and wealth that causes people to seek domination and to lord it over each other. Unless this fundamental lust for domination is overcome, a successful war of liberation will only replace one domination with another. Jesus seeks to model, in his own life, a new concept of leadership based on service to others, even unto death. This is the model that he wishes to impart to his followers. In the new community based on the life of service to others, the lust for domination will be overcome at its source. . . .

Another perspective on christology is being elaborated by liberation theologies. Liberation theologies go back to nineteenth century movements of Christian socialism that began to seek alliances between the gospel and the Left. Liberation theologies base their christologies particularly on the Jesus of the synoptic gospels. Here is a Jesus who does not sacralize existing ruling classes. The messianic prophet proclaims his message as an iconoclastic critique of existing élites, particularly religious élites. The gospel drama is one of prolonged conflict between Christ and those religious authorities who gain their social status from systems of ritualized righteousness. Jesus proclaims an iconoclastic reversal of this system of religious status. The leaders of the religious establishment are blind guides and hypocrites, while the outcasts of the society, socially and morally, prostitutes, publicans, Samaritans, are able to hear the message of the prophet. In Matthew's language, "Truly the tax collectors and the harlots go into the kingdom of God before you," i.e., the scribes and Pharisees (Matt. 21:31). The gospel turns upside down the present order; the first shall be last and the last first.

This reversal of order is not simply a turning upside down of the present hierarchy, but aims at a new order where hierarchy itself is overcome as a principle of rule. This may have been the source of the messianic struggle between Jesus and his own disciples. It certainly has been the root of misunderstanding of Jesus by the church historically. When the sons of Zebedee ask Jesus if they can sit on his left and right hands when he comes into his kingdom, he confronts them with his different vision of the way into the messianic future.

> You know that the rulers of the Gentiles lord it over them, and their great men exercise authority over them. It shall not be so among you; but whoever would be great among you must be your servant, and whoever would be first among you must be your slave; even as the Son of man came not to be served but to serve and to give his life as a ransom for many. (Matt. 20:25–27)

The meaning of servanthood in this oft-quoted and oft-misused text of Jesus cannot be understood either as a sacralized Christian lordship that calls itself "servant," but reproduces the same characteristics of domination, or as the romanticizing of servitude. This is why neither existing lords nor existing servants can serve as a model for this servanthood, but only the Christ, the messianic person, who represents a new kind of humanity. The essence of servanthood is that it is possible only for liberated persons, not people in servitude. Also it exercises power and leadership, but in a new way, not to reduce others to dependency, but to empower and liberate others.

This means, in the language of liberation theology, that God as liberator acts in history to liberate all through opting for the poor and the oppressed of the present system. The poor, the downcast, those who hunger and thirst, have a certain priority in God's work of redemption. Part of the signs of the kingdom is that the lame walk, the blind see, the captives are freed, the poor have the gospel preached to them. Christ goes particularly to the outcasts, and they, in turn, have a special affinity for the gospel. But the aim of this partiality is to create a new whole, to elevate the valleys and make the high places low, so that all may come into a new place of God's reign, when God's will is done on earth.

How does the question of the subjugation and emancipation of women fit into such a vision of the iconoclastic prophetic Christ? This world view is not concerned with the dualism of male and female, either as total groups or as representatives of some cosmic principles that need to be related to each other. But women are not ignored in this vision. Indeed, if one can say that Christ comes to the oppressed and the oppressed especially hear him, then it is women within these marginal groups who are often seen both as the oppressed of the oppressed and also as those particularly receptive to the gospel. The dialogue at the well takes place not just with a Samaritan, but with a Samaritan woman. Not just a Syro-Phoenician, but a Syro-Phoenician woman is the prophetic seeker who forces Jesus to concede redemption to the non-Jews. Among the poor it is widows who are the exemplars of the most destitute; among the moral outcasts it is the prostitutes who represent the bottom of the list. This is not accidental. It means that, in the iconoclastic messianic vision, it is the women of the despised and outcast peoples who are seen as the bottom of the present hierarchy and hence, in a special way, the last who shall be first in the kingdom.

How does this vision of the redemptive work of Christ, that addresses itself particularly to the women among the outcast, differ from those messianic visions of the new age of the "feminine" which we described earlier? It seems to me that it has some affinities with them, in the sense that Christ is seen as critic rather than vindicator of the present hierarchical social order. The meaning of Christ is located in a new future order still to come that transcends the power structures of historical societies, including those erected in the Christian era in "Christ's name."

But this biblical vision also differs in important ways from the romantic vision of the advent of the new age of the feminine. These gnostic and romantic traditions abstract the human person as male and female into a dualism of opposite principles, masculinity and femininity. They give different valuations to each side and then try to set up a scheme to unite the two in a new whole. This sets up an insoluble problem for human personhood until these qualities labelled masculine and feminine are seen as the product of social power relations rather than "nature." "Woman-as-body-sensuality" and "woman-as-pure-altruistic-love" are both abstractions of human potential created when one group of people in power is able to define other groups of people over against themselves. To abstract these definitions into eternal essences is to miss the social context in which these definitions arise.

The world of the gospels returns us to concrete social conditions in which maleness and femaleness are elements of a complex web in which humans have defined status, superiority and inferiority. The gospel returns us to the world of Pharisees and priests, widows and prostitutes, homeless Jewish prophets and Syro-Phoenician women. Men and women interact with each other within a multiplicity of social definitions: sexual status, but also ethnicity, social class, religious office and law define relations with each other. Jesus as liberator calls for a renunciation and dissolution of this web of status relationships by which societies have defined privilege and unprivilege. He speaks especially to outcast women, not as representatives of the "feminine," but because they are at the bottom of this network of oppression. His ability to be liberator does not reside in his maleness, but, on the contrary, in the fact that he has renounced this system of domination and seeks to embody in his person the new humanity of service and mutual empowerment.

Together, Jesus and the Syro-Phoenician woman, the widow and the prostitute, not as male and female principles, but as persons responding authentically to each other, point us to that new humanity of the future. This new humanity is described in simple and earthy terms by Jesus as the time when "all receive their daily bread, when each remits the debts which the others owe to them, when we are not led into temptations (including messianic temptations) but are delivered from evil."

5. HICK: ONE GOD, MANY IMAGES

The excerpts from John Hick can be seen as an attempt to apply Niebuhr's principle of radical monotheism to the world's religions. How, he asks, can we think about the *one* God as revealed in plural ways instead of, as Christians have traditionally thought, only or absolutely in Jesus Christ? Might openness to other manifestations of God help us to speak of God in different images—as "mother," for instance, as well as "father"? And what difference would such an understanding of divine revelation make on the way Christians think of salvation and the relationship of Jesus Christ to the one God? Source: John Hick, *God Has Many Names* (Philadelphia: Westminster Press, 1982), pp. 26–28, 48, 51–52, 66–67, 74–75.

Let us then think of the Eternal One as pressing in upon the human spirit, seeking to be known and responded to by man, and seeking through man's free responses to create the human animal into (in our Judeo-Christian language) a child of God, or toward a perfected humanity. And let us suppose that in that first millennium B.C. human life had developed to the point at which man was able to receive and respond to a new and much fuller vision of the divine reality and of the claim of that reality upon his life. Such a breakthrough is traditionally called revelation, and the revelation was, as I have pointed out, already plural. But should we not expect there to have been *one* single revelation for all mankind, rather than several different revelations? The answer, I suggest, is no—not if we take seriously into account the actual facts of human life in history. For in that distant period, some two and a half thousand years ago, the civilizations of China, of India, and of the Near East could almost have been located on different planets, so tenuous and slow were the lines of communication between them. A divine revelation intended for all mankind but occurring in China, or in India, or in Israel would have taken many centuries to spread to the other countries. But we are supposing that the source of revelation was always seeking to communicate to mankind, and in new ways to as much of mankind as was living within the higher civilizations that had then developed. From this point of view it seems natural that the revelation should have been plural, occurring separately in the different centers of human culture. . . .

And so we come back to our original question, Why should religious faith take a number of such different forms? Because, I would suggest, religious faith is not an isolated aspect of our lives but is closely bound up with human culture and human history, which are in turn bound up with basic geographical, climatic, and economic circumstances. It has been pointed out, for example, that "in nomadic, pastoral, herd-keeping societies the male principle predominates; whereas among agricultural peoples, aware of the fertile earth which brings forth from itself and nourishes its progeny upon its broad bosom, it is the mother-principle which seems important. . . . Among Semitic peoples therefore, whose traditions are those of herdsmen, the sacred is thought of in male terms: God the father. Among Indian peoples whose tradition has been for many centuries, and even millennia, agricultural, it is in female terms that the sacred is understood: God the mother" (Trevor Ling). Again, as has been pointed out by Martin

Prozesky, the Canaanites, and other ancient Near Eastern cultures with a comparable mythology, worshiped a sky god (Baal) and an earth goddess (Anath), whereas the ancient Egyptians, in contrast, had a sky goddess (Nut) and an earth god (Geb). Why was Egypt different in this respect? Is it not because Egypt is in the exceptional position that the fertilizing waters, male by analogy, come from the earth, in the form of the river Nile, whereas in the other countries they come from the sky in the form of rain? Now one could, as I mentioned earlier, react to this kind of evidence by concluding that the belief in God is entirely a human projection, guided by cultural influences. But the alternative interpretation is that there is some genuine awareness of the divine, but that the concrete form which it takes is provided by cultural factors. On this view these different human awarenesses of the Eternal One represent different culturally conditioned perceptions of the same infinite divine reality. . . .

In the light of the phenomenological similarity of worship in these different traditions we have to ask whether people in church, synagogue, mosque, gurdwara, and temple are worshiping different Gods or are worshiping the same God? Are Adonai and God, Allah and Ekoamkar, Rama and Krishna different gods, or are these different names for the same ultimate Being? There would seem to be three possibilities. One is that there exist, ontologically, many gods. But this conflicts with the belief concerning each that he is the creator source of the world. A second possibility is that one faith-community, let us say our own, worships God while the others vainly worship images which exist only in their imaginations. But even within Christianity itself, is there not a variety of overlapping mental images of God—for example, as stern judge and predestinating power, and as gracious and loving heavenly Father—so that different Christian groups, and even different Christian individuals, are worshiping the divine Being through their different images of him? And do not the glimpses which I have just offered of worship within the various religious traditions suggest that our Christian images overlap with many non-Christian images of God? If so, a third possibility must seem the most probable, namely, that there is but one God, who is maker and lord of all; that in his infinite fullness and richness of being he exceeds all our human attempts to grasp him in thought; and that the devout in the various great world religions are in fact worshiping that one God, but through different, overlapping concepts or mental icons of him. . . .

But let me now turn to the effects which a pluralist view of religion has upon one's understanding of and relationship to one's own tradition. However imperfectly (and in fact very imperfectly) this is reflected in my own life, I feel irrevocably challenged and claimed by the impact of the life and teaching of Jesus; and to be thus decisively influenced by him is, I suppose, the basic definition of a Christian. How then is my Christian faith changed by acceptance of the salvific character of the other world religions?

The older theological tradition of Christianity does not readily permit religious pluralism. For at its center is the conviction that Jesus of Nazareth was God—the second Person of a divine Trinity living a human life. It follows from this that Christianity, and Christianity alone, was founded by God in person on the only occasion on which he has ever become incarnate in this world, so that Christianity has a unique status as the way of salvation provided and appointed by God himself. If this claim is to have real substance and effect, it follows that the salvation thus made possible within Christianity cannot also be possible outside it. This conclusion was drawn with impeccable logic in the Roman dogma *Extra ecclesiam nulla salus* (Outside the church, no salvation), with its nineteenth-century Protestant missionary equivalent (Outside Christianity, no salvation). But in the light of our accumulated knowledge of the other great world faiths this conclusion has become unacceptable to all except a minority of dogmatic diehards. For it conflicts with our concept of God, which we have received from Jesus, as the loving heavenly Father of *all* mankind; could such a Being have restricted the possibility of salvation to those who happen to have been born in certain countries in certain periods of history?

But perhaps salvation is not the issue. Perhaps salvation is taking place, not only within Christianity but also outside it, while the unique Christian gospel is that God became man in Jesus to make this possible. The doctrine of atonement thus becomes central. This suggestion appeals to some as a means of acknowledging God's saving work throughout mankind while retaining the dogma of the unique centrality of Christ as the only savior of the world. But in doing so it sacrifices the substance of the older position. For the nerve of the old dogma was the imperative which it generated to convert all people to faith in Jesus as their lord and savior: "No one comes to the Father, but by me" and "There is salvation in no one else, for there is no other name under heaven given among men by which we must be saved." That nerve is cut when we acknowledge the other great world religions as also areas of divine salvation. The other kind of attempt to have it both ways, exemplified by Karl Rahner's picture of devout persons of other faiths as "anonymous Christians," is too manifestly an ad hoc contrivance to satisfy many. For it is as easy, and as arbitrary, to label devout Christians as anonymous Muslims, or anonymous Hindus, as to label devout Hindus or Muslims as anonymous Christians.

Because such responses are inadequate, it seems to me necessary to look again at the traditional interpretation of Jesus as God incarnate. Such a reconsideration is in any case required today by the realization that the historical Jesus almost certainly did not in fact teach that he was in any sense God; and also by the fact that Christian thought has not yet, despite centuries of learned attempts, been able to give any intelligible content to the idea that a finite human being, genuinely a part of our human race, was also the infinite, eternal, omnipotent, omniscient creator of everything other than himself. The proper conclusion to draw, as it seems to me, is that the idea of divine incarnation is a metaphorical (or, in technical theological language, a mythological) idea. When a truth or a value is lived out in a human life, it is a natural metaphor to speak of its being incarnated in that life. Jesus lived in full openness to God, responsive to the divine will, transparent to the divine purpose, so that he lived out the divine agape within human history. This was not a matter of his being of the same substance as God the Father, or of his having two complete natures, one human and the other divine. Agape is incarnated in human life whenever someone acts in selfless love; and this occurred in the life of Jesus to a startling and epoch-making degree. Whether he incarnated self-giving love more than anyone else who has ever lived, we cannot know. But we do know that his actual historical influence has been unique in its extent. . . .

Indeed one may say that the fundamental heresy is precisely to treat the incarnation as a factual hypothesis! For the reason why it has never been possible to state a literal meaning for the idea of incarnation is simply that it has no literal meaning. It is a mythological idea, a figure of speech, a piece of poetic imagery. It is a way of saying that Jesus is our living contact with the transcendent God. In his presence we find that we are brought into the presence of God. We believe that he is so truly God's servant that in living as his disciples we are living according to the divine purpose. And as our sufficient and saving point of contact with God there is for us something absolute about him which justifies the absolute language which Christianity has developed. Thus reality is being expressed mythologically when we say that Jesus is the Son of God, God incarnate, the Logos made flesh.

When we see the incarnation as a mythological idea applied to Jesus to express the experienced fact that he is our sufficient, effective, and saving point of contact with God, we no longer have to draw the negative conclusion that he is man's one and only effective point of contact with God. We can revere Christ as the one through whom we have found salvation, without having to deny other points of reported saving contact between God and man. We can commend the way of Christian faith without having to discommend other ways of faith. We can say that there is salvation in Christ without having to say that there is no salvation other than in Christ.

6. KAUFMAN: DIVINE POWER, HUMAN RESPONSIBILITY, AND THE NUCLEAR THREAT

If there is one overriding issue facing our earth, it is undoubtedly nuclear disaster. Gordon Kaufman addresses the issue directly: How can theology become part of the solution, rather than be part of the problem? It will remain part of the problem until imperialistic, triumphalist models of God, which suggest that God is responsible for averting nuclear destruction, are exchanged for new models that focus accountability on human beings. His call to theologians as the guardians of religious language to revise their most precious symbols of God, Christ, and Torah is eloquent and sobering. Source: Gordon D. Kaufman, "Nuclear Eschatology and the Study of Religion," *Journal of the American Academy of Religion*, 51 (March 1983): 4–9.

The religious eschatology of the West was undergirded by faith in an active creator and governor of history, one who from the beginning was working out purposes which were certain to be realized as history moved to its consummation. The end of history, thus—whether viewed as ultimate catastrophe or ultimate salvation—was to be God's climactic act. This consummation was something that the faithful could live with—even look forward to with hope—for it would be the moment when God's final triumph over all evil powers was accomplished.

The end of history which we in the late twentieth century must contemplate, however—an end brought about by nuclear holocaust—is conceived primarily not as God's doing but as ours. Moreover, it is not part of a grand plan bringing about the salvation of humanity; it is, rather, the extinction—the total obliteration—of humanity. Not only the ending of all our individual hopes and aspirations—a finality which each of us individually must face as we contemplate our own deaths—but an ending of all hopes and all aspirations, indeed, of all hopers and aspirers, of all future generations who could carry on the quests and projects, the values and meanings, the institutions and ways of life in which humankind has invested so much over many thousands of years. . . .

With all our talk about matters of ultimate concern, about sin and evil, about the way human life must be grounded in faith and hope, about the symbolical schemes and ritualistic practices in and through which humans find meaning in life, about God and the importance, or lack of importance, which belief in God has had, or must have, for human beings—with all this talk and inquiry and investigation and research on questions which we in the field of religion like to say are matters of life-and-death importance for human beings, very little attention has been paid to what is perhaps the most momentous *change* in the human religious situation since symbolical frames of orientation were invented: the possibility that we humans, by ourselves, will utterly destroy not only ourselves but our species, all future generations, thus bringing the entire human project, through which and for which many hundreds of generations have suffered, to an abrupt and final halt. Though some occurrences in recent history—such as the Nazi holocaust or the Cambodian massacres, or earlier, the attempted obliteration of American Indian cultures—certainly demonstrate vividly the human capacity for massive evil, they barely foreshadow the kind of finality we are here trying to contemplate. Why have we students of religion not been examining, from our special point of view, this momentous religious fact right before our eyes? Why have we not sought to interpret the nature of human religiousness through it, and sought to interpret it in terms of the modes of understanding and insight made available to us by the religious traditions of humankind? I would like, today, to suggest some of the implications which it seems to me our new religious situation has for religion studies and for theology. . . .

It is important that we contrast our situation today with the eschatological visions found in many religious communities from ancient Israel to the present: in most cases there was an expectation that a faithful remnant would survive the catastrophe and, indeed, be glorified; in even the bleakest visions of that dark day, there was the satisfaction that God's righteous will would at least prevail and that God's glory and honor would be vindicated. So for traditional eschatology there was always some positive meaning—some humanly significant meaning—in the consummating events of history. But our situation is different. The potential catastrophe that we are here called upon to contemplate is empty of any human meaning whatsoever. About all that we can imagine here is a picture of this earth becoming a barren desert, devoid of life like the moon above us, and with an atmosphere filled with poisonous gases. The only thing human about this event is that we humans will be the ones who have done it, we will be responsible for having brought on the catastrophe; when it happens, nothing human, nothing humanly significant whatsoever, will remain. How are we to think such an utterly abstract notion, a notion of an earth from which the human has been totally and irrevocably removed? And how are we to take such an idea seriously? It is hardly surprising that most people don't. . . .

Of all the world religions, few have emphasized human creativity and responsibility as have those traditions grounded in the Bible. Yet not even Western religious traditions have contemplated human powers and responsibilities of anything like the horrific scope and magnitude which we must consider here: humankind was never believed to have the power utterly to destroy itself; that power lay with God alone. If we wish to interpret our catastrophic event in terms of these traditions, two alternatives appear to be open to us. Either we can assert that the ultimate catastrophe, if it comes, is in some significant sense

God's will and God's doing, that the annihilation of humanity which God had contemplated during the time of Noah is now coming to pass through a nuclear holocaust instead of a flood. Or we may hold that God, as the redeemer and savior of humankind as well as our creator, has so bound Godself to humanity and the human enterprise—in the covenant made with us in Jesus Christ, as Karl Barth would say—that this utterly calamitous self-destruction of humanity will never be allowed to occur. Each of these alternatives affirms the ultimate sovereignty of God over the events of history—an indispensable point for biblical faith. This provides a ground for human hope in face of this potential catastrophe, and it implies that the proper human action here—as always—is to be conceived in terms of obedience to the divine will. But clearly neither of these interpretations grants what is central and novel in this potential event as it confronts our consciousness today, namely, that it will be we human beings who are absolutely and fully responsible if this catastrophe occurs, that this event confronts us as an act of human doing not of divine will, and that both our actions and our hopes with respect to it, therefore, must be directed primarily toward the transformation of our human institutions and policies.

Some fundamentalists on the far religious right, following out the implications of the biblical apocalyptic imagery of an earthly holocaust as the ultimate expression of God's sovereignty over history, are apparently willing to go so far as to suggest that a nuclear disaster, if it ever comes, could only be an expression of the purposes of God; hence, any who work to prevent such a climax to human history are in fact guilty of opposing God's will. Along with such convictions, as one might expect, goes the demand that America arm itself to the teeth in preparation for the coming Armageddon. But surely to take such a position is not only an ultimate evasion of our responsibility as human beings; it is demonically to invoke the divine will as a justification for that very evasion.

The other direction one can go with traditional theological interpretation, holding that God's providential care will surely not allow us to destroy ourselves in a nuclear holocaust, does not push us toward this sort of demonic extreme; but it also has the effect of cutting the nerve of human responsibility with its assurance that, however horrible a nuclear war might be and however much we are obliged to work against such a calamity, ultimately we can be confident that we humans will not—on our own—be able to bring human history to its end.

Obviously, nuanced variations on these theological alternatives can be developed and they can certainly provide powerful incentives to struggle against a nuclear disaster—as much contemporary peace and disarmament work of religious groups shows—but all such interpretations confront a serious problem: they are attempting to grasp our new religious situation—in which human power and responsibility confront us as so overwhelming and frightening—in terms of a symbolism of divine sovereignty which really cannot contain or interpret this idea, and which thus helps to conceal the true nature of our predicament rather than illuminate it. The stark facts of total human responsibility for the future of humanity, which a potential nuclear catastrophe symbolizes, call into question all this traditional talk—held together so tightly and meaningfully in the symbol of the divine sovereignty—of God's power and purposes and love as the proper and only adequate ground for hope in such a desperate situation. These facts demand that we ask much more seriously than many have yet done whether it is not necessary to reconsider some of the most fundamental axioms of Western religious symbolism and faith. Humanity's "coming of age," to use Bonhoeffer's phrase, means that traditional images of divine providential care have become not only outmoded; they have become misleading and dangerous and must be thoroughly reworked. The personalistic conception of God, so powerfully presented by the traditional images of Christian and Jewish piety, seems less and less defensible in face of the issues humanity today confronts—not only the nuclear crisis, but the Nazi holocaust, our ecological problems, the population explosion, the decisions forced upon us by modern biological science; and the anthropocentric, even henotheistic, forms which these faiths have so often taken historically, far from being salvific of the human, now appear to be part of the problem. If radically transformative moves are not, or cannot be, made in these faiths, these traditions, one wonders whether their resources will be capable of grasping and illuminating the full dimensions of the situation with which we must come to terms.

ACKNOWLEDGMENTS

The excerpt from Schubert M. Ogden, "What Is Theology?" *The Journal of Religion* 52 (January 1972). © 1972 by The University of Chicago. All rights reserved. Used by permission.

From CALVIN: INSTITUTES OF THE CHRISTIAN RELIGION, edited by John T. McNeill and translated by Ford Battles (Volume XX: The Library of Christian Classics). Copyright © MCMLX W. L. Jenkins. Reprinted and used by permission of The Westminster Press, Philadelphia, PA.

Excerpts from Charles Hodge, *Systematic Theology* (Grand Rapids: Wm. B. Eerdmans, 1960). Used by permission.

Selections taken from FOUNDATIONS OF CHRISTIAN FAITH by Karl Rahner published and copyright 1978 by Darton, Longman and Todd Limited, London. English translation copyright © 1978 by The Crossroad Publishing Company. Reprinted by permission of the publishers.

Excerpts from David Kelsey, "The Bible and Christian Theology," *Journal of the American Academy of Religion* (September 1980), are reprinted by permission of Scholars Press on behalf of the American Academy of Religion.

From CHRISTOLOGY OF THE LATER FATHERS, edited by Edward Rochie Hardy and Cyril C. Richardson (Volume III: The Library of Christian Classics). Published in the U.S.A. by The Westminster Press, 1954. Used by permission.

Selections from *Monologium* in St. Anselm translated by S. N. Deane. Copyright 1903 by Open Court Publishing Company. Reprinted by permission of Open Court Publishing Company, La Salle, Ill.

Excerpts from Thomas Aquinas, SUMMA THEOLOGICA, ed. Herbert MacCabe (London: Eyre and Spottiswoode, 1964) vols. 3, 30, and 46, are reprinted by permission of the publisher.

Excerpt from Charles Hartshorne, *The Divine Relativity*, pp. 18–24. Copyright © 1948 Yale University Press. Used by permission.

ACKNOWLEDGMENTS

The excerpt from *The Humanity of God* by Karl Barth. Copyright C. D. Deans 1960. Published by John Knox Press. Used by permission.

Selection from Paul Tillich, *The Courage To Be* (New Haven: Yale University Press, 1952). Copyright 1952, by Yale University Press. All rights reserved. Used by permission.

Augustine, *Lectures on the Gospel According to St. John,* trans. John Gibb and James Innes, in *Nicene and Post-Nicene Fathers,* First Series (Grand Rapids: Wm. B. Eerdmans, 1960). Reprinted by permission of the publisher.

Excerpts from *Luther's Works,* vol. 26. © 1963 Concordia Publishing House. Used by permission.

The excerpts from Karl Barth, *Church Dogmatics,* trans. G. W. Bromiley (Edinburgh: T. & T. Clark, 1956), vols. 1/1, 1/2, and 4/1, are reprinted by permission of the publisher.

The excerpt from *The Meaning of Revelation* by H. Richard Niebuhr is reprinted with permission of Macmillan Publishing Company. Copyright 1941 by Macmillan Company, renewed 1969 by Florence Niebuhr, Cynthia M. Niebuhr, and Richard R. Niebuhr.

Selections from Augustine, *The City of God* in *The Fathers of the Church* series, translated by G. G. Walsh, G. Monahan and D. J. Honan (Washington, D.C.: Catholic University of America Press, 1952) are used by permission of the copyright holder.

Benedict de Spinoza, from *Spinoza: Selections,* edited by John Wild. Copyright 1930 Charles Scribner's Sons; copyright renewed. Reprinted with the permission of Charles Scribner's Sons.

The selections from G. W. F. Hegel, *Lectures on the Philosophy of Religion,* ed. Peter C. Hodgson (Berkeley: University of California Press, 1984), Vols. 1 and 3, are reprinted by permission of the publisher.

The selections from Lewis S. Ford, "Divine Persuasion and the Triumph of the Good," in *Process Philosophy and Christian Thought,* ed. Delwin Brown, Ralph James, and Gene Reeves (New York: Bobbs-Merrill, 1971), are reprinted by permission of the publisher.

Selections are reprinted from Paul Tillich, *Systematic Theology,* Volume 1: *Reason and Revelation, Being and God* (Chicago: University of Chicago

Press, 1951). Copyright 1951 by The University of Chicago. All rights reserved. Published 1951. Used by permission.

Excerpts from Friedrich Schleiermacher, *The Christian Faith*, ed. H. R. Mackintosh and J. S. Stewart (Edinburgh: T. & T. Clark, 1928), are reprinted by permission of the publisher.

Excerpts from Reinhold Niebuhr, *The Nature and Destiny of Man*. Copyright 1949 Charles Scribner's Sons; copyright renewed. Reprinted with the permission of Charles Scribner's Sons.

From AUGUSTINE: EARLIER WRITINGS, edited by John H. S. Burleigh (Volume VI: The Library of Christian Classics). Published simultaneously in Great Britain and the United States of America by the S.C.M. Press, Ltd., London, and The Westminster Press, Philadelphia, PA. Used by permission.

The selection from F. R. Tennant, *The Origin and Propagation of Sin*, 2d ed. (Cambridge: Cambridge University Press, 1906), is reprinted by permission of the publisher.

Søren Kierkegaard, *The Sickness Unto Death: A Christian Psychological Exposition for Upbuilding and Awakening*, ed. by Howard V. Hong and Edna H. Hong. Copyright © 1983 by Princeton University Press. Excerpt, pp. 80–82, reprinted by permission of Princeton University Press.

Abridged from pp. 151–155 in *The Symbolism of Evil* by Paul Ricoeur, Translated by Emerson Buchanan, Volume 17 of The Religious Perspective Series, Planned and Edited by Ruth Nanda Anshen. Copyright © 1967 by Paul Ricoeur. By permission of Harper & Row, Publishers, Inc.

Excerpt from *Love Almighty and Ills Unlimited* by Austin Farrer. Copyright © 1961 by Austin Farrer. Reprinted by permission of Doubleday & Company, Inc.

Excerpts from "The Creed of Nicaea," translation adapted from *Creeds of the Churches*, ed. John H. Leith (New York: Doubleday, 1963). Reprinted by permission of the copyright holder John H. Leith, Professor, Union Theological Seminary, Richmond, Va.

The translation of the "Chalcedonian Definition" is adapted from *Documents of the Christian Church*, 2d ed., ed. Henry Bettenson (London: Oxford University Press, 1963). Reprinted by permission of the publisher.

ACKNOWLEDGMENTS

Excerpted from ANSELM OF CANTERBURY, Vol. III, trans. by J. Hopkins and H. Richardson (The Edwin Mellen Press, Box 450, Lewiston, New York: 1976), pp. 129–36. Used by permission.

The selection from Jurgen Moltmann, "The 'Crucified God': God and the Trinity Today" in *New Questions on God*, ed. J. B. Metz (Edinburgh: T. & T. Clark, 1972), is reprinted by permission of CONCILIUM.

Selections from Cyprian, *On the Unity of the Catholic Church*, in *The Ante-Nicene Fathers*, Vol. 5 (Grand Rapids: Wm. B. Eerdmans, 1955–56), and from Justin Martyr, *Dialogue with Trypho, Second Apology* and *Hortatory Address to the Greeks*, in ANF, Vol. 1, are reprinted by permission of the publisher.

The selection from Thomas Aquinas, "Exposition on the Apostle's Creed," in *Theological Texts*, translated with notes and an introduction by Thomas Gilby (London: Oxford University Press, 1955), is reprinted by permission of the publisher.

"Chapter XVII. Of the Catholic and Holy Church of God, and of the One Only Head of the Church" from "The Second Helvetic Confession, 1566" reprinted from REFORMED CONFESSIONS OF THE 16TH CENTURY, Edited, with Historical Introductions, by Arthur C. Cochrane. Copyright © MCMLXVI W. L. Jenkins. Reprinted and used by permission of The Westminster Press, Philadelphia, PA, and SCM Press Ltd., London.

Selections from Peter Paris, "The Social World of the Black Church," *The Drew Gateway* 52:3 (Spring 1982), are reprinted by permission of the publisher.

Selections from Gustavo Gutiérrez, *A Theology of Liberation: History, Politics and Salvation*, trans. Caridad Inda and John Eagleson (Maryknoll, N.Y.: Orbis Books, 1973; London: SCM Press, 1974), are reprinted by permission of Orbis Books and SCM Press.

The excerpt taken from *The World as Sacrament* by Alexander Schmemann, published and copyright 1966 by Darton, Longman and Todd, London; and published in the United States under the title *For the Life of the World: Sacraments and Orthodoxy* by St. Vladimir's Seminary Press, Crestwood, N.Y. Reprinted by permission of the copyright holders, Darton, Longman and Todd, and Juliana Schmemann.

410

ACKNOWLEDGMENTS

The selection by Isaac of Syria is reprinted by permission of Faber and Faber Ltd from *Early Fathers from the Philokalia*, translated by E. Kadloubovsky and G. E. H. Palmer (London: Faber and Faber, 1954).

Excerpts from *The Collected Works of St. John of the Cross* trans. by K. Kavanaugh and O. Rodriguez (Washington, D.C.: Institute of Carmelite Studies, 1973) and *The Collected Works of St. Teresa of Avila*, vol. 1, trans. by K. Kavanaugh and O. Rodriguez (Washington, D.C.: Institute of Carmelite Studies, 1976). Reprinted by permission of the publisher.

A selection is reprinted from William Law, *A Serious Call to a Devout and Holy Life*. Copyright 1978 by the Missionary Society of St. Paul the Apostle in the State of New York. All rights reserved. Used by permission of the publisher, Paulist Press.

Selections are reprinted with permission of Macmillan Publishing Company from *A Theology for the Social Gospel* by Walter Rauschenbusch. Copyright 1917 by Macmillan Publishing Co., Inc., renewed 1945 by Pauline E. Rauschenbusch.

The selection from Rowan Williams is taken from *Christian Spirituality* published and copyright 1979 by Darton, Longman and Todd Limited, London, and 1980 by John Knox Press, Atlanta. Used by permission of the publishers.

From EARLY CHRISTIAN FATHERS, translated and edited by Cyril C. Richardson (Volume I: The Library of Christian Classics). Published in the U.S.A. in MCMLIII by The Westminster Press, Philadelphia, PA. Used by permission.

Selections are reprinted from Paul Tillich, *The Protestant Era*, translated and with a concluding essay by James Luther Adams. Copyright 1948 by The University of Chicago. All rights reserved. Published 1948. Composed and printed by The University of Chicago Press, Chicago, Illinois, U.S.A. Used by permission.

From THE IDEA OF GOD AND HUMAN FREEDOM, by Wolfhart Pannenberg, translated from the German by R. A. Wilson. © SCM Press Ltd 1973, and published in Great Britain under the title BASIC QUESTIONS IN THEOLOGY, Volume Three. Published in the U.S.A. in 1973 by The Westminster Press. Used by permission of Westminster Press and SCM Press.

From *God of the Oppressed* by James H. Cone. Copyright © 1975 Winston/Seabury Press. Published by Winston/Seabury Press (formerly published by The Seabury Press), 430 Oak Grove, Minneapolis, MN 55403. All rights reserved. Used with permission.

Selections from To CHANGE THE WORLD by Rosemary Radford Ruether. Copyright © 1981 by the author. Reprinted by permission of The Crossroad Publishing Company and SCM Press Ltd.

From GOD HAS MANY NAMES, by John Hick. © John Hick 1980, 1982. Used by permission of The Westminster Press, Philadelphia, PA and Macmillan Publishers Ltd., London and Basingstoke.

The excerpt from Gordon Kaufman, "Nuclear Eschatology and the Study of Religion," *Journal of the American Academy of Religion* 51 (March 1983) is reprinted by permission of Scholars Press on behalf of the American Academy of Religion.

Selections from pp. 31–34 from *Radical Monotheism and Western Civilization* by H. Richard Niebuhr. Copyright © 1943, 1952, 1955, 1960 by H. Richard Niebuhr. Reprinted by permission of Harper & Row, Publishers Inc.

Selections from pp. 86–94 from *Christ and Adam* by Karl Barth (Trans. by T. A. Smail). Copyright © 1956, 1957 by Harper & Row, Publishers, Inc. Originally published in *Scottish Journal of Theology: Occasional Papers*. Reprinted by permission of Harper & Row, Publishers, Inc. and Scottish Academic Press (Journals) Limited.

Selections from *Treasure in Earthen Vessels: The Church as a Human Community* by James M. Gustafson (New York: Harper & Brothers, 1961). Used by permission of the author.

Excerpts from Wolfhart Pannenberg, "Dogmatic Theses on the Doctrine of Revelation," in *Revelation as History*, edited by Wolfhart Pannenberg, translated by David Granskou (New York: Macmillan, 1968). Reprinted by permission of Vandenhoeck and Ruprecht, Göttingen, Federal Republic of Germany.

Selections from Matthew Tindal, "Christianity as Old as Creation," in *Deism: An Anthology*, ed. Peter Gay (Princeton: D. Van Nostrand Co., 1968). Originally published 1730.

Excerpts reprinted from AUGUSTINE: LATER WORKS, edited by John Burnaby (Volume III: "The Library of Christian Classics"). Reprinted and used by permission of The Westminster Press, Philadelphia, PA.

ACKNOWLEDGMENTS

Selection from *Religion Within the Limits of Reason Alone* by Immanuel Kant, translated by Theodore M. Greene and Hoyt H. Hudson (New York: Harper & Row, 1960). Reprinted by permission of Open Court Publishing Co., La Salle, Ill.

From *Existence and Faith: Shorter Writings of Rudolf Bultmann*. Copyright © 1960 by Meridian Books, Inc. Reprinted by arrangement with New American Library, New York, N.Y.

Selections from Rudolf Bultmann, *History and Eschatology* (Edinburgh: Edinburgh University Press, 1957). Originally the Gifford Lectures.

Selections from Jürgen Moltmann, "Resurrection as Hope," in *Religion, Revolution, and the Future* (New York: Charles Scribner's Sons, 1969).

Excerpts from Ernst Troeltsch, "Christianity Among World Religions," in *Christian Thought: Its History and Application*, ed. Baron F. von Hugel (London: University of London Press, 1923).

INDEX OF AUTHORS
AND SELECTIONS

Authors and works are referenced to our chapters and selections. The numbers following the titles refer either to the chapters and books or to the pages and volumes from which the selections are taken (chapter and book references are not preceded by a comma). Complete bibliographical information is given at the beginning of each selection.

Ambrose
  St. Ambrose on the Sacraments and on the Mysteries, 86–93
  Chap. X, Sel. 2

Anselm
  Cur Deus Homo in *Anselm of Canterbury*, 3:129–36
  Chap. VIII, Sel. 4
  Monologium 16–18, 25
  Chap. III, Sel. 2

Athanasius
  "*Orations Against the Arians: Book III*" in *Christological Controversy*, 90–96
  Chap. VIII, Sel. 2

Augustine
  The City of God 11.4, 6, 16–18
  Chap. V, Sel. 1
  The City of God 13.2, 3, 24; 14.1, 5, 6, 11, 13, 27
  Chap. VI, Sel. 1
  The City of God 22.30
  Chap. XII, Sel. 3
  Lectures on the Gospel According to St. John 7.20–21
  Chap. IV, Sel. 1
  On Free Will, in *Earlier Writings*, 165–69
  Chap. VII, Sel. 1
  The Spirit and the Letter, in *Later Works*, 197–98, 236
  Chap. VII, Sel. 1

Barth, Karl
  Christ and Adam, 86–94
  Chap. VI, Sel. 3
  Church Dogmatics, 1/1:191, 193–94, 196
  Chap. IV, Sel. 4
  Church Dogmatics, 1/2:280, 297–98, 299–300, 309–10, 325–27, 338, 353–54
  Chap. XIII, Sel. 3
  Church Dogmatics, 4/1:128–37
  Chap. VIII, Sel. 7
  The Humanity of God, 47–52
  Chap. III, Sel. 5

Bultmann, Rudolf
  "The Concept of Revelation in the New Testament," in *Existence and Faith*, 85–88
  Chap. IV, Sel. 5
  History and Eschatology, 151–55
  Chap. XII, Sel. 5
  Kerygma and Myth, 34–43
  Chap. VIII, Sel. 6

Calvin, John
  Institutes of the Christian Religion 1.6–7

Chap. II, Sel. 2
Institutes of the Christian Religion
1.16
Chap. V, Sel. 2

Chalcedonian Definition
Chap. VIII, Sel. 3

Cobb, John B., Jr.
Beyond Dialogue, 47–52, 141–43
Chap. XIII, Sel. 5

Cone, James
God of the Oppressed, 45–46, 52–56
Chap. XIV, Sel. 2

Cyprian
On the Unity of the Catholic Church
4–6
Chap. IX, Sel. 1

Cyril of Jerusalem
St. Cyril of Jerusalem's Lectures on the Christian Sacraments, 59–67
Chap. X, Sel. 1

Farley, Edward
Theologia, 31–44, 162, 165–69
Chap. I, Sel. 1

Farrer, Austin
Love Almighty and Ills Unlimited,
49–56
Chap. VII, Sel. 7

Ford, Lewis S.
"Divine Persuasion and the Triumph of the Good," in *Process Philosophy and Christian Thought*, 288–91,
297–98
Chap. V, Sel. 5

Gregory of Nyssa
"An Answer to Ablabius," in *Christology of the Later Fathers*, 259–64
Chap. III, Sel. 1

Gustafson, James
Treasure in Earthen Vessels, 100–102,
108–10
Chap. IX, Sel. 5

Gutiérrez, Gustavo
A Theology of Liberation, 6–11

Chap. XIV, Sel. 3
A Theology of Liberation, 256–59,
260, 261, 267–69
Chap. IX, Sel. 7

Hartshorne, Charles
The Divine Relativity, 18–24
Chap. III, Sel. 4

Hegel, G. W. F.
Lectures on the Philosophy of Religion,
1: 307–9; 3: 271–74, 291–94
Chap. V, Sel. 4

Hick, John
God Has Many Names, 26–28, 48,
51–52, 66–67, 74–75
Chap. XIV, Sel. 5

Hodge, Charles
Systematic Theology, 1:151, 152,
153–54, 155, 156–57, 163, 165,
166
Chap. II, Sel. 4

Irenaeus
Against Heresies 5.32–33, 36
Chap. XII, Sel. 1

Isaac of Syria
Early Fathers from the Philokalia,
183–87
Chap. XI, Sel. 1

John of the Cross
Ascent of Mount Carmel 8–9
Chap. XI, Sel. 3

Justin Martyr
Dialogue with Trypho 10–13
Chap. XIII, Sel. 1
Hortatory Address to the Greeks 20,
22–23
Chap. XIII, Sel. 1
Second Apology 13
Chap. XIII, Sel. 1

Kant, Immanuel
Religion within the Limits of Reason Alone, 180–90
Chap. X, Sel. 4

Kaufman, Gordon D.
"Nuclear Eschatology and the Study of

Religion," *Journal of the American Academy of Religion*, 51:4–9
Chap. XIV, Sel. 6

Kelsey, David
"The Bible and Christian Theology," *Journal of the American Academy of Religion*, 48:393–99, 400–401
Chap. II, Sel. 6

Kierkegaard, Søren
The Sickness Unto Death, 80–82
Chap. VII, Sel. 4

Law, William
A Serious Call to a Devout and Holy Life 4
Chap. XI, Sel. 4

Luther, Martin
"Against Latomus," in *Luther's Works*, 32:223–29
Chap. VII, Sel. 2
"The Babylonian Captivity of the Church," in *Luther's Works*, 36:58–74
Chap. X, Sel. 3
"Lectures on Galatians," in *Luther's Works*, 26:399–402
Chap. IV, Sel. 2

Möhler, Johann Adam
Symbolism, 349–52, 358–60
Chap. II, Sel. 3

Moltmann, Jürgen
"The 'Crucified God': God and the Trinity Today," in *New Questions on God*, 31–35
Chap. VIII, Sel. 8
"Resurrection as Hope," in *Religion, Revolution, and the Future*, 60–62
Chap. XII, Sel. 8

Nicene Creed
Chap. VIII, Sel. 1

Niebuhr, H. Richard
The Meaning of Revelation, 109–16
Chap. IV, Sel. 8
Radical Monotheism and Western Culture, 31–34
Chap. XIV, Sel. 1

Niebuhr, Reinhold
The Nature and Destiny of Man, 1:169–70, 182–83, 258–60, 269–72, 274–76
Chap. VI, Sel. 4
The Nature and Destiny of Man, 1:188–94
Chap. VII, Sel. 5

Ogden, Schubert
"What Is Theology?" *The Journal of Religion*, 52:22–36
Chap. I, Sel. 2

Origen
On First Principles 3.6.1, 3–5
Chap. XII, Sel. 2
On First Principles 4.1–3
Chap. II, Sel. 1

Pannenberg, Wolfhart
"Dogmatic Theses on the Doctrine of Revelation," in *Revelation as History*, 135–39
Chap. IV, Sel. 7
"Eschatology and the Experience of Meaning," in *The Idea of God and Human Freedom*, 196–99
Chap. XII, Sel. 7
"Toward a Theology of the History of Religions," in *Basic Questions in Theology*, 2:92–96, 110–15
Chap. XIII, Sel. 4

Paris, Peter
"The Social World of the Black Church," *The Drew Gateway*, 52:3:1–2, 4–9
Chap. IX, Sel. 6

Rahner, Karl
Foundations of Christian Faith, 26, 28–38, 42–43
Chap. VI, Sel. 5
Foundations of Christian Faith, 126–30
Chap. IV, Sel. 6
Foundations of Christian Faith, 371, 373–78
Chap. II, Sel. 5

Foundations of Christian Faith,
411–15, 427–28
Chap. X, Sel. 6

Rauschenbusch, Walter
A Theology for the Social Gospel, 13,
131, 133–37, 142–43
Chap. XI, Sel. 5

Ricoeur, Paul
The Symbolism of Evil, 151–55
Chap. VII, Sel. 6

Ruether, Rosemary Radford
To Change the World, 14–15, 53–56
Chap. XIV, Sel. 4

Schleiermacher, Friedrich
The Christian Faith, § 4
Chap. VI, Sel. 2
The Christian Faith, § 100
Chap. VIII, Sel. 5
The Christian Faith, § 113
Chap. IX, Sel. 4
The Christian Faith, §§ 157–59
Chap. XII, Sel. 4

Schmemann, Alexander
The World as Sacrament, 29–55
Chap. X, Sel. 5

Second Helvetic Confession 17
Chap. IX, Sel. 3

Spinoza, Benedict de
*Short Treatise on God, Man, and His
Well-Being* 8, 3–6
Chap. V, Sel. 3

Tennant, F. R.
The Origin and Propagation of Sin,
24–34
Chap. VII, Sel. 3

Teresa of Avila
Life 22
Chap. XI, Sel. 3

Thomas Aquinas
"Exposition on the Apostles' Creed,"
in *Theological Texts,* 340–43
Chap. IX, Sel. 2
Summa Theologica 1a. 14, 5–6
Chap. III, Sel. 3
Summa Theologica 1a2ae. 106, 1;
2a2ae. 182, 4
Chap. XI, Sel. 2

Tillich, Paul
The Courage to Be, 182–90
Chap. III, Sel. 6
"Kairos," in *The Protestant Era,* 33,
35–38
Chap. XII, Sel. 6
Systematic Theology, 1:252–54,
261–63, 264, 266–67
Chap. V, Sel. 6

Tindal, Matthew
"Christianity as Old as Creation," in
Deism: An Anthology, 112–13,
117–20
Chap. IV, Sel. 3

Troeltsch, Ernst
"Christianity Among World Reli-
gions," in *Christian Thought: Its
History and Application,* 9–27
Chap. XIII, Sel. 2

Williams, Rowan
Christian Spirituality, 176–79
Chap. XI, Sel. 6

*Key theological resources
from Fortress Press—*
ð

Christian Theology
An Introduction to Its Traditions and Tasks
Peter C. Hodgson and Robert H. King, Editors
The widely acclaimed and popular restatement of theology
in its modern context, newly updated by the editors.
416 pages, ISBN 0-8006-2867-5
ð

Readings in Christian Theology
Peter C. Hodgson and Robert H. King, Editors
A rich selection from classical and contemporary
sources on central doctrines of Christian faith
432 pages, ISBN 0-8006-1849-1
ð

Reconstructing Christian Theology
Rebecca S. Chopp and Mark Lewis Taylor, Editors
A liberating pedagogy, which tackles and reconstructs
major Christian doctrines in light of significant
social or cultural challenges.
400 pages, ISBN 0-8006-2696-6

Printed in the United States
135591LV00006B/1/A